THE RIGHTEOUS MAN
SHALL LIVE BY HIS FAITH

MEDITATIONS OF THE HEART
52 WEEKLY DEVOTIONS

BY ROBERT ALDERSON

TRILOGY

The Righteous Man Shall Live by His Faith: Meditations of the Heart

Trilogy Christian Publishers A Wholly Owned Subsidary of Trinity Broadcasting Network

2442 Michelle Drive Tustin, CA 92780

Cover design by: Natalee Groves

For information about special discounts for bulk purchases, please contact Trilogy Christian Publishing.

Manufactured in the United States of America

10 9 8 7 6 5 4 3 2 1

Library of Congress Cataloging-in-Publication Data is available.

ISBN: 979-8-88738-960-8

E-ISBN: 979-8-88738-961-5

To my readers,

I want to thank you for acquiring my book, *The Righteous Man Shall Live by His Faith*. This effort has been an amazing journey as God has been revealing truths progressively about living in God's righteousness. This endeavor has created in me a deeper appreciation of the New Testament relationship with God, a spiritual relationship. And since it has been such a blessing for me, I am convinced many others will also benefit from these perspectives.

It would be a great blessing to further the expansion of these truths if you would consider leaving a review at amazon.com after reading at least a portion by signing into your account, click "Returns & Orders," locate the book, then click "Write a product review," and finally select an overall rating. Your efforts will help others looking at purchasing the book to gain a measure of comfort that the book addresses the subject thoughtfully and accurately.

If you wish, contact me at pastorbill@rwalderson.com or visit rwalderson.com. You will find my blogs posted, as well as links to my weekly podcasts.

Many blessings,
R. W. (Pastor Bill) Alderson.

Endorsement

I finished your phenomenal book last evening. I am beyond blessed, humbled & honored to be asked to proofread what is, in my opinion, a perfectly written book. I smiled and cried (deeply moved) and praised God while reading it. Words fail me in an attempt to express how beautifully written and meaningful this is for anyone reading it.

This book made me fall in love with my Savior all over again. What a wonderful way to meditate each week of the year, taking a chapter at a time; however, I can see this as a weekly Bible study or for our weekly date night meditation & prayer. Worth its weight in gold, filled with pearls of wisdom. I felt privileged to enter the Holy of Holies and find my Beloved.

—Cathy Caron

TABLE OF CONTENTS

FOREWORD

If you want to understand what it is to have a relationship with the living God who created the universe with His word, this is a great resource. Man's relationship to and with God is laid out in the Bible. Is it possible to be a friend of God? This Christian life is likened to a walk. Walking with God is a huge part of our relationship with and to God. How can two walk together? They must agree. Faith in the promise and the one that keeps the promise is the way the righteous man lives. Without faith, he cannot please God. This book shows the legal precedence for the basis of our faith directly from the Scriptures. It's a systematic and spiritual defense of what we believe and why, so that we can walk by faith.

"Always be ready to give an answer for the hope that is within you" (1 Peter 3:15, paraphrased NASB). This book builds the case for the hope we have. Studying the basis for a defense of our belief system builds our faith. I must know why I believe the Scripture so that when the world attacks truth, my faith isn't shattered. I need a firm foundation of truth that causes me to live a faith that is pleasing to God. Living by my own faith and not that of someone else builds a real relationship with God. Enoch walked with God. Abraham was a friend of God. David was a man after God's heart. All these men had their own faith that flew in the face of conventional wisdom. They knew God, and they believed He could be trusted. Walking in that faith propelled them to heights in their relationship with God, which was seemingly unattainable but is available to each believer through His Word.

I've known Pastor Bill for more than thirty-five years. Throughout, he has stayed faithful to God through tragedy and trial. His willingness to praise God in any state he finds himself in is inspiring.

His consistency in the Word of God is unparalleled. His passion for the depth of the Word of God is incessant. His ability to teach it to anyone who is willing to listen is an asset to the body of Christ. What he writes on paper will be written in the souls of those who read it simply because it is the communication of the Word of God. Nothing else.

—John Stropparo

PREFACE

My wife and I are celebrating our forty-sixth wedding anniversary on December 18th. She has been a tremendous support to me both on a personal and spiritual level. The nature of the relationship has changed over the years as we have dealt with many challenges, including the loss of a two-year-old son and how we have come together within the trials. As each of us has grown in our relationships with God, it has been a process of getting to know her and the things that make her happy while still being honest about myself and who I am and marrying our priorities together. It is about learning which battles are worth fighting and which never need to be fought. It mirrors the relationship the believer has with his God. Knowing God goes beyond church attendance and "following the rules." It is learning how to respond to the Lord's unconditional love, as demonstrated in Calvary (Romans 5:8).

My six children and ten grandchildren are an amazing blessing to my life. As Solomon wrote in Psalm 127:3–5,

> Behold, children are a gift of the Lord, The fruit of the womb is a reward. Like arrows in the hand of a warrior, So are the children of one's youth. How blessed is the man whose quiver is full of them.

They add so much texture to my life as they face many of the same conflicts and struggles to find their own victories.

I dedicate this book to Dr. Carl H. Stevens, my spiritual father and the one who not only taught me the truth of Scripture but lived it and modeled it to show many of us that it was possible. He exemplified what it meant to walk by his faith. He manifested what righteousness looks like when an imperfect man chooses to walk in the righteousness of the

Righteous One. He was totally devoted to studying the Word of God and serving Him.

Many years ago, God gave him the vision to establish a worldwide ministry that would prioritize teaching the Word of God and introduce many to a personal knowledge of God. I am the by-product of that vision, having responded to God's call to attend Bible college and become an ordained pastor. The ministry has works happening in eighty countries, having established more than 750 churches, many with Bible colleges, and intent on raising up native pastors to further the work in their own countries.

Dr. Stevens understood that when Jesus made the statement "It is finished" (John 19:30), He was not just speaking of the conclusion of His earthly ministry. He was telling us that the new relationship with God in Christ is superior to the covenant made with Moses nearly 3,500 years ago, known as the old covenant. In Romans 8:3–4,

> For what the Law could not do, weak as it was through the flesh, God did: sending His own Son in the likeness of sinful flesh and as an offering for sin, He condemned sin in the flesh, so that the requirement of the Law might be fulfilled in us, who do not walk according to the flesh but according to the Spirit.

The finished work of Christ opens up a spiritual relationship with God as each believer learns how to be led and guided by the Holy Spirit.

Pastor, as many of us affectionately referred to him over the years, emphasized that studying the Bible categorically provides the believer with a much clearer understanding of God's thoughts. Through the spiritual life in Christ, believers learn how to think with God. As Paul says in 1 Corinthians 2:14–16,

> But a natural man does not accept the things of the Spirit of God, for they are foolishness to him; and he cannot understand them, because they are spiritually appraised. But he who is spiritual appraises all things, yet he himself is appraised by no one. For WHO HAS KNOWN THE MIND OF THE LORD, THAT HE WILL INSTRUCT HIM? But we have the mind of Christ.

The righteous man lives by his faith as he thinks with God. Pastor Stevens was my example.

Introduction

"Righteous Man." (It is living water being poured into an earthen
vessel that is quite broken ~me.) Cathy Caron.

"Behold, as for the proud one, His soul is not right within him; But
the righteous will live by his faith" (Habakkuk 2:4).

In Habakkuk 1, the prophet asks God to explain why the Lord would
use such a wicked nation, Babylon, as His instrument of justice toward
His people. This does not compute! Yahweh's answer only came after
Habakkuk waited a season. God's answer to the believer often comes
after a season of waiting (Isaiah 40:31). He contrasts the utter wickedness
of the Babylonians to the man who walks by his faith. A more accurate
translation may be, "The just man, or the righteous man, shall live by
his confidence in God." The Lord would eventually restore the Jewish
people to their land. The Bible Knowledge Commentary captures the
essence of God's answer:

> Yahweh then declared that a righteous person, by stark contrast, will
> live by his faith (emûnah, "steadfastness or faithfulness"). A righteous
> Israelite who remained loyal to God's moral precepts and was humble

before the Lord enjoyed God's abundant life. To "live" meant to experience God's blessing by enjoying a life of security, protection, and fullness. Conversely, an apparently victorious but proud and perverse Babylonian would die. Faithfulness (NIV marg.) and faith are related. One who trusts in the Lord is one who relies on Him and is faithful to Him.

A Foundational Statement

This clause, "the righteous will live by his faith," is a foundational statement tied directly to the gospel by Paul in Romans 1:16–17, who repeated the clause in Galatians 3:11 (and also Hebrews 10:38, if you believe Paul wrote Hebrews). This expression also became the watchword of the Reformation, helping Martin Luther to appreciate the truth of justification by faith. "This text," said Luther, "was to me the true gate of Paradise."

In the third century, Rabbi Simla noted that Moses gave 365 prohibitions and 248 positive commands. David reduced them to eleven commands in Psalm 15; Isaiah made them six (33:14–15); Micah bound them into three (6:8); and Habakkuk condensed them all to one, namely—"The righteous shall live by faith" (from P. L. Tan, Encyclopedia of 7700 illustrations. Garland, TX: Bible Communications, #1495).

The Old Testament saints could not comprehend that this clause is the doorway into a higher life with God, that is, eternal life, and provides each believer a higher quality of life. His human limitations no longer have to limit him, but he can participate in God's life and His ability based on the believer's willingness to trust the Righteous One, the fullness of grace. "As a result of the anguish of His soul, He will see it and be satisfied; by His knowledge the Righteous One, My Servant, will justify the many, As He will bear their iniquities" (Isaiah 53:11). The sacrifice of the Righteous One satisfies the demands of a Holy God.

Knowing Christ

More than that, I count all things to be loss in view of the surpassing value of knowing [*gnoesis*—knowledge by experience rather than intuition] Christ Jesus my Lord, for whom I have suffered the loss of all things, and count them but rubbish so that I may gain Christ, and may be found in Him, not having a righteousness of my own derived from the Law [self-righteousness], but that which is through faith in Christ, the righteousness which comes from God on the basis of faith, that I may know Him and the power of His resurrection and the fellowship of His sufferings, being conformed to His death; in order that I may attain to the resurrection from the dead.

Philippians 3:8–11

The apostle Paul recognizes in the above passage that the real treasure of this relationship "in Christ" is the experience of knowing Him beyond the Law of Moses he had previously treasured. The Law was the avenue that allowed him to succeed as a Pharisee and Jewish leader since he could perform to earn recognition. He understood that all of his abilities and accomplishments through the Law were rubbish and an impediment to knowing Jesus Christ as Lord. This word, *gnoesis*, emphasizes understanding rather than sensory perception and embraces every organ and mode of knowledge (i.e., seeing, hearing, experience, etc.). This type of knowledge implies verification by the eye or other objective observation. Ultimately, it speaks of the deepest kind of relationship, a connection to "the righteousness which comes from God based on faith."

Out of Faith, into Faith

Paul further explains in Romans 4:4–5 that the righteousness of God cannot be earned but must be received as a gift based on faith.

Now to the one who works, his wage is not credited as a favor, but as what is due. But to the one who does not work, but believes in Him who justifies the ungodly, his faith is credited as righteousness.

It is God that justifies or declares the believer righteous; man's role is to accept God's standards of living. God's righteousness produces a life defined by integrity and blameless conduct. According to Romans 1:17, "For in it [the gospel] the righteousness of God is revealed from faith to faith; as it is written, 'BUT THE RIGHTEOUS man SHALL LIVE BY FAITH.'" The original Greek could be better translated as "by or out of faith into faith." When the believer exercises his faith in a given situation, it leads to another opportunity to trust God.

Consider Abraham when God called him to offer his promised son to the Lord. Genesis 22:1–3 tells us that it was a test. Abraham passed the test by rising early in the morning without complaint and taking Isaac up to Mount Moriah, to the very spot where Jesus would be offered for the sins of the world nearly 1,900 years later. In Hebrews 11:17–19,

> By faith Abraham, when he was tested, offered up Isaac, and he who had received the promises was offering up his only begotten son; it was he to whom it was said, "IN ISAAC YOUR DESCENDANTS SHALL BE CALLED." He considered that God is able to raise people even from the dead, from which he also received him back as a type.

Since God had made all kinds of promises related to Abraham's seed through Isaac, Abraham was convinced that God would need to raise Isaac from the dead.

Security in the Lord

> Trust [*batach*—the feeling of safety and security when one can rely on someone else] in the Lord and do good; Dwell in the land and cultivate faithfulness [friendship]. Delight yourself in the Lord; And He will give you the desires of your heart. Commit [entrust] your way to the Lord, Trust also in Him, and He will do it. He will bring forth your righteousness as the light And your judgment as the noonday. Rest [*damam*—the absence of emotional distress and churning, the ability to relax] in the Lord and wait patiently for Him; Do not fret because of him who prospers in his way, Because of the man who carries out wicked schemes. …But the humble will inherit the land And will delight themselves in abundant prosperity.
>
> Psalm 37:3–7, 11

In Psalm 37, David is communicating the various aspects of the ability of faith and trust; it takes the believer on a journey to believe God for more. In his preoccupation with God's life, the humble believer finds his security in the Lord and His provisions and finds delight in His friendship. He can wait for God to give him what the Lord wishes him to have at the proper time. The passage connects this trust to a righteousness that defines his new life in the Lord. The believer shares in the Lord's righteousness, having set aside his desires. The result is rest and the ability to relax in any situation. Jeremiah 17:8 tells us that the man who trusts the Lord…

> Will be like a tree planted by the water, That extends its roots by a stream And will not fear when the heat comes; But its leaves will be green, And it will not be anxious in a year of drought Nor cease to yield fruit.

A Right Path

One of the most quoted Scripture passages is Proverbs 3:5–6, "Trust in the Lord with all your heart and do not lean on your own understanding. In all your ways acknowledge Him, and He will make your paths straight [*yasar*—smooth, upright]." God removes obstacles, making the way smooth or right. It begs the question: what role does the believer play in directing his own path? Proverbs 16:9 clarifies this issue, "The mind of man plans his way, but the Lord directs [*kun*—makes firm, establishes] his steps." The believer may have specific ideas about what he should do, but he defers the final decision to the Lord.

This principle plays itself out in many different ways. For example, I recently needed to purchase a new vehicle for my wife after her car was "totaled" in an accident. We did not believe we should take on a new car payment, so we were restricted to what we could afford based on the amount we would receive from the insurance company. We started looking and found a used car at a local dealer and went to check it out. We wanted something else, so they showed us a different make of car that we both liked. The dealer was pressuring us to take out a temporary loan to purchase the vehicle that day, but we believed that if God wanted us to have it, it would be available when we had all the funds.

On the way to purchase the car about one week later, we found out about a newer car of the same make and model that another dealer offered for much less than the one we planned to purchase. It turns out it had more features for less money and was available because we were willing to wait and trust God. Walking by faith has incredible benefits.

Lord of All

The decision to trust God for every detail of life is not based on some feeling that overwhelms the believer to do the right thing, but a choice to let God be God and accept whatever happens as His right. If Paul was right when he declared that the believer is no longer his own, he was bought with a price, then allowing the Lord to be Lord is its reasonable conclusion. Hudson Taylor is quoted as saying, "He is either Lord of all or He is not Lord at all." Faith in God is a decision of the heart and takes courage. It is the doorway into the believer's promised land. Paul said to his shipmates as the ship was ready to run aground, "Therefore, keep up your courage, men, for I believe God that it will turn out exactly as I have been told" (Acts 27:25).

> Good and upright is the Lord; Therefore, He instructs sinners in the way. He leads the humble in justice, And He teaches the humble His way. All the paths of the Lord are lovingkindness and truth To those who keep His covenant and His testimonies.
>
> Psalm 25:8–10

What Follows

The following fifty-two chapters, one for each week of the year, reveal various aspects of the righteous man, who lives his life through his faith in the one who has created a righteous path. As Paul defines it in Romans 6:17–18,

> But thanks be to God that though you were slaves of sin, you became obedient from the heart to that form of teaching to which you were committed, and having been freed from sin, you became slaves [voluntarily under the dominion] of righteousness.

What Is Salvation?

Chapter 1: Born of God

But as many as received Him, to them He gave the right to become children of God, even to those who believe in His name, who were born, not of blood nor of the will of the flesh nor of the will of man, but of God.

John 1:12–13

We see from an examination of different New Testament Scripture writers that each one has particular insights that others do not. For example, if you want to understand the role and importance of God's grace, you will consult the apostle Paul and his letters. James, the half-brother of Jesus, had an understanding of the power of the tongue like no other author. The apostle John is the one who provides the deepest understanding of the new relationship with God in Christ, being born of God. The account from John 3 of Jesus's meeting with Nicodemus is not covered by any other writer.

John testifies in verse 13 above that being born of God is not the result of anyone's genealogy (i.e., born of Jewish descent), human will (effort), or human choice (decision). God's will and only God's will is the creator of this new relationship in Christ, by faith in what He did. "Just as He chose us in Him before the foundation of the world" (Ephesians 1:4). This means that each one born of God is individually a child of God; God has no grandchildren. John recognized that to be born of God is to be born from above.

Born from above by Faith

Jesus answered and said to him, "Truly, truly, I say to you, unless one is born again [*anoethen*—from above] he cannot see the kingdom of God." Nicodemus said to Him, "How can a man be born when he is old? He cannot enter a second time into his mother's womb and be born, can he?" Jesus answered, "Truly, truly, I say to you, unless one is born of water and the Spirit he cannot enter into the kingdom of God. That which is born of the flesh is flesh, and that which is born of the Spirit is spirit. Do not be amazed that I said to you, 'You must be born again [from above].' The wind blows where it wishes and you hear the sound of it, but do not know where it comes from and where it is going; so is everyone who is born of the Spirit."

John 3:3–8

Although a seasoned Pharisee and well-respected teacher, Nicodemus had no clue what this new relationship with God would look like. The concept of being born from above was foreign to him. The Jewish perspective had been that being born Jewish and "keeping the law" was enough to guarantee an eternal relationship with God. But Paul testified that this approach falls short of the life defined by being born of God. In Galatians 3:23–24,

But before faith came, we were kept in custody under the law, being shut up to the faith which was later to be revealed. Therefore, the Law has become our tutor to lead us to Christ, so that we may be justified by faith.

The Law is a transitionary step to eternal life in Christ. To be born of God is to be born of the Holy Spirit.

In John 3:13, Jesus tells us that "no one has ascended into heaven, but He who descended from heaven: the Son of Man." The spiritual life is the result of God coming to us and not man reaching God. This is the exact mistake that the people of Babel, led by Nimrod, made in trying to "make for ourselves a name" (Genesis 11:4). The tower of Babel was man's attempt, through a human effort, to bridge the gap between earth and heaven. Man always tries to accomplish things, even religious matters, by human effort, without God's help. In this way, man can take credit for his work. This is why salvation is a work of God alone, and it is the Son of God who delivers salvation to man by grace from heaven to Earth. No matter how good man's efforts may be, they can never measure up to the standard God's justice demands (Isaiah 64:6).

A Living Hope

Blessed be the God and Father of our Lord Jesus Christ, who according to His great mercy has caused us to be born again [*anagennaoe*—to be reborn, regenerated] to a living hope through the resurrection of Jesus Christ from the dead, to obtain an inheritance which is imperishable and undefiled and will not fade away, reserved in heaven for you.

1 Peter 1:3–4

Peter speaks of this reality in the introduction of his first letter to Christians scattered throughout Asia Minor. He says that we are born of God "to a living hope," connecting each believer to the life of Christ and all that it entails. It is "Christ in you, the hope of glory" (Colossians 1:27); He is the blessed hope, "who gave Himself for us to redeem us from every lawless deed, and to purify for Himself a people for His own possession, zealous for good deeds" (Titus 2:14). In 1 John 3:2–3, the Holy Spirit tells us that the believer is purified when his hope is fixed on Christ and, "We know that when He appears, we will be like Him because we will see Him just as He is."

Peter connects the new birth to "the living and enduring word of God" (1 Peter 1:23), an imperishable seed. He quotes Isaiah 40:6–8 in verses 24–25,

ALL FLESH IS LIKE GRASS, AND ALL ITS GLORY LIKE THE FLOWER OF GRASS. THE GRASS WITHERS, AND THE FLOWER FALLS OFF, BUT THE WORD OF THE LORD ENDURES FOREVER.

As Peter concludes, "And this is the word which was preached to you." For the true believer, the new birth connects him to eternity by the eternal *Word of the Lord.*

Walk by the Spirit

John introduces the relationship between the new birth and sin in 1 John 3:9–10,

No one who is born of God practices sin, because His seed abides in him; and he cannot sin, because he is born of God. By this the children of God and the children of the devil are obvious: anyone who does not practice righteousness is not of God, nor the one who does not love his brother.

Of course, this passage is very controversial, suggesting to some that a true believer has won the complete victory over the sin nature so he cannot sin. There are so many verses saying the very opposite that contradict this interpretation.

To understand the meaning, one needs to consider what took place at the moment of salvation. The 1 John 3 passage above tells us that a synonym for being born of God is being born of the Spirit (verse 8). The human spirit, dead or dormant in each person before salvation, comes alive and is now able to hear from and discern the Holy Spirit (1 Corinthians 2:14, Romans 8:16). According to Proverbs 20:27, "The spirit of man is the lamp of the Lord, searching all the innermost parts of his being." After salvation, the believer still must choose who will be the lord of his life, Jesus Christ and His Spirit, or someone else (the flesh). In Galatians 5:16–17,

> But I say, walk by the Spirit, and you will not carry out the desire of the flesh. For the flesh sets its desire against the Spirit, and the Spirit against the flesh; for these are in opposition to one another, so that you may not do the things that you please.

The conclusion we may draw is that man cannot sin while he is operating under the authority and leading of the Holy Spirit. The onus is on the righteous man to decide which force he will be subject to, the Holy Spirit or the flesh (see Romans 6:16–19). According to *Barnes' Notes*, 1 John 3:9 can be understood in light of these two observations:

1. That the germ or seed of religion implanted in the soul abides there as a constant, vital principle so that he who is born of God cannot become habitually a sinner.
2. That it will so continue to live there that he will not fall away and perish. The idea is clearly that the germ or principle of piety so permanently abides in the soul [spirit] that he who is renewed never can become again characteristically a sinner.

Victory over the Evil One

If anyone sees his brother committing a sin not leading to death, he shall ask and God will for him give life to those who commit sin not leading to death. There is a sin leading to death; I do not say that he should make request for this. All unrighteousness is sin, and there is a sin not leading to death. We know that no one who is born of God sins; but He who was born of God keeps him, and the evil one does not touch him. We know that we are of God, and that the whole world lies in the power of the evil one.

1 John 5:16–19

John provides a further definition of the effect of sin on the believer's life in the above passage. He addresses believers (brothers) and the power of sin in another believer's life. John encourages him to pray for those who live in unrighteousness, which is sin. He also speaks of "a sin leading to death." What John wishes to teach is that there is a power (law) of sin and death (see Romans 8:2) that works against the righteous one, but there is also a power that keeps or protects him (the law of the Spirit of life in Christ Jesus). The world is subject to the power of the evil one, but the one born of God has the protection of God working on his behalf. In 1 Peter 1:5, we "are protected by the power of God through faith."

God Is Love

The principle of agape (unconditional, self-sacrificing) love is directly connected to the one born of God. In 1 John 4:7–9 (emphasis added by the author),

Beloved, let us love one another, for love is from God; and everyone who loves [*agapao*] is born of God and knows [*ginosko*—determined or governed by love—Kittels] God. The one who does not love does not know God, for *God is love*. By this the love of God was manifested in us, that God has sent His only begotten Son into the world so that we might live through Him.

The one born of God loves God and loves his neighbor (Matthew 22:37–39). Since God is love, the ordained relationship the righteous man has with Him is defined and governed by that love and results in a desire to keep His commandments. In 1 John 2:3–5 (emphasis added by the author),

> By this we know that we have come to know Him, if we keep His commandments. The one who says, "I have come to know Him," and does not keep His commandments, is a liar, and the truth is not in him; but whoever keeps His word, *in him the love of God has truly been perfected.*

The new covenant relationship with God begins with faith in Jesus as the Messiah, and this relationship is ruled by the love (*agape*) of God. That love produces love for other righteous ones as well as a desire to honor and keep His commandments. That love manifested through the life of genuine righteous ones overcomes the world. Ultimately, this perfect position before God is the manifestation of faith, hope, and love, "but the greatest of these is love" (1 Corinthians 13:13).

> Whoever believes that Jesus is the Christ is born of God, and whoever loves the Father loves the child born of Him. By this we know that we love the children of God, when we love God and observe His commandments. For this is the love of God, that we keep His commandments; and His commandments are not burdensome. For whatever is born of God overcomes the world; and this is the victory that has overcome the world—our faith.
>
> 1 John 5:1–4

Chapter 2: An Anatomy of Salvation

What are the conditions for eternal salvation according to the Bible? The passage that comes immediately to mind is Ephesians 2:8–9 (emphasis added by the author): "For by grace you have been saved through faith; and that not of yourselves, *it is the gift of God*; not as a result of works, so that no one may boast." Grace is another word for a free gift, and faith means to trust or be firmly persuaded. It involves a free gift and includes trust in something or someone. In John 3:16, that someone is "His only begotten Son," and is a clear reference to Jesus Christ. When one trusts in Jesus Christ as "His only begotten Son," he is ready to receive a free gift, a gift that human works cannot receive. It is the gift of salvation in Ephesians 2:8, but this gift may also be referred to as eternal life (John 3:16). And what about the gift of the Holy Spirit (Acts 2:38)? This is an amazing gift!

In John 4, Jesus and His disciples were traveling to Galilee from Judea, and He made a point to travel through Samaria, a route not normally traveled by a good Jew. This was intentional because He had a divine appointment with a Samaritan (Gentile) woman. In verse 10, Jesus spoke to her, "If you knew the gift of God, and who it is who says to you, 'Give Me a drink,' you would have asked Him, and He would have given you living water." But, of course, Jesus was teaching her, a Gentile, about salvation and receiving eternal life (verse 14). He was teaching her that the elements of salvation are the recognition of the Giver, who He is, and that He has a free gift for her.

Later in the conversation, she recognizes Him as a prophet (verse 19), and then in verses 25–26, Jesus confirms that He is the Messiah. How do we know she got saved? In verses 28–29, "So the woman left her waterpot, and went into the city and said to the men, 'Come, see a man who told me all the things that I have done; this is not the Christ, is it?'" She became the first missionary in the New Testament age. She accepted the free gift when she recognized the Giver.

The Simplicity of the Gospel

This is the simplicity of the gospel. Saul of Tarsus was on his way to Damascus as an esteemed Pharisee when something profound took place. He tells the story this way in Acts 26:14–16,

> And when we had all fallen to the ground, I heard a voice saying to me in the Hebrew dialect, 'Saul, Saul, why are you persecuting Me? It is hard for you to kick against the goads.' And I said, 'Who are You, Lord?' And the Lord said, 'I am Jesus whom you are persecuting. But get up and stand on your feet; for this purpose, I have appeared to you, to appoint you a minister and a witness not only to the things which you have seen, but also to the things in which I will appear to you.'

At that moment, Saul realized that Jesus of Nazareth was the Messiah and Jesus was elevating Saul into his gift. The manifestation of that gift in soon-to-be Paul's life was the incredible ministry God was calling him to, that he would be the apostle to the Gentiles.

There's another example to consider here. It's found in Acts 16 when Paul and Silas are imprisoned in a Philippian jail. The reasons why are not important to this conversation. God decided that Paul and Silas were no longer to remain in jail, so He sent an earthquake to shake the foundations of the prison house, and the prison doors were opened. The jailer woke up to see this miraculous event and drew his sword to kill himself, believing the magistrate would have him put to death since the prisoners were escaping. In verses 28–29, "But Paul cried out with a loud voice, saying, 'Do not harm yourself, for we are all here!' And he called for lights and rushed in, and trembling with fear he fell down before Paul and Silas." His question to them still sounds today: "Sirs, what must I do to be saved?"

Their answer also rings true today: "Believe in [*epi*—on] the Lord Jesus, and you will be saved, you and your household." This jailer and his whole household believed in Jesus as Lord and were gloriously saved.

They acknowledged the Giver and received the gift of life, eternal life. It's so simple yet so profound.

The Gift Is Free

Paul teaches that "the wages of sin is death, but the free gift of God is eternal life *in Christ Jesus our Lord*" in Romans 6:23 (emphasis added by the author). Eternal life, the free gift, is found "in Christ Jesus our Lord." Paul uses this terminology, "in Christ" or "in Him," more than 150 times to emphasize that the believer's connection to Jesus is not religious but rather all about relationship and an exchange of life. What is the evidence of that life? It is in the relationship of believers among themselves (1 John 3:14). See Bishop Stephen Neil's comment:

> In the fellowship of those who are bound together by personal loyalty to Jesus Christ, the relationship of love reaches an intimacy and intensity unknown elsewhere. Friendship between the friends of Jesus of Nazareth is unlike any other friendship, and this ought to be the normal experience within the Church. Where it is experienced, especially across the barriers of race, nationality, and language, it is one of the most convincing evidences of the continuing activity of Jesus among men.

This means that being "in Christ" has supernatural implications as the righteous man shares in the life of Christ and with each other.

There is so much more to the free gift. In Romans 5:15–17 (emphasis added by the author),

> But *the free gift* is not like the transgression. For if by the transgression of the one the many died, much more did the grace of God and *the gift* by the grace of the one Man, Jesus Christ, abound to the many. *The gift* is not like that which came through the one who sinned; for on the one hand the judgment arose from one transgression resulting in condemnation, but on the other hand *the free gift* arose from many transgressions resulting in justification. For if by the transgression of the one, death reigned through the one, much more those who receive the abundance of grace and of *the gift of righteousness* will reign in life through the One, Jesus Christ.

This gift is not only free but much more, abounding to many. This gift solves the transgression problem and becomes the gift of righteousness, resulting in the believer "reigning in life through the One, Jesus Christ." What a gift!

Chapter 3: Adopted or Orphaned

At the Last Supper, Jesus consoled His disciples that He would be leaving them but would not leave them as orphans (John 14:18). He told them that the world would not see Him, but they would. He was trying to get them to see that a new relationship was in order, that they would be sons, adopted sons.

Paul reveals this principle of adoption in a number of his letters. In Romans 8:15–17,

> For you have not received a spirit of slavery leading to fear again, but you have received a spirit of adoption as sons by which we cry out, "Abba! Father!" The Spirit Himself testifies with our spirit that we are children of God, and if children, heirs also, heirs of God and fellow heirs with Christ, if indeed we suffer with Him so that we may also be glorified with Him.

Although the believer is not a son by blood, adoption means he has the same rights as a full-blooded son, including being an heir. The Aramaic word "Abba" could be better translated as "Daddy" since it means that our relationship with our heavenly Father is just like a child's.

Father to the Fatherless

God promises in Psalm 68:5 that He is a father to the fatherless. In Deuteronomy 10:18, "He executes justice for the orphan and the widow." In the New Testament, He tells believers that true religion in the sight of our God and Father is "to visit orphans and widows in their distress" (James 1:27). The Father wants righteous ones to recognize their sonship.

In Ezekiel 28:16, Lucifer, otherwise known as Satan, was kicked out of heaven from the mountain of God because he had an "I" problem. In Isaiah 14:13–14,

But you said in your heart, 'I will ascend to heaven; I will raise my throne above the stars of God, And I will sit on the mount of assembly In the recesses of the north. I will ascend above the heights of the clouds; I will make myself like the Most High.'

Because he got too wrapped up in himself and his beauty, he lost his high position. Since he cannot be a son, he now wishes everyone to believe they are orphans. He does it by getting man to be centered on self.

There is a story about a Jewish man who wrote a letter to his rabbi because he was unhappy and needed guidance in getting his life on track. The letter read: "I need your help. I wake up every day sad and anxious. I have difficulty concentrating. I find it hard to pray. I feel that life has lost its joy and meaning. I need help." The rabbi delivered his reply without writing a single word. Instead, the rabbi took a red pen and circled the first word of every sentence: "I."

Godly Discipline

Jeremiah writes in Lamentations 5 that the Jews in their captivity in Babylon have become like orphans and widows. In verses 1–9 (emphasis added by the author),

> Remember, O Lord, what has befallen us; Look, and see our reproach! Our inheritance has been turned over to strangers, Our houses to aliens. *We have become orphans without a father*, Our mothers are like widows. We have to pay for our drinking water, Our wood comes to us at a price. Our pursuers are at our necks; We are worn out, there is no rest for us. We have submitted to Egypt and Assyria to get enough bread. Our fathers sinned and are no more; It is we who have borne their iniquities. Slaves rule over us; There is no one to deliver us from their hand. We get our bread at the risk of our lives Because of the sword in the wilderness.

They could not see their heavenly Father amid their estrangement from their God away from the homeland. They did not appreciate that the Father disciplines His sons.

> And you have forgotten the exhortation which is addressed to you as sons, "MY SON, DO NOT REGARD LIGHTLY THE DISCI-

PLINE OF THE LORD, NOR FAINT WHEN YOU ARE RE-
PROVED BY HIM; FOR THOSE WHOM THE LORD LOVES
HE DISCIPLINES, AND HE SCOURGES EVERY SON WHOM
HE RECEIVES." It is for discipline that you endure; God deals with
you as with sons; for what son is there whom his Father does not discipline? But if you are without discipline, of which all have become
partakers, then you are illegitimate children and not sons.

Hebrews 12:5–8

Being disciplined by the Lord does not confirm that we are orphans,
but it is clear evidence that we, like the Jews (Exodus 4:22), are adopted
sons. When life gets hard, and we think we are somehow being punished,
it is most likely a lie. The discipline of the Lord is not punishment but
rather training. The Greek word translated as "discipline" is *paideia*, and
it can also mean "education by training." The Septuagint, the Greek translation of the Old Testament, uses this same Greek word when translating
Proverbs 22:6, "Train up a child in the way he should go, Even when he
is old, he will not depart from it." God is always trying to prepare His
people for the road ahead, and He does it by training.

Finding Sonship

But when the fullness of the time came, God sent forth His Son,
born of a woman, born under the Law, so that He might redeem
those who were under the Law, that we might receive the adoption as
sons. Because you are sons, God has sent forth the Spirit of His Son
into our hearts, crying, "Abba! Father!" Therefore, you are no longer a
slave, but a son; and if a son, then an heir through God.

Galatians 4:4–7

The fullness of time has come in the form of Jesus Christ. In our
relationship with Him, we find our sonship. In that sonship, we are not
operating under a set of rules and regulations that are intended to keep
us in line. Instead, we find that the love of God that caused Him to adopt
us as sons is now the primary motive for living within the family unit.
We recognize our role as sons, representing a king and His kingdom, and
understand that when our lives glorify the king as sons, we confirm our
position as heirs of the kingdom.

One of the marks of our sonship is our concern and care for widows and orphans. James 1:27 says, "Pure and undefiled religion in the sight of our God and Father is this: to visit orphans and widows in their distress, and to keep oneself unstained by the world." The Lord has a special heart for the fatherless, desiring to be a father to anyone willing to acknowledge His lordship. "A father of the fatherless and a judge for the widows, is God in His holy habitation" (Psalm 68:5). Sonship is not just a title but is, more importantly, a way of life. "Vindicate the weak and fatherless; Do justice to the afflicted and destitute. Rescue the weak and needy; Deliver them out of the hand of the wicked" (Psalm 82:3–4).

Chapter 4: A Galilean Wedding

It is no coincidence that Jesus performed His first miracle at a Galilean (Cana) wedding. The wedding was the most important event in the Galilean villages on Jesus's day since it was to be celebrated by all. The entire church age, as defined by the new covenant established by Jesus at His first coming, is predicated on the traditional wedding feast of the first century. By examining the elements of this wedding, the believer in Christ can begin to appreciate the sanctity of the relationship with Christ, His completed work, and His promises.

The wedding began with a betrothal. The bridegroom's father would select a bride for his son, and the bridegroom would obtain a marriage covenant. The father of the bride and bridegroom would agree upon a dowry to be given by the bridegroom to the bride as a consideration in case of the abandonment or divorce of the bride. The bridegroom selected a ring and took a cup of wine to offer to the bride, and her acceptance represented a legally binding covenant contract. Upon its acceptance, the bridegroom would acknowledge to all in attendance that he would not partake of the wine until the consummation of the wedding, to take place a year later at the feast.

Getting Ready

Between the betrothal and the feast, the bride and her bridesmaids selected the wedding clothing in preparation for the wedding. This could take many months since the linens and fabrics may be available elsewhere. The bride's primary interest is getting ready for the wedding and her new life in a new place. Once the bride and bridesmaids acquired their wedding clothes, they would wait in their wedding clothes to be alerted by a shofar (trumpet) that the bridegroom was coming for his bride. At the same time, the bridegroom returned home to prepare the wedding chambers. Neither the bridegroom nor the bride would know the exact date; only the bridegroom's father would know. So, the bride and bridegroom would be waiting for the notification that the time had come.

During the middle of a night, only known to the father of the bridegroom, he would notify his son to go get his bride. Then, the bridegroom sounded the shofar, and the bride and bridesmaids joined him in the street for the wedding procession, ensuring they had enough oil to light the lamps. The bridegroom would then place the bride in a seat to be carried to the wedding chamber, where the marriage is consummated.

Chosen by the Father

The betrothal period is a reference to Jesus's first coming, while the wedding feast is a picture of the Marriage Supper of the Lamb (Revelations 19:7–9), to occur shortly after His return for His bride (the rapture). The father of the bridegroom is God the Father, who "chose us in Him before the foundation of the world, that we would be holy and blameless before Him" (Ephesians 1:4). Also, 2 Corinthians 11:2, "For I betrothed you to one husband, so that to Christ I might present you as a pure virgin." We become the chosen ones when we accept the cup of the new covenant (salvation by grace through faith) during the betrothal period. The disciples drank this cup of the new covenant at the Last Supper. At the same time, Jesus (the bridegroom) said, "For I say to you, I will not drink of the fruit of the vine from now on until the kingdom of God comes" (Luke 22:18). The dowry represents the price paid by the bridegroom and His Father, namely the blood (Ephesians 5:25).

Between the betrothal and the feast, the bridegroom prepares the new home for his bride as John 14:2–3 says,

> In My Father's house are many dwelling places; if it were not so, I would have told you; for I go to prepare a place for you. If I go and prepare a place for you, I will come again and receive you to Myself, that where I am, there you may be also.

He then waits for his father to tell him when to go get his bride. In Matthew 24:36, "But of that day and hour no one knows, not even the angels of heaven, nor the Son, but the Father alone."

The Signs of the Times

At the same time, the bride is preparing for the wedding ceremony, finding the needed linens for the dress. This speaks of the believer following the apostle's instructions, "not as in my presence only, but now much more in my absence," working out his salvation with fear and trembling (Philippians 2:12). When the signs of the times suggest Jesus's return is near, he is "on the alert, for you do not know which day your Lord is coming" (Matthew 24:42). Jesus challenged His disciples in this passage to be ready.

At a time determined by the Father, Jesus will return for His bride,

> For the Lord Himself will descend from heaven with a shout, with the voice of the archangel and with the trumpet of God, and the dead in Christ will rise first. Then we who are alive and remain will be *caught up together with them in the clouds* to meet the Lord in the air, and so we shall always be with the Lord.
>
> 1 Thessalonians 4:16–17
(emphasis added by the author)

The bride of Christ is those both alive and dead at His appearing. Just as the bridegroom carries his bride to the wedding chamber, the bride of Christ will be "caught up together" in the clouds.

The Oil and the Holy Spirit

The bride and her maids needed to have oil to light the lamps. The oil is a reference to the anointing and the Holy Spirit. For the bride to be allowed to enter the chamber, she needed the oil of the Holy Spirit. The message Jesus gave to His disciples in Matthew 25:1–13 about ten virgins speaks to this principle. Five of the ten virgins were prudent to bring flasks of oil, while the others did not. Only those with oil were allowed into the wedding feast. A Galilean wedding would last seven days, so the door is shut for seven days. The seven days represent a pre-tribulation rapture since, in this context, the seven days represent the seven-year Great Tribulation. Jesus warns His disciples in verse 13 to be on alert. I conclude that the prudent virgins are true believers in Jesus, having received the Holy Spirit as a promise (Ephesians 1:13–14), while the others are the Jews, who were not yet willing to recognize Jesus as their Messiah. They will get another chance during the Great Tribulation.

Conclusion

Believers in Christ, His bride, can expect that the bridegroom is preparing their future homes in heaven. He is coming soon to receive us so that we can begin to enjoy all the blessings promised to us as new covenant believers, including an inheritance. Preparation requires us to be ever conscious of His imminent return, as Titus 2:13–14 encourages,

> Looking for the blessed hope and the appearing of our great God and Savior, Christ Jesus, Who gave Himself for us to redeem us from every lawless deed, and to purify for Himself a people for His own possession, zealous for good deeds.

The Sinfulness of Mankind

Chapter 5: The Corruption of Mankind

> For the creation was subjected to futility, not willingly, but because of Him who subjected it, in hope that the creation itself also will be set free from its slavery to corruption into the freedom of the glory of the children of God. For we know that the whole creation groans and suffers the pains of childbirth together until now.
>
> Romans 8:20–22

When God created the garden of Eden, He made it a perfect place to live. After creating man, He empowered him with the ability to exercise dominion over the garden and everything in it. The Lord gave Adam great freedom in fulfilling his responsibilities, with one exception, "From any tree of the garden you may eat freely; but from the tree of the knowledge of good and evil you shall not eat, for in the day that you eat from it *you will surely die*." (Genesis 2:16–17) (emphasis added by the author).

As we know, this one prohibition created an opportunity for sin (Romans 7:7–12), and Satan used it as a means of deception, and mankind still lives with the consequences of Adam and Eve's decision. According to Genesis 3:6–7 (emphasis added by the author),

> When the woman saw that the tree was good for food, and that it was a delight to the eyes, and that *the tree was desirable to make one wise* [*sakal*—to act with insight, prudence], she took from its fruit and ate; and she gave also to her husband with her, and he ate. Then the eyes of both of them were opened.

Curses

As a result, not only did God curse Satan, Adam, and Eve, but He also cursed the ground. According to Jamieson Fausett and Brown Commentary:

In the rich and smiling garden of Eden, the vigorous and prolific soil yielded a spontaneous produce, and the industry of man was confined to the easy and pleasant work of checking or regulating the luxuriant growth of vegetation. This state, because anything we are told to the contrary, would have been perpetuated but for the disobedience of rebellious man, who, with the solemn warning of the penal consequences still ringing in his ears, transgressed, and with the loss of his innocence forfeited the happy place of his primeval abode. The awful curse of an offended God fell not, however, upon Adam himself, as it did upon the serpent, but upon the ground 'for his sake.'

Therefore, it would be necessary to expel them from Eden so their sin might not be immortalized. In Genesis 3:23, "Therefore the Lord God sent him out from the garden of Eden, to cultivate the ground from which he was taken." Cherubim were stationed at the entrance to keep mankind from his paradise for a time. Adam and Eve must leave paradise for a corrupted (cursed) world. Man would now face the results of Adam's sin, illustrated in the life of his son, Cain. Without a provision for sin, Cain would commit a heinous crime by murdering his brother out of jealousy. The Lord addressed it with him in Genesis 4:7 (emphasis added by the author),

If you do well, will not your countenance be lifted up? And if you do not do well, sin is crouching at the door; and its desire is for you, *but you must master [masal—to rule, reign, have dominion over] it.*

Of course, Cain was not able to rule over or master his sin. By inheritance, we all face the same challenges.

The Coming Flood

According to Josephus, Adam had been warned by God of two judgments, one by fire and another *by the violence and quantity of water* (Antiquities 1.2.3). God never told him which one would come first. It would be 1,656 years from creation until the flood when the corruption of sin became more and more consuming. It ultimately resulted in a deeper corruption, brought on by demonic forces and documented in Genesis 6:1–8 (emphasis added by the author),

Now it came about, when men began to multiply on the face of the land, and daughters were born to them, that the sons [*ben*—offspring, descendants] of God [Elohim] saw that the daughters of men [*adam*—mankind] were beautiful; and they took wives for themselves, whomever they chose. Then the Lord said, "My Spirit shall not strive with man forever, because he also is flesh; nevertheless, his days shall be one hundred and twenty years." The Nephilim were on the earth in those days, and also afterward, when the sons of God came in to the daughters of men, and they bore children to them. Those were the mighty men who were of old, men of renown. Then the Lord saw that the wickedness of man was great on the earth, and *that every intent of the thoughts of his heart was only evil continually.* The Lord was sorry that He had made man on the earth, and *He was grieved in His heart.* The Lord said, "I will blot out man whom I have created from the face of the land, from man to animals to creeping things and to birds of the sky; for I am sorry that I have made them." But Noah found favor in the eyes of the Lord.

This passage suggests there was a further attempt to immortalize man's sin through a demonic attempt to pervert mankind in a greater way, an organized conspiracy among evil forces to corrupt mankind and the animal world. The conspiracy was that the promise of Genesis 3:15, "And I will put enmity Between you and the woman, And between your seed and her seed; He shall bruise you on the head, And you shall bruise him on the heel," would never be fulfilled.

Testaments of the Patriarchs

According to the legend in the Talmud of the orthodox Jews and the Essene community, all of the patriarchs from Adam to Aaron (thirty-seven or more) were prophets, and all wrote testaments for their posterity. From the Testament of Noah, as preserved in the Dead Sea Scrolls, we find out that Noah was taught from birth the ways of righteousness and was faithful to walk in God's instructions. From Column 6 of that testament, we learn:

After many years, about ten jubilees, when my sons should have been married, the Lord appeared to me in a vision. He showed me the conduct of the sons of heaven. I thought about the vision... the great

Holy One sent the Watcher to instruct me. In the vision, he said, in a loud voice, "they are talking about you, Noah" … I considered their behavior and knew who would succeed. After two weeks… bore witness to all the blood shed by the Nephilim, I waited until… the daughters of men whom the holy ones made unclean by divination. I went and asked one of them… I, Noah, found grace, prominence, and righteousness in the eyes of the Lord… to cattle, wild animals, birds and even humans… the entire deed was very…

According to the Book of Enoch, chapter 6:1–5, it is reported:

And it came to pass when the children of men had multiplied that in those days were born unto them beautiful and comely daughters. And the angels, the children of the heaven, saw and lusted after them, and said to one another: 'Come, let us choose us wives from among the children of men and beget us, children.' And Semajaza, who was their leader, said unto them: 'I fear ye will not indeed agree to do this deed, and I alone shall have to pay the penalty of a great sin.' And they all answered him and said: 'Let us swear an oath, and all bind ourselves by mutual imprecations not to abandon this plan but to do this thing.' Then sware they all together and bound themselves by mutual imprecations upon it.

According to chapter 7:1–6,

And all the others together with them took unto themselves wives, and each chose for himself one, and they began to go in unto them and to defile themselves with them, and they taught them charms and enchantments, and the cutting of roots, and made them acquainted with plants. And they became pregnant, and they bare great giants, whose height was three thousand ells: Who consumed all the acquisitions of men. And when men could no longer sustain them, the giants turned against them and devoured mankind. And they began to sin against birds, and beasts, and reptiles, and fish, and to devour one another's flesh and drink the blood. Then the earth laid accusations against the lawless ones.

The Purity of Kind

Hebrews 11:7 gives us a further definition of this reality,

> By faith Noah, being warned by God about things not yet seen, in reverence prepared an ark for the salvation of his household, by which he condemned the world, and became an heir of the righteousness which is according to faith.

Humanity was warned of the coming judgment, but only Noah, his wife, three sons, and their wives were delivered from this judgment. The lesson to be learned is that God intends that mankind keeps each of his "kind" pure. Noah was instructed in Genesis 7:14–15,

> They and every beast after its kind, and all the cattle after their kind, and every creeping thing that creeps on the earth after its kind, and every bird after its kind, all sorts of birds. So, they went into the ark to Noah, by twos of all flesh in which was the breath of life.

This principle applies to mankind as well, as Ezra 9:1–4 conveys,

> Now when these things had been completed, the princes approached me, saying, "The people of Israel and the priests and the Levites have not separated themselves from the peoples of the lands, according to their abominations, those of the Canaanites, the Hittites, the Perizzites, the Jebusites, the Ammonites, the Moabites, the Egyptians and the Amorites. "For they have taken some of their daughters as wives for themselves and for their sons, so that the holy race has intermingled with the peoples of the lands; indeed, the hands of the princes and the rulers have been foremost in this unfaithfulness." When I heard about this matter, I tore my garment and my robe, and pulled some of the hair from my head and my beard and sat down appalled. Then everyone who trembled at the words of the God of Israel on account of the unfaithfulness of the exiles gathered to me, and I sat appalled until the evening offering.

Ezra was instructing men to remain holy, to be set apart, and not to intermarry with anyone not of his kind. In Ezra 9:12,

> So now do not give your daughters to their sons nor take their daughters to your sons, and never seek their peace or their prosperity, that

you may be strong and eat the good things of the land and leave it as an inheritance to your sons forever.

Peter helps us understand further details of this intended corruption in 2 Peter 2:4–9,

> For if God did not spare angels when they sinned, but cast them into hell and committed them to pits of darkness, reserved for judgment; and did not spare the ancient world, but preserved Noah, a preacher of righteousness, with seven others, when He brought a flood upon the world of the ungodly; and if He condemned the cities of Sodom and Gomorrah to destruction by reducing them to ashes, having made them an example to those who would live ungodly lives thereafter; and if He rescued righteous Lot, oppressed by the sensual conduct of unprincipled men (for by what he saw and heard that righteous man, while living among them, felt his righteous soul tormented day after day by their lawless deeds), then the Lord knows how to rescue the godly from temptation, and to keep the unrighteous under punishment for the day of judgment.

A Scattering

It took more than two hundred years since the flood for the third judgment of God to visit mankind. This judgment came in the form of a scattering of the people and confusion of their language, as reported in Genesis 11:1–9 (emphasis added by the author),

> Now the whole earth used the same language and the same words. It came about as they journeyed east, that they found a plain in the land of Shinar and settled there. They said to one another, "Come, let us make bricks and burn them thoroughly." And they used brick for stone, and they used tar for mortar. They said, "Come, let us *build for ourselves a city* and a tower whose top will reach into heaven, *and let us make for ourselves a name*; otherwise, we will be scattered abroad over the face of the whole earth." The Lord came down to see the city and the tower which the sons of men had built. The Lord said, "Behold, they are one people, and they all have the same language. And this is what they began to do, and now nothing which they purpose to do will be impossible for them. "Come, let Us go down and there confuse their language so that they will not understand one another's speech."

So, the Lord scattered them abroad from there over the face of the whole earth; and they stopped building the city. Therefore, its name was called Babel, because there the Lord confused the language of the whole earth; and from there the Lord scattered them abroad over the face of the whole earth.

In this passage, the people were organized in the land of Shinar and conspired to build themselves a city with "a tower whose top will reach into heaven" to demonstrate to God that they could do it without God, to establish a name for themselves. It reminds me of Lucifer's declaration in Isaiah 14:14, "I will make myself like the Most High." Genesis 11:4 tells us that they were concerned about being scattered abroad, so they understood this was contrary to God's will. In Proverbs 18:11, "A rich man's wealth is his strong city, And like a high wall in his own imagination." It teaches that man's abilities, apart from God, produce only an image of strength. When men come together to conspire against God, it reflects an uncontrollable spirit. According to Proverbs 25:28, "Like a city that is broken into and without walls Is a man who has no control over his spirit." When man operates outside God's authority, he sets himself up for judgment. The Lord had to scatter the people while confusing their languages; He will always come against unholy alliances. In Psalm 127:1, "Unless the Lord builds the house, they labor in vain who build it."

A Man of Promise

The immediate conclusion to this problem would come through a man named Abram, later called Abraham by God, who would receive promises from God of blessings and a charge to leave his home for a new land, a promised land. It would be there that Abraham would begin to realize the promised blessings. The solution to the corruption of mankind is a walk of faith, choosing to believe God for His promises as revealed in His Word. In Hebrews 11:9–10 (emphasis added by the author),

By faith he lived as an alien in the land of promise, as in a foreign land, dwelling in tents with Isaac and Jacob, fellow heirs of the same promise; for *he was looking for the city which has foundations, whose architect and builder is God.*

When the believer follows the leading of God by His Holy Spirit, he trusts in God's provisions for life instead of his resources.

The promises God made to Abraham, Isaac, and Jacob redound to the new covenant believer as Paul defines in Romans 4:13 (emphasis added by the author), "For the promise to Abraham or to his descendants that he would be heir of the world was not through the Law, but *through the righteousness of faith.*" When mankind places its trust in God's promises, it walks in God's righteousness with all of its provisions for life. Moses spoke about Israel being separated for an inheritance in Deuteronomy 32:8–9,

> When the Most High gave the nations their inheritance, When He separated the sons of man, He set the boundaries of the peoples According to the number of the sons of Israel. For the Lord's portion is His people; Jacob is the allotment of His inheritance.

When man allows God to define the boundaries of his life, he becomes the Lord's portion (*heleq*—possession).

The motives that caused Babel to construct its tower still exist today. Prophesy tells us that when the antichrist appears, he will use his authority to establish a one-world government (see Revelation 13), and most of the world will follow him. Peter tells us that the provisions of God are available to all who believe. In 1 Peter 2:9–10,

> But you are A CHOSEN RACE, A royal PRIESTHOOD, A HOLY NATION, A PEOPLE FOR God's OWN POSSESSION, so that you may proclaim the excellencies of Him who has called you out of darkness into His marvelous light; for you once were NOT A PEOPLE, but now you are THE PEOPLE OF GOD; you had NOT RECEIVED MERCY, but now you have RECEIVED MERCY.

This has always been God's plan for man to overcome corruption.

CHAPTER 6: MASTERING SIN

We are introduced to the concept of sin early in the Scriptures, in Genesis 3, with the fall of Adam and Eve. Their reaction to their sin was to hide (verse 8). Then in chapter 4, Cain has a face-to-face run-in with sin, and his reaction is anger. The Lord warned him that "sin is crouching at the door and its desire is for you."

Sin is everything in the disposition and purpose and conduct of God's moral creatures that is contrary to the expressed will of God. It represents the central struggle of man. As a result, there are many manifestations of sin, as many as there are people. And according to Genesis 4, it has an energy unto itself with some type of agenda. In this case, sin wants to master Cain, so the Lord encourages Cain, "You must master it." Although it was not directly stated, it was understood that any offering to God had to be "firstlings," meaning that God deserves our best. When Abel offered his best while Cain's offering was "the fruit of the ground," the Lord had regard for Abel's offering but not Cain's. Cain's response was to kill his brother out of jealousy.

Your Sin Will Find You Out

This condition of sin is something we all wrestle with, and it cannot be hidden for long. In fact, it says in Numbers 32:23, "But if you will not do so, behold, you have sinned against the Lord, and be sure your sin will find you out." And then there is Proverbs 13:21, which says, "Adversity pursues sinners, But the righteous will be rewarded with prosperity."

This wild animal (sinful nature) that we have to face and manage creates all kinds of havoc in our lives. This defilement also has major consequences for the way we approach God. When God was speaking to Moses from the burning bush in Exodus 3:5, God told him to "remove your sandals from your feet, for the place on which you are standing is holy ground." Removal of sandals was the means by which the individual would confess personal defilement and conscious unworthiness to stand in His presence. Approaching God requires the recognition of not only His holiness but also a man's sinfulness. David spoke of his need to acknowledge his sin before God in Psalm 32. In verse 3, his body wasted away through groanings when he kept silent about his sin. In verse 5, "I acknowledged my sin to You, And my iniquity I did not hide; I said, 'I will confess my transgressions to the Lord,' and You forgave the guilt of my sin." God resists the proud and gives grace to the humble (James 4:6).

Buried with Him through Baptism

It was God's intention right from the beginning, before the foundation of the world, that Jesus Christ would solve that problem (Revelation 13:8). Paul explains in Romans 6:4–7 how we receive the provision of that work so as to be delivered from the power of sin, that is the sin nature that wishes to make us slaves:

> Therefore, we have been buried with Him through baptism into death, so that as Christ was raised from the dead through the glory of the Father, so we too might walk in newness of life. For if we have become united with Him in the likeness of His death, certainly we shall also be in the likeness of His resurrection, knowing this [experientially], that our old self was crucified with Him, in order that our body of sin might be done away with [made inoperative], so that we would no longer be slaves to sin; for he who has died is freed from sin.

So how do we, as those living in the twenty-first century, become united with Christ in His death? I have a personal experience that may illustrate the answer.

Spiritual DNA

My uncle Maurice Belanger was a Marine airplane mechanic on Midway Island in June 1942 when the Japanese struck American forces by surprise, killing many servicemen and civilians, my uncle included. It is noteworthy that many historians believe that the Battle of Midway

Island was the turning point in America's fight to win the war against the Japanese. The day after my uncle died, American dive bombers took on Japanese aircraft carriers and aircraft and stopped them from taking control of the island. Maurice Belanger, along with thousands of other servicemen who lost their lives in the fight for liberty, are heroes. We celebrate their sacrifice.

Although I never knew him, I am connected to Uncle Maurice by DNA. I celebrate his sacrifice and what he stood for. My grandparents received a memorium from President Franklin Roosevelt in recognition of their loss, and it included these words:

> HE STANDS IN THE UNBROKEN LINE OF PATRIOTS WHO HAVE DARED TO DIE THAT FREEDOM MIGHT LIVE, AND GROW, AND INCREASE ITS BLESSINGS. FREEDOM LIVES AND THROUGH IT HE LIVES IN A WAY THAT HUMBLES THE UNDERTAKINGS OF MOST MEN.

We are connected to the death and, therefore, the resurrection of Christ through our spiritual DNA, working in us through faith in His person and work. Paul recognizes in Romans 6:6 that we know by our spiritual experience that "our old self was crucified with Him" so that we no longer need to be slaves to that sinful nature. Paul summarizes this treatise in verses 17 and 18 when he says,

> But thanks be to God that though you were slaves of sin, you became obedient from the heart to that form of teaching to which you were committed, and having been freed from sin, you became slaves of righteousness.

Obedience from the heart to what we have been taught is the standard for our freedom from the power of sinful nature. Then we become slaves of righteousness!

CHAPTER 7: WHAT IS REPENTANCE?

In Matthew 3:1–2, we are told that the ministry of John the Baptist is best characterized in his statement, "Repent, for the kingdom of heaven is at hand." Once he was put into prison, Jesus picked up John's mantle, signifying the beginning of His public ministry as Matthew gives the following testimony:

> Now when Jesus heard that John had been taken into custody, He withdrew into Galilee; and leaving Nazareth, He came and settled in Capernaum, which is by the sea, in the region of Zebulun and Naphtali. This was to fulfill what was spoken through Isaiah the prophet: "THE LAND OF ZEBULUN AND THE LAND OF NAPHTALI, BY THE WAY OF THE SEA, BEYOND THE JORDAN, GALILEE OF THE GENTILES— THE PEOPLE WHO WERE SITTING IN DARKNESS SAW A GREAT LIGHT, AND THOSE WHO WERE SITTING IN THE LAND AND SHADOW OF DEATH, UPON THEM A LIGHT DAWNED." From that time Jesus began to preach and say, "Repent, for the kingdom of heaven is at hand."
>
> Matthew 4:12–17

The Greek word for repent is *metanoeoe*, and it is the combination of two words: *meta*, denoting a change of place or condition, and *noeoe*, which means to exercise the mind, to think, or comprehend. It basically refers to regret or sorrow accompanied by a true change of heart. Regret can mean sorrow because you got caught, but repentance moves forward to a restored relationship. Some theologians identify this distinction as between "attrition," remorse caused by fear of punishment or a loss of blessing, and "contrition," genuine repentance. Contrition includes deep remorse for having offended God. King David spoke of this in Psalm 51:10 and 17, "Create in me a clean heart, O God, And renew a steadfast spirit within me. …The sacrifices of God are a broken spirit; A broken and contrite heart, O God, You will not despise."

Genuine Repentance

The quote Jesus made in Matthew 4 is from Isaiah 9:1–2 and identifies "THE LAND OF ZEBULUN AND THE LAND OF NAPHTALI," referencing the very land not only of Jesus's childhood but also about two-thirds of His public ministry. The light that would shine from Jesus's ministry would represent a total change of mind and direction from the teaching of the Pharisees and Sadducees. Paul illustrates what genuine repentance looks like in his second letter to the Corinthians:

> For though I caused you sorrow by my letter, I do not regret it; though I did regret it—for I see that that letter caused you sorrow, though only for a while— I now rejoice, not that you were made sorrowful, but that you were made sorrowful to the point of repentance; for you were made sorrowful according to the will of God, so that you might not suffer loss in anything through us. For the sorrow that is according to the will of God produces a repentance without regret, leading to salvation, but the sorrow of the world produces death. For behold what earnestness this very thing, this godly sorrow, has produced in you: what vindication of yourselves, what indignation, what fear, what longing, what zeal, what avenging of wrong! In everything you demonstrated yourselves to be innocent in the matter.
>
> 2 Corinthians 7:8–11

Billy Graham and other evangelical leaders many years ago started using the sinner's prayer as an avenue to deliver the gospel to the world and lead unbelievers into a saving grace. It begins with an acknowledgment to God of the sinful condition each person faces and the need for forgiveness. The potential believer then commits to turning from personal sins to invite Jesus into his heart and life.

> Dear Lord Jesus, I know that I am a sinner, and I ask for Your forgiveness. I believe You died for my sins and rose from the dead. I turn from my sins and invite You to come into my heart and life. I want to trust and follow You as my Lord and Savior. In Your Name. Amen.
>
> Billy Graham

Salvation by Grace, Through Faith

Other evangelical programs like the Four Spiritual Laws promoted by Bill Bright and Campus Crusade for Christ or the Romans Road to Salvation emphasize a recognition that "all have sinned and fall short of the glory of God" (Romans 3:23). This premise is the foundation for the need for repentance. However, is repentance a requirement for salvation? A number of passages dealing with salvation do not mention repentance as a must, including Ephesians 2:8–9, "For by grace you have been saved through faith; and that not of yourselves, it is the gift of God; not as a result of works, so that no one may boast." The environment for salvation is grace, God's work alone, and it must be by faith and given as a free gift. The Philippian jailor (Acts 16:30–31) asked what he needed to do to be saved, and Paul's answer was to "believe in the Lord Jesus Christ, and you will be saved." In John 4:10, Jesus introduced salvation and eternal life to a Samaritan woman with two requirements, to know (*eido*—perceive) the gift of God (i.e., salvation) and "who it is who says to you, 'Give Me a drink.'" Repentance is not included. To receive eternal life, she needed only to recognize the Giver and that He had a free gift to give.

The Reformation Study Bible, R. C. Sproul General Editor, on page 2059, has an article dealing with and entitled Repentance. In it, the writer's take is that repentance is the result of regeneration and not the cause:

> Repentance is not the cause of new birth or regeneration; it is the fruit of regeneration. Though repentance begins with regeneration, it is an attitude and action that must be repeated throughout the Christian life. As we continue to sin, we are called upon to repent as we are convicted of our sin by the Holy Spirit.

Repentance Implied

Many evangelical Christians might say that, although not outwardly stated, repentance is implied as necessary for anyone to become a Christian. When Saul of Tarsus received Christ and His commission to be the apostle to the Gentiles in Acts 9:4–6, there was no mention of repentance. Paul's testimony in 1 Timothy 1:16 is, "For this reason I found mercy, so that in me as the foremost [sinner], Jesus Christ might demonstrate His perfect patience as an example for those who would believe in Him for eternal life." He was saying that his salvation required his recognition as being a sinner and that he needed mercy, an implication of repentance. His salvation as an enemy of Jesus Christ became an example to many of the transforming power of being born from above. The greatness of salvation is exemplified in the supernatural ability of God to change lives.

There are some passages that suggest that repentance is a necessity for salvation, including Acts 2:37–38,

> Now when they heard this, they were pierced to the heart, and said to Peter and the rest of the apostles, "Brethren, what shall we do?" Peter said to them, "Repent, and each of you be baptized in the name of Jesus Christ for the forgiveness of your sins; and you will receive the gift of the Holy Spirit."

The rich man in Luke 16:27–31 pleaded with Abraham to send someone to his five brothers and warn them; then, they would repent. "But he said to him, 'If they do not listen to Moses and the Prophets, they will not be persuaded even if someone rises from the dead.'" Being a child of Abraham would not be enough to qualify. As the passage below confirms, there must be good fruit, and good fruit comes after the roots of the tree (i.e., old covenant) are cut down. True repentance is all about leaving behind the old ways.

Step of Faith Based on Reason

> So, he began saying to the crowds who were going out to be baptized by him, "You brood of vipers, who warned you to flee from the wrath to come? Therefore, bear fruits in keeping with repentance, and do not begin to say to yourselves, 'We have Abraham for our father,' for I say to you that from these stones God is able to raise up children to Abraham. Indeed, the axe is already laid at the root of the trees; so every tree that does not bear good fruit is cut down and thrown into the fire."

Luke 3:7–9

Jesus says in Matthew 9:13, "I did not come to call the righteous, but sinners." Repentance begins when a person comes to his senses to understand that his current condition (a sinner) has been a snare (2 Timothy 2:25–26) and is keeping him from realizing the quality-of-life God has prepared for him. This realization means he is now willing to move on from the allegiances and alliances that have defined his condition. A religious man must be willing to turn away from the religious system that keeps him in bondage. This is where faith begins, and it is a step of faith based on reason and not a blind leap, as Francis Schaeffer taught. It is a willingness to trust in some promises made by an unknown or little-known entity that stepping away from the current environment will not result in death. It is based on the hope of a new and meaningful life.

> Or do you think lightly of [*kataphroneo*—take lightly, despise] the riches of His kindness and tolerance and patience, not knowing that the kindness of God leads you to repentance? But because of your stubbornness and unrepentant heart you are storing up wrath for yourself in the day of wrath and revelation of the righteous judgment of God.
>
> Romans 2:4–5

The above passage tells us that it is the kindness of God that leads one to repentance. Paul is addressing the religious Hebrew who is stubbornly holding on to his own conventions in spite of the manifestations of God's grace happening all around him. It represents a journey from taking God's kindness for granted to accepting and receiving it personally. Paul understood that his call was to "solemnly testify to both Jews and Greeks of repentance toward God and faith in our Lord Jesus Christ" (Acts 20:21).

Unloading Burdens

True repentance is the process of unloading burdens. "Blessed be the Lord, who daily bears our burden, the God who is our salvation. Selah" (Psalm 68:19). Through the prophet Ezekiel, the Lord tried to warn the people by having the prophet carry baggage on his shoulder "like the baggage of an exile" (Ezekiel 12:6–7). Unloading the baggage of one's sin on another is to share his burden. "Take My yoke upon you and learn from Me, for I am gentle and humble in heart, and YOU WILL

FIND REST FOR YOUR SOULS. For My yoke is easy and My burden is light" (Matthew 11:29–30). Being yoked up to Christ means he finds rest. Observe the following:

There is a Jewish tale about a merchant named Yankel who carried his wares from town to town. One day, as a horse-drawn wagon passed by Yankel, the owner recognized him and offered him a ride. Yankel gratefully accepted the offer, but a few moments later, the wagon owner noticed that Yankel was still carrying his burden on his shoulders. "Yankel," he said, "why don't you put your bags down?" "Oh, it's all right," Yankel replied. "I don't want to be in any trouble." "Yankel, you fool!" the owner exclaimed. "My horses are pulling everything in the wagon whether or not you are carrying them. Put down your bags and stop carrying all this unnecessary baggage!"

Repentance After Regeneration

The greatest work of repentance is accomplished after regeneration. It is turning back to God, unloading the burden of sins on the one who wishes to bear it. In Isaiah 30:15,

> For thus the Lord God, the Holy One of Israel, has said, "In repentance [*subah*—turning back to God] and rest you will be saved [delivered],
> In quietness and trust is your strength." But you were not willing.

Repentance is a willingness to turn back to God, who has already proven that His love is complete.

CHAPTER 8: A TALE OF TWO TAMARS

It is actually reported that there is immorality among you, and immorality of such a kind as does not exist even among the Gentiles, that someone has his father's wife. You have become arrogant and have not mourned instead, so that the one who had done this deed would be removed from your midst. For I, on my part, though absent in body but present in spirit, have already judged him who has so committed this, as though I were present. In the name of our Lord Jesus, when you are assembled, and I with you in spirit, with the power of our Lord Jesus, I have decided to deliver such a one to Satan for the destruction of his flesh, so that his spirit may be saved in the day of the Lord Jesus. Your boasting is not good. Do you not know that a little leaven leavens the whole lump of dough?

1 Corinthians 5:1–6

In his first address to the church in Corinth, Paul thought it of great importance to address the principle of sin (leaven) and its effect on the church's spiritual health. He used the example of the man having an open affair with his stepmother without the church calling it out as such. Even though Paul was absent from the congregation, he used his status to encourage the church to excommunicate the man until there would be repentance. The principle is that outward sin will reproduce itself, so it must be arrested.

In the Old Testament, two individuals named Tamar will help further illustrate the point. The story of the first Tamar, one of David's children and the sister of Absalom and Amnon, is a tragedy. It illustrates some of the dysfunctionality of David's family. It involves Amnon and his physical lust for his half-sister, Tamar. Tamar was a virgin, and Amnon and his uncle Shimeah hashed up a plot to pretend an illness to get Tamar to come to him alone in his bedroom for comfort. She brought food to feed him, and he grabbed her to violate her, and she resisted.

Tamar & Amnon

However, he would not listen to her; since he was stronger than her, he violated her and lay with her. Then Amnon hated her with a very great hatred; *for the hatred with which he hated her was greater than the love with which he had loved her.* And Amnon said to her, "Get up, go away!" But she said to him, "No, because this wrong in sending me away is greater than the other that you have done to me!" Yet he would not listen to her. Then he called his young man who attended him and said, "Now throw this woman out of my presence, and lock the door behind her." Now she had on a long-sleeved garment; in this manner, the virgin daughters of the king dressed themselves in robes. Then his attendant took her out and locked the door behind her. *Tamar put ashes on her head and tore her long-sleeved garment which was on her; she put her hand on her head and went away, crying aloud as she went.*

2 Samuel 13:14–19
(emphasis added by the author)

After this cruel act, Amnon compounded his cruelty by having Tamar thrown out of his presence since his hatred for her was more intense than his prior love. It is the testimony of the power of sin in a person's life. She was advertising her violation by putting ashes on her head and tearing her garment. Her brother, Absalom, recognized the matter and asked Tamar to stay with him and be silent until another time. In verse 20, "So Tamar remained and was desolate [devastated, deserted] in her brother Absalom's house." As it turns out, David found out and was angry but did not act to address it. After two full years, Absalom arranged for his brother Amnon to be killed for his treatment of Tamar. When sin is allowed to fester, it reproduces itself, often even worse than the original indiscretion.

Tamar & Judah

The second Tamar was the wife of Er, Judah's oldest son, and expected to produce children to carry on the name.

Now Judah took a wife for Er, his firstborn, and her name was Tamar. But *Er, Judah's firstborn, was evil in the sight of the Lord,* so the Lord took his life. Then Judah said to Onan, "Go in to your brother's wife, and perform your duty as a brother-in-law to her, and raise up offspring for your brother." Onan knew that the offspring would not be his; so, when he went in to his brother's wife, he wasted his seed on the ground to not give offspring to his brother. But what he did was displeasing in the sight of the Lord; so, He took his life also. Then Judah said to his daughter-in-law Tamar, "Remain a widow in your father's house until my son Shelah grows up"; for he thought, "I am afraid that he too may die like his brothers." So, Tamar went and lived in her father's house. …Now it was about three months later that Judah was informed, "Your daughter-in-law Tamar has played the harlot, and behold, she is also with child by harlotry." Then Judah said, "Bring her out and let her be burned!" It was while she was being brought out that she sent to her father-in-law, saying, "I am with child by the man to whom these things belong." And she said, "Please examine and see, whose signet ring and cords and staff are these?" Judah recognized them, and said, "*She is more righteous than I, inasmuch as I did not give her to my son Shelah.*"

Genesis 38:6–11, 24–26
(emphasis added by the author)

When the Lord took Er because he was evil, it was understood that the next son, Onan, would become the father of Tamar's offspring. Onan did not want to give offspring to his brother through Er's widow; he would not willingly impregnate Tamar. The Lord took Onan's life as well, leaving only a much younger brother, Shelah, to fulfill the obligation to Tamar. Judah promised Tamar to wait for Shelah to come of age and go back to her father to wait. Judah was afraid the same fate would occur with his youngest son, so he had no intention of fulfilling this obligation. So, Tamar came up with a plan to trick Judah by disguising herself as a prostitute, and she got pregnant. Judah did not admit to it until his signet ring and cords and staff were produced by Tamar to prove that he was the father. Do we believe that one wrong justifies another?

The Genealogy of David

Why is this story important? Because the Messiah would come through the seed of Judah. In Revelation 5:5, Jesus is referred to as the Lion of Judah. Tamar was now pregnant with twins, the firstborn being Perez, who would become the ancestor of David. In Ruth 4:18–22,

> Now these are the generations of Perez: to Perez was born Hezron, and to Hezron was born Ram, and to Ram, Amminadab, and to Amminadab was born Nahshon, and to Nahshon, Salmon, and to Salmon was born Boaz, and to Boaz, Obed, and to Obed was born Jesse, and to Jesse, David.

God's will would be realized in spite of the sin in the camp. Judah would recognize Tamar as "more righteous than I, inasmuch as I did not give her to my son Shelah." The bloodline would continue, even through sinful men. The Bible is filled with flawed people whom God uses to fulfill His greater purpose.

In 2 Corinthians 5:18, "All these things are from God." And 2 Corinthians 4:15 says, "For all things are for your sakes." And then there is Romans 8:28, "And we know that God causes all things to work together for good to those who love God." The Greek word *sunergeo* (present active indicative) is translated as "work together" and means "to cooperate, with the end goal being the believer's good." This principle is the essence of divine providence, that none of us needs to take matters of injustice into our own hands since God's plan is that He will do it. A great example of one who lived by this principle was Joseph, Jacob's eleventh son.

Joseph's Integrity

Now Joseph had been taken down to Egypt; and Potiphar, an Egyptian officer of Pharaoh, the captain of the bodyguard, bought him from the Ishmaelites, who had taken him down there. *The Lord was with Joseph, so he became a successful man.* And he was in the house of his master, the Egyptian. Now his master saw that the Lord was with him and how the Lord caused all that he did to prosper in his hand. So, Joseph found favor in his sight and became his personal servant, and he made him overseer over his house, and all that he owned he put in his charge. It came about that from the time he made him overseer in his house and over all that he owned, the Lord blessed the Egyptian's house on account of Joseph; thus, the Lord's blessing was upon all that he owned, in the house and in the field. So he left everything he owned in Joseph's charge, and with him there, he did not concern himself with anything except the food which he ate.

Genesis 39:1–6
(emphasis added by the author)

The biography of Joseph, a type of Christ, is the story of a man who suffered severe injustices, from being sold into slavery to false accusations about an attempted rape by Potiphar's wife and having to spend many years in prison. Yet his response, as indicated in Genesis 39, is to commit himself to be faithful despite his difficulties. Verse 2 tells us that "the Lord was with Joseph, so he became a successful man." As a result, Potiphar put everything in his charge; the only thing Potiphar decided was the food he ate. Jesus is also trustworthy to each believer despite our injustices or troubles since He understands our plight. Hebrews 4:15 says, "For we do not have a high priest who cannot sympathize with our weaknesses, but One who has been tempted in all things as we are, yet without sin." The ultimate answer to our sin condition is our willingness to trust our high priest.

Issues Governing Salvation

CHAPTER 9: SALVATION & FREE WILL

As Moses lifted up the serpent in the wilderness, even so must the Son of Man be lifted up; so that *whoever believes* will in Him have eternal life. For God so loved the world, that He gave His only begotten Son, that *whoever believes* in Him shall not perish, but have eternal life.

John 3:14–16
(emphasis added by the author)

Christianity is split over the role of a man's free will in receiving salvation. Most of Christianity is derived from four basic doctrinal positions: Universalism, Calvinism, Arminianism, and Pelagianism. Understanding the differences and the role that free will plays in salvation provide a framework to appreciate the dynamics of a deeper relationship with God through the new covenant. Unfortunately, many heresies were born in the first and second centuries, and they have perverted the gospel in a way that distorts the character and nature of God.

A Brief History

Gnosticism—a prominent heretical movement of the late first and second-century Christian church, partly of pre-Christian origin. The gnostic doctrine taught that the world was created and ruled by a lesser divinity, the demiurge, and that Christ was an emissary of the remote supreme divine being, esoteric knowledge (gnosis) of whom enabled the redemption of the human spirit.

One of the Gnostic schools was the Valentinians, who taught that some men were predestined to hell without choice. Another school, known as the Basilideans, taught that everyone was born sinless and needed no savior unless they fell into sin later in life. Although the whole church strongly condemned these positions, another cult, the Manicheans, revived the Valentinian positions and added to them around 250 AD. A century later, Augustine was born and became a Manichean for ten years before converting to Christianity.

In 417 AD, a new Gnostic cult, Pelagianism, led by a British bishop named Pelagius, revived many of the elements of the Basilideans, particularly that man is born free from sin and needs no savior unless he later sins. Pelagius also claimed that humankind could decide between good and evil and that his choice achieved salvation. Augustine, going back to his Manichean roots, claimed that humankind were slaves to sin and could not choose to do anything except what was evil. Salvation was not something a person could choose for himself. God must first give that person grace to choose what is good. The controversy did not end in the fifth century but has sprung up multiple times throughout history and continues to be an ongoing debate in Christendom today. Augustinianism was later revived and perfected by John Calvin during the Protestant Reformation.

The Birth of Arminianism

When Calvin died, his mantle was continued by Theodore Beza, and this doctrine dominated Europe for years. One of Beza's students, Jacob Arminius, researched the ancient church and found that Calvinism had deep ties to Valentinian Gnostics teaching which had been condemned by the church many years earlier. Instead of accepting the doctrine that man was totally depraved, meaning he could not freely choose salvation, Arminius believed man could freely choose salvation as God's gift; that instead of unconditional election, election is conditioned on a man's faith alone; that instead of limited atonement, salvation is for everyone, not just for the elect. He believed God draws all individuals to Himself through His Son and by His grace. Calvinism teaches the perseverance of the saints, otherwise known as eternal security, while most Arminians believe that salvation can be lost.

A Christian Landscape

- Universalism: Everyone is born saved, and no one can lose their salvation. No human will ever go to hell.

- Calvinism: God chose a few people and compelled them to be saved. God has predestined all others to hell.
- Arminianism: Everyone is born with a sin nature and is, therefore, on their way to hell. God enables everyone, at some time in their life, to understand God's gift of salvation. He gives each person the free will to accept or reject the gift.
- Pelagianism: Everyone is born sinless and is therefore saved and on their way to heaven. They have no need for a savior unless they sin sometime in their life.

Much of Christianity begins with one of the above doctrines or some combination. For example, Southern Baptists are basically Arminian, but they have adopted the perseverance of the saints (eternal security), unlike pure Arminianism. Calvinism is the central doctrine of Presbyterian churches and other reformed churches, although pure Calvinism has been modified recently. The crux of the matter revolves around the issue of free will.

Foreknowledge

For those whom He *foreknew*, He also predestined to become conformed to the image of His Son, so that He would be the firstborn among many brethren; and these whom He predestined, He also called; and these whom He called, He also justified; and these whom He justified, He also glorified. What then shall we say to these things? If God is for us, who is against us?

Romans 8:29–31
(emphasis added by the author)

Most modern denominations believe true believers are predestined for salvation (Acts 13:48). According to the above passage, foreknowledge is the basis of predestination, then called, then justified, and then glorified by God. Calvinists believe that it is individuals that God foreknew, not the body of Christ, that is, those who would receive Jesus as Savior. They see foreknowledge as referring to a person, not an event (an individual moment of accepting Jesus). One problem with this position is that the early church fathers understood foreknowledge as speaking of an event.

Examples

Justin Martyr

So that, in consequence of these events, we know that Jesus foreknew what would happen after Him, as well as in consequence of many other events which He foretold would befall those who believed on and confessed Him, the Christ.

Dialogue with Trypho
Chapter 35

I can demonstrate that they were types, symbols, and declarations of those things which would happen to Christ, of those whom it was foreknown were to believe in Him, and of those things which would also be done by Christ Himself.

Dialogue with Trypho
Chapter 42

Irenaeus

God only blinds the minds of those who choose not to believe and have already rejected Him. In Romans 1, those who would not retain God in their knowledge He gave them over to a reprobate mind. In 2 Thessalonians 2, strong delusion is sent to believe the lie. God knows the number of those who will not believe, since He foreknows all things, and has given them over to unbelief. God has foreknowledge of all things.

Against Heresies

Tatian

"Jesus created men and angels with free will. Jesus had foreknowledge of what free agents would do. There is no such thing as fate" (*Greeks*, chapter 7).

Clement of Alexandria

"Again, prophesy is foreknowledge; and knowledge, the understanding of prophesy; being the knowledge of those things known before by the Lord who reveals all things" (*Stromata*, chapter 12).

Origen

"[God] knows the secret things of the heart and foreknows the future" (*On First Principles* 3:13).

Modern Calvinism and Free Will

Concerning salvation, the question then becomes, what do human beings desire? The Arminian believes that some desire to repent and be saved. Others choose to flee from God and thus reap eternal damnation. Why different people have different desires is never made clear by the Arminian. The Calvinist holds that all human beings desire to flee from God unless and until the Holy Spirit performs a work of regeneration. That regeneration changes our desires so we will freely repent and be saved. It is important to note that even the unregenerate are never forced against their will. Their wills are changed without their permission, but they are always free to choose as they will.

Reformation Study Bible
Free Will, page 1353

The above quote comes from an article entitled Free Will, found in *The Reformation Study Bible*, edited by R. C. Sproul and published in 2016. It confirms the basic Calvinist position that "all human beings desire to flee from God unless and until the Holy Spirit performs a work of regeneration." According to this viewpoint, a man's salvation is predetermined or predestinated, and no man can choose God prior to this regeneration work of the Holy Spirit. This position differs from most modern denominations, which recognize man's free will to choose God. Deuteronomy 30:19–20 (emphasis added by the author) gives us a clear picture of what that choice looks like:

I call heaven and earth to witness against you today, that I have set before you life and death, the blessing and the curse. So, *choose life* [*bahar*—a choice which is based on a thorough examination of the situation and not an arbitrary whim] in order that you may live, you and your descendants, by loving the Lord your God, by obeying His voice, and by holding fast to Him; for this is your life and the length of your days, that you may live in the land which the Lord swore to your fathers, to Abraham, Isaac, and Jacob, to give them.

Regeneration and the Choice

Most modern Christianity believes that man is born into sin and needs a savior. According to Romans 3:10–11, "THERE IS NONE RIGHTEOUS, NOTE EVEN ONE; THERE IS NONE WHO UNDERSTANDS, THERE IS NONE WHO SEEKS FOR GOD." If the work of redemption does not precede man's choice to accept the finished work of Christ (as Calvinism teaches), then how does God draw men to Himself? The Scriptures are filled with examples of the unbeliever who faces God and makes his choice for God, becoming His servant instead of an enemy. Saul of Tarsus is a prime example.

> As he was traveling, it happened that he was approaching Damascus, and suddenly a light from heaven flashed around him; and he fell to the ground and heard a voice saying to him, "Saul, Saul, why are you persecuting Me?" And he said, "Who are You, Lord?" And He said, "I am Jesus whom you are persecuting, but get up and enter the city, and it will be told you what you must do."
>
> Acts 9:3–6

The choice to become the apostle Paul happened when he understood that his pursuit of righteousness through the Law of Moses was causing him to be a persecutor of his Messiah instead of a follower. Once the scales of his blindness were removed (verses 17–18), Paul was commissioned to be the apostle to the Gentiles. He came to recognize where his power came from. Saul was on his way to find Christians, "still breathing threats and murder against the disciples of the Lord" (Acts 9:1), when he found the deliverance he was actually looking for. The story below provides some texture:

According to Jewish tradition, they panicked when the Israelites stood at the Red Sea and realized that the Egyptian army was quickly closing in on them. While Moses prayed and everyone else tried to figure out what to do, Nahshon, son of Amminadab (the tribe of Judah), walked straight into the sea with complete faith that God would take care of him. Tradition teaches that when the water reached Nahshon's nose, God told Moses to stop praying, to stretch out his staff, and to split the sea. And that is exactly what happened. Our Jewish tradition teaches that the sea didn't part, and *then* the Israelites walked through it; instead, one Israelite stepped out in faith and walked into the sea, and therefore, it parted.

Conclusion

Nahshon represents the individual who faces a life challenge and steps out in faith for his salvation/deliverance. God allows difficult circumstances to get the potential believer to trust Him for His provision. He meets each person where they are, intending to draw him/her to Jesus. In John 12:32–33, "'And I, if I am lifted up from the earth, will draw all men to Myself.' But He was saying this to indicate the kind of death by which He was to die." The way He suffered and died on our behalf as a demonstration of His love (Romans 5:8) is the genuine drawing card that brings the seeking individual to justification. There he finds peace with God (Romans 5:1). When any individual exercises his free will to trust God, he finds fulfillment in Christ.

CHAPTER 10: FREE WILL

There is much confusion surrounding the words "Calvinism" and "Arminianism" since they have been used throughout the centuries to divide Christians along denominational lines. As a result, they create schisms within the family of God—true believers in Christ, that are very destructive within the body of Christ and its call to evangelize the world with the gospel. This confusion is complicated because the definition of each term is altered from its original meaning, so the labels create more disagreement and dissension than agreement. Therefore, misperceptions make utilizing these terms less advantageous and more divisive.

J. I. Packer wrote a provocative article entitled "Arminianisms" addressing this subject. When comparing the two alternatives, Packer determined:

> To Calvinism, predestination is God's unconditional decision about the destiny of individuals; to Arminianism, it is God's unconditional decision to provide means of grace, decisions about individuals' destiny being secondary, conditional, and consequent upon foresight of how they will use those means of grace. To Calvinism, predestination of individuals means the foreordaining of both their doings (including their response to the Gospel) and their consequent destinies; to Arminianism it means a foreordaining of destinies based on doings foreseen but not foreordained. Arminianism affirms that God predestined Christ to be man's Savior, repentance and faith to be the way of salvation, and the gift of universal sufficient inward grace to make a saving response.

Calvinism vs. Arminianism

I have been trying to wrap my head around the nuances of the conflict and the real issues that separate these two alternatives. In this way, I can move on from these polarizing positions. Since Calvinism subscribes to "predestination of individuals as the foreordaining of both their doings (including their response to the Gospel) and their consequent destinies," this leaves a serious question of the role of a person's free will in accepting the free gift of salvation. Is it genuinely free will or a response to "irresistible grace" based on God's predestination? On the other hand,

> To Arminianism, it is essentially God's unconditional decision to provide means of grace, decisions about individuals' destiny being secondary, conditional, and consequent upon foresight of how they will use those means of grace.

This position presupposes that the believer chooses salvation independent of any holy influence on God's part other than His providence.

> Whereas to Calvinism, election is God's resolve to save, and the cross Christ's act of saving, for Arminianism salvation rests in the last analysis neither on God's election nor on Christ's cross, but on a man's cooperation with grace, which is something that God does not himself guarantee.

To avoid getting lost in the word salad of this exercise, determining the role that both God the Father and God the Son play is understood in light of the principle of the drawing of God, as seen in John 6:44–45 and John 12:32.

> No one can come to Me unless the Father who sent Me draws [*helkoe*—to draw or induce to come] him; and I will raise him up on the last day. It is written in the prophets, 'AND THEY SHALL ALL BE TAUGHT OF GOD.' Everyone who has heard [*akouo*—to comprehend] and learned [*manthano*—to know more fully] from the Father, comes to Me.
>
> John 6:44–45

Drawing

These verses suggest an energy originating with the Father that induces individuals to come to Him. According to John 12:32, that drawing (same Greek word) occurs when Jesus is lifted up, referencing the bronze serpent to which the people needed to look (Numbers 21:9) to heal the serpent's bite. When snake venom compares to man's sin condition, Jesus and His sacrifice become the healing source.

In verse 45, it is the one who comprehends the instructions of God and is motivated to know those instructions more fully is the one who comes to the Father through His Son (John 14:6). According to *Barnes' Notes* regarding this verse:

> In the conversion of the sinner, God enlightens the mind (John 6:45), he inclines the will (Ps 110:3), and he influences the soul by motives, by just views of his law, by his love, his commands, and his threatenings; by a desire of happiness, and a consciousness of danger; by the Holy Spirit applying truth to the mind and urging him to yield himself to the Saviour. So that, while God inclines him and will have all the glory, man yields without compulsion; obstacles are removed, and he becomes a willing servant of God.

Grace vs. Work

This explanation suggests that the drawing energy of the Father characterizes right motives, accurate views of His Word and laws, consequences of ungodly actions, and an intense urging to recognize Jesus as Lord. In this case, God gets the glory for all of His influences while the believer still maintains the free will to resist these urgings if he chooses. This position does not mean that exercising faith is work. According to Jeremiah 31:2–3, this drawing is motivated by His lovingkindness to deliver the believer to find his rest. The grace of God is always the environment whereby salvation is received, based on faith (Ephesians 2:8), and the believer exercises his faith independent of God's complete control over his actions. The strength of the relationship with Christ (in Christ) as new covenant believers is in the structure and power of that relationship, thus guaranteeing a finished work.

> "But what do you think? A man had two sons, and he came to the first and said, 'Son, go work today in the vineyard.' And he answered, 'I will not'; but afterward he regretted it and went. The man came to the second and said the same thing; and he answered, 'I will, sir'; but he did not go. Which of the two did the will of his Father?" They said,

"The first." Jesus said to them, "Truly I say to you that the tax collectors and prostitutes will get into the kingdom of God before you. For John came to you in the way of righteousness and you did not believe him; but the tax collectors and prostitutes did believe him; and you, seeing this, did not even feel remorse afterward so as to believe him."

Matthew 21:28–32

Willing and Obey

Free will is not only an important part of becoming a believer, but it is also critical in determining the quality of the believer's life as he finds his calling and his place in the kingdom of God. In the above parable, Jesus addresses the Pharisees and their questions about where His authority came from. He was teaching that the Pharisees were not accepting the ministry of John the Baptist, while the prostitutes and tax collectors *did believe him*. Exercising free will is not just an agreement in words, but it must also include the completion of the act from a believing heart. Isaiah 1:18–20 speaks to this principle and the blessings related to that completion:

> "Come now, and let us reason together," Says the Lord, "Though your sins are as scarlet, They will be as white as snow; Though they are red like crimson, They will be like wool. If you consent [*abah*—be willing] and obey [*shama*—to hear, pay attention to], You will eat the best of the land; But if you refuse and rebel, You will be devoured by the sword." Truly, the mouth of the Lord has spoken.

God Is Gracious

The completion of exercising one's free will about his relationship with God is obedience (*hupakouoe*—to hearken with stealth, stillness, or attention to respond), an interest in paying close attention to the will and purposes of God. This process is the result of Jesus becoming "high priest according to the order of Melchizedek." In Hebrew 5:9–10, "And having been made perfect, He became to all those who obey [*hupakouoe*] Him the source of eternal salvation."

And the Lord said to me, "Faithless Israel has proved herself more righteous than treacherous Judah. Go and proclaim these words toward the north and say, 'Return, faithless Israel,' declares the Lord; 'I will not look upon you in anger. For I am gracious,' declares the Lord; 'I will not be angry forever. Only acknowledge your iniquity, That you have transgressed against the Lord your God And have scattered your favors to the strangers under every green tree, And you have not obeyed My voice,' declares the Lord. 'Return, O faithless sons,' declares the Lord; 'For I am a master to you, And I will take you one from a city and two from a family, And I will bring you to Zion.'

Jeremiah 3:11–14

The Lord will continue to draw each one to Himself, no matter how much he is faithless, as Judah was, or which Christian doctrines govern his life, Calvinist, Arminian, or whatever. The goal is for the reconciled believer to learn to exercise his will and freely walk with his God.

Chapter 11: The Right to Choose, the Essence of Freedom

In the Garden of Eden, God gave Adam the responsibility to cultivate [*abad*—work] and keep [*samar*—watch, guard, care for] it (Genesis 2:15–17). The Lord would allow him to carry out these requirements by providing all the provisions of life from the trees found in Eden, including the tree of life. There would also be one restriction: "But from the tree of the knowledge of good and evil *you shall not eat*, for in the day that you eat from it you will surely die" (emphasis added by the author). The Lord God (Yahweh Elohim) granted man the right to choose, and man would decide and suffer whatever blessings or curses were attached to his decision. The right to choose is the essence of freedom. Adam could decide for himself the quality of his relationship with God.

> Now the serpent was more crafty than any beast of the field which the Lord God had made. And he said to the woman, "Indeed, *has God said*, 'You shall not eat from any tree of the garden'?" The woman said to the serpent, "From the fruit of the trees of the garden we may eat; but from the fruit of the tree which is in the middle of the garden, God has said, 'You shall not eat from it or touch it, or you will die.'" The serpent said to the woman, "*You surely will not die!* For God knows that in the day you eat from it your eyes will be opened, and you will be like God, *knowing good and evil.*"
>
> Genesis 3:1–5
> (emphasis added by the author)

We know from the above passage that Adam and Eve were deceived into eating from the tree of the knowledge of good and evil. Verse 22 tells us the effect of that decision, "Behold, the man has become like one of Us, knowing good and evil; and now, he might stretch out his hand,

and take also from the tree of life, and eat, and live forever" Once man chose to decide for himself that which is good from that which is evil, God could not allow him to eat from the tree of life and therefore, live forever. "So, He drove the man out; and at the east of the garden of Eden He stationed the cherubim and the flaming sword which turned every direction to guard the way to the tree of life" (verse 24). God intends that He should decide good and evil, but He still gave Adam the right to choose. This prohibition represents the only restriction He gave to Adam in the garden.

Outside of Paradise

Removed from paradise, Adam had to learn how to live in a fallen world and face all that corruption affords, including the murder of his son by his other son. He could decide the standards by which he would live or defer to God's righteousness. The righteousness of God always provides the highest quality of life, but man's right to choose is the essence of his freedom. Unfortunately, the history of mankind since the fall of Adam is a story of continued bad moral choices. God would periodically intervene, first with a flood and later to scatter the people and confuse their language to remind them that He was still in charge and that His standards for living were still the best; He was resetting the human condition.

After four hundred and thirty years of Israel living in Egypt, to the very day, the Lord delivered His people from bondage, led by Moses, to Mount Sinai to receive His law (Exodus 12:40–41). This Mosaic Law addressed both moral and judicial, governmental, ceremonial, and ecclesiastical laws. According to The New Unger's Bible Dictionary, there are four guiding principles found in the Law of Moses:

1. The principle of strict but righteous retribution, the intention being to eliminate evil and produce reverence for the righteousness of the holy God in the heart of the people.
2. The principle that punishment should correspond to the heinousness of the offense, that there shall fall upon the culprit what he has done to his neighbor, and that the punishment

is to be limited to the guilty party and not be extended to his children (Deuteronomy 24:16).

3. The principle that all presumptuous disobedience to God and to His holy ordinances should be punished with unsparing severity.

4. The threat of "a curse and severe punishments from God, the avenger of all evil, for offenses which either escape the eye of civil justice, or which, like apostasy from the Lord to idolatry, may prevail to such a degree that the arm of the earthly magistrate is overpowered and paralyzed by the spirit of the time."

What about the Law of Moses

Because of all of those years of slavery, the people were anxious to live under God's system of perfect justice and perfect righteousness. It begins with the ten commandments (see Exodus 20), which define the righteous relationship with God (the first five) and then with others (six-ten). The 613 laws that make up the entire legal standard are found in Exodus, Leviticus, Numbers, and Deuteronomy and speak to every aspect of life. The people welcomed it initially but found it impossible to keep it completely (James 2:10) without heavy doses of mercy. Each unfulfilled commandment included a consequence that kept the people seeking forgiveness. Consequences are the by-product of a judicial system that provides a right to choose so that man can learn of God's goodness.

> What shall we say then? Is the Law sin? May it never be! On the contrary, I would not have come to know sin except through the Law; for I would not have known about coveting if the Law had not said, "YOU SHALL NOT COVET." But sin, taking opportunity through the commandment, produced in me coveting of every kind; for apart from the Law sin is dead. I was once alive apart from the Law; but when the commandment came, sin became alive and I died; and this commandment, which was to result in life, proved to result in death for me; for sin, taking an opportunity through the commandment, deceived me and through it killed me. So then, the Law is holy, and the commandment is holy and righteous and good.
>
> Romans 7:7–12

Paul found that the Law is the vehicle God uses to expose the existence and the power of sin resident in each person. "For through the Law comes the knowledge of sin" (Romans 3:20). Before his conversion, the righteousness within the Law made him blameless (Philippians 3:6), but since his redemption, he was exposed as being a prisoner of the law of sin and death working within him (Romans 7:23). His new reality changed everything, as being "found in Him, not having a righteousness of my own derived from the Law, but that which is through faith in Christ, the righteousness which comes from God based on faith" (Philippians 3:9). His faith decision to acknowledge Jesus as Messiah allowed him to begin to see things from their proper perspective, that he had been a prisoner. His God was not Yahweh but the Law of Moses. He also recognized a higher law, the law of the Spirit of life in Christ Jesus.

Law of the Spirit of Life in Christ

For the law of the Spirit of life in Christ Jesus has set you free from the law of sin and of death. For what the Law could not do, weak as it was through the flesh, God did: sending His own Son in the likeness of sinful flesh and as an offering for sin, He condemned sin in the flesh, so that the requirement of the Law might be fulfilled in us, who do not walk according to the flesh but according to the Spirit.

Romans 8:2–4

This message became Paul's battle cry. Jesus proclaimed in Luke 4:18,

THE SPIRIT OF THE LORD IS UPON ME, BECAUSE HE ANOINTED ME TO PREACH THE GOSPEL TO THE POOR. HE HAS SENT ME TO PROCLAIM RELEASE TO THE CAPTIVES, AND RECOVERY OF SIGHT TO THE BLIND, TO SET FREE THOSE WHO ARE OPPRESSED.

God always intended that this law of the Spirit of life in Christ Jesus would be man's ultimate solution to life outside of the garden. In a sense, man's garden life is restored when he finds this life in the Holy Spirit, thus overcoming a walk according to the flesh. It is a life that includes the freedom to fail and be restored. "Knowing this, that our old self was crucified with Him, in order that our body of sin might be done away with, so that we would no longer be slaves to sin; for he who has died is freed from sin" (Romans 6:6–7).

You Will Be Free Indeed

So, Jesus was saying to those Jews who had believed Him, "If you continue in My word, then you are truly disciples of Mine; and you will know the truth, and the truth will make you free." They answered Him, "We are Abraham's descendants and have never yet been enslaved to anyone; how is it that You say, 'You will become free'?" Jesus answered them, "Truly, truly, I say to you, everyone who commits sin is the slave of sin. The slave does not remain in the house forever; the son does remain forever. So, if the son makes you free, you will be free indeed."

John 8:31–36

Jesus also tells us that the Word of God is central to the believer finding his freedom. The Word of God defines truth, and "the truth will make you free." This freedom is derived from the Son of God, who provides freedom for all who trust Him and His Word. "But as many as received Him, to them He gave the right to become children of God, even to those who believe in His name" (John 1:12). When man exercises his right to trust Jesus, the Father is glorified, and the believer finds his highest quality of life.

The American Experiment

Thomas Jefferson was the author of The Declaration of Independence, possibly the most important founding document of our nation. In it, he states,

We hold these truths to be self-evident, that all men are created equal, that they are endowed by their Creator with certain unalienable Rights, that among these are Life, Liberty and the pursuit of Happiness. --That to secure these rights, Governments are instituted among Men, deriving their just powers from the consent of the governed.

He confirmed that man has individual rights given by God and must be defended. Many suggest that The Bill of Rights is the most important part of The Constitution of the United States of America since it focuses on individual rights. In his Second Inaugural Address, George W. Bush stated,

> Freedom, by its nature, must be chosen, defended by citizens, and sustained by the rule of law and the protection of minorities. And when the soul of a nation finally speaks, the institutions that arise may reflect customs and traditions very different from our own. America will not impose our own style of government on the unwilling. Our goal instead is to help others find their own voice, attain their own freedom, and make their own way.

The Blessed Nation

This nation was founded on principles documented in the Bible, that a godly nation should stand for those principles. In Psalm 33:12, "Blessed is the nation whose God is the Lord, The people whom He has chosen for His own inheritance." When a country adopts and defends these freedoms, it falls under the wings of His protection. Our nation has experienced that protection since its founding and has been willing to fight to defend those God-given rights. My uncle Maurice Belanger enlisted in the Marines right after Pearl Harbor and was assigned to be an airplane mechanic on Midway Island. He died at the Battle of Midway Island on June 4, 1942. My grandparents received an acknowledgment of his sacrifice entitled "A Grateful Memory" and included the following words from President Roosevelt:

> HE STANDS IN THE UNBROKEN LINE OF PATRIOTS WHO HAVE DARED TO DIE THAT FREEDOM MIGHT LIVE, AND GROW, AND INCREASE ITS BLESSINGS. FREEDOM LIVES AND THROUGH IT HE LIVES- IN A WAY THAT HUMBLES THE UNDERTAKINGS OF MOST MEN.

We are in a new age in America when a broken education system blurs the reasons to defend our nation, and the values that motivated our founding fathers are being corrupted by evil forces, causing Americans to question these values. Yet, freedom is still worth fighting for. As Paul writes in Galatians 5:13–14,

For you were called to freedom, brethren; only do not turn your freedom into an opportunity for the flesh, but through love serve one another. For the whole Law is fulfilled in one word, in the statement, "YOU SHALL LOVE YOUR NEIGHBOR AS YOURSELF."

God's love is the final solution.

Chapter 12: When Willingness Meets Divine Purpose

"This is good and acceptable in the sight of God our Savior, who *desires all men to be saved* and to come to the knowledge of the truth" (1 Timothy 2:3–4) (emphasis added by the author).

A healthy relationship with God begins with the divine truth that He wishes salvation, an eternal relationship with Him, for all men. Acts 2:23 tells us that this was "the predetermined plan and foreknowledge of God" and that God, Himself, through His Son, would need to be the solution. This solution would not be easy, but the result of an extended struggle, culminating in the seed of the woman, Jesus the Messiah, bruising the head of the serpent (Satan) (Genesis 3:15). This solution is intended for everyone, but there is a condition. It is dependent on man's heart attitude toward God.

Godly Fear

Surely His salvation is near *to those who fear [reverence] Him*, That glory may dwell in our land. Lovingkindness and truth have met together; Righteousness and peace have kissed each other. Truth springs from the earth, And righteousness looks down from heaven. Indeed, the Lord will give what is good, And our land will yield its produce. Righteousness will go before Him And will make His footsteps into a way.

Psalm 85:9–13
(emphasis added by the author)

Romans 9:8 tells us that faith in the promises of God, a willingness to trust God for something one could not accomplish on his own, is always the basis of a relationship with God. Psalm 85:9 refers to it as a reverence for God, recognizing Him as Savior and deliverer. Just as Paul wrote of all the fantastic supernatural blessings associated with salvation in Ephesians 1, this psalm gives us an inside view of what salvation looks like. Regarding this passage, Keil and Delitzsch's Commentary on the Old Testament says:

> The glory that has been far removed again takes up its abode in the land. Mercy or loving-kindness walks along the streets of Jerusalem, and there meets fidelity, like one guardian angel meeting the other. Righteousness and peace or prosperity, these two inseparable brothers, kiss each other there and fall lovingly into each other's arms. The poet pursues this charming picture of the future further. After God's *emet*, i.e., faithfulness to the promises, has descended like dew, His faithfulness to the covenant, springs up out of the land, the fruit of that fertilizing influence. And *sedeq*, gracious justice, looks down from heaven, smiling favour and dispensing blessing.

Integrity & Uprightness

What connects the Old Testament believer to these divine realities? According to Isaiah 45:22, "Turn to Me [*panah*—turn the face toward God] and be saved, all the ends of the earth; For I am God, and there is no other." The uniqueness of God makes Him the only source. The fulcrum of the decision centers on man's willingness, a decision of the will, to place his total confidence in the God of Abraham, Isaac, and Jacob. King David understood this principle as a perfect heart, a heart of integrity and uprightness. In 1 Chronicles 29:14–19 (emphasis added by the author),

> But who am I and who are my people that we should be able to offer as generously as this? For all things come from You, and from Your hand we have given You. For we are sojourners before You, and tenants, as all our fathers were our days on the earth are like a shadow, and there is no hope. O Lord our God, all this abundance that we have provided to build You a house for Your holy name, it is from Your hand, and all is Yours. Since I know, O my God, that You try the heart and delight in uprightness [*meyshar*—rightness, equity, smoothness], I, in the integrity [*yoser*—straightness, uprightness] of my heart, have willingly offered all these things; so now with joy I have seen Your people, who

are present here, make their offerings willingly to You. O Lord, the God of Abraham, Isaac and Israel, our fathers, preserve this forever in the intentions of the heart of Your people, and direct their heart to You; and give to my son Solomon *a perfect heart to keep Your commandments*, Your testimonies and Your statutes, and to do them all, and to build the temple, for which I have made provision.

Godly Examples

Second Corinthians 1:12 says it this way:

For our proud confidence [glorying] is this: the testimony of our conscience, that in holiness [*haplotes*—singleness of mind] and godly sincerity [*eilikroneia*—sincerity, purity], not in fleshly wisdom but in [according to] the grace of God, we have conducted ourselves in the world, and especially [more abundantly] toward you.

Paul makes it clear that it must be according to the grace of God, where the divine attributes of holiness and purity become the believer's motivation and an eagerness to represent these attributes as an example to the flock of God (1 Peter 5:2–3). Without this divine exchange of attributes, man will operate in his limited ability and character, where good and evil are not clearly discerned. Isaiah 5:19–21 says (emphasis added by the author):

Who say, "Let Him make speed, let Him hasten His work, that we may see it; And *let the purpose of the Holy One of Israel draw near And come to pass, that we may know it!*" Woe to those who call evil good, and good evil; Who substitute darkness for light and light for darkness; Who substitute bitter for sweet and sweet for bitter! Woe to those who are wise in their own eyes And clever in their own sight!

Fulfillment of the Divine Will

The completion and fulfillment of the divine will are experienced *in Christ* within the new covenant relationship purchased by Jesus at His first coming and as defined by the gospel. It is a mystery to the Old Testament believer but is realized in the fullness of the times, where redemption is complete, where forgiveness is "according to the riches of His grace," as Paul documents in Ephesians 1. Paul used the term "in Christ" or "in

Him" more than 170 times in his letters to identify the spiritual reality of knowing Christ. Jamieson, Fausset, and Brown's Commentary says the following about "in Christ:"

> The repetition of "in Christ" implies the paramount importance of the truth that it is in Him, by virtue of union to Him, the Second Adam, the Restorer ordained for us from everlasting, the Head of redeemed humanity, believers have all their blessings.
>
> Blessed be the God and Father of our Lord Jesus Christ, who has blessed us with every spiritual blessing in the heavenly places *in Christ*, just as He chose us *in Him* before the foundation of the world, that we would be holy and blameless before Him. In love He predestined us to adoption as sons through Jesus Christ to Himself, according to the kind intention of His will, to the praise of the glory of His grace, which He freely bestowed on us *in the Beloved*. *In Him* we have redemption through His blood, the forgiveness of our trespasses, according to the riches of His grace which He lavished on us. In all wisdom and insight He made known to us the mystery of His will, according to His kind intention which He purposed *in Him* with a view to an administration *suitable to the fullness of the times*, that is, the summing up of all things *in Christ*, things in the heavens and things on the earth.
>
> Ephesians 1:3–10
(emphasis added by the author)

Under Compulsion

When Paul accepted the commissioning of God to be the apostle to the Gentiles, he was sacrificing his will to the divine purpose for not only his life but for the very future of the New Testament church. It is not much different than the compulsion Jonah felt after spending time in the big fish. Paul speaks of this dynamic in Philippians 3:12 when he said, "But I press on so that I may lay hold of that for which also I was laid hold of by Christ Jesus." Paul's labor to fulfill his call would be accomplished as he recognized and surrendered to the grace of God. He was acknowledging that it would be the grace of God that was laboring with him (1 Corinthians 15:10).

But I have used none of these things. And I am not writing these things so that it will be done so in my case; for it would be better for me to die than have any man make my boast an empty one. For if I preach the gospel, I have nothing to boast of, *for I am under compulsion*; for woe is me if I do not preach the gospel. For if I do this voluntarily, I have a reward; but if against my will, I have a stewardship entrusted to me. What then is my reward? That, when I preach the gospel, I may offer the gospel without charge, so as not to make full use of my right in the gospel.

1 Corinthians 9:15–18
(emphasis added by the author)

Finding the divine purpose is for all who make a conscious decision of the will to follow Christ no matter what the cost. Paul understood this when he spoke these words in Acts 20:27, "For I did not shrink from declaring to you the whole purpose of God."

Man's willingness meets divine purpose at the cross. The religious man looks up and sees Jesus on the cross, but the spiritual man, in Christ, sees himself on the cross with Christ and, therefore, sees the world from a totally different vantage point, as the resurrected Lord sees it. Believers have…

Been buried with Him through baptism into death, so that as Christ was raised from the dead through the glory of the Father, so we too might walk in newness of life. For if we have become united with Him in the likeness of His death, certainly we shall also be in the likeness of His resurrection.

Romans 6:4–5

Provisions of the Spiritual Life

Chapter 13: By Faith

"A little while, *and you will no longer see Me*; and again, a little while, and you will see Me." Some of His disciples then said to one another, "What is this thing He is telling us, 'A little while, and you will not see Me; and again, a little while, and you will see Me'; and 'because I go to the Father'?" So, they were saying, "What is this that He says, 'A little while'? We do not know what He is talking about." Jesus knew that they wished to question Him, and He said to them, "Are you deliberating together about this, that I said, 'A little while, and you will not see Me, and again a little while, and you will see Me'? Truly, truly, I say to you, that you will weep and lament, *but the world will rejoice*; you will grieve, but your grief will be turned into joy. Whenever a woman is in labor, she has pain, because her hour has come; but when she gives birth to the child, she no longer remembers the anguish because of the joy that a child has been born into the world. Therefore, you too have grief now; *but I will see you again*, and your heart will rejoice, and no one will take your joy away from you."

John 16:16–22
(emphasis added by the author)

On the night before His crucifixion, Jesus had much to say to His disciples to prepare them for what would take place in the coming days. Chapters 13–17 of John's Gospel include many of these instructions. As noted in the above conversation, the disciples were thoroughly confused by His lack of specificity regarding time. The Scriptures are filled with the accounts of many miraculous events when God revealed His supernatural abilities, but unless otherwise stated, the time lapses between the events are left unclear. Jesus gave them a timeline of the coming church age, beginning with His ascension and ending with His second coming. What connects these two major events is *a little while*. What connects spiritual events in a believer's life is *a little while*. Paul tells us in 2 Corinthians

5:7, "For we walk by faith, not by sight." Faith connects one promise of God to the next. "BUT THE RIGHTEOUS man SHALL LIVE BY FAITH" (Romans 1:17).

What Is Faith?

Hebrews 11 is the chapter we go to when we want to read about faith, particularly many Old Testament saints who lived by faith. According to Hebrews 11:1–2 (AMPC) (emphasis added by the author),

> Now faith is the assurance (*the confirmation, the title deed*) of the things [we] hope for, being the proof of things [we] do not see and the conviction of their reality [*faith perceiving as real fact what is not revealed to the senses*]. For by [faith—trust and holy fervor born of faith] the men of old had divine testimony borne to them and obtained a good report {gained approval—NASB}.

Faith confirms that hope for future promises is real.

This amazing chapter defines genuine faith by what it looks like in human events, as expressed by many people of the Bible about whom we know. Hebrews 11:6 (AMPC) also tells us what happens when there is no faith.

> But without faith it is impossible to please and be satisfactory to Him. For whoever would come near to God must [necessarily] believe that God exists and that He is the rewarder of those who earnestly and diligently seek Him [out].

Faith requires two elements: to believe that He exists and that He rewards the ones who earnestly seek Him. In Psalm 58:11, "Surely there is a reward for the righteous."

Faith generates many different kinds of responses. Because it places its confidence in God, there are no restrictions on what can happen. "For nothing will be impossible with God" (Luke 1:37). When there are no restrictions, the believer is free to believe in any outcome. Enoch believed, and he got raptured. Noah constructed a big boat at a time when there had never rained. Abraham left his home to go somewhere without knowing where. Sarah believed she could give birth at ninety years old.

Abraham was willing to sacrifice his promised son. Moses believed that God would part the Red Sea.

> But the truth is that *they were yearning for and aspiring to a better and more desirable country*, that is, a heavenly [one]. For that reason, God is not ashamed to be called their God [even to be surnamed their God—the God of Abraham, Isaac, and Jacob], for He has prepared a city for them.

Hebrews 11:16 (AMPC)
(emphasis added by the author)

Great Faith

And when Jesus entered Capernaum, a centurion came to Him, imploring Him, and saying, "Lord, my servant is lying paralyzed at home, fearfully tormented." Jesus said to him, "I will come and heal him." But the centurion said, "Lord, I am not worthy for You to come under my roof, *but just say the word*, and my servant will be healed. For I also am a man under authority, with soldiers under me; and I say to this one, 'Go!' and he goes, and to another, 'Come!' and he comes, and to my slave, 'Do this!' and he does it." Now when Jesus heard this, He marveled and said to those who were following, "Truly I say to you, *I have not found such great faith with anyone in Israel.*"

Matthew 8:5–10
(emphasis added by the author)

When Jesus came to Earth, He introduced a clear path to that city, not through the Law of Moses. In Galatians 3:24–26,

> Therefore, the Law has become our tutor to lead us to Christ, so that we may be justified by faith. But now that faith has come, we are no longer under a tutor. For you are all sons of God through faith in Christ Jesus.

In the above account, Jesus saw what great faith looked like in a Roman centurion, a non-Jew. He came to Jesus with a significant problem and was willing to accept Jesus at His word! The essence of the believer's faith is his acceptance of the Lord at His word, the Word of God commands great authority.

A Canaanite woman (non-Jew) from the district of Tyre and Sidon demonstrated great faith in Jesus (Matthew 15:21–28). She, too, came to Jesus for mercy, calling Him the Son of David, a term for Messiah. When Jesus said to her, "I was sent only to the lost sheep of the house of Israel," she responded by bowing down before Him, saying, "Lord, help me!" Jesus answered her, "It is not good to take the children's bread and throw it to the dogs." Why would Jesus want to meet a Gentile's needs while He came for the Jews? Interestingly, this statement did not discourage her. Instead, she responded, "Yes, Lord, but even the dogs feed on the crumbs which fall from their masters' table." She gave a sufficient response for Jesus to fulfill her wish. "O woman, your faith is great." But why? It might be that she was not willing to take no for an answer from this God who is not restricting Himself to be the God of the Jews only, but He is the Lord of all.

Little Faith

On that day, when evening came, He said to them, "Let us go over to the other side." Leaving the crowd, they took Him along with them in the boat, just as He was; and other boats were with Him. And there arose a fierce gale of wind, and the waves were breaking over the boat so much that the boat was already filling up. *Jesus Himself was in the stern, asleep on the cushion*; and they woke Him and said to Him, "Teacher, do You not care that we are perishing?" And He got up and rebuked the wind and said to the sea, "Hush, be still." And the wind died down and it became perfectly calm. And He said to them, "Why are you afraid? *Do you still have no faith?*" They became very much afraid and said to one another, "Who then is this, that even the wind and the sea obey Him?"

Mark 4:35–41
(emphasis added by the author)

It appears that Jesus purposely went to sleep in the stern of the boat while the storm was raging to let them know that He would be with them no matter what, even in the midst of difficult circumstances.

For He Himself has said, "I WILL NEVER DESERT YOU, NOR WILL I EVER FORSAKE YOU," so that we confidently say, "THE

LORD IS MY HELPER; I WILL NOT BE AFRAID. WHAT WILL MAN DO TO ME?"

Hebrews 13:5–6

Just as the disciples awoke Jesus to rescue them, the believer is reminded that he, too, awakes the Lord in his prayers for every situation. He does not need to be afraid like the disciples when a miracle is required. The believer's faith depends on his willingness to trust the Lord in all situations. The great psychotherapist Viktor Frankl, who survived the Nazi concentration camps and authored the book *Man's Search for Meaning*, wrote that we must always remember that we do not decide what the circumstances of our lives will be. Whether we will face tragedy or not on any given day is not up to us. The only thing we control is our own reaction and our choices in the face of the circumstances. Faith is a choice.

Looking for the Blessed Hope

Jesus gave some of His last instructions to His disciples in response to their questions regarding the signs of times when He returns. His teachings began with His command in Matthew 24:42 (emphasis added by the author), "Therefore *be on the alert* [pay attention], for you do not know which day your Lord is coming." Faith gets its confidence from both His first coming and the promises of His second coming. Verses 43–44 (emphasis added by the author),

> But be sure of this, that if the head of the house had known at what time of night the thief was coming, he would have been on the alert and would not have allowed his house to be broken into. For this reason, *you also must be ready*; for the Son of Man is coming at an hour when you do not think He will.

Walking by faith keeps the believer prepared at all times.

CHAPTER 14: SPIRITUAL DYNAMICS

My son do not forget my teaching [*torah*—direction, instruction], But let your heart keep my commandments; For length of days and years of life And peace they will add to you. Do not let kindness [lovingkindness] and truth [faithfulness] leave you; Bind them around your neck, Write them on the tablet of your heart. So, you will find favor and good repute In the sight of God and man. Trust in the Lord with all your heart, And do not lean on your own understanding. In all your ways acknowledge Him, And He will make your paths straight. Do not be wise in your own eyes; Fear the Lord and turn away from evil. It will be healing to your body And refreshment to your bones. Honor the Lord from your wealth And from the first of all your produce; So, your barns will be filled with plenty And your vats will overflow with new wine. My son do not reject the discipline of the Lord Or loathe His reproof, For whom the Lord loves He reproves, Even as a father corrects the son in whom he delights.

Proverbs 3:1–12

If you asked ten believers what it takes to live a spiritual life, you would likely get ten different answers. To discover the answer to this question, a close look at the Scriptures gives insight into those dynamics. One passage that provides some perspective is in the first few verses of Proverbs 3. God's gift of wisdom to Solomon is displayed in much of the book of Proverbs.

Divine Instruction

So much of Proverbs focuses on the importance of wisdom and understanding, and this chapter is no different. But before it gets there, it has some important ground to cover. In verses 1 & 2, the key to the length of days (quality) and years of life (quantity) is how one treats God's laws, His instruction, and Bible doctrine. The Hebrew word *torah* is the means by which one can reach a goal or ideal. Solomon says that it is a matter of the heart. According to Jesus, the heart is where your treasure is, where values are determined (Matthew 6:21). When one's priorities are governed by God's priorities (*torah*), great things occur. David found out that when his heart was filled with God's directions, he was delighted to do His will (Psalm 40:8). In Psalm 119:11, "Your word I have treasured in my heart, That I may not sin against You."

Lovingkindness and Truth

Verses 3 & 4 address the benefits of wearing lovingkindness (*hesed*), truth, and faithfulness. These benefits are represented by favor or acceptance or grace (unmerited favor) as well as a good reputation, and the Scripture says these are "in the sight of God and man." It means that God and man will recognize the believer as having a good understanding. So how does this take place? Verse 3 says that we should bind them around our neck to be viewed by others like a necklace and write them on our hearts, making them our highest priorities. *Hesed*, often translated as lovingkindness or mercy, can also mean loyalty. So, this verse speaks to the believer being loyal and faithful to God and being kind and truthful to men. We see these two aspects of the matter in the following verses:

"By lovingkindness and truth iniquity is atoned for, And by the fear of the Lord one keeps away from evil" (Proverbs 16:6).

"Listen to the word of the Lord, O sons of Israel, For the Lord has a case against the inhabitants of the land, Because there is no faithfulness or kindness Or knowledge of God in the land" (Hosea 4:1).

Trust in the Lord

In verses 5–6, the Hebrew word for trust is *batah*, and Zodhiates says it means trust or confidence and "expresses the feeling of safety and security that one can rely on someone or something else." The middle verse in the Bible is Psalm 118:8, which says, "It is better to take refuge in the Lord than to trust in man." It is no coincidence that in the very middle of the Bible is a warning to trust in anyone other than God, even oneself. Putting one's trust entirely in God is to deny any absolute trust in self. Psalm 37:5 says, "Commit your way to the Lord, trust also in Him, and He will do it." Then there is Proverbs 26:12, "Do you see a man wise in his own eyes? There is more hope for a fool than for him." The promise in Proverbs 3:6 is that God will make his paths straight. It means God removes the obstacles, making a smooth path or way of life, or perhaps better, bringing one to the appointed goal.

Fear of the Lord

We observe verses 7–8 emphasizing "the fear of the Lord." This Hebrew word for fear is *yare*, which has a sense of reverence and respect or awe. When the believer fears the Lord, he recognizes that "Behold, the fear of the Lord, that is wisdom; And to depart from evil is understanding" (Job 28:28). When one puts God in first place in his life (Colossians 1:18), the promise is that the believer will experience physical health benefits. In 3 John 1:2, John writes, "Beloved, I pray that in all respects you may prosper and be in good health, just as your soul prospers." John recognizes the relationship between spiritual health and physical health. In his search for meaning in life in Ecclesiastes 12:13, Solomon concluded, "Fear God and keep His commandments, because this applies to every person."

Giving

In verses 9–10, Solomon identifies the importance of giving to the Lord and the spiritual and temporal benefits of its practice. The Hebrew word for honor is *kabed*, which has the idea of something that weighs heavily, and when referring to another person (the Lord), it means to honor, to place in high esteem. The Bible is filled with warnings of not honoring God, and one prominent passage appears in Malachi 3:8–10 when the writer asks the question, "Will a man rob God? Yet you are robbing Me! But you say, 'How have we robbed You?' In tithes and offerings." To dishonor God in our giving is to rob him! On the other hand, He promises that when the believer tests God by giving what God asks, he will receive "a blessing until it overflows." One other biblical point about giving to the Lord: "He who oppresses the poor taunts his Maker, But he who is gracious to the needy honors Him" (Proverbs 14:31). Giving to the Lord includes our support to the needy.

Discipline

Finally, in verses 11–12, the Lord's discipline is emphasized. If the believer is to find depth in his relationship with God, he must be brought there by God. Depending on the situation, this process involves reproof, correction, or even chastisement. Verse 12 reminds us that discipline is for those whom God loves as sons; it is a form of instruction based on a particular need. Eliphaz says in Job 5:17, "Behold, how happy is the man whom God reproves, So do not despise the discipline of the Almighty." Hebrews 12 quotes Proverbs 3:11–12 and says that without discipline, one is considered an illegitimate child and not a son (verse 8). In verse 10, "He disciplines us for our good, so that we may share His holiness." Since the believer is never holy apart from God, this is our means of access in sharing His holiness.

True Spirituality

Come, you children, listen to me; I will teach you the fear of the Lord. Who is the man who desires life And loves length of days that he may see good? Keep your tongue from evil And your lips from speaking deceit. Depart from evil and do good; Seek peace and pursue it.

Psalm 34:11–14

True biblical spirituality does not happen to us by happenstance or all of a sudden but results from a pursuit of truth for a meaningful relationship with God. Proverbs 3 can take us there.

Chapter 15: Eternal Matters

Since the believer's citizenship is heaven (Philippians 3:20), his highest priority is learning to live in a foreign land amid unheavenly standards. That verse tells us that it is heaven "from which also we eagerly wait for a Savior, the Lord Jesus Christ." It's about not getting too comfortable with the surroundings of our temporary home. Paul gives us further perspective on our eternal home in 2 Corinthians 5:1–8 and how we live outside of eternity:

Walking by Faith

For we know that if the earthly tent which is our house is torn down, we have a building from God, a house not made with hands, eternal in the heavens. For indeed in this house, we groan, longing to be clothed with our dwelling from heaven, inasmuch as we, having put it on, will not be found naked. For indeed while we are in this tent, we groan, being burdened, because we do not want to be unclothed but to be clothed, so that what is mortal will be swallowed up by life. Now He who prepared us for this very purpose is God, who gave to us the Spirit as a pledge. Therefore, being always of good courage, and knowing that while we are at home in the body we are absent from the Lord— for we walk by faith, not by sight— we are of good courage, I say, and prefer rather to be absent from the body and to be at home with the Lord.

2 Corinthians 5:1–8

Approaching our life on Earth as if we are living far from home is key to finding real spiritual success; the more connected we are to this world, the more disconnected we are from heaven. Bob Dylan says, "When you ain't got nothin', you got nothin' to lose." The believer who recognizes that his future is heaven can begin to live with this ever-present reality in mind. Paul reminds us that our earthly tent is temporary and that our groanings for that permanent home are also temporary. Living in time and space and mortality does not have to define life's quality. The Holy Spirit is our pledge to the eternal life available to us now, and He is the key to walking by faith and not by sight. His leadership and guidance bring us into all of the truth. Learning to live as ambassadors (2 Corinthians 5:20) means we don't allow our current surroundings to dictate whom we represent.

To Live Is Christ

One's attitude toward death helps to define which kingdom he represents. In Philippians 1:21–23, Paul writes,

> For to me, to live is Christ and to die is gain. But if I am to live on in the flesh, this will mean fruitful labor for me; and I do not know which to choose. But I am hard-pressed from both directions, having the desire to depart and be with Christ, for that is very much better.

Living in Christ is directly related to the work to which we are called while in this world. It is the presentation of the gospel that this physical life is not the end; eternal life has been purchased for all who believe. As a result, the believer takes on God's call by taking on Jesus's ministry. In 2 Corinthians 5:15, "And He died for all, so that they who live might no longer live for themselves, but for Him who died and rose again on their behalf." It's all about eternal priorities.

While waiting for our heavenly home to become our current reality, we learn what it means to be a bondservant of Christ. In Galatians 1:10, Paul realized that seeking the favor of men was not the answer. Instead, we learn to face life's difficulties and challenges as a part of a bigger mission, that the life of the risen Christ would be made manifest to others. In 2 Corinthians 4:8–12,

> We are afflicted [to be compressed] in every way, but not crushed; perplexed [not knowing how to proceed], but not despairing; persecuted, but not forsaken; struck down, but not destroyed; always carrying about in the body the dying of Jesus, so that the life of Jesus also may be manifested in our body. For we who live are constantly

being delivered over to death for Jesus's sake, so that the life of Jesus also may be manifested in our mortal flesh. So death works in us, but life in you.

Paul was testifying that his earthly life would be difficult, but that could not stop him from his ultimate goal of revealing the life of Jesus in the process of being identified with the death of Jesus. Paul further explains this phenomenon in 1 Corinthians 4:9–13:

> For, I think, God has exhibited us apostles last of all, as men condemned to death; because we have become a spectacle to the world, both to angels and to men. We are fools for Christ's sake, but you are prudent in Christ; we are weak, but you are strong; you are distinguished, but we are without honor. To this present hour we are both hungry and thirsty, and are poorly clothed, and are roughly treated, and are homeless; and we toil, working with our own hands; when we are reviled, we bless; when we are persecuted, we endure; when we are slandered, we try to conciliate; we have become as the scum of the world, the dregs of all things, even until now.

Human life is completely segregated from eternal life except for a saving relationship with Jesus Christ. Identification with human struggles is not a curse, as some religious people might believe, but an entry into the eternal. Paul acknowledges that his servanthood to a higher purpose motivates him.

Letters of Christ

The primary source of this life as a servant is the work of the Holy Spirit, writing on human hearts so that we would become letters of Christ to the world. His empowerment enables the believer to become a servant of the new covenant; it is His life and not human performance. Paul's ministry was founded on this power, as he testified in 1 Corinthians 2:3–5,

> I was with you in weakness and in fear and in much trembling, and my message and my preaching were not in persuasive words of wisdom, but in demonstration of the Spirit and of power, so that your faith would not rest on the wisdom of men, but on the power of God.

Believers are directly connected to eternity by the power of God; human effort is futile. Paul tells us in 2 Corinthians 3:5–6 that we are made adequate and sufficient by this eternal power.

> But if the ministry of death, in letters engraved on stones, came with glory, so that the sons of Israel could not look intently at the face of Moses because of the glory of his face, fading as it was, how will the ministry of the Spirit fail to be even more with glory? For if the ministry of condemnation has glory, much more does the ministry of righteousness abound in glory. For indeed what had glory, in this case has no glory because of the glory that surpasses it. For if that which fades away was with glory, much more that which remains is in glory.
>
> 2 Corinthians 3:7–11

Paul's commentary on the contrasts between the old and new covenants in the above passage emphasizes the principle of glory. The Greek word is *doxa*, and its primary meaning is reputation, honor, or splendor. According to Spiros Zodhiates:

> The glory of God must mean His unchanging essence. Giving glory to God is ascribing to Him His full recognition. On the other hand, the true glory of man is the ideal condition in which God created man. This condition was lost in the fall, recovered through Christ, and exists as a real fact in the divine mind. The believer waits for this complete restoration.

To God be the Glory

The old covenant was restricted by man's glory, while the new covenant, under the administration of the Holy Spirit, taps into the full glory of God, Himself. This covenant provides no glory for men since it transcends the natural for the eternal.

A young man went to study in a renowned Jewish school that emphasized character refinement. After a few days, the new student began to imitate what he saw many of the veteran students doing day after day. He sat in his chair, closed his eyes tight, and began to repeat, "I am nothing! I am nothing! I am nothing!" Upon hearing the young man chanting that phrase, an elder classman scolded him by saying, "Who do you think you are? You have to be here at least a year until you can reach the level of being nothing!"

Nothingness is eternal!

CHAPTER 16: DISCERNING GOOD & EVIL

Along the road to spiritual maturity, there are several landmarks a believer must pass through so "that you may be filled up to all the fullness of God" (Ephesians 3:20). One of those is the ability to hear the voice of God in the details of life. Another is the recognition of the sovereignty of God that God is in charge even when things don't go well, and it is okay; trust in God means to trust all of the time. Mature believers must also develop the ability to discern good and evil. Amid a world influenced by Satan and his demons, believers must recognize the intense warfare by the enemy to deceive.

The Greek word translated to discern is *diakrisis*, which means to distinguish or to judge; it does not mean to determine for oneself which is good or evil. In this way, Adam and Eve were challenged in the Garden of Eden, "*From the tree of the knowledge of good and evil you shall not eat, for in the day that you eat from it you will surely die*" (Genesis 2:17) (emphasis added by the author). By deceiving Eve to eat of that tree, the serpent promised them that "your eyes will be opened, and you will be like God, *knowing good and evil*" (Genesis 3:5) (emphasis added by the author). Since God never intended that man would decide for himself what is good and evil, He had to excommunicate Adam and Eve from the Garden so as not to allow their sin to be immortalized. In verse 22 (emphasis added by the author),

> Then the Lord God said, "Behold, the man has become like one of Us, *knowing good and evil*; and now, he might stretch out his hand, and also take from the tree of life, and eat, and live forever.

His provision would come 4,000 years later on Calvary.

Solomon's Gift

In 1 Kings 3:9 (emphasis added by the author), Solomon recently became king and asked God to "give Your servant an understanding heart to judge Your people *to discern between good and evil*. For who is able to judge this great people of Yours?" He understood that if he was going to be a successful leader, Solomon needed this ability, and he didn't have it. So, God blessed Solomon with a wise, discerning heart, riches, and honor. As a result, Solomon became world renowned for his wisdom and wealth, God's gifts to Solomon.

Trained in Righteousness

In the New Testament age, believers have access to this gift to discern good and evil. The writer of Hebrews gives us insight into the importance and the process of discerning good and evil. In Hebrews 5:12, he recognizes Hebrew Christians as having become dull of hearing,

> For though by this time, you ought to be teachers, you have need again for someone to teach you the elementary principles of the oracles of God, and you have come to need milk and not solid food.

Growing in the discernment of good and evil is directly related to a growing capacity for the Word of God and, particularly, God's righteousness. These Christians were not accustomed to and inexperienced in the word of righteousness, that is, the goal of living in God's righteousness (verse 13); they were still infants.

Verse 14 contains the key to the whole thing (emphasis added by the author), "But solid food is for the mature, who because of practice *have their senses trained to discern good and evil*," who can make appropriate moral choices. Kenneth Wuest translates the verse this way (emphasis added by the author):

> But solid food belongs to those who are [spiritually] mature, to those who *on account of long usage have their powers of perception exercised* to the point where they can discriminate between both that which is good in character and that which is evil.

Exercised

This Greek word for exercise is a metaphor taken from the athlete or contenders in the Grecian games, who were wont to employ all their powers, skill, and agility in mock fights, running, wrestling, etc., that they might be better prepared for the actual contests when they took place. It speaks to the fact that applying God's Word is a participation sport and requires a total commitment to the excellence God has called us. It represents not just traditional religious activity but may also encompass simple things like how we speak to someone in the grocery check-out lane. In Romans 1:17, "For in it [the gospel] the righteousness of God is revealed from faith to faith; as it is written, 'BUT THE RIGHTEOUS man SHALL LIVE BY FAITH.'" Living in God's righteousness is a moment-by-moment event and is revealed from faith to faith.

Pressing On

Hebrews 6:1 continues the process in this way (emphasis added by the author),

> Therefore, leaving the elementary teaching about the Christ, let us *press on* [be carried forward] to maturity, not laying again a foundation of repentance from dead works and of faith toward God.

This verb is a present passive subjunctive and is better translated as "let us be carried" and gives the thought of personal surrender to an active influence. It means that God is moving forward with those committed to maturity. This maturity is the wonder of spiritual life. God provides the energy; we accept the process.

"Do not be overcome by evil but overcome evil with good" (Romans 12:21). Discerning good and evil allows the believer to recognize warfare and, therefore, to overcome evil with good.

Natural Man	Carnal Christian	Spiritual Christian	Rewarded Christian
	Struggle	Maturity	Rest
	Exodus Generation	Second Generation	
	In the Wilderness	Across the Jordan	Receiving the Inheritance
Exodus 1–11	Exodus 12; Deuteronomy 34	Joshua 1–11	Joshua 12–22
Non-Christian	Carnal Christian	Warfare	Victory
Egypt	Wilderness	Canaan	
In the World	In the Kingdom		At the Table
1 Corinthians 2:14	1 Corinthians 3:1–3	Romans 12:1–2	2 Corinthians 5:10; 1 Corinthians 3:13–14

The best book I've ever read on the subject of the finished work of Christ is *The Reign of the Servant Kings*, written by Joseph Dillow. On page 100, he includes the above diagram to illustrate the relationship between the journeys of the children of Israel and the Christian life. This illustration is worth a closer look.

The four columns show the four different states of any person from a New Testament Christian perspective. They include the natural man (unregenerate, unsaved), the carnal Christian (saved but not spiritual, of the flesh), the spiritual Christian, and the rewarded Christian. The diagram compares each of these New Testament conditions to the plight of the Jewish people, from bondage in Egypt to finding their inherited land in Canaan. Scripture is full of these biblical illustrations of spiritual principles.

Natural Man

In 1 Corinthians 2:14, Paul says, "But a natural man does not accept the things of the Spirit of God, for they are foolishness to him; and he cannot understand them, because they are spiritually appraised." This man is comparable to the Jew still in Egypt's bondage, as illustrated in the first eleven chapters of Exodus. He has never acknowledged Jesus as Savior and is preoccupied with his worldly presence and priorities. The Jews were dealing not only with the bondage of Egypt but also with the plagues God was bringing against the Egyptians and their land and people. The natural man is subject to his environment and his desires.

Carnal Christian

Paul explains the carnal Christian in 1 Corinthians 3:1–3,

And I, brethren, could not speak to you as to spiritual men, but as to men of flesh, as to infants in Christ. I gave you milk to drink, not solid food; for you were not yet able to receive it. Indeed, even now you are not yet able, for you are still fleshly. For since there is jealousy and strife among you, are you not fleshly, and are you not walking like mere men?

Carnal Christianity represents a true believer who has yet to find deliverance from the power of the sinfulness of his nature. The power of his fleshly desires continues to govern his life despite the presence of the Holy Spirit. His life is defined by continuous struggle, similar to the Jews represented by Exodus 12 (the introduction of the Passover lamb—a picture of salvation) and Deuteronomy 34 (all of their wanderings in the wilderness). These people never made it to the promised land since they believed the bad report of the ten spies in Numbers 13–14. They never find a home in their faith in God but constantly complain about their situation. They are in the kingdom but unable to find absolute joy in their salvation, so they continue to wander.

Spiritual Christian

The spiritual Christian has found deliverance from the power of his nature, the world, and the devil. This person finds his promised land, just as the second-generation Jews did in Joshua 1–11. Romans 12:1–2 says,

> Therefore, I urge you, brethren, by the mercies of God, to present your bodies a living and holy sacrifice, acceptable to God, which is your spiritual service of worship. And do not be conformed to this world, but be transformed by the renewing of your mind, so that you may prove what the will of God is, that which is good and acceptable and perfect.

The spiritual Christian has crossed the Jordan River into the promised land and recognizes that the quality of his life is not derived from his circumstances but has allowed the Holy Spirit to lead, direct, and guide his life and decisions. He recognizes worldly warfare and pursues spiritual maturity through his surrender to the will of God. He has made himself available for God's purposes.

Rewarded Christian

The final step to complete maturity in Christ is the rewards associated with that reality. These rewards are not only in the next life, but many are for our current existence. In 2 Corinthians 5:10, "For we must all appear before the judgment seat of Christ, so that each one may be recompensed for his deeds in the body, according to what he has done, whether good or bad." Then there is 1 Corinthians 3:13–14,

> Each man's work will become evident; for the day will show it because it is to be revealed with fire, and the fire itself will test the quality of each man's work. If any man's work which he has built on it remains, he will receive a reward.

The Jewish counterpart to this state appears in Joshua 12–22, where the twelve tribes receive their promised lands. The New Testament equivalent to accepting the inheritance of land is faith-rest. As New Testament believers are rewarded for their works in heaven, they also find the victorious life in their ability to rest in any situation. The apostle Paul says this in Philippians 4:11–13,

> Not that I speak from want, for I have learned to be content in whatever circumstances I am. I know how to get along with humble means, and I also know how to live in prosperity; in any and every circumstance I have learned the secret of being filled and going hungry, both of having abundance and suffering need. I can do all things through Him who strengthens me.

The victorious life depends only on God at His banquet table.

Chapter 18: Categorical Doctrine

You, however, continue in the things you have learned and become convinced of, knowing from whom you have learned them, and that from childhood you have known the sacred writings which are able to give you the wisdom that leads to salvation through faith which is in Christ Jesus. All Scripture [*graphe*—that which is written] is inspired by God [*theopneústou*—God-breathed] and profitable [advantageous] for teaching [doctrine], for reproof, for correction, for training in righteousness; so that the man of God may be adequate, equipped for every good work.

2 Timothy 3:14–17

There are sixty-six books of the Christian Bible recognized by the Christian community as canon, meaning an acknowledgment as inspired by God and, thus, given divine authority. Paul understood the importance of this when he wrote the following in 1 Thessalonians 2:13 to the church:

For this reason, we also constantly thank God that when you received the word of God which you heard from us, you accepted [*dechomai*— accept an offer readily] it not as the word of men, but for what it really is, the word of God, which also performs its work [*energeo*—effective, operative work] in you who believe.

As quoted above, *all Scripture* is God-breathed and has a divine purpose: doctrine, reproof, correction, and training in righteousness. If the believer is to receive everything God intends, he needs to accept it as if God spoke it. "So will My word be which goes forth from My mouth; It will not return to Me empty, Without accomplishing what I desire, And without succeeding in the matter for which I sent it" (Isaiah 55:11).

The Mind of the Lord

Now we have received, not the spirit of the world, but the Spirit who is from God, so that we may know the things freely given to us by God, which things we also speak, not in words taught by human wisdom, but in those taught by the Spirit, combining [*sugkrinoe*—joining together] spiritual thoughts with spiritual words. But a natural man does not accept the things of the Spirit of God, for they are foolishness to him; and he cannot understand them, because they are spiritually appraised. But he who is spiritual appraises all things, yet he himself is appraised by no one. For WHO HAS KNOWN THE MIND OF THE LORD THAT HE WILL INSTRUCT HIM? But we have the mind of Christ.

1 Corinthians 2:12–16

We understand from the above passage that the Word of God is ultimately taught by the Spirit of God to each true believer; the non-believer cannot understand them since he cannot discern the Holy Spirit. By joining together spiritual thoughts with spiritual words, the Holy Spirit creates in the believer the mind of the Lord, the mind of Christ. According to Jamieson, Fausset, and Brown's Commentary,

> Expounding the Spirit-inspired Old Testament by comparison with the Gospel revealed by the same Spirit, conversely illustrating the Gospel mysteries by comparing them with the Old Testament types.

The organized thoughts of God, as taught by the Spirit, give believers the ability to think with God, His thoughts as confirmed by His Word.

Seeking the Truth

Be diligent [*spoudazoe*—diligent, eager, earnest] to present yourself approved to God as a workman who does not need to be ashamed, accurately handling [*orthotomeoe*—correctly teaching] the word of truth.

2 Timothy 2:15

To properly understand Scripture, the believer seeks truth expressed in the entire Bible as a laborer, pursuing God's complete thoughts on a subject. It requires diligence and an eagerness to discover the deeper understanding God intends each believer to find. Scripture is filled with historical accounts of events, while the deeper meaning of those accounts requires a systematic pursuit and an intensity, a seeking to find it. According to Proverbs 8:17, "I love those who love me, And those who diligently seek me will find me." It is a pursuit of the heart and a journey driven by love. There is a reward at the end of that journey; it is to know Him.

Paul writes in 1 Timothy 4:6,

> In pointing out these things to the brethren, you will be a good servant of Christ Jesus, constantly nourished on the words of the faith and of the sound [good] doctrine [*didaskalia*—instruction, that which is taught] which you have been following.

Paul wanted Timothy to appreciate the importance of sound doctrine as a good servant of Christ Jesus. In his second letter, Paul warns Timothy of the spiritual warfare surrounding this journey:

> For the time will come when they will not endure sound doctrine; but wanting to have their ears tickled, they will accumulate for themselves teachers in accordance to their own desires, and will turn away their ears from the truth and will turn aside to myths.
>
> 2 Timothy 4:3–4

Paul writes to Titus of purity or soundness in doctrine that demonstrates a ministry above reproach (Titus 2:7–8).

Methods of Preaching

There are three basic methods that preachers have used to prepare and deliver their sermons: expository, categorical or topical, and textual. The most common of these today is expository, presenting the meaning and intent of a particular biblical text and providing commentary and examples to make the passage clear and understandable. The intent is to "expose" the meaning of the Bible, verse by verse.

To prepare an expository sermon, the preacher starts with a passage of Scripture and then studies the grammar, the context, and the historical setting of that passage to understand the author's intent. In other words, the expositor is also an exegete—one who analyzes the text carefully and objectively. Once the preacher understands the meaning of the passage, he then crafts a sermon to explain and apply it.

Topical Sermons

In a topical sermon, the preacher starts with a topic/category and then finds passages in the Bible that address it. The focal point is a clear presentation of the category in a way that provides a depth of understanding of that subject which usually includes passages from both the Old and New Testaments. If the believer is to understand the mind of Christ related to a category, he needs to combine or join together *spiritual thoughts with spiritual words.*

Textual preaching dominated the homiletical landscape in the latter half of the 1800s and the first half of the 1900s and remains popular in some circles today. At the dawn of the twenty-first century, when topical preaching and expository preaching get most of the press in America, what is the role of textual preaching? That question can be answered only after defining what textual preaching is. In a textual sermon, the preacher uses a text as a springboard for discussing a particular point.

According to John Broadus, a Southern Baptist preacher and seminary president, a subject or topical (categorical) sermon is structured according to the nature of the subject rather than the biblical text(s) on which it is based. He notes that the Bible does "not present truth in a succession of logical propositions," so when the preacher needs to present a doctrine or moral issue, the topical form works well. However, while the sermon must be faithful to Scripture, its structure does not take its cue from the biblical text(s) on which it is based.

Benefits & Shortcomings

In both topical and textual sermons, the Bible passage is used as support material for the topic. In expository sermons, the Bible passage is the topic, and support materials are used to explain and clarify it. Each method has its benefits and shortcomings and should be chosen based on the particular intent. Many preachers like me will combine these three in the same sermon, taking advantage of the benefits and avoiding many of the downfalls. Sticking to only one method can be shortsighted.

Finding categorical doctrine is the process of acquiring God's organized thoughts that enables the believer to think with God in an accurate light. It provides the ability to reciprocate and receive God's thoughts in an absolute category as set forth in the Word of God. There are no prerequisites other than an honest effort to study and meditate on Scripture categorically. Consider the following:

Albert Einstein once said, "Everybody is a genius. But if you judge a fish by its ability to climb a tree, it will live its whole life believing that it is stupid." This comes from a genius—a genius who didn't talk until he was four or read until he was seven. Einstein's teachers labeled him "slow" and "mentally handicapped." He may have been last in his class to do what the rest could, but certainly, Einstein wasn't any less than his peers. He just had his own way of thinking —a way of thinking that would earn him the Nobel Prize and change the way we understand our world.

The Victorious Life

You shall therefore *impress* [*sim*—place, fix] these words of mine on your heart and on your soul; and you shall bind them as a sign on your hand, and they shall be as frontals on your forehead. You shall teach them to your sons, talking of them when you sit in your house and when you walk along the road and when you lie down and when you rise up. You shall write them on the doorposts of your house and on your gates, so that your days and the days of your sons may be multiplied on the land which the Lord swore to your fathers to give them, as long as the heavens remain above the earth. For if you are careful to *keep* [*shamar*—maintain, observe for a purpose] all this commandment which I am commanding you to do, to love the Lord your God, to walk in all His ways and hold fast to Him, then the Lord will drive out all these nations from before you, and you will dispossess nations greater and mightier than you. Every place on which the sole of your foot treads shall be yours; your border will be from the wilderness to Lebanon, and from the river, the river Euphrates, as far as the western sea. No man will be able to stand before you; the Lord your God will lay the dread of you and the fear of you on all the land on which you set foot, as He has spoken to you.

Deuteronomy 11:18–25
(emphasis added by the author)

Thinking with God's thoughts is the doorway into the victorious life over the sin nature and an avenue into intimacy with Him in all circumstances. Psalm 119:11 (emphasis added by the author), "*Your word I have treasured* [*sapan*—conceal something of great value] *in my heart, That I may not sin against You.*" Take note of the following verses and the importance of meditation:

> This book of the law [*torah*—doctrine] shall not depart from your mouth, but you shall *meditate* [*hagah*—ponder] on it day and night, so that you may be careful to do according to all that is written in it; for then you will make your way prosperous, and then you will have success.
>
> Joshua 1:8
> (emphasis added by the author)

> But his delight is in the law of the Lord, And in His law, he *meditates* day and night. He will be like a tree firmly planted by streams of water, Which yields its fruit in its season And its leaf does not wither; And in whatever he does, he prospers.
>
> Psalm 1:2–3
> (emphasis added by the author)

"One thing I have asked from the Lord, that I shall seek: That I may dwell in the house of the Lord all the days of my life, To behold the beauty of the Lord And to *meditate* in His temple" (Psalm 27:4) (emphasis added by the author).

> Therefore, putting aside all filthiness and all that remains of wickedness, *in humility* receive the word implanted [*emphutos*—engrafted from another source], which is able to save your souls.
>
> James 1:21
> (emphasis added by the author)

The humble heart is the environment through which the Word of God does its work.

CHAPTER 19: BIBLICAL PROSPERITY

In Matthew 6:24, Jesus taught that we could not serve (*douleuo*—to be subjected to) two masters, referring to God versus riches (*mammon*—the God of materialism), that we will love the one and hate the other. This teaching had in mind that there are two economies, one defined by the material realm and a different economy represented by the authority of God.

Economy can be defined as "the wealth and resources of a country or region, especially in terms of the production and consumption of goods and services." It includes the systems and processes associated with the accumulation of material things. The believer needs to understand that to find God's riches, he must apply different principles than the world system, and those principles are found in the Scriptures. To find the fullness of God's economy is to use these principles as a way of life.

Fear of the Lord

In Proverbs 22:4 (emphasis added by the author), Solomon teaches, "The reward of *humility and the fear of the Lord* Are riches, honor and life." Another translation says, "Humility is the fear of the Lord." This principle of the fear of the Lord is a central theme to a quality (right) relationship with God. It means that one sees the Lord with great reverence and awe, and this takes one to a place where walking in God's ways is not a chore but a delight. In Psalm 128:1–6 (emphasis added by the author),

> How blessed is everyone *who fears the Lord, Who walks in His ways.* When you shall eat of the fruit of your hands, You will be happy [state of bliss] and it will be well with you. Your wife shall be like a fruitful vine Within your house, Your children like olive plants Around your table. Behold, for thus shall the man be blessed Who fears the Lord. The Lord bless you from Zion, *And may you see the prosperity of*

Jerusalem all the days of your life. Indeed, may you see your children's children. Peace be upon Israel!

How critical is the fear of the Lord and biblical prosperity? According to Psalm 128, it is the avenue to God's blessings, to *walk in His ways.* It is the environment that creates bliss as one enjoys the fruitfulness of one's work as well as from his wife and children. These blessings are recognized to come from the Lord's holy hill, Zion, and these blessings flow to the Jewish nation (i.e., Jerusalem). Finally, the blessings associated with the fear of the Lord flow to future generations. Psalm 25:13 says it is where God's instruction is received, and in verse 14, God reserves His secrets for those who fear Him.

Meditation

This *book of the law shall not depart from your mouth*, but you shall meditate on it day and night, so that you may be careful to do according to all that is written in it; *for then you will make your way prosperous* [accomplish satisfactorily what is intended], and then you will have success [prudence, give insight].

Joshua 1:8
(emphasis added by the author)

Finding biblical prosperity involves the Word of God as a central part of a believer's life. Now that Moses was gone and Joshua was in charge, Joshua needed to get established in his ability to be led by God. The Lord was teaching him that it would be his willingness to meditate on His Word, day and night, to make his way what God had purposed for Him and His people. Psalm 1 has a similar instruction that consistent meditation on *His law* produces a fruitful life, "like a tree firmly planted by streams of water, which yields its fruit in its season and *its leaf does not wither*; and *in whatever he does, he prospers*" (emphasis added by the author).

The Lord Will Command the Blessing

Now it shall be, if you diligently obey the Lord your God, being careful to do all His commandments which I command you today, the Lord your God will set you high above all the nations of the earth. All these *blessings* [God's favor] will come upon you and overtake you if you obey the Lord your God: Blessed shall you be in the city and blessed shall you be in the country. Blessed shall be the offspring of your body and the produce of your ground and the offspring of your beasts, the increase of your herd and the young of your flock. Blessed shall be your basket and your kneading bowl. Blessed shall you be when you come in and blessed shall you be when you go out. The Lord shall cause your enemies who rise up against you to be defeated before you; they will come out against you one way and will flee before you seven ways. *The Lord will command the blessing upon you* in your barns and in all that you put your hand to, and He will bless you in the land which the Lord your God gives you. *The Lord will establish you as a holy people to Himself,* as He swore to you, if you keep the commandments of the Lord your God and walk in His ways. So, all the peoples of the earth will see that you are called by the name of the Lord, and they will be afraid of you. *The Lord will make you abound in prosperity, in the offspring of your body and in the offspring of your beast and in the produce of your ground,* in the land which the Lord swore to your fathers to give you. The Lord will open for you His good storehouse, the heavens, to give rain to your land in its season and to bless all the work of your hand; and you shall lend to many nations, but you shall not borrow. The Lord will make you the head and not the tail, and you only will be above, and you will not be underneath, if you listen to the commandments of the Lord your God, which I charge you today, to observe them carefully, and do not turn aside from any of the words which I command you today, to the right or to the left, to go after other gods to serve them.

Deuteronomy 28:1–14
(emphasis added by the author)

Deuteronomy 28 begins with fourteen verses addressing God's blessings and then thirty-six verses dealing with curses. He begins the chapter by laying the foundation for God's blessings or favor: the believer's diligent obedience to the Lord's commandments. The Hebrew word for diligent obedience is *shama*, and its basic meaning is to listen to. This word introduces the Jewish daily prayers known as the Shema, "Hear, O Israel," which are prayed day and night (Deuteronomy 6:4). It means paying close attention to God's instructions to honor them. It is a listening of the heart that elicits a corresponding response.

The following verses of this passage identify all the amazing ways Elohim brings favor and prosperity to those who diligently obey, including in the city and the country. This passage speaks of the all-encompassing ways that He blesses a man's life with abundance. He even promises to make this believer "the head and not the tail." He adds to the condition by saying this man does not turn aside from any of His commandments "to the right or the left," meaning it is a full commitment.

Seeking the Lord

We can learn from the example of King Uzziah as revealed in 2 Chronicles 26:1–5 and the principle of seeking the Lord (emphasis added by the author):

> And all the people of Judah took Uzziah, who was sixteen years old, and made him king in the place of his father Amaziah. He built Eloth and restored it to Judah after the king slept with his fathers. Uzziah was sixteen years old when he became king, and he reigned fifty-two years in Jerusalem; and his mother's name was Jechiliah of Jerusalem. He did right in the sight of the Lord according to all that his father Amaziah had done. He continued to seek God in the days of Zechariah, who had understanding through the vision of God; and *as long as he sought the Lord, God prospered him.*

The Hebrew word *darash* speaks of an inquiry with intensity, a pursuit to understand as to obey. It is this attitude that allowed Uzziah to receive God's blessings. Verse 4 above tells us that he "did right in the sight of the Lord according to all his father Amaziah had done" and continued seeking understanding from God in every situation. He realized that his prosperity would not continue once he stopped seeking the Lord.

Choose Life

Biblical prosperity is the result of the right choices. In Deuteronomy 30:15–20 (emphasis added by the author):

See, I have set before you today life and prosperity, and death and adversity; in that I command you today to *love the Lord your God, to walk in His ways and to keep His commandments and His statutes and His judgments*, that you may live and multiply, and that the Lord your God may bless you in the land where you are entering to possess it. But if your heart turns away and you will not obey but are drawn away and worship other gods and serve them, I declare to you today that you shall surely perish. You will not prolong your days in the land where you are crossing the Jordan to enter and possess it. I call heaven and earth to witness against you today, that I have set before you life and death, the blessing and the curse. *So, choose life in order that you may live, you and your descendants, by loving the Lord your God, by obeying His voice, and by holding fast to Him*; for this is your life and the length of your days, that you may live in the land which the Lord swore to your fathers, to Abraham, Isaac, and Jacob, to give them.

It always comes down to a choice. The believer gets to decide how much of God's abundance he enjoys. He must understand that there are forces present that wish to keep him from an abundant life and destroy his quality of life. When the believer makes God his highest priority, he enters into a loving relationship with his God and is guaranteed the highest quality of life. As 3 John 1:2 says, "Beloved, I pray that in all respects you may prosper and be in good health, *just as your soul prospers.*"

Chapter 20: The Lord Reigns

"Say among the nations, 'The Lord reigns; Indeed, the world is firmly established [*kun*—fixed, steadfast], it will not be moved; He will judge the peoples with equity [righteously]'" (Psalm 96:10).

Scripture is clear that creation is the work of God, but what role does He play after creation is complete? Does He play an active role in the events of man, or does He stand back and watch, with little to do with day-to-day details? The answer to these questions can determine the quality of the relationship man can have with his God. According to the psalmist above, Yahweh reigns or rules over a world that He firmly established by judging the people righteously. Colossians 1:17 tells us, "He is before all things [preexistent], and in Him all things hold together [*sunistemi*—join together parts into a whole, keep in order]." In Hebrews 1:3, He "upholds [*pheroe*—governs] all things by the word of His power." These verses testify of God's active role in man's affairs.

In Him

The God who made the world and all things in it, since He is Lord of heaven and earth, does not dwell in temples made with hands; nor is He served by human hands, as though He needed anything, since He Himself gives to all people life and breath and all things; and He made from one man every nation of mankind to live on all the face of the earth, having determined their appointed times and the boundaries of their habitation, that they would seek God if perhaps they might grope [*pselaphao*—to feel for or after an object] for Him and find Him, though He is not far from each one of us; for *in Him we live and move and exist*, as even some of your own poets have said, 'For we also are His children.'

Acts 17:24–28
(emphasis added by the author)

While in Athens, Paul engaged with some Epicurean and Stoic philosophers, who brought him to Mars Hill. There, Paul would explain to them what the gospel was all about; he used the occasion to describe the *strange deities* he was preaching. In light of an altar to an Unknown God, Paul began teaching them about this God. The above passage utilizes the philosophers' perspective to provide a foundation for the God of the Bible. He would determine "their appointed times and the boundaries of their habitation." According to *Barnes' Notes*:

> Their limits and boundaries as a people: by customs, laws, inclinations, and habits, He has fixed the boundaries of their habitations and disposed them to dwell there. We may learn:
> (1) That the revolutions and changes of nations are under the direction of infinite wisdom.
> (2) People should not be restless and dissatisfied with where God has located them.
> (3) That God has given sufficient limits to all so that it is not needful to invade others; and,
> (4) That wars of conquest are evil. God has given people their places of abode, and we have no right to disturb them or attempt to displace them violently. This strain of remark by the apostle was also opposed to all the notions of the Epicurean philosophers and yet so obviously true and just that they could not gainsay or resist it.

A Greater Zeus

Paul quotes from Epimenides, from the poem "Minos" and addresses Zeus as follows (emphasis added by the author):

> They fashioned a tomb for you, holy and high one,
> Cretans, always liars, evil beasts, idle bellies.
> But you are not dead: you live and abide forever,
> *For in you we live and move and have our being.*

Many did not believe in Zeus' immortality. Epimenides wrote that Zeus was not only immortal but was the source of life. Paul was comparing their perception of Zeus to the God of Abraham, Isaac, and Jacob, who "does not dwell in temples made with hands, nor is He served by human hands, as though He needed anything." Man's boundaries and habitations are ordained by God's perfect plan to create a need for God and, therefore, a desire to seek after Him. This seeking requires faith beyond the five senses "if perhaps they might grope for Him and find Him, though He is not far from each one of us." This verse creates the picture of a blind man recognizing the existence of God but not being able to see Him, so he feels for or after Him. The conclusion of that search is to find the one in whom "we live and move and exist."

The progression Paul speaks of begins with life "in Him." This is terminology he uses more than 170 times in his letters, referring to each true believer's ordained relationship to the person and work of Christ. In seeking, he experiences a supernature life (*zoe*), the life of Christ, which is offered as an exchange for natural life (Galatians 2:20). Embracing this *zoe* life causes him to be guided by the movement of Jesus and into His work, stepping outside of the work created by human agenda and energy. The result is a new existence and a new identity in Christ.

Seeking First the Kingdom

In the Sermon on the Mount, Jesus explains that the believer can count on God's provisions for food, clothing, and shelter when he seeks first the kingdom of God and His righteousness (Matthew 6:25–34). When prioritizing God's kingdom and righteousness over his individual interests, one is acknowledging the Lord's kingship and holiness. In Matthew 13:44, Jesus teaches that the issue comes down to where one's treasure is. "The kingdom of heaven is like a treasure hidden in the field, which a man found and hid again; and from joy over it he goes and sells all that he has and buys that field." A willingness to die to personal interests for the sake of this new life connects the righteous one to the life of the Son of God. In Galatians 2:20, "The life which I now live in the flesh I live by faith in the Son of God, who loved me and gave Himself up for me." Faith in His Son defines that new life.

There is a Jewish teaching that talks about two shapes—the circle and the line. The circle represents our physical existence. This is why the earth was created round. However, if we live simply on the earthly level, we will go around and around the circle but never get anywhere. This is the life where we wake up and go through the daily routine—and repeat it again and again and again. This is a life devoid of meaning. We age, but we don't change. We go through time, but we don't grow with time.

The line, however, is symbolic of progression and connection. As we grow, we come closer to God. This is why human beings were created in the form of a line. Sure, we may have circular elements, and indeed, our lives require physical cycles and routines, but our overall form, from top to bottom, is a line. This teaches us that while we live in the circle of the earth, our job is to grow up and out like a line. We can and must live a meaningful life growing closer to what is beyond the earth—to God.

Judging Righteously

We give thanks to You, O God, we give thanks, for Your name is near; Men declare Your wondrous works. "When I select an appointed time, It is I who judge with equity [rightness]. The earth and all who dwell in it melt; It is I who have firmly set [*takan*—weighing to establish] its pillars. Selah. I said to the boastful, 'Do not boast,' and to the wicked, 'Do not lift up the horn [strength]; do not lift up your horn on high, do not speak with insolent pride.'" For not from the east, nor from the west, nor from the desert comes exaltation, but God is the Judge; He puts down one and exalts another. For a cup is in the hand of the Lord, and the wine foams; It is well mixed, and He pours out of this; surely all the wicked of the earth must drain and drink down its dregs. But as for me, I will declare it forever; I will sing praises to the God of Jacob. And all the horns of the wicked He will cut off, but the horns of the righteous will be lifted up.

Psalm 75

Psalm 75 is written by Asaph and refers to the Lord as Ruler among the nations, asserting that He will, in due time, take vengeance on those in rebellion against Him. It speaks of pillars on which the earth is established, with a judge who sets things in their proper order according to His righteousness and justice. He identifies the boastful and those who rely on their strength, resulting in pride. He speaks of a cup of wine that foams and is well-mixed, a reference to His judgment and a cup of wrath (see Psalm 60:3). He upholds the world through His attention to both the righteous and the wicked.

According to Hebrews 11:3,

By faith we understand that the worlds were prepared [*katartizoe*— establish, arrange, set in order] by the word [*rhema*—that which is spoken] of God, so that what is seen was not made out of things which are visible.

It speaks of the critical role played by His Word in keeping things in their proper order. Our success is dependent upon our life of faith in Him and His Word.

CHAPTER 21: THREE COATS

The life of Joseph, Jacob's eleventh son, gives us insight into the journey a believer takes to find the victorious life in Christ. Joseph's three coats or garments best demonstrate it. These three coats represent three different critical times in the life of a believer in his pursuit of getting to know God and experiencing His blessings. New Testament believers can benefit significantly from a close look at Joseph's life.

The first coat to consider appears in Genesis 37 and Jacob's gift to his son of a coat of many colors. Verses 3–4 say (emphasis added by the author),

> Now Israel loved Joseph more than all his sons, because he was the son of his old age; and *he made him a varicolored tunic* [coat]. His brothers saw that their father loved him more than all his brothers; and so they hated him and could not speak to him on friendly terms.

The Hebrew word *passim* means richly ornamented and made with many colors, a highly esteemed garment. The fact that Jacob gave it only to Joseph created all kinds of jealousy among his brothers and caused a severe reaction that would affect Joseph's entire future.

Coat of Salvation

What is the significance of this magnificent coat? The coat of many colors signifies an individual's salvation and the ramifications of that choice.

In Zechariah 3:1–5, we have the account of Joshua, the high priest standing before the angel of the Lord (most` likely an appearance of Jesus) with Satan accusing him of being "clothed with filthy garments." Jesus says, "Remove the filthy garments from him." Jesus then says, "I have taken your iniquity away from you and will clothe you with festal robes." This clearly references the gospel of salvation available to believers in the new covenant.

In Revelation 3:18, Jesus's letter to the church at Laodicea advises them to "buy from Me gold refined by fire so that you may become rich, and *white garments* [garments of salvation] so that you may clothe yourself" (emphasis added by the author). The fact that Joseph's brothers rejected him because of his coat is also how the world can treat new believers in Christ. In Joseph's case, his brothers had him sold into slavery.

Coat of Injustice

As a slave, Potiphar, an Egyptian officer of Pharaoh, purchased Joseph and brought him to his house to be his servant in Genesis 39. Joseph was highly successful as Potiphar's overseer since "the Lord was with Joseph," to the point that Potiphar "left everything he owned in Joseph's charge; and with him there he did not concern himself with anything except the food which he ate" (verse 6). The second coat/garment is found in verse 12 when Joseph tries to get away from Potiphar's wife, who wants Joseph to "lie with me." When he refuses, she grabs his garment and then accuses him of trying to lie with her. Joseph spent at least two years in jail because he was falsely accused. The second coat is the coat of injustice.

There are many difficulties one faces in life that can be characterized as unjust and undeserved. Learning how to meet these injustices is part of the maturity process. The believer is taught that "'vengeance is mine, I will repay,' says the Lord;" God will deal with it, so he should let it ride. This requires real intestinal fortitude and genuine faith in God. In James 1:12, the Bible says, "Blessed is a man *who perseveres under trial*; for once he has been approved, he will receive the crown of life which the Lord has promised to those who love Him" (emphasis added by the author). Spiritual maturity requires accepting injustices in life as a part of a larger master plan by the God in whom "all things hold together" (Colossians

1:17). This dynamic may also be referred to as His sovereignty. In Psalm 115:3, God does whatever He pleases. Are we willing to accept that?

Coat of the Overcomer

Genesis 41:38–44 relates the account of Joseph's third coat. It comes about as a result of Joseph's perseverance with injustice. He has spent many years in prison but does not, by all accounts, react but accepts it and finds peace during the greatest trials. As a result, God uses him mightily. He gets out of jail when God gives him the interpretation of Pharaoh's dream, while none of his reliable leaders can provide the answer. In verse 38, "Then Pharaoh said to his servants, 'Can we find a man like this, in whom is a divine spirit?'" Pharaoh concluded that since Joseph accomplished this, he was discerning and wise, and Pharaoh would elevate Joseph to be his second in command. In verse 42 (emphasis added by the author), "Then Pharaoh took off his signet ring from his hand and put it on Joseph's hand *and clothed him in garments of fine linen* and put the gold necklace around his neck."

To the Laodicean church in Revelation 3:21, Jesus says, "He who overcomes, I will grant to him to sit down with Me on My throne, as I also overcame and sat down with My Father on His throne." Just like Joseph would assist Pharaoh in reigning over Egypt, the overcomer sits down with the Father on His throne. Those present at the marriage supper of the lamb will be clothed with fine linen, which speaks of the righteous acts of the saints (Revelation 19:7–8). Ultimately, God wants those who endure to reign with Him (2 Timothy 2:12).

Reigning in Life

For if by the transgression of the one, death reigned through the one, much more those who receive the abundance of grace and of the gift of righteousness *will reign in life through the One, Jesus Christ.*

Romans 5:17
(emphasis added by the author)

The ones who endure are the ones who receive and accept "the abundance of grace and of the gift of righteousness."

Chapter 22: Forgetting the Lord

Beware that you do not forget the Lord your God by not keeping His commandments and His ordinances and His statutes which I am commanding you today; otherwise, when you have eaten and are satisfied, and have built good houses and lived in them, and when your herds and your flocks multiply, and your silver and gold multiply, and all that you have multiplies, *then your heart will become proud and you will forget the Lord your God* who brought you out from the land of Egypt, out of the house of slavery. He led you through the great and terrible wilderness, with its fiery serpents and scorpions and thirsty ground where there was no water; He brought water for you out of the rock of flint. In the wilderness He fed you manna which your fathers did not know that He might humble you and that He might test you, to do good for you in the end. *Otherwise,* you may say in your heart, 'My power and the strength of my hand made me this wealth.' But you shall remember the Lord your God, for *it is He who is giving you power to make wealth,* that He may confirm His covenant which He swore to your fathers, as it is this day. It shall come about if you ever forget the Lord your God and go after other gods and serve them and worship them, I testify against you today that *you will surely perish.* Like the nations that the Lord makes to perish before you, so you shall perish because you would not listen to the voice of the Lord your God.

Deuteronomy 8:11–20
(emphasis added by the author)

This important passage, written a few weeks before Moses' death, was given as a warning about the dangers of putting one's trust in man's ability and circumstances instead of completely trusting God. The middle verse in the Bible is Psalm 118:8, and it is no coincidence that it speaks of this principle: "It is better to take refuge in the Lord than to trust in man." In verse 14 above, the consequence of not trusting in the Lord is a proud heart, removing consciousness of the Lord from the forefront of the believer's mind. It opens the door for intense spiritual warfare as the devil ignites in the flesh covetousness, craving with intensity instead of waiting on God (Psalm 106:13–14). Hezekiah succumbed to this principle in 2 Chronicles 32:25–26 when he "gave no return for the benefit he received, *because his heart was proud*; therefore wrath came on him and Judah and Jerusalem" (emphasis added by the author).

They Quickly Forgot

This was a consistent problem with Israel throughout Old Testament times, but the Lord did not abandon them *for the sake of His name* (Psalm 106:7–15). Upon experiencing God's deliverance, the people "believed His words; They sang His praise" only for a short season (verse 12). "They quickly forgot His works; They did not wait for His counsel, But craved [coveted] intensely in the wilderness, And tempted God in the desert," and the Lord brought a new trial for the people to bear (verse 13). As verse 7 states, "They did not remember Your abundant kindnesses." According to Isaiah 17:10–11,

> For you have forgotten the God of your salvation And have not remembered the rock of your refuge. Therefore, you plant delightful plants And set them with vine slips of a strange god. In the day that you plant it you carefully fence it in, And in the morning, you bring your seed to blossom; But the harvest will be a heap In a day of sickliness and incurable pain.

The natural man is looking to establish his own significance through human effort, and this process generally results in a competition to achieve something God wishes to give the believer freely. Paul wrote the church at Corinth and addressed this principle in 1 Corinthians 4:6–7 (emphasis added by the author) when he said,

> Now these things, brethren, I have figuratively applied to myself and Apollos for your sakes, so that in us you may learn not to exceed what is written, so that no one of you will become arrogant in behalf of one against the other. For who regards you as superior? *What do you have*

that you did not receive? And if you did receive it, why do you boast as if you had not received it?

Drifting Away

The carnal (fleshly) mind is also subject to this phenomenon. In Hebrews 2:1, the writer warns the believer of a "drifting away" from the faith. The Greek word used is *pararreoe*, and it means a slipping away, a gradual and almost unnoticeable movement as a result of a deviation from the truth. The solution to this spiritual warfare is to pay closer attention (*prosechoe*—to hold the mind in a particular direction) "to what we have heard." In Deuteronomy 4:9, Moses writes,

> Only give heed to yourself and keep your soul diligently, so that you do not forget the things which your eyes have seen, and they do not depart from your heart all the days of your life; but make them known to your sons and your grandson.

The spiritual principle being taught is an attention of the heart to divine instruction as the Holy Spirit illuminates truth in the inner man. Without this approach, we are subject to slackness in our relationship with God. This may be the most important theme addressed in the book of Hebrews.

The successful believer has learned how to wait on the Lord. It means that he has access to supernatural strength so that he does not tire. In Isaiah 40:28–31:

> Do you not know? Have you not heard? The Everlasting God, the Lord, the Creator of the ends of the earth Does not become weary or tired. His understanding is inscrutable. He gives strength to the weary, And to him who lacks might He increases power. Though youths grow weary and tired, And vigorous young men stumble badly, Yet those who wait for the Lord Will gain new strength; They will mount up with wings like eagles, They will run and not get tired, They will walk and not become weary.

An Inspiring Story

There is an inspiring story about an Israeli couple, Shlomo and Shiraz, who had struggled for years with fertility issues. Finally, after six years of disappointment, the couple found out that they were expecting twins! Their prayers had been answered abundantly, and when the time came, two healthy children—one girl and one boy—were born. But the story does not stop there.

Shortly after the birth of the twins, Shlomo and Shiraz discovered that their son had Down syndrome. However, these joy-filled parents explained how they never felt despair from the news—only endless love and gratitude for the gift of their child. Shiraz admits that without the six hard years of longing for a child, she may not have been able to handle the news as gracefully as she did. In fact, studies have shown that approximately one-third of parents who give birth to children with Down syndrome abandon their babies in the hospital. But for Shlomo and Shiraz, their son was a gift that they greatly cherished, even if he came in packaging that was different than expected.

As this story illustrates, the difficulties one may face in waiting on the Lord may be a silver lining. The Grateful Dead sing about this in their song "Touch of Grey," "Every silver lining's got a touch of grey." The specific challenges we face in waiting for God to ultimately resolve the challenge may be the very thing we need to keep moving forward in faith. In 1 Corinthians 10:13,

> No temptation has overtaken you, but such as is common to man; and God is faithful, who will not allow you to be tempted beyond what you are able, but with the temptation will provide the way of escape also, so that you will be able to endure it.

Walk by the Spirit

We are talking about the employment of spiritual laws that supersede natural laws, which limit man's ability and can subject him to the sin nature that desires to control him. Galatians 5:16–18 tells us that the solution is to "walk by the Spirit, and you will not carry out the desire of the flesh." When man is freed from his limitations by relating to God through the Spirit and not the Law of Moses, he finds victory. "But if you are led by the Spirit, you are not under the Law."

> *Unless the Lord builds the house*, They labor in vain who build it; Unless the Lord guards the city, The watchman keeps awake in vain. It is vain for you to rise up early, To retire late, To eat the bread of painful labors; For He gives to His beloved even in his sleep.

Psalm 127:1–2
(emphasis added by the author)

Chapter 23: God's Perfect Justice

Job's struggle, which many scholars believe happened around the time of Abraham, can be interpreted in many ways. First, it appears that the trial had a strong flavor of undeserved suffering, which makes it difficult to interpret God's intended motive for permitting it. The trial began when God allowed Satan certain liberties in Job's life that resulted in the loss of his possessions and his ten children. God then allowed Satan to attack Job's physical body, and it seems that this second trial was harder for Job to accept than the first.

Ultimately, it brought Job to question God's justice. In Job 16:12–13, Job says,

> I was at ease, but He shattered me, And He has grasped me by the neck and shaken me to pieces; He has also set me up as His target. His arrows surround me. Without mercy He splits my kidneys open; He pours out my gall on the ground.

Job was looking for relief and found none. He was relying on his integrity and not God's. The Lord was teaching him that Job didn't have what it took to be righteous before God.

Contending with the Almighty

Throughout the first thirty-seven chapters, God remained silent to Job. Finally, in chapter 38, the Lord answers Job out of the whirlwind. He starts by challenging Job to "gird up your loins like a man," meaning that God would speak some very challenging words and Job should be prepared. He then proceeded to ask him sixty-five questions in chapters 38 and 39 about Job's fitness in deciding perfect justice, including,

> Where were you when I laid the foundation of the earth? Tell Me, if you have understanding, Who set its measurements? Since you know. Or who stretched the line on it? On what were its bases sunk? Or who laid its cornerstone?

> Job 38:4–6

We see Job's response in chapter 40 that he is brought to his knees.

The Lord begins chapter 40 by saying, "Will the faultfinder contend with the Almighty? Let him who reproves God answer it." Job's reaction is found in Job 40:4, "Behold, I am insignificant [*qalal*—trifling, slight]; what can I reply to You? I lay my hand on my mouth." However, this did not end the conversation as God continued questioning Job's ability to administer perfect justice.

Questioning Justice

> Then the Lord answered Job out of the storm and said, "Now gird up your loins like a man; I will ask you, and you instruct Me. Will you really annul My judgment? Will you condemn Me that you may be justified? Or do you have an arm [strength] like God, and can you thunder with a voice like His? Adorn yourself with eminence and dignity and clothe yourself with honor and majesty. Pour out the overflowings of your anger, and look on everyone who is proud, and make him low. Look on everyone who is proud, and humble him, and tread down the wicked where they stand. Hide them in the dust together; bind them in the hidden place. *Then* I will also confess to you, *that your own right hand can save you.*"

> Job 40:6–14
> (emphasis added by the author)

After again warning Job to gird up his loins, the Lord immediately addresses the issue of His justice. He accuses Job of attempting to reverse His judgments, condemning God in the process of justifying himself. This lays the foundation for God's questioning of Job's ability to be the author or administrator of perfect justice. Does Job have the strength, voice, eminence, and dignity, as well as the ability to consistently apply justice in every situation? Is he able to humble the proud and tread down the wicked? If this is so, then Job can save himself. Otherwise, questioning the Lord's ability to accomplish all of these perfectly is fool's gold. In Romans 9:19–21, Paul says it this way,

> You will say to me then, "Why does He still find fault? For who resists His will?" On the contrary, who are you, O man, who answers back to God? The thing molded will not say to the molder, "Why did you make me like this," will it? Or does not the potter have a right over the clay, to make from the same lump one vessel for honorable use and another for common use?

Being the Creator has its advantages.

Full Retraction

The Lord refers to two created beings, a behemoth (maybe a hippopotamus) and a leviathan (could be a crocodile), as a means of illustrating that any massive, strong, powerful being or created thing cannot overcome His perfect plan. These conversations put Job entirely on his knees before God. In Job 42:1–6 (emphasis added by the author),

> Then Job answered the Lord and said, "I know that You can do all things, And that no purpose of Yours can be thwarted. 'Who is this that hides counsel without knowledge?' *Therefore,* I have declared that which I did not understand, Things too wonderful for me, which I did not know." 'Hear, now, and I will speak; I will ask You, and You instruct me.' "I have heard of You by the hearing of the ear; But now my eye sees You; *Therefore,* I retract, And I repent in dust and ashes."

These two "therefores" are the conclusions that this man referred to in Job 1:1 as blameless, upright, fearing God, and turning away from evil needed something more to experience the entire nature of God. Job was coming to understand that questioning justice, the plan of God for each man, was a dangerous occupation.

Job's testimony of his trial may be likened to Abraham's challenge to believe in God for his entire future, accepting the Lord's command to leave his home for a "promised land," far away from his homeland. Letting go of any control over personal life choices to make God's plan superior is the avenue into a more profound experience with God. It is to acknowledge that God knows best that His program for the believer, exercised by faith, will turn out in his favor. Abraham went so far in his faith in God as to be willing to sacrifice the son God promised him based on God's request. These made Abraham the father of our faith (Romans 4:16). Job had learned that accepting God at His word and not questioning Him when great difficulties arose would bring him to the place where God would bless with eternal (not just temporal) blessings.

Divine Ability

The Law of Moses was unable to fulfill God's perfect justice for Israel because it "was weak through the flesh" (Romans 8:3), meaning that it takes more than natural ability or complete devotion to perfect. In Isaiah 11:3–5, Scripture reveals that the Holy Spirit will empower the coming Messiah to provide perfect justice since,

> He will delight in the fear of the Lord, and He will not judge by what His eyes see, nor make a decision by what His ears hear; but with righteousness He will judge the poor and decide with fairness for the afflicted of the earth; and He will strike the earth with the rod of His mouth, and with the breath of His lips He will slay the wicked. Also, righteousness will be the belt about His loins, and faithfulness the belt about His waist.

Perfect justice requires divine ability. Since Jesus the Messiah is the mediator of the new covenant, it is only through the new covenant relationship with God that the believer finds perfect justice. It is the place where the believer can trust the Lord for His perfect plan.

Song of Solomon is a picture of the relationship between Jesus (the bridegroom) and each believer (the bride). It reveals that God's love for the believer and his corresponding love for his Lord is the source of a fruitful life. In Song of Solomon 2:3, "Like an apple tree among the trees of the forest, So is my beloved among the young men. In his shade I took great delight and sat down, And his fruit was sweet to my taste." This verse tells us that God's commandments, represented by the trees of the forest, provide shade (religious protection), but the apple tree (the new covenant relationship to God) is where the sweet fruit (quality of life) is found. Job found the apple tree at the end of his trial when he accepted the perfect plan.

Justice for All

In Matthew 12, Jesus healed the man with a withered hand on the Sabbath, and the Pharisees made a big deal about it—what a surprise! In verses 18–21, Jesus revealed that this was in fulfillment of Isaiah 42:1–4 (emphasis added by the author),

> BEHOLD, MY SERVANT WHOM I HAVE CHOSEN; MY BE-LOVED IN WHOM MY SOUL is WELL-PLEASED; I WILL PUT MY SPIRIT UPON HIM, AND *HE SHALL PROCLAIM JUS-TICE TO THE GENTILES.* HE WILL NOT QUARREL, NOR CRY OUT; NOR WILL ANYONE HEAR HIS VOICE IN THE STREETS. A BATTERED REED HE WILL NOT BREAK OFF, AND A SMOLDERING WICK HE WILL NOT PUT OUT, *UNTIL HE LEADS JUSTICE TO VICTORY.* AND IN HIS NAME THE GENTILES WILL HOPE.

Perfect justice is not a set of rules and regulations to follow, but rather it is following God's laws (instructions), written on human hearts, learning to trust the one who will not break the battered reed or put out the smoldering wick. Ultimately, justice finds victory!

Paul tells us in Romans 1:20,

> For since the creation of the world His invisible attributes, His eternal power and divine nature, have been clearly seen, being understood through what has been made, so that they are without excuse.

The promise is that the Lord reveals Himself through things created, including His master plan for each believer's life. To understand this reality is to recognize that His control over details of life, namely His perfect justice, is a means by which each believer fully appreciates His ability and His personal love.

Fully Confirmed

The Lord reigns, He is clothed with majesty; The Lord has clothed and girded Himself with strength; Indeed, the world is firmly established, it will not be moved. Your throne is established from of old; You are from everlasting. The floods have lifted up, O Lord, The floods have lifted up their voice, The floods lift up their pounding waves. More than the sounds of many waters, Than the mighty breakers of the sea, The Lord on high is mighty. *Your testimonies are fully confirmed;* Holiness befits Your house, O Lord, forevermore.

Psalm 93:1–5
(emphasis added by the author)

Chapter 24: Make Your Days Count

As I get older and older, the passage of time becomes more apparent, and my awareness of time more relevant. To the young person, time is something that is in abundance, and to guard or protect it is not so important. Solomon spent a great deal of Ecclesiastes considering the dynamics of time and its effect on his pursuit of a meaningful life. Gleaning biblical principles helps the believer become a good manager of the time God afforded him, which makes life on Earth purposeful.

No Regrets

A few years ago, a nurse working in palliative care found herself having profound conversations with her patients. The result was a book, *The Top Five Regrets of the Dying*. From what the dying wished they had done differently; the living could learn precious lessons about the changes they should make in their own lives—before it's too late. They express the need to value time more wisely.

Here are the five regrets.

"I wish I'd had the courage to live a life true to myself."

"I wish I hadn't worked so hard."

"I wish I'd had the courage to express my feelings."

"I wish I had stayed in touch with my friends."

"I wish that I had let myself be happier."

Moses addresses time concerning man's days (lifetime) in Psalm 90:10–12,

> As for the days of our life, they contain seventy years, Or if due to strength, eighty years, Yet their pride is but labor and sorrow; For soon it is gone and we fly away. Who understands the power of Your anger And Your fury, according to the fear that is due You? So teach

us [make us know] to number our days [appreciate the passage of time], That we may present to You a heart of wisdom [carry wisdom into the heart].

To number our days is to recognize the passage of time to make each day matter the most. If each day is a gift from God, it has great value, and God wishes us to treat it that way. This is the wisdom of the heart.

Seasons of Life

In Ecclesiastes 3:1, Solomon introduces a discussion of time when he says, "There is an appointed [opportune] time for everything [actions & events]. And there is a time [as a duration] for every event [activity—what one desires] under heaven." The essence of this verse is that God has given time as a gift to be managed to discern its most significant meaning and find His will amid its details. It also brings up the idea of seasons of life when conditions or events govern different periods of life: "A time to kill and a time to heal; A time to tear down and a time to build up. A time to weep and a time to laugh; A time to mourn and a time to dance" (verses 3–4). The summary of the passage is found in verse 11, where God has made everything beautiful or appropriate in its time. Therefore, man finds the highest quality of life when he seeks God's purpose for each day.

Solomon also discusses time in Ecclesiastes 7:8, "The end of a matter is better than its beginning; Patience of spirit is better than haughtiness of spirit." So, patience is a virtue; learning how to wait gives one the fullness of life! And then there is Ecclesiastes 8:5–6,

> He who keeps a royal command experiences no trouble [harm], for a wise heart knows the proper time and procedure. For there is a proper time and procedure for every delight, though a man's trouble [misery] is heavy upon him.

The king's command (i.e., government regulation) is worth heeding, resulting in temporal benefits (no harm). Everything has a time and procedure or method, and the circumstances surrounding the event do not govern it. In Ecclesiastes 7:14, God has made both the day of prosperity and adversity "so that man will not discover anything that will be after him." Walking by faith usually means not knowing where I'm going. Current circumstances of life are not an indication of the future.

The Effects of Aging

It used to be that the elders in our society were generally recognized with respect and treated with dignity for their wisdom and experience. I believe that, for the most part, our society no longer acknowledges the elderly as ones to honor but more like ones to tolerate. Solomon addresses this subject in Ecclesiastes 12:5,

> Furthermore, men are afraid of a high place and terrors on the road [elderly fears]; the almond tree blossoms [white hair], the grasshopper drags himself along [physical disabilities], and the caperberry is ineffective [diminished appetites]. For man goes to his eternal home while mourners go about in the street.

The progression of aging, the effect of time on man, creates all kinds of infirmities, both physical and psychological. In a society that values the aging ones, these conditions are to be accepted and not discarded as those with little value. God speaks about the elderly in this way in Psalm 92:13–14, "They will flourish in the courts of our God. They will still yield fruit in old age; They shall be full of sap and very green." In God's eyes, man can be fruitful until the end; life has great value in its totality.

Redeeming the Time

The apostle Paul expresses the same principle that man should manage time wisely. In Ephesians 5:15–16, he says, "Therefore be careful how you walk, not as unwise men but as wise, making the most of your time, because the days are evil." To redeem the time has the idea of purchasing and setting free. When the believer recognizes the need to value his time and acts on that need, he is set free from the world's evil influences. Jesus addressed this principle at the end of His Sermon on the Mount when He said in Matthew 7:13–14,

> Enter through the narrow gate; for the gate is wide and the way is broad that leads to destruction, and there are many who enter through

it. For the gate is small and the way is narrow that leads to life, and there are few who find it.

The narrow gate is the pathway governed by the Holy Spirit and the perfect will of God. The choices we make to live while being led by God determine the quality of the time we have received.

Robert Frost, the famous American poet, wrote a notable poem dealing with choices we make in the direction of our lives when he wrote: "The Road Not Taken." Although not a Christian according to his writings, this poem communicates a biblical principle:

The Road Not Taken

Two roads diverged in a yellow wood,
Then took the other, as just as fair,
And sorry I could not travel both
And having perhaps the better claim,
And be one traveler, long I stood

Because it was grassy and wanted wear.
And looked down one as far as I could
Though as for that the passing there
To where it bent in the undergrowth;
Had worn them really about the same,

And both that morning equally lay
I shall be telling this with a sigh
In leaves, no step had trodden black.
Somewhere ages and ages hence:
Oh, I kept the first for another day!

Two roads diverged in a wood, and I—
Yet knowing how way leads on to way,
I took the one less traveled by,
I doubted if I should ever come back.
And that has made all the difference.

The believer's walk with God is not defined by the exact steps of other believers gone before us. Instead, it is finding the unique pathway prepared before us by God, so it is a road less traveled. Although we recognize the biblical foundations of our lives as provided by the apostles and prophets and learn to follow God by watching others, it is up to us, as led by the Holy Spirit, to find the particular steps He has prepared beforehand, which we should walk. Identifying that path is more complex and usually requires much experience, but in the end, those choices will make all the difference.

The Great I Am

Just like Jesus was crucified between two thieves, the present is also being stolen from the believer by the past and the future. Too many are driven either by the failures of the past or the unknowns of the future, and this robs them of the joy in the relationship God has intended. You see, He told Moses in Exodus 3 that His name is "I Am that I Am," and means He is the God of the present moment and, therefore, every moment. Jesus acknowledged that His name is also "I Am" when he told the Jewish leadership that "before Abraham was born, I am" (John 8:58). Ultimately, God meets each of us in the present moment, learning to "cease striving and know that I am God" (Psalm 46:10) is our place of rest. Jesus taught His disciples to "seek first His kingdom and His righteousness" and "do not worry about tomorrow" (Matthew 6:33–34), meaning His presence is in the present moment.

Chapter 25: The Foolishness of God

Where is the wise man? Where is the scribe? Where is the debater of this age? Has not God made foolish the wisdom of the world? For since in the wisdom of God the world through its wisdom did not come to know God, God was well-pleased through the foolishness of the message preached to save those who believe. For indeed Jews ask for signs and Greeks search for wisdom; but we preach Christ crucified, to Jews a stumbling block and to Gentiles foolishness, but to those who are the called, both Jews and Greeks, Christ the power of God and the wisdom of God. Because *the foolishness* [*moeros*—silly, stupid, foolish] *of God* is wiser than men, and the weakness of God is stronger than men.

1 Corinthians 1:20–25
(emphasis added by the author)

In the above passage, Paul tries to get the Corinthians to understand that the avenue to comprehending the highest priorities of God does not take one through the wisdom of the world. He says that salvation has been removed from man's ability to think on his own and instead established on the foundation of faith in something or someone outside himself (verse 21). In verse 23, "but we preach Christ crucified," it was His life crucified as an offering that should be the object of that faith. The emphasis is on the plan of the Father executed by the Son on behalf of those, both Jews and Greeks, who would place their confidence in the fulfillment of that plan by a crucified Christ. Man's ability or efforts are not part of the equation. In fact, "God has chosen the foolish things of the world to shame the wise" (verse 27).

Blow the Trumpets

Now Jericho was tightly shut because of the sons of Israel; no one went out and no one came in. The Lord said to Joshua, "See, I have given Jericho into your hand, with its king and the valiant warriors. *You shall march around the city, all the men of war circling the city once. You shall do so for six days.* Also, seven priests shall carry seven trumpets of rams' horns before the ark; then on the seventh day you shall march around the city seven times, and the priests shall blow the trumpets. It shall be that when they make a long blast with the ram's horn, and *when you hear the sound of the trumpet, all the people shall shout with a great shout;* and the wall of the city will fall down flat, and the people will go up every man straight ahead."

Joshua 6:1–5
(emphasis added by the author)

The Lord intended that the Jews would begin to take control and possess their promised land city by city, beginning with Jericho. In taking Jericho, God's plan was to demonstrate how much the people needed to trust in God's plan, no matter how foolish it might seem. As the above passage states, God gives specific instructions to march around the city's walls each day for six days, with seven priests carrying seven trumpets. On the seventh day, the people would march around the city seven times, then the priests would blow the trumpets, and the walls would fall down flat. I'm sure this plan was not related to any known military strategies for winning any military battle; instead, this plan encouraged a willingness to completely trust in God, no matter how foolish it may seem.

Outnumbered

There are similar events in Scripture where God commanded the Jews facing an adversarial enemy to do something contrary to wise military counsel. This is the basis of real faith, trusting God when it appears there can be no victory in any situation, no matter how grave it may be. Another example appears in 2 Chronicles 20, where the Jews faced the armies of Ammon, Moab, and Mount Seir. In verse 20, King Jehoshaphat says, "Listen to me, O Judah and inhabitants of Jerusalem, put your trust in the Lord your God and you will be established. Put your trust in His prophets and succeed." The Lord's commandment was for the king to choose singers who would go before the army to sing praises to God in holy attire and give thanks for the upcoming victory. Foolishness to man, yet it was God's perfect plan. Verses 22–23 say (emphasis added by the author),

> *When they began singing and praising, the Lord set ambushes against the sons of Ammon, Moab and Mount Seir, who had come against Judah; so they were routed.* For the sons of Ammon and Moab rose up against the inhabitants of Mount Seir destroying them completely; and when they had finished with the inhabitants of Seir, they helped to destroy one another.

Their enemies destroyed each other without any military effort from the army.

> Then Jerubbaal (that is, Gideon) and all the people who were with him, rose early and camped beside the spring of Harod; and the camp of Midian was on the north side of them by the hill of Moreh in the valley. The Lord said to Gideon, "*The people who are with you are too many for Me to give Midian into their hands,* for Israel would become boastful, saying, 'My own power has delivered me.' Now therefore, come, proclaim in the hearing of the people, saying, '*Whoever is afraid and trembling, let him return and depart from Mount Gilead.*'" So 22,000 people returned, but 10,000 remained. Then the Lord said to Gideon, "*The people are still too many;* bring them down to the water, and I will test them for you there. Therefore, it shall be that he of whom I say to you, 'This one shall go with you,' he shall go with you; but everyone of whom I say to you, 'This one shall not go with you,' he shall not go." So he brought the people down to the water. And the Lord said to Gideon, "You shall separate everyone who laps the water with his tongue as a dog laps, as well as everyone who kneels to drink." Now the number of those who lapped, putting their hand to their mouth, was 300 men; but all the rest of the people kneeled to drink water. The Lord said to Gideon, "*I will deliver you with the 300 men who lapped and will give the Midianites into your hands*; so, let all the other people go, each man to his home." So the 300 men took the people's provisions and their trumpets into their hands. And Gideon sent all the other men of Israel, each to his tent, but retained the 300 men; and the camp of Midian was below him in the valley.

> Judges 7:1–8
> (emphasis added by the author)

Gideon's 300 Men

Another example comes to view in the account of Gideon above. The Lord explains that His purpose is to keep the people from becoming boastful, thus taking credit for the victory that will only be attributable to God. God told Gideon that the 32,000 troops assembled to fight the Midianite army were too many, even though vastly outnumbered. As a result, 22,000 people returned, leaving 10,000 to fight. As it turns out, even 10,000 was too many for the Lord, so He devises a test to determine which of the remaining would be worthy of this fight. In verse 5, "You shall separate everyone who laps the water with his tongue as a dog laps, as well as everyone who kneels to drink." Only 300 men qualified, while the rest kneeled to drink. Only those who were watchful would be useful.

God instructed Gideon to break the men into three groups of a hundred each and would carry trumpets and empty jars with torches inside as their weapons while the Lord would fulfill His promise to "give the Midianites into your hands." The three groups would be night watchmen, each group taking a different shift and were told in verse 20,

> When the three companies blew the trumpets and broke the pitchers, they held the torches in their left hands and the trumpets in their right hands for blowing, and cried, "A sword for the Lord and for Gideon!"

This commotion demonstrated their trust in the Lord while creating confusion within the Midianite army, and they fled.

A Contemporary Illustration

Here's a story from Israel's not-so-distant past. In the spring of 2003, Israel was fighting a war against terrorism. The Israel Defense Forces (IDF) were reasonably successful, but a few battles were hard to win. One such fight took place in Jenin, a Palestinian stronghold. The Israeli fighters described an incident where the morale was very low. Many soldiers had already lost their lives, and as a last resort, an Israeli general had threatened over the loudspeaker to send in F-16 fighter jets. It was an empty threat that neither the soldiers nor the terrorists took seriously.

That is, until a loud booming sound was heard moments later. At first, the soldiers were confused, but then they realized the sound was thunder, even though it was spring, and in Israel, it almost never rains in the spring. The terrorists were not as wise. They immediately surrendered. When asked why, they said, "We heard the sound of fighter jets and knew we were defeated." God's thunder won the battle. A modern-day miracle!

Ultimately, the Lord always teaches His people to "Trust in the Lord with all your heart And do not lean on your own understanding. In all your ways acknowledge Him, And He will make your paths straight" (Proverbs 3:5–6). It is about learning to trust in the promises of God, no matter what.

Chapter 26: The Weakness of God

Where is the wise man? Where is the scribe? Where is the debater of this age? Has not God made foolish the wisdom of the world? For since in the wisdom of God the world through its wisdom did not come to know God, God was well-pleased through the foolishness of the message preached to save those who believe. For indeed Jews ask for signs and Greeks search for wisdom; but we preach Christ crucified, to Jews a stumbling block and to Gentiles foolishness, but to those who are the called, both Jews and Greeks, Christ the power of God and the wisdom of God. Because the foolishness of God is wiser than men, and *the weakness* [*asthenos*—without strength, powerless] *of God* is stronger than men.

1 Corinthians 1:20–25
(emphasis added by the author)

In the above passage, Paul tries to get the Corinthians to understand that the avenue to comprehending God's highest priorities does not take one through the wisdom of the world. In fact, he says that salvation has been removed from the plane of man's ability to think on his own and instead established on the foundation of faith in something or someone outside himself (verse 21). In verse 23, "But we preach Christ crucified," it was His life crucified as an offering that should be the object of that faith. The emphasis is on the plan of the Father executed by the Son on behalf of those, both Jews and Greeks, who would place their confidence in the fulfillment of that plan by a crucified Christ. Man's ability or efforts are not part of the equation. In fact, "God has chosen the weak things of the world to shame the things which are strong" (verse 27).

Despised and Forsaken

For He grew up before Him like a tender shoot, And like a root out of parched ground; He has no stately form or majesty That we should look upon Him, Nor appearance that we should be attracted to Him. *He was despised and forsaken of men*, A man of sorrows and acquainted with grief; And like one from whom men hide their face, He was despised, and we did not esteem Him. *Surely our griefs He Himself bore*, And our sorrows He carried; Yet we ourselves esteemed Him stricken, Smitten of God, and afflicted. But He was pierced through for our transgressions, He was crushed for our iniquities; The chastening for our well-being fell upon Him, And by His scourging we are healed. All of us like sheep have gone astray, Each of us has turned to his own way; But the Lord has caused the iniquity of us all To fall on Him. He was oppressed and He was afflicted, Yet He did not open His mouth; Like a lamb that is led to slaughter, And like a sheep that is silent before its shearers, So He did not open His mouth.

Isaiah 53:2–7
(emphasis added by the author)

Although the Old Testament predicted a coming Messiah who would rule as a king with full authority, numerous passages, particularly from Isaiah, characterize another coming of Messiah as a suffering servant. The most recognizable of these is found in the above passage and illustrates the weakness of the Messiah at His first coming, as a lamb led to the slaughter. He was rejected by His people (John 1:11), "He was despised, and we did not esteem Him," "yet we ourselves esteemed Him stricken, Smitten of God, and afflicted." He accepted the divine judgment from His Father, including physical beatings, as a substitute for each one of us. In addition, He chose to stay quiet despite the false claims against Him. He demonstrated complete weakness.

A Bondservant

The apostle Paul characterizes this weakness in Philippians 2 as emptying Himself of His deity to accept the role as a bondservant (*doulos*—a slave, one who is in a permanent relation of servitude to another, his will being altogether consumed in the will of the other—Zodhiates). It demonstrated a humility that Paul recognized as a necessary mindset to experience the fullness of God (verses 3–5). In verse 9, "For this reason also, God highly exalted Him, and bestowed on Him the name which is above every name." The greatness of the work of Jesus Christ at His first coming is characterized by His willing weakness to accept the perfect plan of the Father on behalf of the world.

> And when I came to you, brethren, I did not come with superiority of speech or of wisdom, proclaiming to you the testimony of God. For I determined to know nothing among you except Jesus Christ, and Him crucified. I was with you in weakness and in fear and in much trembling, and my message and my preaching were not in persuasive words of wisdom, but in demonstration of the Spirit and of power, so that your faith would not rest on the wisdom of men, but on the power of God.
>
> 1 Corinthians 2:1–5

The Gospel

Paul, the five-star general of the New Testament age, gives us insight into how each of us can connect to this weakness in the above passage. He recognized that his ability to have an effective ministry was to manifest the power of the Holy Spirit, which would only take place in weakness. In this way,

> My message and my preaching were not in persuasive words of wisdom, but in demonstration of the Spirit and of power, so that your faith would not rest on the wisdom of men, but on the power of God.

The source of that weakness can be found in verse 2, where he makes a judicial judgment that the weakness of Christ (Christ crucified) and the message of the gospel, that He had accomplished full redemption (John 19:30) for everyone and can be received based on faith alone.

Moses acknowledged his weakness before God in Exodus 4 when he testified, "Please, Lord, I have never been eloquent, neither recently nor in time past, nor since You have spoken to Your servant; for I am slow of speech and slow of tongue" (verse 10). How would he be God's spokesman before Pharaoh with such a weakness? The Lord answered that Moses' weakness would be God's avenue to allow Him to speak. Verse 12: "Now then go, and I, even I, will be with your mouth, and teach you what you are to say." The Lord had earlier illustrated how that would take place in verses 1–5 (emphasis added by the author):

> Then Moses said, "What if they will not believe me or listen to what I say? For they may say, 'The Lord has not appeared to you.'" The Lord said to him, "What is that in your hand?" And he said, "A staff." Then He said, "Throw it on the ground." So he threw it on the ground, and it became a serpent; and Moses fled from it. But the Lord said to Moses, "Stretch out your hand and grasp it by its tail"—so he stretched out his hand and caught it, and it became a staff in his hand— *"that they may believe that the Lord, the God of their fathers, the God of Abraham, the God of Isaac, and the God of Jacob, has appeared to you."*

Wait for the Lord

The fact is that the Lord is more than capable of managing His plan. In Acts 5, the Christian leaders were commanded not to proselytize, but they did. Complaints were brought to the Jewish leadership that action was necessary. Gamaliel, a highly respected teacher of the Law, testified that it was unnecessary to take action since "if it is of God, you will not be able to overthrow them; or else you may even be found fighting against God" (verse 39). He also cited a false teacher named Theudas, who had four hundred followers, yet when Theudas was killed, the movement died on its own.

> Do you not know? Have you not heard? The Everlasting God, the Lord, the Creator of the ends of the earth Does not become weary or tired. His understanding is inscrutable. He gives strength to the weary, And to him who lacks might He increases power. Though youths grow weary and tired, And vigorous young men stumble badly, Yet those who wait for the Lord Will gain new strength; They will mount up with wings like eagles; They will run and not get tired; They will walk and not become weary.
>
> Isaiah 40:28–31

Success in serving God does not depend on natural or acquired ability but rather the willingness to wait on God. The manifestation of God's weakness is clearly seen in man's willingness to be weak so that God can be strong in us (2 Corinthians 12:9–10). He is aware of the need and is able to meet the need in His timing and manner. It represents a simple life.

The Simpleton & the Sophisticate

Rabbi Nachman of Breslov, the famous eighteenth-century Ukrainian teacher, shared many stories as a form of teaching biblical concepts. One of his more famous tales is "The Simpleton and the Sophisticate." The story compares the lives of two different men—one simple and one sophisticated.

The simple man doesn't have much and isn't one of the best in his trade. Yet, he is always happy and satisfied with what he has. He is honest and straight as an arrow in all his dealings with others. He is also confident and peaceful with who he is and has no need to pretend to be anyone or anything different.

The sophisticated man, on the other hand, is knowledgeable, well-traveled, and worldly. He excels in many areas and is clever about how to make more money and do things better. Yet, he is never satisfied with himself or with what he has. He has this nagging feeling that he should be more and have more. Ultimately, his depression and sense of failure lead to a bitter life. Conversely, the simple man rises to prominence because of his reliability and reputation for integrity.

The moral of the story? The simple life is the best life.

Chapter 27: Our Great High Priest

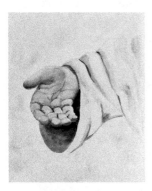

One of the offices Messiah holds in the new covenant is that of the high priest, but it is not based on the position derived from Aaron, but rather after the order of Melchizedek. In Hebrews 7:1–2 (emphasis added by the author),

For this Melchizedek, king of Salem, *priest of the Most High God*, who met Abraham as he was returning from the slaughter of the kings and blessed him, to whom also Abraham apportioned a tenth part of all the spoils, was first of all, by the translation of his name, *king of righteousness*, and then also king of Salem, which is *king of peace*.

This priesthood is different in that it is an eternal priesthood and not derived from the Law of Moses since Jesus, of the tribe of Judah and not Levi, had fulfilled the Law (Matthew 5:17). Because Melchizedek is referred to as both king of righteousness and peace, this priesthood becomes the source for the righteousness and peace of the believer-priest. Romans 5:1 tells us that we have been justified [(declared righteous) by faith, and therefore, we have the righteousness and peace belonging to Christ.

In Hebrews 1:3, "When He had made purification of sins, He sat down at the right hand of the Majesty on high." This position, at the right hand of His Father, is the place of authority, acceptance, and honor. David identifies it in Psalm 110:1 as where His Son is given authority over His enemies, thus acknowledging Him as Lord. It means that the mediator of the new covenant, our great high priest (Hebrews 4:14–16), really cares when He sympathizes with our weaknesses since He was tempted as a man, yet He remained sinless. Therefore, His throne is a throne of grace, and He is able to dispense mercy and grace to help in our time of need when we approach Him with confidence. In Ephesians 1:19–20,

> And what is the surpassing greatness of His power toward us who believe. These are in accordance with the working of the strength of His might which He brought about in Christ, when He raised Him from the dead and seated Him at His right hand in the heavenly places.

This priesthood can accomplish everything asked of it since it is limited only by God's unlimited power.

A Royal Priesthood

> But you are A CHOSEN RACE, A royal PRIESTHOOD, A HOLY NATION, A PEOPLE FOR God's OWN POSSESSION, so that you may proclaim the excellencies of Him who has called you out of darkness into His marvelous light; for you once were NOT A PEOPLE, but now you are THE PEOPLE OF GOD; you had NOT RECEIVED MERCY, but now you have RECEIVED MERCY.
>
> 1 Peter 2:9–10

Peter acknowledges that as chosen ones (Ephesians 1:4), the believer is automatically part of "a royal priesthood" and a holy nation, meaning that he has been set apart for a divine purpose as "a people for God's own possession." This divine purpose is "so that you may proclaim the excellencies of Him who has called you out of darkness into His marvelous light," and this empowerment only happens to the one who has accepted his position as a priest by receiving His mercy. The new covenant believer-priest recognizes that he belongs to God and derives his accountability from that position. God has commissioned New Testament believers into His army of servant priests.

No Rest

As a believer-priest, the new covenant believer accepts his accountability to the high priest. In Colossians 2:13–14,

> When you were dead in your transgressions and the uncircumcision of your flesh, He made you alive together with Him, having forgiven

us all our transgressions, having canceled out the certificate of debt consisting of decrees against us, which was hostile to us; and He has taken it out of the way, having nailed it to the cross.

As a result of this greatest work, the believer-priest is tuned into the voice of God, unlike the Jews in the wilderness, who were not listening to God and became disobedient. The ten spies and the people refused to accept that God was greater than their enemies in the promised land, and therefore they missed their rest. Psalm 95:10–11, "For forty years I loathed that generation, And said they are a people who err in their heart, And they do not know My ways. Therefore, I swore in My anger; Truly they shall not enter into My rest."

The writer of Hebrews addresses this matter in Hebrews 3:18–19, "And to whom did He swear that they would not enter His rest, but to those who were disobedient? So we see that they were unable to enter because of unbelief." There is a direct relationship between unbelief and disobedience. Psalm 106:25 says they grumbled in their tents and were not listening to God's voice. When the high priest speaks, the believer-priest not only listens but also mixes faith with what he hears. The relationship to the Word of God is an essential element for the believer finding God's rest (Hebrews 4:2). In verse 3 (emphasis added by the author),

> For we who have believed enter that rest, just as He has said, "AS I SWORE IN MY WRATH, *THEY SHALL NOT ENTER MY REST*," although His works were finished from the foundation of the world.

The rest of the high priest is available to each believer-priest who trusts His finished work (John 19:30) and His truth, the Word of God (John 17:17).

Sabbath Rest

When Hebrews 4:9 says, "So there remains a Sabbath rest for the people of God," it was not just referring to the future kingdom age when Messiah would be in total control, but to all of His people who recognize His lordship as high priest in every age. The Greek word is *sabbatismós*, which means keeping the day of rest as a time when the believer ceases labor. Verse 10 suggests that this word, derived from the Hebrew *shabbat*, references the eternal rest that all believers will experience when God completes His work, and he can enter God's rest. It is different from the other word (*katapausis*) in this passage, translated as rest, and speaks about a ceasing to work. Psalm 46:10 says, "Cease striving and know that I am God." This Sabbath rest is the beginning of the believer finding an inner rest, where he learns to rest in the work of God.

Inner Rest

Come to Me, all who are weary and heavy-laden, and *I will give you rest*. Take My yoke upon you and learn [*mathete*] from Me, for I am gentle and humble in heart, and YOU WILL FIND REST FOR YOUR SOULS. For My yoke is easy and My burden is light.

Matthew 11:28–30
(emphasis added by the author)

The rest Jesus refers to here is that inner rest that each believer receives from Jesus through being "yoked up" with Him in His work. It happens when the believer becomes His student, His disciple (*mathete*), and prioritizes His words. He also places Himself under the authority of the Word of God, which is "living and active and sharper than any two-edged sword, and piercing as far as the division of soul and spirit, of both joints and marrow, and able to judge the thoughts and intentions of the heart" (Hebrews 4:12). He allows the Word of God to become his judge so that his thoughts and intentions are disclosed and brought to light. It is a place of safety.

God gave King David a glimpse of this eternal rest when he wrote Psalm 16. In verses 8–11 (emphasis added by the author):

I have set the Lord continually before me; because He is at my right hand, I will not be shaken. Therefore, my heart is glad and my glory rejoices; My flesh also will dwell securely. for You will not abandon my soul to Sheol; nor will You allow Your Holy One to undergo decay. You will make known to me the path of life; *In Your presence is fullness of joy*; In Your right hand there are pleasures forever.

David refers to a present rest and a future rest. In either case, it is in God's presence where he finds his rest. So, our great high priest is an ever-present reality to the one who makes His life and words his priority.

Chapter 28: Like a Weaned Child

O Lord, my heart is not proud, nor my eyes haughty; Nor do I involve myself in *great matters*, Or in things too difficult for me. Surely, I have composed and quieted my soul; Like a weaned child rests against his mother, *My soul is like a weaned child within me.* O Israel, hope in the Lord From this time forth and forever.

Psalm 131
(emphasis added by the author)

Psalm 131 is a psalm of David and became one of the fifteen Songs of Degrees sung by pilgrims on their way to Jerusalem to celebrate the Jewish feasts. We are not sure what event caused its writing, but we know it speaks to the believers' hope in the Lord. David starts by telling of the condition of his heart that it is not proud nor eyes haughty to look down on others. Approaching God requires a proper attitude not only toward Him but toward others as well. Paul references this attitude in Philippians 2:3–8.

Humility of Mind

Do nothing from selfishness or empty conceit, but with humility of mind regard one another as more important than yourselves; do not merely look out for your own personal interests, but also for the interests of others. *Have this attitude* in yourselves which was also in Christ Jesus, who, although He existed in the form of God, did not regard equality with God a thing to be grasped, but emptied Himself, taking the form of a bond-servant, and being made in the likeness of men. Being found in appearance as a man, *He humbled Himself* by becoming obedient to the point of death, even death on a cross.

Philippians 2:3–8
(emphasis added by the author)

David had to exercise great humility during his life, especially as King Saul was pursuing to kill him. In this psalm, David testifies that his humility was augmented by his decision not to get involved in matters of great significance or things he could not manage. In Psalm 139:4–6, he writes,

> Even before there is a word on my tongue, Behold, O Lord, You know it all. You have enclosed me behind and before and laid Your hand upon me. Such knowledge is too wonderful for me; It is too high, I cannot attain it.

He recognized that there is so much above and beyond him and that the Lord has everything in hand. Therefore, he can quiet his soul in faith-rest. It is in this mindset he found his hope in God.

An Illustration

A story is told about a ninety-two-year-old woman as she entered the nursing home where she would spend the rest of her life. After waiting patiently in the lobby, she was told that her room was ready. An attendant escorted the lady to her room, and as she slowly edged her walker toward the elevator, he described the room to her. "I love it!" she exclaimed with the enthusiasm of a child who had just received the most wonderful birthday gift. "But Mrs. Jones, you haven't even seen it yet!" the man replied. "That has nothing to do with it," she said.

The elderly woman continued: "Joy is something you decide on ahead of time. Whether I like my room or not doesn't depend on how the furniture is arranged...*it's how I arrange my mind.* I have already decided to love it. It's a decision I make every morning when I wake up. Each day is a gift, and as long as my eyes open, I'll focus on the new day."

This remarkable woman had arrived at a secret that gave her freedom from the overwhelming effects of details of life that she could not influence. The victory was found in the right arrangement of her mind. David found this reality in seeing himself as a weaned child. This references the innocence associated with young children as they face the world without the mother's breast for protection and nourishment. In Isaiah 11:8–9, the

Lord tells us about the conditions found during the millennial kingdom when he says,

> The nursing child will play by the hole of the cobra, And the weaned child will put his hand on the viper's den. They will not hurt or destroy in all My holy mountain, For the earth will be full of the knowledge of the Lord As the waters cover the sea.

The authority of King Jesus has overcome the world's power.

Innocence

The innocence of a child is the pathway to the fullness of God's kingdom. Jesus rebuked His disciples for not recognizing this principle. In Matthew 19:13–14,

> Then some children were brought to Him so that He might lay His hands on them and pray; and the disciples rebuked them. But Jesus said, "Let the children alone, and do not hinder them from coming to Me; for the kingdom of heaven belongs to such as these."

In Matthew 11:25, Jesus teaches that the Father has hidden the important matters of the kingdom from the wise and intelligent and instead revealed them to infants, little ones. Simple faith bases its hope on the Lord.

> And said, "Truly I say to you, unless you are converted and become like children, you will not enter the kingdom of heaven. Whoever then humbles himself as this child, he is the greatest in the kingdom of heaven."

> Matthew 18:3–4

CHAPTER 29: THE AUTHORITY OF HUMILITY

When we see that *humility* is something infinitely deeper than contrition and accept it as our participation in the life of Jesus, we shall begin to learn that it is our true nobility and that to prove it in being servants of all is the highest fulfillment of our destiny, as men created in the image of God.

This is a quote from Andrew Murray (emphasis added by the author) and his book *Humility*, and it captures the essence of the importance of humility. It means that humility is not just a critical part of our relationship with Jesus but also the foundation of our relationship with others. Peter strongly encourages every believer to "clothe yourselves with humility toward one another" (1 Peter 5:5) since God is watching and "gives grace to the humble." So what is humility?

Humility is the quality of being humble. Dictionary definitions accentuate humility as a low self-regard and sense of unworthiness. In a religious context, humility can mean recognition of a self-concerning God. Outside of a religious context, humility is being "unselved," a liberation from the consciousness of self, and a form of temperance that is neither having pride nor indulging in self-deprecation. It is defined most clearly concerning Jesus, as found in Philippians 2. In verses 3–5,

Do nothing from selfishness or empty conceit, but with humility of mind regard one another as more important than yourselves; do not merely look out for your interests, but also for the interests of others. Have this attitude in yourselves which was also in Christ Jesus.

This humility, exemplified by Jesus's public ministry, is motivated by self-sacrificing love.

God Does the Exalting

The Father honors those who operate in humility. Proverbs 22:4 says, "The reward of humility and the fear of the Lord Are riches, honor and life." He says that the humility of Jesus will be highly exalted, the Father bestowing on Him the name above every name (Philippians 2:9–11). The truth is it is best when the Father is the one who does the exalting, which takes the pressure off the individual. Consider 1 Peter 5:6, "Therefore humble yourselves under the mighty hand of God, that He may exalt you at the proper time." The contrast here is that the believer humbles himself to be brought low, and God will do the exalting, the lifting up. This is one way that God gets the glory in any situation.

A Roman centurion came to Jesus asking for healing for his servant in Matthew 8:5–10. This soldier, not a Jew, said to Jesus, "Lord, *I am not worthy* for You to come under my roof, but just say the word, and my servant will be healed" (emphasis added by the author). Then he explained to Jesus what he was thinking, "For I also am a man under authority, with soldiers under me; and I say to this one, 'Go!' and he goes, and to another, 'Come!' and he comes, and to my slave, 'Do this!' and he does it." This man, like many in military service, understood authority. This non-Jew recognized the authority of Jesus and that when He spoke that his servant was healed, His words were sufficient. Jesus acknowledged this centurion's recognition of God's authority when He said, "Truly I say to you, I have not found such great faith with anyone in Israel." The believer's faith demands that he wait for God to bring about His will in any given situation, and the result will be greater than anything man can accomplish. Psalm 27:14 says, "Wait for the Lord; Be strong and let your heart take courage; Yes, wait for the Lord."

Moses and Paul

Let's look at a couple of examples of this kind of humility in Scripture. Moses spent forty years in the backside of the desert after running for his life, and then God spoke to him through a burning bush (Exodus 3). God would use this man, Moses, to lead His people from their bondage in Egypt into the land promised to Abraham. Why Moses? Numbers

12:3 answers, "(Now the man Moses was very humble, more than any man who was on the face of the earth)." Moses was able to speak with God's authority because of his humility. In this environment, the Lord gave Moses authority to confront Pharoah and lead His people. In Exodus 4:1–5, the Lord changed Moses' staff into a serpent and then back to a staff. He was proving to Moses that Moses would speak with His authority, as He says in verse 5, "That they may believe that the Lord, the God of their fathers, the God of Abraham, the God of Isaac, and the God of Jacob, has appeared to you."

Another example is the apostle, Paul. In 1 Corinthians 2:1–5, Paul's testimony is that:

> And when I came to you, brethren, I did not come with superiority of speech or of wisdom, proclaiming to you the testimony of God. For I determined to know nothing among you except Jesus Christ, and Him crucified. I was with you in weakness and in fear and in much trembling, and my message and my preaching were not in persuasive words of wisdom, but in demonstration of the Spirit and of power, so that your faith would not rest on the wisdom of men, but on the power of God.

Paul concluded that for him to fulfill the call of God on his life, it would only happen when he acknowledged his weakness before God in humility so that God would be strong in his weakness (see 2 Corinthians 12:9–10). The demonstration of God's power, God's ability, and God's authority would cause men to put their faith in God and not man. The humility of man is the doorway into the authority of God.

A Bag of Chickens Becomes a Herd of Goats

A story is told about a great sage, Rabbi Chanina Ben Dosa, who lived in Galilee about two thousand years ago. Rabbi Chanina was known for his saintliness and also for his extreme poverty. One day, a merchant was on his way to the market when he put down his bag of chickens next to a dilapidated house and went through the neighborhood in search of some food. The man got his food, but then he couldn't find the house where he had left his chickens. Rabbi Chanina's wife heard the chickens and brought them into her home that night.

To make a long story short, Rabbi Chanina and his family cared for the chickens, awaiting their owner's return, for many years. During that time, the chickens laid many eggs. Rabbi Chanina could not afford eggs, and his whole yard was covered in them! *But he would not touch them because they were not his.* Those eggs became more chickens, and soon there were so many chickens that Rabbi Chanina had to trade them in for goats, which became more goats until there was a large herd.

One day, a man walked by Rabbi Chanina's house and said, "That's the house! That's where I lost my chickens many years ago!" Rabbi Chanina heard the man's words and quickly opened the door. "If you are the man who left chickens here, I have something to show you...." And with that, Rabbi Chanina gave the man a small fortune, an entire herd of goats!

This Rabbi recognized through his poverty (humility) not to accept anything that did not belong to him but became a steward of it, accountable to God for it. This way, the bag of chickens was multiplied into a herd of goats. This principle can apply to many different aspects of life, but it means that when the believer waits for God to give something, it will be much greater than when he takes that thing for himself. When God gets the glory due Him, the believer gets exalted.

The Great Commission

Jesus commended His authority to His disciples just before His ascension in Matthew 28:18–20 when He said (emphasis added by the author),

> *All authority* has been given to Me in heaven and on earth. Go therefore and make disciples of all the nations, baptizing them in the name of the Father and the Son and the Holy Spirit, teaching them to observe all that I commanded you; and lo, I am with you always, even to the end of the age.

When the disciple goes in the name of the Father and the Son and the Holy Spirit, he goes under the authority of the trinity to accomplish the great commission that all nations would hear the gospel and become disciples, revealing the authority of humility.

CHAPTER 30: BE STRONG & COURAGEOUS

A test was once conducted where ten high school students were placed in one room and shown three lines of varying lengths. The students were told to raise their hands when the instructor pointed to the longest line. In reality, only one student was being tested. Nine of the students had been instructed beforehand to raise their hands when the instructor pointed to the second longest line. Seventy-five percent of the time, the students being tested retracted the right answer when they saw that no one else agreed with them. The researchers concluded that most people would rather be popular than be right.

This condition is a symptom of today's society and is caused by a lack of conviction in the truth. When peer pressure supersedes doing the right thing, we become part of the herd and subject to various influences, many being very destructive. The apostle Paul tells us,

> But the Spirit explicitly says that in later times some will fall away from the faith, paying attention to deceitful spirits and doctrines

of demons, by means of the hypocrisy of liars seared in their own conscience as with a branding iron.

1 Timothy 4:1–2

Having the courage to stand for one's convictions is not an accident but the result of a decision to stand for important things.

From Moses to Joshua

Now it came about after the death of Moses the servant of the Lord, that the Lord spoke to Joshua the son of Nun, Moses' servant, saying, "Moses My servant is dead; now therefore arise, cross this Jordan, you and all this people, to the land which I am giving to them, to the sons of Israel. Every place on which the sole of your foot treads, I have given it to you, just as I spoke to Moses. From the wilderness and this Lebanon, even as far as the great river, the river Euphrates, all the land of the Hittites, and as far as the Great Sea toward the setting of the sun will be your territory. No man will be able to stand before you all the days of your life. Just as I have been with Moses, I will be with you; I will not fail you or forsake you. *Be strong* [*hazaq*—to be strong, courageous] *and courageous* [*amas*—to be strong, determined, courageous], for you shall give this people possession of the land which I swore to their fathers to give them. Only *be strong and very courageous*; be careful [observe] to do according to all the law which Moses My servant commanded you; do not turn from it to the right or to the left, so that you may have success wherever you go. This book of the law shall not depart from your mouth, but you shall meditate on it day and night, so that you may be careful to do according to all that is written in it; for then you will make your way prosperous, and then you will have success. Have I not commanded you? *Be strong and courageous!* Do not tremble or be dismayed, for the Lord your God is with you wherever you go."

Joshua 1:1–9
(emphasis added by the author)

The story of the transfer of the leadership of the Jews from Moses to Joshua is a good case study of this subject. The above passage reveals several issues related to this event. First, Joshua is now in charge as the previous leader is dead. After forty years of wandering, it is time to take the people into their promised land. Joshua had demonstrated his worthiness as the leader after serving Moses as his servant as well as being one of the two of twelve spies that supported the immediate occupation of Canaan some thirty-eight years earlier (Numbers 13 & 14). Deuteronomy 34:9 tells us (emphasis added by the author), "Now Joshua the son of Nun was *filled with the spirit of wisdom*, for Moses had laid his hands on him; and the sons of Israel listened to him and did as the Lord had commanded Moses." Joshua's commitment to follow the Lord was complete or total, with all his heart. In Joshua 14:8 (emphasis added by the author), "Nevertheless my brethren who went up with me made the heart of the people melt with fear; *but I followed the Lord my God fully.*"

The promises the Lord made to Joshua exemplify the confidence that Caleb and Joshua demonstrated in the Lord. "Every place on which the sole of your foot treads, I have given it to you, just as I spoke to Moses." He further promised to give them the land as He had promised to Abraham, Isaac, and Jacob. "No man will be able to stand before you all the days of your life" (verse 5). He promised to be their strength and protector against all of their enemies. This reminds me of Psalm 121, one of the fifteen songs of degrees, sung by travelers on their way to Jerusalem to celebrate major Jewish festivals, a psalm of recognizing the Lord as keeper. In verses 7–8, "The Lord will protect you from all evil; He will keep your soul. The Lord will guard your going out and your coming in from this time forth and forever." It was sung as Mount Zion, symbolic of God's presence, came into view from a distance on the last evening of the trek.

Real Strength and Courage

In Joshua 1:6, 7, and 9, the Lord emphasizes the principle of courage, demonstrating strength in all situations. The Hebrew words *hazaq* and *amas* mean the same things, strength, and courage, determination. Yahweh has given them the basis for this strength and courage: His promises to His people that He would protect them from every enemy. His strength becomes the believers' strength when they exercise genuine faith. In Ephesians 6:10 (emphasis added by the author), "Finally, *be strong* [*dunamis*—God's ability] *in the Lord* and the strength [*kratos*—strength or might] of His might [*ischus*—physical strength]." In the new covenant age in which we belong, this faith is predicated on God's grace, His free gift. In 2 Timothy 2:1 (emphasis added by the author), "You therefore, my son, *be strong in the grace that is in Christ Jesus.*" The believer's ability is directly tied to receiving God's ability on the basis of faith. Paul further states in 2 Corinthians 12 that God's strength is perfected in his own weakness.

We can trust the Lord because He has proven His faithfulness repeatedly. When addressing those in captivity in Isaiah 41:10–14, He made the following promises,

> 'Do not fear, for I am with you; do not anxiously look about you, for I am your God. I will strengthen you, surely, I will help you, Surely I will uphold you with My righteous right hand.' Behold, all those who are angered at you will be shamed and dishonored; Those who contend with you will be as nothing and will perish. You will seek those who quarrel with you, but will not find them, Those who war with you will be as nothing and non-existent. For I am the Lord your God, who upholds your right hand, Who says to you, 'Do not fear, I will help you.' "Do not fear, you worm Jacob, you men of Israel; I will help you," declares the Lord, "and your Redeemer is the Holy One of Israel."

Pay Close Attention

The history of the Hebrew nation is filled with many events of God moving miraculously to protect and deliver them, yet they "drifted" in their faith. In Hebrews 2:1, the writer warns the believer of a spiritual phenomenon that can happen to anyone. It involves "drifting away" from the faith. The Greek word is *pararreoe*, meaning a slipping away, a gradual and almost unnoticeable movement resulting from a deviation from the truth. The solution to this spiritual warfare is to pay closer attention [*prosechoe*—to hold the mind in a particular direction] "to what we have heard." In Deuteronomy 4:9, Moses writes,

> Only give heed to yourself and keep your soul diligently, so that you do not forget the things which your eyes have seen and they do not depart from your heart all the days of your life; but make them known to your sons and your grandsons.

The spiritual principle taught is an attention of the heart to divine instruction as the Holy Spirit illuminates' truth in the inner man. Without this approach, we are subject to slackness in our relationship with God. This may be the most important theme addressed in the book of Hebrews.

Our Inheritance Is Rest

Therefore, let us fear if, while a promise remains of entering His rest, any one of you may seem to have come short of it. For indeed we have had good news preached to us, just as they also; *but the word they heard did not profit them, because it was not united by faith in those who heard.* For we who have believed enter that rest, just as He has said, "AS I SWORE IN MY WRATH, THEY SHALL NOT ENTER MY REST," although His works were finished from the foundation of the world. For He has said somewhere concerning the seventh day: "AND GOD RESTED ON THE SEVENTH DAY FROM ALL HIS WORKS"; and again, in this passage, "THEY SHALL NOT ENTER MY REST." Therefore, since it remains for some to enter it, and those who formerly had good news preached to them failed to enter because of disobedience, He again fixes a certain day, "Today," saying through David after so long a time just as has been said before, "TODAY IF YOU HEAR HIS VOICE, DO NOT HARDEN YOUR HEARTS." For if Joshua had given them rest, He would not have spoken of another day after that. *So there remains a Sabbath rest for the people of God.* For the one who has entered His rest has himself also rested from his works, as God did from His. Therefore, let us be diligent [earnest, eager] to enter that rest, so that no one will fall through following the same example of disobedience [willful unbelief].

Hebrews 4:1–11
(emphasis added by the author)

The writer of Hebrews testifies that how the believer receives the Word of God determines his ability to rest, in contrast to the Jews, who wandered forty years in the wilderness. This rest, *katapausis*, is a ceasing from labor and represents the eternal state all believers will experience in the presence of God. It means that there is nothing more the believer must do to gain God's approval; His work is complete, perfect, and finished. As quoted above in Joshua 1:8, an emphasis is made on the Word of God, meditating on it day and night, "so that you may be careful to do according to all that is written in it; for then you will make your way prosperous, and then you will have success." This meditation produces an awareness of evil and a conviction to "watch the path of your feet And all your ways will be established" (Proverbs 4:26).

Hold Fast

> Take care, brethren, that there not be in any one of you an evil, un-believing heart that falls away from the living God. But encourage one another day after day, as long as it is still called "Today," so that none of you will be hardened by the deceitfulness of sin. For we have become partakers of Christ if we hold fast the beginning of our assurance firm until the end.
>
> Hebrews 3:12–14

Becoming partakers of Christ, a union of principle and priority with Savior and Lord, is the result of a choice to live in an awareness of evil and the things present that are intended to rob the believer of his faith in the living God. It is a community effort as each encourages others *day after day* in the excellencies of our God. It reminds me of a *Peanuts* cartoon, where Lucy demands that Linus change the TV channel, threatening him with her fist. "What makes you think that you can walk in here and take over?" Linus asks. "These five fingers," says Lucy. "Individually, they're nothing, but when I curl them together like this into a single unit, they form a weapon that is terrible to behold." Linus, defeated, replies, "Which channel do you want?" Then he looks at his own fingers and says, "Why can't you guys get organized like that?" The community of believers is a support system to help keep each holding fast to the faith. The body of Christ should be recognized as a fist, not just a bunch of fingers.

Chapter 31: A Consecrated Life

In Exodus 19:10–11, the Lord said to Moses,

> Go to the people and consecrate them today and tomorrow and let them wash their garments; and let them be ready for the third day, for on the third day the Lord will come down on Mount Sinai in the sight of all the people.

The Hebrew word for consecrate is *qadash*, meaning to set apart as holy. Yahweh wanted the people to be prepared for the perfect justice of God as represented by His law by setting themselves apart. This setting apart would allow them to draw near with a true heart in full assurance of faith, having their hearts sprinkled from an evil conscience and their bodies washed with pure water (Hebrews 10:22). It means the believer can approach the Lord on His terms.

> Cry loudly, do not hold back; Raise your voice like a trumpet, And declare to My people their transgression And to the house of Jacob their sins. Yet they seek Me day by day and delight to know My ways, As a nation that has done righteousness And has not forsaken the ordinance of their God. They ask Me for just decisions, They delight in the nearness of God. 'Why have we fasted, and You do not see? Why have we humbled ourselves [*anah*—denied ourselves] and You do not notice?' Behold, on the day of your fast you find your desire, And drive hard all your workers. Behold, you fast for contention and strife and to strike with a wicked fist. You do not fast like you do today to make your voice heard on high. Is it a fast like this which I choose, a day for a man to humble [*anah*—deny] himself? Is it for bowing one's head like a reed And for spreading out sackcloth and ashes as a bed? Will you call this a fast, even an acceptable day to the Lord? Is this not the fast which I choose, To loosen the bonds of wickedness, To undo the bands of the yoke [*motah*—forces that oppress God's people], And

to let the oppressed go free And break every yoke? Is it not to divide your bread with the hungry And bring the homeless poor into the house; When you see the naked, to cover him, And not to hide yourself from your own flesh? Then your light will break out like the dawn, And your recovery will speedily spring forth; And your righteousness will go before you; The glory of the Lord will be your rear guard. Then you will call [*qara*—summon], and the Lord will answer; You will cry, and He will say, 'Here I am.' If you remove the yoke from your midst, The pointing of the finger and speaking wickedness, And if you give yourself to the hungry And satisfy the desire of the afflicted, Then your light will rise in darkness And your gloom will become like midday. And the Lord will continually guide you, And satisfy your desire in scorched places, And give strength to your bones; And you will be like a watered garden, And like a spring of water whose waters do not fail. Those from among you will rebuild the ancient ruins; You will raise up the age-old foundations, And you will be called the repairer of the breach, The restorer of the streets in which to dwell.

Isaiah 58:1–12

The Truth about Fasting

Isaiah 58 addresses the principle of fasting (Hebrew *sum*, to "cover" the mouth, Greek. *nesteuo*, to "abstain") and the lamentation of the people that they were faithful in fasting and other religious duties and God was not acknowledging or responding to their cries. Interestingly, fasting was not a religious requirement of the Law of Moses but was introduced after the return from captivity. The only reference to the principle from Mount Sinai is found in Leviticus 23:27 concerning the Day of Atonement when it says you "shall humble your souls [*anah*—deny yourselves] and present an offering by fire to the Lord." This word is repeated in the above passage as the people boast of their religious works and self-denial so that the Lord will answer their petitions. In the process, the Lord was exposing their unrighteousness. As verse 4 highlights, "You fast for contention and strife and to strike with a wicked fist." God was revealing to them that their religious activities would be worthless apart from an interest in caring for others. James 1:27 says it this way, "Pure and undefiled religion in the sight of our God and Father is this: to visit orphans and widows in their distress, and to keep oneself unstained by the world."

This principle was communicated to the people by other prophets, as well. In Micah 6:6–8 (emphasis added by the author),

> With what shall I come to the Lord And bow myself before the God on high? Shall I come to Him with burnt offerings, With yearling calves? Does the Lord take delight in thousands of rams, In ten thousand rivers of oil? Shall I present my firstborn for my rebellious acts, The fruit of my body for the sin of my soul? He has told you, O man, what is good; And what does the Lord require of you But to *do justice* [bring justice to those who have experienced injustice], *to love kindness, And to walk humbly with your God?*

Weightier Provisions

These verses tell us that religious activity is no substitute for the believer's interest in caring for others' needs and walking before God with humility. Jesus exposed this same issue to the scribes and Pharisees in Matthew 23:23 (emphasis added by the author) when He said,

> Woe to you, scribes and Pharisees, hypocrites! For you tithe mint and dill and cummin and have neglected the weightier provisions of the law: *justice and mercy and faithfulness*; but these are the things you should have done without neglecting the others.

The prophet Isaiah highlighted the matter in Isaiah 29:13 when the Lord said, "Because this people draw near with their words And honor Me with their lip service, But they remove their hearts far from Me, And their reverence for Me consists of tradition learned by rote." The issues that separate the believer from his God are always a matter of the heart.

So much of church activity today is preoccupied with religious activities (i.e., fasting) and other programs that are intended to bring the believer closer to God. Still, Scripture says it will not produce the expected results apart from a total heart commitment, a consecrated life. Isaiah 58:6, above, addresses the principle of yokes that bind the people into wickedness, forces that oppress God's people. The solution is found in verse 7: divide your bread with the hungry, invite the homeless into the house, etc. The promise is that "your righteousness will go before you;

The glory of the Lord will be your rear guard" (verse 8). As a result, the Lord will say, "Here I am."

Belonging to the Lord

The consecrated life recognizes that he is no longer his own; he was bought with a price (1 Corinthians 6:19–20) and now belongs to the Lord. It means that he is available to be used by God for any purpose, especially when others' needs become apparent. Isaiah characterizes this life with the Jew's attitude toward the Sabbath in Isaiah 58:13–14,

> If because of the sabbath, you turn your foot From doing your own pleasure on My holy day, And call the sabbath a delight, the holy day of the Lord honorable, And honor it, desisting from your own ways, From seeking your own pleasure And speaking your own word, Then you will take delight in the Lord, And I will make you ride on the heights of the earth; And I will feed you with the heritage of Jacob your father, For the mouth of the Lord has spoken.

When we treat each day as the Jews recognize the Sabbath, as holy unto the Lord, we embrace the consecrated life. The governing attitude is the turning of the foot (i.e., walking) from doing one's own pleasures, *desisting from one's own ways, and seeking one's own happiness.* According to Exodus 31:13, when the Jew honors the Lord by observing the Sabbath, the Lord sanctifies him, making him "ride on the heights of the earth." It means that when he gives himself "to the hungry And satisfies the desire of the afflicted, Then your light will rise in darkness And your gloom will become like midday" (Isaiah 58:10). It reminds me of a quote by a famous Jewish Rabbi.

Rabbi Abraham Isaac Kook, the first Chief Rabbi of Israel and one of the most influential rabbis of the twentieth century. Rabbi Kook wrote,

> Every person is required to know that there is a candle burning inside of him, and his light isn't like anyone else's light, and there is no one who doesn't possess a light. Every single person is required to understand that it is his obligation to work on revealing his light, and to make it into a great torch, shedding light on the whole world.

A Watered Garden

The Lord also promised that a consecrated life is one that receives His guidance and is satisfied in scorched places, "and you will be like a watered garden, And like a spring of water whose waters do not fail" (Isaiah 58:11). Jeremiah 17:7–8 tells us that the one who trusts in the Lord,

> Whose trust is the Lord. For he will be like a tree planted by the water, That extends its roots by a stream And will not fear when the heat comes; But its leaves will be green, And it will not be anxious in a year of drought Nor cease to yield fruit.

The consecrated life is an acknowledgment of the Lord's commitment to the believer and is evidenced by fruitfulness and a life filled with His riches.

> Then the King will say to those on His right, 'Come, you who are blessed of My Father, inherit the kingdom prepared for you from the foundation of the world. For I was hungry, and you gave Me something to eat; I was thirsty, and you gave Me something to drink; I was a stranger, and you invited Me in; naked, and you clothed Me; I was sick, and you visited Me; I was in prison, and you came to Me.' Then the righteous will answer Him, 'Lord, when did we see You hungry, and feed You, or thirsty, and give You something to drink? And when did we see You a stranger, and invite You in, or naked, and clothe You? When did we see You sick, or in prison, and come to You?' The King will answer and say to them, 'Truly I say to you, *to the extent that you did it to one of these brothers of Mine, even the least of them, you did it to Me.*'

Matthew 25:34–40
(emphasis added by the author)

Chapter 32: A Reconciled Mind

When Jesus made His famous statement on the cross, "It is finished," in John 19:30, He said more than that His earthly work was completed. The finished work of Christ addresses the full scope of God's justice in directly dealing with the matter separating man from his God—sin! The Greek word  *katallasso* can be translated as "reconciled" and basically means that God has taken upon Himself the work and has become an atonement. It possesses the idea of a total change not dependent on the receiver. The sense is that God has laid aside or withdrawn His wrath so that man no longer has to worry that the wrath may be restored at some later date based on his failure. "It is finished!"

To experience reconciliation is to believe in and trust in the atoning work of Christ, that Jesus is God, and that His work was enough. In Romans 5:10–11 (emphasis added by the author), Paul writes,

> For if while we were enemies we were reconciled to God through the death of His Son, *much more*, having been reconciled, we shall be saved by His life. And not only this, but we also exult in God through our Lord Jesus Christ, through whom we have now received the reconciliation.

If I am to live in the full (much more) effect of reconciliation, my mind must accept the reality that my previous, current, or future failures cannot revive the wrath of God toward me. My position is secure.

Mind Renewal

The constant reminders of one's shortcomings in daily life can cause him to doubt God's promises, so he needs a renewal of the mind (the organ of mental perception and apprehension). Paul refers to this process in Romans 12:1–2 when he urges us to "present your bodies a living and holy sacrifice" as an integral part of our worship. He continues by recommending separation from this world's influences by keeping on being "transformed by the renewing of your mind," representing a total change in thinking. In the process, the believer proves the will of God by testing.

So long as one remains square in the middle of the influences of this world, his mind will be conformed to its value system. Again, Paul teaches that sanctification, a willingness to be separated from the world for God's purposes, is the will of God (1 Thessalonians 4:3). If one is to come to "know how to possess his own vessel in sanctification and honor" (verse 4), he must prioritize purity as a path of life. The world says that a life of purity is either strange or impossible. In Colossians 1:21–22 (emphasis added by the author),

> And although you were formerly alienated and hostile *in mind*, engaged in evil deeds, yet He has now reconciled you in His fleshly body through death, in order to present you before Him holy and blameless and *beyond reproach*.

Reconciliation is the avenue through which we are seen by God as above reproach. Purity does not happen by accident.

The Promised Land Ahead

Take a look at the Hebrew nation in Exodus 14. God had initiated ten plagues to get Pharaoh to let the people go. Now the Lord is leading them to a place that requires a supernatural result to complete the process. Moses brings them to the edge of the Red Sea, and the Egyptian army is in view, coming after them. The people started complaining that this would be the end of them and that being back in bondage in Egypt would have been better. But God was showing them that He wanted to separate them from their past bondages to a new place. In verses 13–14, Moses said,

> Do not fear! Stand by and see the salvation of the Lord which He will accomplish for you today; for the Egyptians whom you have seen today, you will never see them again. The Lord will fight for you while you keep silent.

The sea parted, the people crossed over, and the sea destroyed Pharaoh's army. A reconciled mind sees the promised land and the divine future in front and the bondages of the past in the rearview mirror. He can see the purity of an ordained life since God did it supernaturally.

> To the pure, all things are pure; but to those who are defiled and unbelieving, nothing is pure, but both their mind and conscience are defiled. They profess to know God, but by their deeds they deny Him, being detestable and disobedient and worthless for any good deed.
>
> Titus 1:15–16

Simplicity and Purity of Devotion

The reconciled mind is secure because of what Christ did and recognizes that purity is not only an option for living but, more importantly, the best option. By God's presence in one's life, he can devote himself to God's will and find that pure pathway to face his current failures (sin) without discouragement. But unfortunately, the serpent who deceived Eve is also at work to remove believers from the "simplicity and purity of devotion to Christ" (2 Corinthians 11:3). There is simplicity in purity.

The result of a reconciled mind is God's ministry for us to affect others' lives. In 2 Corinthians 5:18–19,

> Now all these things are from God, who reconciled us to Himself through Christ and gave us the ministry of reconciliation, namely, that God was in Christ reconciling the world to Himself, not counting their trespasses against them, and He has committed to us the word of reconciliation.

Verse 18 speaks of a ministry to the world and is defined by God's work to reconcile the world to Himself. The ministry that God has had

to us becomes our ministry to others. And it is all possible through a
reconciled mind.

CHAPTER 33: FIRST LOVE

To the angel of the church in Ephesus write: The One who holds the seven stars in His right hand, the One who walks among the seven golden lampstands, says this: 'I know your deeds and your toil and perseverance, and that you cannot tolerate evil men, and you put to the test those who call themselves apostles, and they are not, and you found them to be false; and you have perseverance and have endured for My name's sake, and have not grown weary. But I have this against you, that you have left [*aphiemi*—to send away, to dismiss] *your first love*. Therefore remember [*mnemoneuoe*—call to mind, bear in mind] from where you have fallen, and repent and do the deeds you did at first; or else I am coming to you and will remove your lampstand out of its place—unless you repent. Yet this you do have, that you hate the deeds of the Nicolaitans, which I also hate. He who has an ear, let him hear what the Spirit says to the churches. To him who overcomes, I will grant to eat of the tree of life which is in the Paradise of God.'

Revelation 2:1–7

As part of the revelation that God gave to John on the island of Patmos, He addressed seven unique churches that existed at the time, including the church at Ephesus, founded by Paul on his second missionary journey and pastored by Timothy and, later, John. It was from this location that the other six churches were planted. Many of the epistles were written to or about Ephesus (Ephesians; 1 & 2 Timothy; 1, 2, & 3 John; Revelation), which speaks to its influence and importance in the first century. In Ephesians 1:15–16, Paul writes,

For this reason I too, having heard of the faith in the Lord Jesus which exists among you and *your love for all the saints*, do not cease giving thanks for you, while making mention of you in my prayers.

This church began as a model church.

Endurance for My Name's Sake

Many scholars recognize these seven different churches as typical of various churches in each age. In addition, they see these seven churches representing the general spirit of churches of different ages since the institution of the church at Pentecost. The first of the letters is to Ephesus, representing churches during the apostolic age (first and early second centuries). The seventh of these churches is Laodicea which characterizes churches in current times. With the advent of heresies introduced in the latter part of the first century, the four Gospels and apostolic letters were circulating among the churches, teaching sound doctrine. A church needed to stand firm on accurate teaching to maintain the power and authority of Christ that it represented.

This brings us to the above address in Revelation 2. Jesus identifies in verses 2 and 3 that they were a church that persevered and did not tolerate *evil men*, those who represented themselves as prophets but were false teachers. He commends them for having "endured for My name's sake and have not grown weary." They remained faithful to this calling, but in verse 4 (emphasis added by the author), they "have left [*aphiemi*—to send away, to dismiss] *your first love.*" This word *aphiemi* means it is not by accident. What is first love? There is no other place in Scripture that speaks directly to this principle for us, so we must look deeper.

The Zeal of Youth

Now the word of the Lord came to me saying, "Go and proclaim in the ears of Jerusalem, saying, 'Thus says the Lord, "I remember concerning you the devotion of your youth, The love of your betrothals, your following after Me in the wilderness, Through a land not sown. Israel was holy to the Lord, The first of His harvest. All who ate of it became guilty; Evil came upon them," declares the Lord.'" Hear the word of the Lord, O house of Jacob, and all the families of the house of Israel. Thus says the Lord, "What injustice did your fathers find in Me, that they went far from Me and walked after emptiness and became empty? They did not say, 'Where is the Lord Who brought us up out of the land of Egypt, Who led us through the wilderness, through a land of deserts and of pits, through a land of drought and of deep darkness, through a land that no one crossed and where no man dwelt?'"

Jeremiah 2:1–6

In the above passage, the Lord exposes to Israel that they had similar troubles to the Ephesus church. In the beginning, they had a zeal, a holiness to the Lord, a devotion found in youth, and an intensity to follow Him "in the wilderness through a land not sown." In verse 6, the people lost sight of the Lord, the one who had delivered them from all sorts of enemies. They began pursuing other gods, resulting in an emptiness that caused them to forsake their divine provisions. Jesus pledged in Matthew 24:12–13, "Because lawlessness is increased, most people's love will grow cold. But the one who endures to the end, he will be saved." It is a conscious decision to live outside of God's governing love. Endurance is the result of a devotion to that love.

What Is First Love?

According to The Bible Exposition Commentary:

What is "first love"? It is the devotion to Christ that so often characterizes the new believer: fervent, personal, uninhibited, excited, and openly displayed. It is the "honeymoon love" of the husband and wife (Jer 2:1–2). While it is true that mature married love deepens and grows richer, it is also true that it should never lose the excitement and wonder of those "honeymoon days." When a husband and wife begin to take each other for granted, and life becomes routine, then the marriage is in danger.

In Joshua 5:6,

For the sons of Israel walked forty years in the wilderness, until all the nation, that is, the men of war who came out of Egypt, perished because they did not listen to the voice of the Lord, to whom the Lord had sworn that He would not let them see the land which the Lord had sworn to their fathers to give us, a land flowing with milk and honey.

They had forgotten their vows, their daily recognition of God's abundant love; *Ahavah Rabba, which opens,* "With an abundant love You love us, oh Lord our God," is a daily prayer accompanying the Shema, a quote from Deuteronomy 6:4–5. They remind the Jewish believer that God's love should be his motivation. In 2 Corinthians 5:14–15,

> For the love of Christ controls [*sunechoe*—compels] us, having concluded this, that one died for all, therefore all died; and He died for all, so that they who live might no longer live for themselves, but for Him who died and rose again on their behalf.

Real Warfare

There is real warfare centered on man's motivation. Hebrews 12:3 tells us that the consideration of the suffering and sacrifice of Christ keeps our hearts from growing weary.

A story is told about a man who took his aircraft out for a ride. In his plane was a cable that ran from the control stick all the way to the tail of the airplane, which controlled the direction of the plane. On that particular day, the man heard a strange noise. To his horror, he discovered that the source of the noise was a rat that was steadily eating away at the cable.

The man quickly realized that if the rat continued to chew through the cord, the plane would surely crash. The man thought quickly and turned the plane into a sharp climb. He knew the rat could not live at the higher altitude because of the lack of oxygen. As he climbed higher in the sky, the rat died, and the man was saved from certain death.

This story illustrates the warfare we all face in our pursuit of God. The solution for this man was to climb higher, to ascend to a higher spiritual plane, and this happens when the man sets his mind on things above (Colossians 3:2). It is faith in the character and nature of God: His love. True faith in God works through His love (Galatians 5:6). Paul understood this principle clearly when he wrote 1 Corinthians 13, the (agape) love chapter. He begins the chapter with the following:

> If I speak with the tongues of men and of angels, but do not have love, *I have become a noisy gong or a clanging cymbal.* If I have the gift of

prophecy and know all mysteries and all knowledge; and if I have all faith, so as to remove mountains, but do not have love, *I am nothing.* And if I give all my possessions to feed the poor, and if I surrender my body to be burned, but do not have love, *it profits me nothing.*

1 Corinthians 13:1–3
(emphasis added by the author)

An Engaged Heart

Jesus exposes the downfall of the Jews in Matthew 15 when He quotes from Isaiah 29:13,

> Then the Lord said, "Because this people draw near with their words And honor Me with their lip service, But they remove their hearts far from Me, And their reverence for Me consists of tradition learned by rote [repetition]."

When the heart is not engaged, the result is a lot of religion without any benefit to the believer. Paul warned the Corinthians of this process in 2 Corinthians 11:3 when he said, "But I am afraid that, as the serpent deceived Eve by his craftiness, your minds will be led astray from the simplicity and purity of devotion [*hagnotes*—sincerity, purity] to Christ."

Getting back to our original passage in Revelation 2, Jesus exhorted the church to remember, to call to mind where you started in your relationship with God, and get back to your labors, motivated by God's love that defined the church in its formative stages. If not, Jesus promised to remove their lampstand from its place. We can look back in history and see that this church did continue and was later the scene of a major church council (431 AD), but after the fifth century, both the church and the city declined. The immediate area has been uninhabited since the fourteenth century.

Loving the Unlovely

So, when they had finished breakfast, Jesus said to Simon Peter, "Simon, son of John, do you love Me more than these?" He said to Him, "Yes, Lord; You know that I love You." He said to him, "*Tend My lambs.*" He said to him again a second time, "Simon, son of John, do you love Me?" He said to Him, "Yes, Lord; You know that I love You."

He said to him, "*Shepherd My sheep.*" He said to him the third time, "Simon, son of John, do you love Me?" Peter was grieved because He said to him the third time, "Do you love Me?" And he said to Him, "Lord, You know all things; You know that I love You." Jesus said to him, "*Tend My sheep.*"

John 21:15–17
(emphasis added by the author)

Jesus left Peter, soon to be the church's leader, with this important lesson. To love God is to love the people God places in his path. Peter was deeply challenged in this, especially in his Old Testament attitude towards the Gentiles, and Paul would call him on this in Galatians 2:11–14. First love is a love for neighbor, even the unlovely, anyone near, regardless of his heritage, looks, attributes, or background. The parable of the Good Samaritan clearly illustrates this reality. Love never fails.

Chapter 34: Spiritual Character

But I say, walk by the Spirit, and you will not carry out the desire of the flesh. For the flesh sets its desire against the Spirit, and the Spirit against the flesh; for these are in opposition to one another, so that you may not do the things that you please. But if you are led by the Spirit, you are not under the Law.

Galatians 5:16–18

Galatians 5 has become a treatise on spiritual life. Paul identifies the Holy Spirit as the source of spiritual life and character. Jesus said in John 3:6 (emphasis added by the author), "That which is born of the flesh is flesh, and *that which is born of the Spirit is spirit.*" He was teaching that no matter how hard the flesh tries to be spiritual, he will always fall short of the glory of God (Romans 3:23). It then becomes necessary for the believer to develop a living relationship with the Holy Spirit to find the quality of life purchased for each believer by Jesus Christ at Calvary. To walk by the Spirit means to live daily life under His influence. Without His ability, each one is subject to being controlled by the desires of the flesh. The Holy Spirit's leading takes the believer beyond the ability of the Law of Moses or any religious system.

Spiritual Fruit

In verses 22–23, Paul lays out the method the Spirit uses to empower believers in His character by introducing the fruit of the Spirit. "But the fruit of the Spirit is love." It is a list of nine fruit, but the original Greek uses the singular form of the verb "to be," suggesting that the eight other fruit following love are subsets of love, *agape*, God's love, a self-sacrificing love. We believe this to be true since God is love (1 John 4:8, 16); everything He does is based on that love.

But the fruit of the Spirit is love [self-sacrificing], joy [gladness], peace [concord, agreement between persons], patience [forbearance, a person who is able to avenge himself yet refrains from doing so], kindness [lovingkindness in action, opposite of severity], goodness [benevolence, active goodness], faithfulness [trustworthy, reliable], gentleness [submissive to God and His Word]], self-control [curbing fleshly impulses]; against such things there is no law. Now those who belong to Christ Jesus have crucified the flesh with its passions and desires. *If we live by the Spirit, let us also walk* [keep in step] *by the Spirit.* Let us not become boastful, challenging one another, envying one another.

Galatians 5:22–26
(emphasis added by the author)

Walking by the Spirit

This list follows the fifteen works of the flesh, the products of the human condition that each one faces every day. Fruit can only be produced by life in the Spirit and is possible when the believer puts on the new man, submitting his will to that of the Holy Spirit. Living by the Spirit means walking by the Spirit. According to Jamieson, Fausset, and Brown's Commentary,

> Let our practice correspond to the ideal principle of our spiritual life-namely, our standing by faith as dead to, and severed from, sin and the law's condemnation. 'Life by the Spirit' is not an occasional influence, but an abiding state.

Ephesians 4:22–24 says,

> That, in reference to your former manner of life, you lay aside the old self, which is being corrupted in accordance with the lusts of deceit, and that you be renewed in the spirit of your mind, and put on the new self, which in the likeness of God has been created in righteousness and holiness of the truth.

Partakers of the Divine Nature

The three major sources of New Testament theology come from Paul, John, and Peter. Paul uses the term "in Christ" or "in Him" to define this new spiritual relationship known as the new covenant. John's preferred terminology is "born again," "born from above," or "born of God." Peter also uses "born again," but he has a deeper description of the process, likened to Paul's commentary on the fruit of the Spirit, and found in 2 Peter 1.

> Simon Peter, a bond-servant and apostle of Jesus Christ, to those who have received a faith of the same kind as ours, by the righteousness of our God and Savior, Jesus Christ: Grace and peace be multiplied to you in the knowledge of God and of Jesus our Lord; seeing that *His divine power* [Holy Spirit] has granted to us everything pertaining to life and godliness, through the true knowledge [full, complete] of Him who called us *by His own glory and excellence*. For by these He has granted to us His precious and magnificent promises, so that *by them* you may become *partakers of the divine nature*, having escaped the corruption that is in the world by lust.
>
> 2 Peter 1:1–4
> (emphasis added by the author)

Peter addresses believers in Jesus Christ, "A faith of the same kind as ours," and a faith received "by the righteousness of our God and Savior, Jesus Christ." Like Paul, his hope is that believers would experience God's grace and peace, "multiplied to you in the knowledge of God and of Jesus our Lord." According to Ellicott's Commentary, "Grace is the peculiar state of favour with God and Christ, into which the sincere Christian is admitted. Peace is the state of mind resulting from the sense of that favour." Peter lays the foundation of a true spiritual relationship with God when he references *His divine power*, represented by the Holy Spirit, who "has granted to us everything pertaining to life and godliness." This is Peter's unique expression of the quality of the new covenant. By His glory and excellence, the new covenant believer is granted precious promises through which he is a participant in the divine nature.

Applying All Diligence

Now for this very reason also, applying [adding more] all diligence [zeal, earnest effort], in your faith [firm persuasion, conviction, belief in truth] supply [support, provide lavishly] moral excellence [virtuous action], and in your moral excellence, knowledge [spiritual knowledge], and in your knowledge, self-control [curbing fleshly desires], and in your self-control, perseverance [bearing up under, related to circumstances], and in your perseverance, godliness [devotion to God], and in your godliness, brotherly kindness [a fervent, practical care for others], and in your brotherly kindness, love [agape]. For if these qualities are yours and are increasing, they render you neither useless nor unfruitful in the true knowledge [full, complete] of our Lord Jesus Christ. For he who lacks these qualities is blind or short-sighted, *having forgotten his purification from his former sins.* Therefore, brethren, be all the more diligent to make certain about His calling and choosing you; for as long as you practice these things, you will never stumble; for in this way the entrance into the eternal kingdom of our Lord and Savior Jesus Christ will be abundantly supplied to you.

2 Peter 1:5–11
(emphasis added by the author)

Like the description of the fruit of the Spirit, Peter lists nine virtues that help define the fullness of the new covenant relationship. He starts with diligence [*spoude*—zeal, earnest effort]. According to Ellicott's Commentary,

Bringing in all diligence to the side of God's gifts and promises, making your contribution in answer to His. He has made all things possible for you, but they are not yet done, and you must labor diligently to realize the glorious possibilities opened out to you.

The premise is that Christianity is not passive but requires the believer's effort in the form of diligence, given the foundation of a perfect relationship with God "in Christ." The following eight virtues flow from an earnest effort by each believer to walk in that perfect position. Just as the perfect position begins with *agape* love in Galatians 5:22, a believer is to furnish, supply, or support his life through diligence with these virtues.

Spiritual Qualities

Galatians 5:22–23	Second Peter 1:5–7
Agape—self-sacrificing, unconditional love.	Diligence—zeal, earnest effort.
Joy—deep, abiding gladness.	Faith—firm persuasion, trust, belief in truth.
Peace—inner repose, quietness.	Moral excellence—virtuous action, good conduct.
Longsuffering—forbear under provocation.	Knowledge—knowledge by the Holy Spirit.
Kindness—lovingkindness in action.	Self-control—curbing fleshly impulses.
Goodness—character in action, energized.	Perseverance—bearing up under (circumstances).
Faithfulness—trustworthy, reliable.	Godliness—Godly devotion.
Gentleness—submissive to God & His Word.	Brotherly kindness—fervent care for others.
Self-control—curbing fleshly impulses.	Love—self-sacrificing, highest good for others.

God's intention is that "these qualities are yours and are increasing; they render you neither useless nor unfruitful in the true knowledge [full, complete] of our Lord Jesus Christ." God wishes that we would not be "blind or short-sighted, having forgotten his purification from his former sins." Therefore, He wishes the believer to use that diligence to make certain about his calling and election through the exercise of these spiritual qualities that confirm salvation. One's godly behavior is a warranty deed for himself that Jesus Christ has cleansed him from his past sins and, therefore, that he has been, in fact, called and chosen by God. This believer will not stumble. According to Kenneth Wuest's translation of 2 Peter 1:11, "For in this way the entrance shall be richly provided for you into the eternal kingdom of our Lord Jesus Christ." The Lord richly provides the entrance of His kingdom to those who operate in the spiritual qualities of a walk led by His Spirit.

But we should always give thanks to God for you, brethren beloved by the Lord, because God has chosen you from the beginning for salvation through sanctification by the Spirit and faith in the truth. It was for this He called you through our gospel, *that you may gain the glory of our Lord Jesus Christ*. So then, brethren, stand firm and hold to the traditions which you were taught, whether by word of mouth or by letter from us.

2 Thessalonians 2:13–15
(emphasis added by the author)

In the believer's pursuit of a deeper relationship with Christ, he finds His glory!

CHAPTER 35: FROM REJECTION TO WORSHIP

Jacob's eleventh son, Joseph, is a picture of one who overcame rejection and became Egypt's second most powerful man. His life is a testimony of how God can use anyone to be victorious despite incredible opposition and betrayal by even his own family.

> Now Joseph had been taken down to Egypt; and Potiphar, an Egyptian officer of Pharaoh, the captain of the bodyguard, bought him from the Ishmaelites, who had taken him down there. The Lord was with Joseph, so he became a successful man. And he was in the house of his master, the Egyptian. Now his master saw that the Lord was with him and how the Lord caused all that he did to prosper in his hand. So Joseph found favor in his sight and became his personal servant, and he made him overseer over his house, and all that he owned he put in his charge.
>
> Genesis 39:1–4

Having been rejected by his brothers, Joseph was sold into slavery in Egypt. What is striking about him is his response. Joseph did not resist or complain but accepted his situation. As a result, God had His divine hand on Joseph's life and made Joseph successful in Potiphar's house as God prospered Potiphar. This scenario would repeat itself as Joseph would spend many years in an Egyptian prison for things he did not do. Not only did Potiphar's wife make false accusations, but Joseph also accurately interpreted the dreams of his fellow prisoners without receiving credit. Eventually, Pharaoh discovered Joseph's abilities, and Joseph was made a minister in Pharaoh's house. God is present in every situation, even in the biggest injustices.

Rejected by Men

Joseph is a type of Christ who…

Was despised and forsaken of men, A man of sorrows and acquainted with grief; And like one from whom men hide their face He was despised, and we did not esteem Him. Surely our griefs He Himself bore, And our sorrows He carried; Yet we ourselves esteemed Him stricken, Smitten of God, and afflicted.

Isaiah 53:3–4

He identifies with those who have been rejected.

Jacob referred to Joseph in Genesis 49:22–24 as "a fruitful bough by a spring," and although he was attacked, "his bow remained firm and his arms were agile, from the hands of the Mighty One of Jacob." Jacob recognized God's hand in Joseph's life. In Genesis 33:18–20, Jacob purchased a piece of ground in Shechem that became the place of Joseph's burial in Joshua 24:32. This connection of Joseph to Shechem would play itself out in an important New Testament event.

Rejected in Relationships

Jesus and His disciples met a Samaritan woman at a well located in Sychar, formerly Shechem, near the parcel of ground Jacob gave to his son Joseph. John 4 provides us with the exchange between Jesus and this woman. At Jacob's well, Jesus introduced the woman to the concept of eternal life by utilizing the water in the well as an illustration. Jesus explained to her in verses 13–14,

Everyone who drinks of this water will thirst again; but whoever drinks of the water that I will give him shall never thirst; but the water that I will give him will become in him a well of water springing up to eternal life.

When the woman said she wanted this living water, it prompted a conversation about her husband. Jesus revealed to her that the woman had had five husbands, and the man she now lived with was not her husband. It is traditionally assumed that the Samaritan woman was a woman of ill repute. But what if that understanding needs to be revised?

There are several arguments for believing that the Samaritan woman was not of questionable character but rather one who suffered much in her married life. First, it is not likely that a woman is far advanced in years to have had five husbands living in adultery. Secondly, if she were an adulteress, Jesus would have most likely reproved her for her fornication. Also, when Jesus told her of her history with her husband, one would expect her to acknowledge her guilt before Him, but instead, the conversation was about where worship should take place, Mount Zion or Mount Gerizim. Finally, it is very odd that a woman of questionable character would have had such influence on the people of her city on her testimony alone. Nevertheless, the fact remains that women did not initiate divorce during this time and in this culture.

True Worshippers

> Jesus said to her, "Woman, believe Me, an hour is coming when neither in this mountain nor Jerusalem will you worship the Father. You worship what you do not know; we worship what we know, for salvation is from the Jews. But an hour is coming, and now is when the true worshipers will worship the Father in spirit and truth; for such people the Father seeks to be His worshipers. God is spirit, and those who worship Him must worship in spirit and truth."
>
> John 4:21–24

When the Woman brought up worship, Jesus took the opportunity to teach her that true worship has nothing to do with location but is a matter of the heart, defined by spirit and truth. The Greek word for worship is *proskuneo* and means to recognize a superior due reverence and homage, to kiss the hand. It is likened to a dog licking the hand of his master. Since God is spirit, true worship of Him is spiritual and according to truth, the Word of God (John 17:17). This woman finally recognized Jesus as the Messiah and left her waterpot to share her faith with others in her city. The account tells us that many believed. As she met her people, Jesus instructed His disciples that the fields were white for harvest. Jesus said in verses 36–38,

> Already he who reaps is receiving wages and is gathering fruit for life eternal; so that he who sows and he who reaps may rejoice together.

For in this case the saying is true, 'One sows and another reaps.' I sent you to reap that for which you have not labored; others have labored and you have entered into their labor.

True worship includes a willingness to share one's faith with others, whether fruit is visible or not. It represents a co-laboring with the Lord in His work to draw people to Himself.

Much of worship in Old Testament times, particularly after the exile, was centered on prayer. The Jew would express his worship in personal prayers, as exemplified in Daniel 6:10,

> Now when Daniel knew that the document was signed, he entered his house (now in his roof chamber he had windows open toward Jerusalem); and he continued kneeling on his knees three times a day, praying and giving thanks before his God, as he had been doing previously.

Worship would also encompass congregational prayer during times of religious gatherings. The issue emphasized by Jesus to the Samaritan woman is that worship is not religious activity as much as it is an expression of devotion to God, who is the believer's provision for everything. Jesus used the parable of the Pharisee and the tax collector. Worship of God is the means of honestly approaching God in prayer so that the believer humbles himself and God is exalted.

> Two men went up into the temple to pray, one a Pharisee and the other a tax collector. The Pharisee stood and was praying this to himself: 'God, I thank You that I am not like other people: swindlers, unjust, adulterers, or even like this tax collector. I fast twice a week; I pay tithes of all that I get.' But the tax collector, standing some distance away, was even unwilling to lift up his eyes to heaven, but was beating his breast, saying, 'God, be merciful to me, the sinner!' I tell you; this man went to his house justified rather than the other; for everyone who exalts himself will be humbled, but he who humbles himself will be exalted.
>
> Luke 18:10–14

According to William Temple,

> Worship is the submission of all our nature to God. It is the quickening of conscience by His holiness, the nourishment of the mind with His

truth, the purifying of the imagination of His beauty, the opening of the heart to His love, the surrender of the will to His purpose.

When the believer is totally submitted to God's will, His divine empowerment will accomplish His purposes, and others will be watching. Jesus identifies with those who have been rejected or betrayed and desires to use that rejection to reveal His heart to all.

CHAPTER 36: THE SECRET PLACE

The Lord is my light and my salvation; Whom shall I fear? The Lord is the defense of my life; Whom shall I dread? When evildoers came upon me to devour my flesh, My adversaries, and my enemies, they stumbled and fell. Though a host encamp against me, My heart will not fear; Though war arise against me, In spite of this, I shall be confident. One thing I have asked from the Lord, that I shall seek: That I may dwell in the house of the Lord all the days of my life, *To behold the beauty of the Lord, And to meditate in His temple.* For in the day of trouble, He will conceal me in His tabernacle; In the secret place of His tent, He will hide me; He will lift me up on a rock.

Psalm 27:1–5
(emphasis added by the author)

One of my favorite passages in Scripture appears in Psalm 27. David testifies to his relationship with God as a place of protection and a place reserved specifically for him. God wants each believer to recognize that he is special. In verse 4, David seeks his own dwelling as being in the house of the Lord, in His temple, all the days of his life. In verse 5, he refers to it as "the secret place of His tent" where God will hide him. The secret place is where God hides His people within their dynamic relationship with Him. This special place was found in David's pursuit of God's presence through a heart of devotion. Although not a physical place, it is where the believer beholds the beauty of the Lord, where he meditates on His Word.

The Fear of the Lord

Psalm 31 is another written by David, and he says in verses 19–20,

> How great is Your goodness, Which You have stored up for those who fear You, Which You have wrought for those who take refuge in You, Before the sons of men! You hide them in the secret place of Your presence from the conspiracies of man; You keep them secretly in a shelter from the strife of tongues.

This secret place is only for those who fear Him, who revere Him, and willingly acknowledge His goodness. In the secret place, there is a clear sense of protection from those who would attack the righteous, particularly from slanders and scourging of the tongue.

In Ezekiel 7:20–22, God speaks about the wicked concerning the temple as transforming "the beauty of His ornaments into pride." God says they take the beautiful things of His and make them detestable. When a man intends his will to undermine God's purposes, it creates all kinds of evil. This pride also leads to varying forms of idolatry, a personal attack against the holiness of God. In verse 22, God says, "I will also turn My face from them, and they will profane My secret place; then robbers will enter and profane it." The wicked are always trying to pervert that which God has made beautiful.

A Place of Protection

David is famous for writing two particular psalms, Psalms 51 and 32, in response to coming clean with the Lord for his major indiscretions with Bathsheba and Uriah. In his effort to repent of these failures, he expressed confidence in God's willingness to offer forgiveness and provide David with a "hiding place" to protect him from trouble. In Psalm 32:6–7,

> Therefore, let everyone who is godly pray to You in a time when You may be found; Surely in a flood of great waters, they will not reach

him. *You are my hiding place*; You preserve me from trouble; You surround me with songs of deliverance.

Of course, these words are the title of a hymn and a book about Corrie Ten Boom's life and have special meaning.
In Psalm 61:1–4,

Hear my cry, O God; Give heed to my prayer. From the end of the earth, I call to You when my heart is faint; Lead me to the rock that is higher than I. For You have been a refuge for me, A tower of strength against the enemy. Let me dwell in Your tent forever; Let me take refuge in the shelter of Your wings.

The secret place is a shelter under His wings and supported by the Lord's faithfulness, providing the believer with refuge from and strength against his enemies. God calls the believer to reside there, to dwell richly there.

All Things Are Possible with God

I recently heard about a conversation that a rabbi who heads up a lifesaving organization had with a board member. After reviewing the rabbi's ambitious goals, the board member said, "Maybe we need to rein in those goals. You can't save the entire world!"

The rabbi replied, "The reason you think that we can't save everyone is that you think *you* can save 300 lives. If you realized that you can't even lift your finger without God's help, let alone save even one life, then you would understand that if God can help us save 300 people, He can help us save a million."

When we realize that we can't do a single thing without God, we finally understand anything is possible with God.

In John 15:5, Jesus said, "Without Me, you can do nothing." In Isaiah 45:3, God promises, "I will give you the treasures of darkness And hidden wealth of secret places, So that you may know that it is I, The Lord, the God of Israel, who calls you by your name." He promises to go before us and make the rough places smooth. Psalm 91:1, it is the shelter of the Most High, the shadow of the Almighty. Our connection to the secret place is our confidence in God's ability and His heart of love on behalf of His people.

Life in the Spirit

This heart is expressed in Song of Solomon in 2:13–14,

'The fig tree has ripened its figs, And the vines in blossom have given forth their fragrance. Arise, my darling, my beautiful one, And come along!' O my dove, in the clefts of the rock, In the secret place of the steep pathway, Let me see your form, Let me hear your voice; For your voice is sweet, And your form is lovely.

The bridegroom expresses to His bride the fruitfulness of life when the believer finds resurrection life, life in the Spirit. This life exists on the other side of the cross, in the clefts of the rock, where she leaves behind her own interest to accept the bridegroom's complete will. Here the bridegroom (Jesus) is preoccupied with the bride's (believer's) voice and ultimate appearance.

The New Testament revelation of the secret place is communicated by the apostle Paul. Philippians 4:12 says,

I know how to get along with humble means, and I also know how to live in prosperity; in any and every circumstance I have learned the secret of being filled and going hungry, both of having abundance and suffering need.

He spoke about contentment (verse 11), where the believer's happiness is not defined by his circumstances but rather by his security in God, realized in the secret place. Finally, Paul tells us that "we have this treasure in earthen vessels [jars of clay] so that the surpassing greatness of the power will be of God and not from ourselves" (2 Corinthians 4:7). The greatness of God manifests itself most clearly when the believer recognizes he is just a jar of clay. Out of that realization comes the greatness of His power for others to see.

CHAPTER 37: PEACE WITH GOD

"Therefore, having been justified [*aorist* passive participle—declared righteous] by faith, we have peace with God through our Lord Jesus Christ" (Romans 5:1).

The above verse tells us that the true believer, who has been declared righteous by faith, is intended by God to live in peace. The Greek word translated as peace is *eirene*, and it has multiple meanings and applications. The primary meaning is that which is the opposite of war. It can mean harmony between individuals. Another meaning might be tranquility, a state of peace. It also has a sense of health, welfare, or prosperity, every kind of good. We can also understand *eirene* in light of the Hebrew word *shalom*, which stands for wholeness, soundness, hence health, well-being, or prosperity. It is through our Lord [*Kurios*—master, supreme, sovereign one] Jesus [*Iesous*—God saves] Christ [*Christos*—anointed one, Messiah] that this peace comes to him. The one who recognizes Him as Lord, Savior, and Messiah experiences peace and all of its implications.

Imputed Righteousness

The doctrine of justification [*dikaiosis*] is addressed most completely by Paul in his letters. In Romans 4, he ties the doctrine directly to Abraham and his willingness to trust God despite impossible situations. In Genesis 15:6, "Then he believed in the Lord, and He reckoned it to him as righteousness." Romans 4:4–5 reveals that any payment for work is considered a wage, "but to the one who does not work, but believes in Him who justifies the ungodly, his faith is credited [*logizomai*—counted, imputed] as righteousness." This righteousness means that the believer is perfect in his position (state), but faith in life's details determines his experience. In Romans 1:17, "For in it [the gospel—Jesus paid the full price] the righteousness of God is revealed from faith to faith; as it is written, 'BUT THE RIGHTEOUS man SHALL LIVE BY FAITH.'" The believer is accepted into a perfect relationship with God by faith. He then realizes the Lord's righteousness each time he exercises faith in the Lord. It is not dependent on keeping the Law of Moses.

> I will hear what God the Lord will say, For He will speak peace [*shalom*—peace, tranquility, wholeness] to His people, to His godly ones; But let them not turn back to folly. Surely His salvation is near to those who fear Him, That glory may dwell in our land. Lovingkindness and truth have met together; *Righteousness and peace have kissed each other.*
>
> Psalm 85:8–10

Peace Fulfilled

The above passage is an Old Testament reference to the coming new covenant in Christ, where the attributes of the new birth come together in a spiritual connection to God's perfect justice. It anticipates the Messiah's arrival and His mighty accomplishments at Calvary. According to John Gill's Exposition of the Old and New Testaments, when righteousness and peace kiss each other:

> Righteousness may intend the essential justice of God, which will not admit of the pardon and justification of a sinner, without a satisfaction; wherefore Christ was set forth to be the propitiation for sin, to

declare and manifest the righteousness of God, his strict justice; that he might be just, and appear to be so, when he is the justifier of him that believes in Jesus.

Romans 3:25–26

"Righteousness and peace or prosperity, these two inseparable brothers, kiss each other there and fall lovingly into each other's arms" (Keil and Delitzsch's Commentary on the Old Testament). Justification provides an environment where he experiences peace with God. According to the Jewish tradition, there are three symbols for peace: the river, the bird, and the kettle.

The Work of Righteousness

Then justice will dwell in the wilderness And righteousness will abide in the fertile field. And the work [*maaseh*—work, labor] of righteousness will be peace, and the service [bodah—work, service] of righteousness, quietness and confidence forever. Then my people will live in a peaceful habitation, and in secure dwellings and in undisturbed resting places.

Isaiah 32:16–18

The above passage is a prophecy looking to the kingdom age, the 1,000-year reign of Christ following the seven-year tribulation. When Jesus is reigning, the characteristic of that reign will be righteousness and justice. "Righteousness and justice are the foundation of Your throne" (Psalm 89:14). This principle also applies to the church age. In the passage above, the Hebrew words used for "work" and "service" have a similar meaning, with *bodah* having broader implications of work. Keil and Delitzsch's Commentary on the Old Testament says that these two Hebrew words "denote the fruit or self-reward of work and painstaking toil." Righteousness cultivates an environment where the people sense God's protection "in a peaceful habitation, secure dwellings, and in undisturbed resting places." James 3:18 characterizes this work as, "And the seed whose fruit is righteousness is sown in peace by those who make peace." Peace is contagious.

Three Symbols

A river was traditionally used as a means of connection between one town and another. It was a way for people to do business with each other and meet one another. A river is also, of course, a source of life for people, their livestock, and their crops.

A bird makes its home on land but can fly high up in the sky. It lives in both heaven and Earth as it travels between the two.

The kettle takes two opposing forces and brings them together to create something good. Fire wants to boil away water; water seeks to extinguish a fire. However, when a kettle comes between them, both thrive and create a substance that contributes to mankind.

We learn from all three symbols that peace does not mean sameness. The two towns do not merge. They share a river. Heaven and Earth, the spiritual and material worlds, are harmonized within the bird who lives in both, yet they remain two separate realms. Finally, water and fire reach their higher purpose so long as they remain separated by the kettle.

Jesus Is Our Peace

For He Himself is our peace, who made both groups into one and broke down the barrier of the dividing wall, by abolishing in His flesh the enmity, which is the Law of commandments contained in ordinances, so that in Himself He might make the two into one new man, thus establishing peace, and might reconcile them both in one body to God through the cross, by it having put to death the enmity. AND HE CAME AND PREACHED PEACE TO YOU WHO WERE FAR AWAY, AND PEACE TO THOSE WHO WERE NEAR.

Ephesians 2:14–17

Since peace is manifested in the person of Jesus Christ, its implications go far beyond peace with God. It means that Jesus, a Jew, as the Jewish Messiah, connects the Jew and Gentile into one family by "one new man, thus establishing peace" through the cross. Peace is the basis of brotherhood within the body of Christ since He abolishes enmity in Christ. The tranquility of unity through the Holy Spirit keeps the believer moving forward, pressing on "toward the goal for the prize of the upward call of God in Christ Jesus" (Philippians 3:14).

Peace, Peace

For thus says the high and exalted one Who lives forever, whose name is Holy, "I dwell on a high and holy place, And also with the contrite and lowly of spirit In order to revive the spirit of the lowly And to revive the heart of the contrite. For I will not contend forever, Nor will I always be angry; For the spirit would grow faint before Me, And the breath of those whom I have made. Because of the iniquity of his unjust gain, I was angry and struck him; I hid My face and was angry, And he went on turning away in the way of his heart. I have seen his ways, but I will heal him; I will lead him and restore comfort to him and to his mourners, Creating the praise of the lips. *Peace, peace to him who is far and to him who is near*," Says the Lord, "and I will heal him." But the wicked are like the tossing sea, For it cannot be quiet, And its waters toss up refuse and mud. "There is no peace," says my God, "for the wicked."

Isaiah 57:15–21
(emphasis added by the author)

The Lord desires His people to experience His peace. As the God of peace (Hebrews 13:20), He draws His people into the pathway of peace, where a forgiving God is always looking to offer His peace "to him who is far and to him who is near." Ultimately, the contrite and lowly heart finds the God of peace.

A Zionist Dream

In 1903, Joseph Chamberlain, the British Colonial Secretary, made an offer to Theodore Herzl and his Zionist group. The British were prepared to give the Jews 5,000 square miles in Uganda, Africa, to serve as a Jewish homeland. The proposal evoked a fierce debate. On the one hand, the land would provide the Jews with a homeland where they would be free to live in peace and protect themselves from danger.

On the other hand, it fell far short of the Zionist dream to return to the ancient homeland of the Jews—Israel. Thankfully, the offer was declined because the land was deemed unsuitable. However, the question remained: Even though the historical homeland of the Jews is Israel, does it matter where the Jewish homeland is today?

There is peace offered by the world, but it will never measure up to the quality of peace the believer experiences in his relationship with God. "The steadfast of mind You will keep in perfect peace [*shalom, shalom*], Because he trusts in You" (Isaiah 26:3). A perfect peace, in Hebrew *shalom, shalom*, is the Lord's heart toward all His people, Jew or Gentile. "Peace I leave with you; My peace I give to you; not as the world gives do I give to you. Do not let your heart be troubled, nor let it be fearful" (John 14:27).

CHAPTER 38: SERVICE IN THE KINGDOM

In Mark 10, James and John confront Jesus with a request to be able to sit on His right and left hand in glory. This request Jesus could not grant, and His explanation came in the form of a question found in verse 38, "You do not know what you are asking. Are you able to drink the cup that I drink, or to be baptized with the baptism with which I am baptized?" They thought they would be able, and Jesus acknowledged that "the cup that I drink you shall drink; and you shall be baptized with the baptism with which I am baptized. But to sit on My right or on My left, this is not Mine to give" (verses 39–40). He was telling them that they would suffer in identification with His suffering, but that would not measure up to the redemptive work Jesus would complete at Calvary. Jesus added, "But it is for those for whom it has been prepared," meaning that the Father would decide who would occupy those seats. This conversation was in preparation for a deeper discussion about servanthood.

> Hearing this, the ten began to feel indignant with James and John. Calling them to Himself, Jesus said to them, "You know that those who are recognized as rulers of the Gentiles lord it over them; and their great men exercise authority over them. But it is not this way among you, *but whoever wishes to become great among you shall be your servant* [*diakonos*—minister, servant, deacon]; and whoever wishes to be first among you shall be *slave* [*doulos*—one who is in a permanent relation of servitude to another, his will being altogether consumed in the will of the other] of all. For even the Son of Man did not come to be served, but to serve, and to give His life a ransom for many."
>
> Mark 10:41–45
> (emphasis added by the author)

Greatness in the Kingdom

In short, Jesus was giving them (and, by extension, you and I) the definition of greatness in the kingdom of heaven and the characteristics of those who would be first. Both revolve around two Greek words: *diakonos* and *doulos*. Greatness centers itself around *diakonos*, translated as servant, minister, or deacon. Its root refers to "waiting on tables" and, by extension, "care for one's livelihood." Greatness in the kingdom of heaven is about developing a willingness to serve the needs of others, making this attitude a habit.

Doulos, translated slave or bondservant, takes service to another level. It encompasses an attitude derived from the submission of one's will to another. Jesus says that the first in the kingdom of heaven is the one who is a *slave of all*. The apostle Paul refers to himself over and over again as a bondservant of Christ, and this is repeated by John, Peter, James, and Jude. A bondslave of God means devotion resulting in total obedience. For example, in 2 Timothy 2:24–25, he is "kind to all, able to teach, patient when wronged, with gentleness correcting those who are in opposition" themselves. His devotion to God is manifested in his compassion toward others.

The Father's Honor

Who, although He existed in the form of God, did not regard equality with God a thing to be grasped, but emptied Himself, *taking the form of a bond-servant* [*doulos*], and being made in the likeness of men. Being found in appearance as a man, He humbled Himself by becoming obedient to the point of death, even death on a cross. For this reason also, God highly exalted Him, and bestowed on Him the name which is above every name, so that at the name of Jesus EVERY KNEE WILL BOW, of those who are in heaven and on earth and under the earth, and that every tongue will confess that Jesus Christ is Lord, to the glory of God the Father.

Philippians 2:6–11
(emphasis added by the author)

According to Paul, Jesus was a bondservant to complete His Father's will. The above passage reveals that it was Jesus's choice to be surrendered to His Father's will, even if it meant suffering and death. Fulfilling the will of God is the ultimate conclusion of a life in complete submission to the Lord. From this lowly place, God is exalted, and we who agree with this life decision will also be exalted as Jesus was. John writes in John 12:24–26 that when a believer chooses to die to his own will and live for someone else, he finds that, in losing his life, he finds eternal life. In verse 26, "If anyone serves Me, he must follow Me; and where I am, there My servant will be also; if anyone serves Me, the Father will honor him."

Joseph, a Type of Christ

Now Joseph had been taken down to Egypt; and Potiphar, an Egyptian officer of Pharaoh, the captain of the bodyguard, bought him from the Ishmaelites, who had taken him down there. The Lord was with Joseph, so he became a successful man. And he was in the house of his master, the Egyptian. Now his master saw that the Lord was with him and how the Lord caused all that he did to prosper in his hand. So, Joseph found favor in his sight and became his personal servant; and he made him overseer over his house, and all that he owned he put in his charge. It came about that from the time he made him overseer in his house and over all that he owned, the Lord blessed the Egyptian's house on account of Joseph; thus, the Lord's blessing was upon all that he owned, in the house and in the field. *So, he left everything he owned in Joseph's charge; and with him there he did not concern himself with anything except the food which he ate.*

Genesis 39:1–6
(emphasis added by the author)

Joseph was purchased as a slave by Potiphar to serve in his house. Because of Joseph's faithfulness, the Lord anointed his work to bless Potipher, and after making Joseph his personal servant, Potipher ultimately put Joseph in charge of his entire household. In the same way, Jesus wants to serve the believer as a slave. Mark 10:45, "For even the Son of Man did not come to be served, but to serve, and to give His life a ransom for many." Jesus has so much to take care of in a believer's life if he would only leave Jesus in charge of his household. Christ's entire public ministry was to demonstrate what He could do for anyone who would believe. *By allowing Jesus to serve the believer, Jesus empowers him to serve others.*

A Slave Loves His Master

If you buy a Hebrew slave, he shall serve for six years; but on the seventh he shall go out as a free man without payment. If he comes alone, he shall go out alone; if he is the husband of a wife, then his wife shall go out with him. If his master gives him a wife, and she bears him sons or daughters, the wife and her children shall belong to her master, and he shall go out alone. But if the slave plainly says, '*I love my master, my wife and my children; I will not go out as a free man*,' then his master shall bring him to God, then he shall bring him to the door or the doorpost. And his master shall pierce his ear with an awl, and he shall serve him permanently.

Exodus 21:2–6

The Law of Moses gives us a glimpse into a bondslave relationship with God in the above passage. A slave is given his freedom (as a believer receives freedom in Christ), but he chooses to stay a slave because of his love for his master. The piercing by an awl symbolized permanent ownership, likened to the fact that the believer is no longer his own since he has been bought with a price (1 Corinthians 6:19–20). Choosing to be a slave is a statement that he acknowledges the master's will as supreme.

Freed from Sin

Do you not know that when you present yourselves to someone as slaves for obedience, you are slaves of the one whom you obey, either of sin resulting in death, or of obedience resulting in righteousness? But thanks be to God that though you were slaves of sin, you became obedient from the heart to that form of teaching to which you were committed, and having been freed from sin, you became slaves of righteousness.

Romans 6:16–18

As Paul reveals in Romans 6, man's curse means slavery to the sin nature imputed to him from Adam. When he becomes a believer in Christ, he has a choice: to continue being a slave to sin or, through obedience, to become a slave of righteousness. An unregenerate man is unaware of his slave condition; he falsely believes he is free. When Jesus enters his life by faith, the believer begins wrestling with this nature that he realizes cannot be controlled. In Romans 7, Paul testifies that he does the things he does not want to do and does not do the things he wishes to do. "Wretched man that I am! Who will set me free from the body of this death?" (Romans 7:24) His answer in verse 25 is the Lord Jesus Christ! Through obedience "from the heart to that form of teaching to which you were committed" *(paradidomai*—entrusted), the believer is freed from sin to become a slave of righteousness. He accepts accountability for the understanding of the truth God has given him as the means of experiencing God's righteousness.

Two Masters

In Luke 16:13, Jesus instructs His disciples that a servant cannot have two masters because he cannot have multiple allegiances, "for either he will hate the one and love the other, or else he will be devoted to one and despise the other." It means that we cannot serve two masters; we are forced to make a choice. Otherwise, we cannot serve at all. Therefore, a servant must have a single allegiance to serve truly.

> Now Moses was faithful in all His house as a servant [menial attendee], for a testimony of those things which were to be spoken later; but Christ was faithful as a Son over His house—whose house we are, if we hold fast our confidence and the boast of our hope firm until the end.
>
> Hebrews 3:5–6

Chapter 39: The Father's Love

For God so loved the world, that He gave His only begotten Son, that whoever believes in Him shall not perish, but have eternal life. For God did not send the Son into the world to judge the world, but that the world might be saved through Him.

John 3:16–17

A Story to Illustrate His Love

After a few of the usual Sunday evening hymns, the church's pastor slowly stood up, walked over to the pulpit, and, before he gave his sermon for the evening, briefly introduced a guest minister who was in the service that evening. In the introduction, the pastor told the congregation that the guest minister was one of his dearest childhood friends and wanted him to have a few moments to greet the church and share whatever he felt would be appropriate for the service. With that, an elderly person stepped up to the pulpit and began speaking.

"A father, his son, and a friend of his son were sailing off the Pacific coast," he began, "when a fast-approaching storm blocked any attempt to get back to the shore. The waves were so high that even though the father was an experienced sailor, he could not keep the boat upright, and the three were swept into the ocean as the boat capsized." The old man hesitated for a moment, making eye contact with two teenagers who were looking somewhat interested in his story for the first time since the service began.

The aged minister continued with his story, "Grabbing a rescue line, the father had to make the most excruciating decision of his life: to which boy he would throw the other end of the lifeline. He only had seconds to make the decision. The father knew that his son was a Christian, and he also knew that his son's friend was not. The agony of his decision could not be matched by the torment of the waves. As the father yelled,

'I love you, son!' he threw out the lifeline to his son's friend. By the time the father had pulled the friend back to the capsized boat, his son had disappeared beneath the raging swells into the black of night. His body was never recovered."

By this time, the two teenagers were sitting up straight in the pew, anxiously waiting for the next words to come out of the old minister's mouth. "The father," he continued, "knew his son would step into eternity with Jesus, and he could not bear the thought of his son's friend stepping into an eternity without Jesus. Therefore, he sacrificed his son to save the son's friend. How great is the love of God that He should do the same for us? Our heavenly Father sacrificed His only begotten Son to save us. I urge you to accept this offer to rescue you and take hold of the lifeline He is throwing out to you in this service." With that, the old man turned and sat down in his chair as silence filled the room.

The pastor again walked slowly to the pulpit and delivered a brief sermon with an invitation at the end. However, no one responded to the appeal. Within minutes after the service ended, the two teenagers were at the old man's side. "That was a nice story," politely stated one of the boys, "but I don't think it was very realistic for a father to give up his son's life in hopes that the other boy would become a Christian."

"Well, you've got a point there," the old man replied, glancing down at his worn Bible. A big smile broadened his narrow face; he once again looked up at the boys and said, "It sure isn't very realistic, is it? But I'm standing here today to tell you that story gives me a glimpse of what it must have been like for God to give up His Son for me. See—I was that father, and your pastor is my son's friend!"

See Him as He Is

See how great [exotic—Wuest] a love the Father has bestowed on us, that we would be called children of God; and such we are. For this reason, the world does not know us, because it did not know Him. *Beloved*, now we are children of God, and it has not appeared as yet what we will be. We know that when He appears, we will be like Him, because we will see Him just as He is.

1 John 3:1–2
(emphasis added by the author)

As the believer recognizes (beholds, sees) the personal love of the Father, a transformation begins to take place; he acknowledges that God's love has welcomed him into the royal family to be His child. This love distinguishes him from the rest of the world so that it will never understand him. Finally, this love guarantees as beloved that each true believer will see God as He is, confirming that he will also be without imperfection or blemish.

If we know that God's love will be the vehicle that God uses to admit each believer into His family, into the beloved (Ephesians 1:6), then we can have confidence that "in the beloved" is a place of protection, a place where God's provisions for the spiritual life are found. In Psalm 36:7–9, David says,

> How precious is Your lovingkindness, O God! And the children of men take refuge in the shadow of Your wings. They drink their fill of the abundance of Your house, And You give them to drink of the river of Your delights. For with You is the fountain of life; In Your light we see light.

God's light becomes the basis for our spiritual sight and life.

CHAPTER 40: PRECIOUS VS. WORTHLESS

We live in a world filled with corruption. In Romans 8:21–22, Paul says,

That the creation itself also will be set free from its slavery to corruption into the freedom of the glory of the children of God. For we know that the whole creation groans and suffers the pains of childbirth together until now.

This condition's culmination does not occur until there are new heavens and a new earth. In the meantime, we are stuck with a world system infected with the influences of the devil's agenda to kill, steal, and destroy. Yet God is still speaking through the prophets and His Son (Hebrews 1:1–2).

In Old Testament times, the prophets were the method God used to encourage and rebuke His people. Jeremiah was commissioned early on to be God's spokesman in one of the most challenging times for the Hebrew nation. He would spend his entire public ministry warning the people of impending judgment, yet they refused to accept his warnings. This is why he is called "the weeping prophet."

God's Spokesman

In Jeremiah 1:9–10, the Lord touched the mouth of Jeremiah as a young man and said (emphasis added by the author),

Behold, *I have put My words in your mouth*. See, I have appointed you this day over the nations and over the kingdoms, To pluck up and to break down, To destroy and to overthrow, To build and to plant.

Early on, God anointed Jeremiah as His spokesman to a nation that would reject His message.

The central theme in any prophet's ministry is his attitude and approach toward the Word of God. In Jeremiah 15:16, Jeremiah's sentiments toward the Word become apparent when he says to the Lord, "Your words were found and I ate them, And Your words became for me a joy and the delight of my heart; For I have been called by Your name, O Lord God of hosts." The Word of God is a matter of the heart, to be ingested like food because of the nourishment it provides and the strength it gives anyone who approaches it this way. In Psalm 1:2–3, the Scriptures say,

> But his delight is in the law of the Lord, And in His law, he meditates day and night. He will be like a tree firmly planted by streams of water, Which yields its fruit in its season, And its leaf does not wither; And in whatever he does, he prospers.

Meditation on the Word of God brings the believer to a new place where life's challenges do not slow him down, and he finds prosperity.

As Jeremiah had to constantly face the rejection of God's words for His people, it was not surprising that he would get discouraged. In Jeremiah 15:18–19, he asks God, "Will You indeed be to me like a deceptive stream With water that is unreliable?" God's response in verse 19 brings the definition, "*If you extract the precious from the worthless*, You will become *My spokesman*" (emphasis added by the author). The prophet's job was not to make the people accept everything God said but to ensure it was communicated clearly. The Lord continued in verse 20, "Then I will make you to this people A fortified wall of bronze; And though they fight against you, They will not prevail over you; For I am with you to save you And deliver you." Amid the wickedness surrounding him, Jeremiah needed to distinguish the precious from the worthless.

The Holy and the Profane

What does it mean to extract the precious from the worthless? Ezekiel 22:26 may provide insight (emphasis added by the author),

> Her priests have done violence to My law and have profaned My holy things; they have made *no distinction between the holy and the profane*, and they have *not taught the difference between the unclean and the*

clean, and they hide their eyes from My sabbaths, and I am profaned among them.

In Ezekiel's day, the priests could not distinguish between the holy and the profane, so they could not teach it to the people. It was corrected in the time of the future temple in Ezekiel 44:23; a wall in this temple separated the holy things from the common ones. People need to be taught the difference between that which is holy or consecrated (set apart) and that which is profane, unholy, or common. According to Psalm 101:2–3, these are a matter of the integrity of the heart; one must decide to "set no worthless thing before my eyes."

Paul's last letter before his martyrdom was his second to Timothy. He instructed Timothy that if anyone separates or cleanses himself from worldly influences, including common, "he will be a vessel for honor, sanctified, useful to the Master, prepared for every good work." The principle of sanctification, set apart for God's purposes, motivates the committed believer to acknowledge the warfare within the culture intended to separate the believer from his God. Even religious activity can be considered worthless when not motivated by God's heart. Isaiah 1:16–17,

> Wash yourselves, make yourselves clean; Remove the evil of your deeds from My sight. Cease to do evil, Learn to do good; Seek justice, Reprove the ruthless, Defend the orphan, Plead for the widow.

Righteous motives are those that encompass a divine result.

Pure and Undefiled Religion

James 1:26–27 (emphasis added by the author),

> If anyone thinks himself to be religious, and yet does not bridle his tongue but deceives his own heart, *this man's religion is worthless*. Pure and undefiled religion in the sight of our God and Father is this: to visit orphans and widows in their distress, and to keep oneself unstained by the world.

James tells us that the purity of religious expression finds itself in its ultimate object, that those of greatest need would be touched and the believer left unscathed by worldly influences.

Chapter 41: Living in Babylon

When I look around at where we are as a society and compare it to where we were thirty years ago, it scares me. So many of our Judeo-Christian norms and standards are dramatically changed; this is a different place. Our Christian values are under severe attack as committed believers are viewed as enemies rather than model citizens. Attitudes about traditional marriage, homosexuality, and even gender have served to turn our world upside down and away from the traditions and biblical standards that have defined our country since before its founding. Add to that the radical movements to control free speech, protect criminal illegals, and accept abortion even up to birth, and our world becomes unrecognizable. I look around and realize I no longer live in Jerusalem but in Babylon.

Babylon's Challenges

The book of Daniel opens up for us the approach that, as boys, he and three of his friends took in learning how to live in a world much different from the places of their births. When Judah was taken captive by Nebuchadnezzar, and many were brought to Babylon, they had to make certain decisions about how they would incorporate their faith in light of a new culture and the new reality of being servants in the royal court. One of those decisions involved their diet. In Daniel 1:8–9,

> But Daniel made up his mind that he would not defile himself with the king's choice food or with the wine which he drank; so, he sought permission from the commander of the officials that he might not defile himself. Now God granted Daniel favor and compassion in the sight of the commander of the officials.

The Babylonian menu was inconsistent with the regular Jewish diet, and Daniel stood by his convictions and gained approval from the leadership. Since Judaism provides strict guidelines about what is acceptable, Daniel decided to honor those restrictions, and God favored him.

The biggest challenge came in the Babylonian requirement to worship the king's golden image in Daniel 3. This practice is clearly idolatry and a direct assault on the foundation of the Jewish faith.

> I am the Lord your God, who brought you out of the land of Egypt, out of the house of slavery. You shall have no other gods before Me. You shall not make for yourself an idol, or any likeness of what is in heaven above or on the earth beneath or in the water under the earth. You shall not worship them or serve them.
>
> Exodus 20:2–5

If their Jewish faith meant anything, they would need to make serious decisions about how much they would allow this new culture to compromise that faith. Their new surroundings challenged Daniel and the three Hebrew boys to place their lives on the line for their faith in God. In Daniel 3, it was the fiery furnace, and in Daniel 6, the lions' den.

Idolatry Takes on Many Forms

In this society, idolatry can take on at least four different forms: materialism, individual pride, or egotism (i.e., obsession with jobs, etc.), mankind's generic abilities (i.e., naturalism, power of science), and reliance on self and self-exaltation. These present ongoing opportunities to compromise individual faith in God by placing faith in man's ability over God. Are we committed to our faith completely, or are there areas we are willing to negotiate? It affects the things we value, the way we vote in elections, and those we support in the public square. For example, if a Christian believes that pro-life issues are important to his faith in God, he should vote accordingly.

The church of Laodicea had some of the same issues America faces today in Revelation 3:14–22. The level of prosperity we have experienced as a nation challenges the convictions we may or may not have as believers. Verse 17 (emphasis added by the author), "Because you say, 'I am rich, and have become wealthy, and *have need of nothing*,' and you do not know that you are wretched and miserable and poor and blind and naked." Jesus addressed the issue of being rich as a major obstacle in walking closely with God. He said that you could not serve two masters in Matthew 6:24,

> No one can serve two masters; for either he will hate the one and love the other, or he will be devoted to one and despise the other. You cannot serve God and wealth [*mammon*—God of materialism].

The Lord had clear instructions for those living in exile in Jeremiah 29:4–11,

> Thus says the Lord of hosts, the God of Israel, to all the exiles whom I have sent into exile from Jerusalem to Babylon, 'Build houses and live in them; and plant gardens and eat their produce. Take wives and become the fathers of sons and daughters and take wives for your sons and give your daughters to husbands, that they may bear sons and daughters; and multiply there and do not decrease. Seek the welfare of the city where I have sent you into exile, and pray to the Lord on its behalf; for in its welfare, you will have welfare.' For thus says the Lord of hosts, the God of Israel, 'Do not let your prophets who are in your midst and your diviners deceive you, and do not listen to the dreams which they dream. For they prophesy falsely to you in My name; I have not sent them,' declares the Lord. For thus says the Lord, 'When seventy years have been completed for Babylon, I will visit you and fulfill My good word to you, to bring you back to this place. For I know the plans that I have for you,' declares the Lord, 'plans for welfare and not for calamity to give you a future and a hope.'

As the saying goes, "This too shall pass." In the meantime, live your life before God, knowing that the Lord has great plans for His people in Jerusalem or Babylon.

Our Spiritual Service of Worship

Living faith in God must include a willingness to serve Him. This service can take on many different forms, but it is the heart of our worship of Him. In Romans 12:1–2 (emphasis added by the author),

> Therefore I urge you, brethren, by the mercies of God, *to present your bodies a living and holy sacrifice, acceptable to God, which is your spir-*

itual service of worship. And do not be conformed to this world, but be transformed by the renewing of your mind, so that you may prove what the will of God is, that which is good and acceptable and perfect.

Since idolatry is inherent in our current society, it becomes all the more important that the expression of our service to and worship of God must include being "transformed by the renewing of your mind" and not allowing the atmosphere to conform us to worldly priorities.

Ultimately, these realities are forcing us to make critical decisions about the importance of our biblical faith. It is no longer easy to sit on the fence, being wishy-washy about life decisions that challenge our faith in God. As God spoke to Israel in Deuteronomy 30:19 (emphasis added by the author), "I call heaven and earth to witness against you today, that I have set before you life and death, the blessing and the curse. *So, choose life so that you may live.*"

CHAPTER 42: WALKING IN THE LAW

The word "law" is used in many different ways in the Scriptures, so it is important to understand its meaning in its context. Identifying the context of a particular word, verse, or passage in the Bible is a primary principle that should govern one's interpretation of the Word of God. For example, when Psalm 119:1 says that the blessings of God are for those who walk in the law of the Lord, was He talking about the ten commandments and other dos and don'ts given to Moses? Or is He speaking of something more fundamental than living under a bunch of rules and regulations?

> How blessed are those whose *way* [*derek*—the pathways of life] is blameless [*tamiym*—linked to truth, virtue, uprightness], Who walk in the *law* [*torah*—instruction, direction, doctrine] of the Lord. How blessed are those who observe His *testimonies*, Who seek Him with all their heart. They also do no unrighteousness; They walk in His *ways*.
>
> Psalm 119:1–3
> (emphasis added by the author)

There is no consensus as to the author of Psalm 119, but it is very evident that its theme is the Word of God, and the writer uses many different synonyms to communicate deeper spiritual truths regarding the role it should play in a believer's life. These synonyms include not only law but also a commandment, a precept, a statute, a testimony, an ordinance, a judgment, a way, and a word. A closer look at the original Hebrew language helps us understand the nuances of each term. For instance, the Hebrew for "law" is "*torah*," and its primary meaning is instruction or direction. When I apply that meaning to Psalm 119:1, it takes on the idea of being willing to be taught by God within the details of my life and the way I conduct myself. The Hebrew poetic language also uses the repetition of compatible thoughts to reinforce the meaning. Those who walk in the Law are those whose way, by extension, is blameless or virtuous.

Living under the authority of God's instruction allows Him to direct the believer through the valleys and mountaintop experiences. It acknowledges that the blessed one is never alone but walks through the valley of the shadow of death and fears no evil since He walks with him. His only fear is associated with the fear of the Lord, a reverence or high respect for Him and His ways.

There Is Only One Lawgiver and Judge

One way to know that the believer is employing these truths is seen in the way he treats others. James' letter says, "He who speaks against a brother or judges his brother, speaks against the law and judges the law; but if you judge the law, you are not a doer of the law but a judge of it" (James 4:11). Walking in the Law is not a religious thing to be imposed on others, but a way of life that can draw others to the one who continuously directs lives. This type of walk makes faith in God real and is proven by how we treat others and how they react to this life.

Abiding in the Vine

When Jesus walked the earth, He made a profound statement in John 14:6 (emphasis added by the author) when asked about the way to go: "*I am the way*, and the truth, and the life; no one comes to the Father but through Me." In this passage, Philip asks Jesus to "show us the Father," and Jesus answers that to come to know Jesus by His words and ways is to come to know the Father. He teaches them about the principle of abiding, that just as Jesus was abiding in His Father and therefore doing the works of His Father, they could participate in those works. Jesus said that those who believe in and put their trust in Him would participate in greater works than those Jesus performed (John 14:12).

In John 15, Jesus gives us more insight into abiding when He speaks about the relationship between the grapevine and its branches. Since the life source of the branch comes from the vine, it cannot survive without the vine. In verse 5, He says, "I am the vine, you are the branches; he who abides in Me and I in him, he bears much fruit, for apart from Me you can do nothing." There is an exchange of life between the vine and its branches. When the branch recognizes the quality of this relationship and all its possibilities, it is a game changer. Practically speaking, this relationship is fulfilled in the believer's willingness to walk in the law of the Lord. He understands that instruction, directed by the Word of God and His Spirit, produces much fruit, represented by His works, the Father's works. In verse 8, this fruit proves to the Father that we are a disciple.

> The law of the Lord is perfect, *restoring the soul*; The testimony of the Lord is sure, *making wise the simple*. The precepts of the Lord are right, *rejoicing the heart*; The commandment of the Lord is pure, *enlightening the eyes*. The fear of the Lord is clean, *enduring forever*; The judgments of the Lord are true; *they are righteous altogether*. They are more desirable than gold, yes, than much fine gold; Sweeter also than honey and the drippings of the honeycomb.
>
> Psalm 19:7–10
> (emphasis added by the author)

Psalm 19 gives us further insight into the ability and character of the law of the Lord. Not only does it restore the soul, but it also makes wise the simple, rejoices the heart, and enlightens the eyes. This supernatural work of God by His Word endures forever and is righteous altogether. Our challenge is to give in to its calling and benefit from all its strengths and outpourings.

CHAPTER 43: PRIESTHOOD OF THE BELIEVER

One of the essential principles derived from the Protestant Reformation is the priesthood of the believer. Martin Luther wanted Christians to understand that, in God's eyes, the people were not second-class citizens compared to the clergy or the nobility. Instead, new covenant believers are all saints, kings, and priests. There are three fundamental principles of the Protestant Reformation: the supremacy of the Scriptures over tradition, the supremacy of faith over works, and the supremacy of the Christian people over an exclusive priesthood. The first may be called the objective, the second the subjective, and the third the social or ecclesiastical principle.

While Martin Luther did not use the exact phrase "priesthood of all believers," he infers a general priesthood in Christendom in his 1520 "To the Christian Nobility of the German Nation." He said that all Christians "are truly of the spiritual estate, and there is no difference among them, save of office alone." When Paul says that believers are part of one body, one Lord, by one Spirit, one baptism, and called in one hope of your calling (Ephesians 4:4–6), he means that there is no distinction, that we are all one in Christ (Galatians 3:28). Luther continues,

> It is faith that makes men priests, faith that unites them to Christ, and gives them the indwelling of the Holy Spirit, whereby they become filled with all holy grace and heavenly power. The inward anointing - this oil, better than any that ever came from the horn of bishop or pope - gives them not the name only, but the nature, the purity, the power of priests; and this anointing have all they received who are believers in Christ.

A Royal Priesthood

But you are A CHOSEN RACE, A royal PRIESTHOOD, A HOLY NATION, A PEOPLE FOR God's OWN POSSESSION, so that you may proclaim the excellencies of Him who has called you out of darkness into His marvelous light; for you once were NOT A PEOPLE, but now you are THE PEOPLE OF GOD; you had NOT RECEIVED MERCY, but now you have RECEIVED MERCY.

1 Peter 2:9–10

Peter acknowledges that as chosen ones (Ephesians 1:4), the believer is automatically part of "a royal priesthood" and a holy nation, meaning that he has been set apart for a divine purpose as "a people for God's own possession." This divine purpose is "so that you may proclaim the excellencies of Him who has called you out of darkness into His marvelous light," and this empowerment only happens to the one who has accepted his position as a priest by receiving His mercy. The new covenant believer-priest recognizes that he belongs to God and derives his accountability from that position. New Testament believers are commissioned into God's army of servant priests.

Spiritual Sacrifices

As part of a holy nation, the believer-priest has been set apart for God's purposes. In 1 Peter 2:5, "You also, as living stones, are being built up as a spiritual house for a holy priesthood, to offer up spiritual sacrifices acceptable to God through Jesus Christ." The old covenant priest was charged with the job of offering animal sacrifices on behalf of the people in the tabernacle/temple to atone for sins. The new covenant priesthood begins with the offering of self to God, which is our spiritual service of worship (Romans 12:1). From this place, he can become, like Paul, a spiritual sacrifice to others through faith in the high priest, Jesus Christ. Philippians 2:17, "But even if I am being poured out as a drink offering upon the sacrifice and service of your faith, I rejoice and share my joy with you all." The impartation of God's life is realized when a man sees the sacrifice of the Lord through the investment of the priesthood into others.

The old covenant priest was not only responsible for animal sacrifices, but he also burned the incense (a picture of prayer) on the altar of incense, signifying Jesus as our intercessor (Hebrews 7:25). He cleaned and trimmed the lamps of the golden lampstand, which references Jesus as the light of the world (John 8:12). He put the bread of the presence on the table every Sabbath, pointing to Jesus as the bread of life (John 6:35). In the same way, the new covenant priest is a minister to others through prayer (1 Timothy 2:1–2), declaring the light of the gospel (1 Corinthians 9:16), and encouraging others in the bread of God's Word (Matthew 4:4). And just as the old covenant priest was anointed with oil to fulfill his office, so the new covenant priest is anointed with God's power through the Holy Spirit (1 Corinthians 2:4–5).

Missions

Jesus speaks to the apostle John about this new covenant priesthood in Revelation 1:6, "And He has made us to be a kingdom, priests to His God and Father—to Him be the glory and the dominion forever and ever. Amen." The ultimate purpose of the priesthood is that God gets the glory and is recognized as the ultimate authority over man and all things (dominion). Beyond the new covenant offices of apostles, evangelists, and pastor-teacher that resemble the office of priests, maybe the greatest example of the new covenant believer-priest is the missionary. Christian missions employ believers of all shapes and sizes in missionary work all over the world in fulfillment of Acts 1:8. They sacrifice their own lives to serve the Lord as soul winners, teachers, and other efforts intended to meet human needs by sharing the gospel, praying for the greatest needs of the people, and imparting life through the Word of God. In reality, a missionary is anyone who lays down his/her life to follow God's will in serving human needs, no matter the place.

This new covenant priesthood is not reserved strictly for the church age but is also intended for the new covenant of the kingdom age to come on behalf of the Jewish nation. Isaiah 61:6 says, "But you will be called the priests of the Lord; You will be spoken of as ministers of our God. You will eat the wealth of nations, And in their riches you will boast." Revelation 5:8 and 20:6 say that these priests would reign with Christ for a thousand years. That's us, the overcomers from the church age who have chosen to live a life of service for the sake of a higher purpose, God's agape love for the world (John 3:16), to disciple all nations in Christ's stead. Psalm 4:3, "But know that the Lord has set apart the godly man for Himself; The Lord hears when I call to Him."

Chapter 44: The Prophets' Dilemma

In 2 Peter 1:21 (emphasis added b no prophecy was ever made by an act of human will, but men *moved* by the Holy Spirit spoke from God." This verse teaches that the human writers of the Scriptures did not receive their words by some method of dictation, but the truths they spoke of were ingested into their lives organically, and the result was that each one provided a distinct perspective on the truths they reported. For evidence of this, we need only look at the differences in reporting of and emphasis for the same or similar events of the four gospels.

Abraham Heschel wrote two incredible books entitled *The Prophets I & II*. In them, he examined the biographies and writings of many Old Testament prophets to ascertain a description of their "consciousness" as they reported God's thoughts, which resulted in Holy Scripture. According to his introduction,

> The inquiry, then, was aimed, not at psychological motives to be looked for in the pre-prophetic background of the prophet's life, but at motives which consciously given, even if not explicitly stated...

The uniqueness of each Scripture writer's experience and mindset provides the rich canvas through which God delivers His truth and character to those who feed on the Scriptures.

Jeremiah's Laments

One of the most notable of these Old Testament prophets is Jeremiah, who warned Judah again and again of God's judgment with little positive response from the people. Their rejection of his messages weighed heavily on his temperament and entire public ministry as he became known as the "weeping prophet." His second writing is entitled "Lamentations," crying out to God on behalf of a fallen people. We find some of these emotions expressed in Jeremiah 20, where he is brought by God into His lamentations for His people.

> O Lord, You have deceived [enticed, seduced] me and I was deceived; You have overcome [raped] me and prevailed. I have become a laughingstock all day long; Everyone mocks me. For each time I speak, I cry aloud; I proclaim violence and destruction, Because for me the word of the Lord has resulted In reproach and derision all day long. But if I say, "I will not remember Him Or speak anymore in His name," Then in my heart it becomes like a burning fire Shut up in my bones, And *I am weary of holding it in*, And I cannot endure it. For I have heard the whispering of many, "Terror on every side! Denounce him; yes, let us denounce him!" All my trusted friends, watching for my fall, say: "Perhaps he will be deceived [enticed], so that we may prevail against him And take our revenge on him."

Jeremiah 20:7–10
(emphasis added by the author)

Weariness

God's passion, His pathos toward His own in anticipation of their coming exile in Babylon produced a shared emotion on behalf of His prophet in identification with the Lord's desire to save them from their impending losses. Those shared emotions created this dilemma inside and produced unexplainable conflict. In verse 7, Jeremiah accuses God of seduction and rape in getting him to continue the Lord's ministry despite severe rejection. The only message he has for them is gloom and doom. In response to this dilemma, Jeremiah contemplates keeping quiet but then acknowledges that in his heart, "It becomes like a burning fire Shut up in my bones; And I am weary of holding it in." Although he expresses his desire to be quiet, the pathos of God would not allow it. The prophet recognized that the Lord's heart for His people overruled his own internal conflict.

A further expression of this dilemma appears in Jeremiah 25:15–16,

> For thus the Lord, the God of Israel, says to me, "Take this cup of the wine of wrath from My hand and cause all the nations to whom I send you to drink it. They will drink and stagger and go mad because of the sword that I will send among them."

The prophet's connection to the heart of God is an all-encompassing one; it is likened to eating and drinking (see Jeremiah 15:16), some of the basic necessities of human life. The man of God recognizes that rejection by even friends is to be expected when operating under the passion and purposes of God. After all, Elohim is the one who sees the end from the beginning (Isaiah 46:10).

Clinging to God

> Then the word of the Lord came to me, saying, "Thus says the Lord, 'Just so will I destroy the pride of Judah and the great pride of Jerusalem. This wicked people, who refuse to listen to My words, who walk in the stubbornness of their hearts and have gone after other gods to serve them and to bow down to them, let them be just like this waistband which is totally worthless. For as the waistband clings to the waist of a man, so I made the whole household of Israel and the whole household of Judah cling to Me,' declares the Lord, 'that they might be for Me a people, for renown, for praise and for glory; but they did not listen.'"

Jeremiah 13:8–11

God's command to Jeremiah in chapter 13 began with, "Go and buy yourself a linen waistband and put it around your waist, but do not put it in water." Afterward, He told the prophet to hide the waistband in the cleft of the rock, most likely in Parah. God then commands Jeremiah to dig up the waistband and finds it ruined and totally worthless. The Lord was illustrating to Judah that so long as they were attached to the Lord through Jeremiah's waistband (public ministry, teaching), they would be protected. But once they rejected Jeremiah's waistband, they would be rejected by the Lord. The waistband had to be first worn by Jeremiah, speaking of the ministry of the Lord through Jeremiah; the waistband was worn around the midsection to signify the essence of the man. Then, so long as the people listened to the Lord as revealed through the life of Jeremiah, they would be accepted. But that is not how things turned out.

Like a Mighty Warrior

But the Lord is with me like a dread champion [mighty warrior]; Therefore, my persecutors will stumble and not prevail. They will be utterly ashamed, because they have failed, With an everlasting disgrace that will not be forgotten. Yet, O Lord of hosts, You who test the righteous, Who see the mind and the heart; Let me see Your vengeance on them; For to You I have set forth my cause. Sing to the Lord, praise the Lord! For He has delivered the soul of the needy one From the hand of evildoers.

Jeremiah 20:11–13

The world in which man occupies is controlled by "the prince of the power of the air," who has his own agenda and manages his own system (cosmos) apart from the will and purposes of God. Therefore, the environment in which the believer operates is in opposition to the world just as the Spirit is in opposition to the flesh (Galatians 5:17). The believer has a mighty warrior on his side to be the defender, and He is the one who rights all that is wrong. The world presents all kinds of trials and tests that the Lord uses to try men's hearts for His purposes and to "deliver the soul of the needy." It represents the integration of God's life within man (theandric action) to expose wickedness wherever it is found.

Partakers of the Divine Nature

The last and greatest of the Old Testament prophets was John the Baptist. His public ministry as the forerunner of the Messiah was short-lived but presented to the Jews of Jesus's day the integration of God's life into a man's life in a profound way. According to Matthew 3:4, he wore "a garment of camel's hair and a leather belt around his waist; and his food was locusts and wild honey." He lived a wilderness life, apart from society, and was used mightily to bring many to repentance of sin through baptism in the Jordan River. I know some believers with this same spirit and commitment to the divine cause. They have consciously forsaken even the simplest of worldly benefits for the divine cause. They have embraced the higher life without regret and are experiencing theandric action. Pastor Carl Stevens, who coined the phrase, defined theandric action as "the fulness to overflowing of God's divine nature in the human vessel surrendered to the plan of God."

After John's imprisonment, he sent word to Jesus through the disciples with a question, "Are You the Expected One, or shall we look for someone else?" (Matthew 11:3). Jesus's response was to have his followers tell John the miracles they observed. He then spoke these words in verses 7–11 (emphasis added by the author):

> What did you go out into the wilderness to see? A reed shaken by the wind? But what did you go out to see? A man dressed in soft clothing? Those who wear soft clothing are in kings' palaces! But what did you go out to see? A prophet? Yes, I tell you, and *one who is more than a prophet*. This is the one about whom it is written, 'BEHOLD, I SEND MY MESSENGER AHEAD OF YOU, WHO WILL PREPARE YOUR WAY BEFORE YOU.' Truly I say to you, among those born of women there has not arisen anyone greater than John the Baptist! Yet the one who is least in the kingdom of heaven is greater than he.

John the Baptist was more than a prophet. He paved the way for all those who wish to be greater in the kingdom by seeking a higher life. The believer's connection to this higher life relates to his relationship to Calvary's cross. The apostle Paul defines it this way in Galatians 2:20,

> I have been crucified with Christ; and it is no longer I who live, but Christ lives in me; and the life which I now live in the flesh I live by faith in the Son of God, who loved me and gave Himself up for me.

The cross connects the believer directly to Christ's life, His attitudes, and His priorities and creates a heart of service for His will. The higher life results from a believer partaking in the divine nature (2 Peter 1:4).

CHAPTER 45: WALK BEFORE GOD

Question: how does a fallen man walk before a holy God in a corrupt world? This may be God's greatest miracle. Yet, it was what God intended for man all along. The failure of Adam and Eve was repeated from generation to generation in different ways until Enoch came along. The Bible tells us that "Enoch walked with God; and he was not, for God took him" (Genesis 5:24). God honored Enoch's walk by taking him home early. The next time we see this quality of relationship with God is with Abram in Genesis 17.

In this chapter (verses 1–2), God wishes to establish a covenant relationship with Abram when He says,

> Now when Abram was ninety-nine years old, the Lord appeared to Abram and said to him, "I am God Almighty; Walk before Me, and be blameless [*tamiym*—linked to truth, virtue, uprightness]. I will establish My covenant between Me and you, And I will multiply you exceedingly."

This covenant was between God and Abram and depended on Abram's belief in God's promises. At the same time, God changed Abram's name to Abraham, meaning father of many nations. God told Abraham that walking before God was a byproduct of a committed covenant relationship with Him.

One of the most interesting people in the Bible is King David. He was a man after God's heart (Acts 13:22), so he was favored by God, but he also had many shortcomings, just like you and me. This is why his life and writings are so meaningful to believers. Despite all of his failures, he learned to walk before his God. David was a man of action, a man of experience, and his psalms are the honest communications of his struggles to God. Learning to walk before God is not an academic pursuit but rather a process of trying on all the elements of our salvation "with fear and trembling."

God Is for Me

You have taken account of my wanderings; Put my tears in Your bottle. Are they not in Your book? Then my enemies will turn back in the day when I call; *This I know that God is for me.* In God, whose word I praise, In the Lord, whose word I praise, In God I have put my trust, I shall not be afraid. What can man do to me? Your vows are binding upon me, O God; I will render thank offerings to You. For You have delivered my soul from death, Indeed my feet from stumbling, So that I may walk before God In the light of the living.

Psalm 56:8–13
(emphasis added by the author)

David is willing to admit that his life is filled with wanderings (traveling about with no home and no goals), and this has caused many tears that God has captured in a bottle and recorded in His Book of Remembrance. In verse 9, he concludes that God is for him. Paul says it this way in Romans 8:31, "What then shall we say to these things? If [since] God is for us, who is against us?" This confidence in God's attitude toward His people becomes foundational for man to walk before his God. David sees that God is keeping track of his own tears created by times when he is not on track with God. Psalm 116:7–9,

Return to your rest, O my soul, For the Lord has dealt bountifully with you. For You have rescued my soul from death, My eyes from tears, My feet from stumbling. I shall walk before the Lord In the land of the living.

The psalmist understood that nothing could separate him from God's love, not even his own failures (see Romans 8:37–39).

The Light of the Living

In Psalm 56:13 above, David learned to walk before God "in the light of the living." This phrase speaks to the fact that so long as the light of God is with us, we learn to walk in that light. In John 12:35–37,

So Jesus said to them, "For a little while longer the Light is among you. Walk while you have the Light, so that darkness will not overtake you; he who walks in the darkness does not know where he goes. While you have the Light, believe in the Light, so that you may become sons of Light."

Jesus was speaking about His light, that in Him was found the knowledge and the ability to walk with Him in this world, in the land of the living. He wants His followers to be sons of His light. To the nation of Israel in the last days, Isaiah says, "Come, house of Jacob, and let us walk in the light of the Lord" (Isaiah 2:5).

In Isaiah 38:3, Hezekiah became deathly ill, and God spoke to him through Isaiah to get his house in order. Hezekiah prayed to the Lord, "Remember now, O Lord, I beseech You, how I have walked before You in truth and with a whole heart, and have done what is good in Your sight." God's answer was to give him an additional fifteen years to live; He said to Hezekiah, "I have heard your prayer, I have seen your tears" (verse 5). He understood that walking before the Lord meant walking in truth and with the whole heart, holding nothing back. It is crying to God in Psalm 142:5, "You are my refuge, My portion [*heleq*—a piece of territory] in the land of the living." When the Lord is my portion, I am only interested in what proceeds from Him.

Psalm 119:57, "The Lord is my portion; I have promised to keep Your words." The ultimate measure of walking before God is a commitment to keep His words in a covenant relationship with Him.

Heroes of the Faith

CHAPTER 46: HUDSON TAYLOR— THE HEART OF MISSIONS

One of the greatest missionaries of the modern Christian age is (James) Hudson Taylor, who spent fifty-one years as a missionary to China and established the China Inland Missions, now known as OMF International. This society was responsible for bringing over 800 missionaries to the country who began 125 schools and directly resulted in 18,000 Christian conversions, as well as establishing more than 300 stations of work with more than 500 local helpers in all eighteen provinces. Taylor's methods included dressing like a native and exhibiting a deep passion for reaching remote people groups within China. In addition, he promoted a new approach to world missions, namely "Faith missions," the sending of missionaries with no promises of temporal support but instead a reliance "through prayer to move Men by God." Hudson Taylor's attitude and focus revolutionized modern missions. He was completely committed to his call. Here's an illustration of that attitude:

The Turkey Prince is a Jewish tale told by Rabbi Nachman of Breslov in the eighteenth century. The story is about a prince who goes insane, believing that he is a turkey. He takes off his clothing, sits under the table, and eats crumbs off the floor. The king and queen are horrified. Many try to heal their son, but none are successful until one day when a wise man comes to town and says that he can heal the prince.

This man takes off his own clothing and sits together with the prince on the floor, claiming to be a turkey, too. Gradually, the prince accepts the man as a friend and trusts him. The wise man then suggests to the prince that turkeys can also wear clothing and eat at a table. Step by step, the wise man is able to get the prince to act normally until the prince is completely cured.

All Things to All Men

Effective missions meet people right where they are. The apostle Paul understood this principle clearly when he offered the following in 1 Corinthians 9:18–23:

> What then is my reward? That, when I preach the gospel, I may offer the Gospel without charge, so as not to make full use of my right in the gospel. For though I am free from all men, I have made myself a slave to all, so that I may win more. To the Jews I became as a Jew, so that I might win Jews; to those who are under the Law, as under the Law though not being myself under the Law, so that I might win those who are under the Law; to those who are without law, as without law, though not being without the law of God but under the law of Christ, so that I might win those who are without law. To the weak I became weak, that I might win the weak; I have become all things to all men, so that I may by all means save some. I do all things for the sake of the gospel, so that I may become a fellow partaker of it.

This reference to Paul is derived from his understanding of God's heart for people as a servant. He expressed this heart in Philippians 2:6–8 when, in referring to Jesus, he said,

> Although He existed in the form of God, did not regard equality with God a thing to be grasped, but emptied Himself, taking the form of a bond-servant, and being made in the likeness of men. Being found in appearance as a man, He humbled Himself by becoming obedient to the point of death, even death on a cross.

This agape love of God for the people of the world (so loved—John 3:16) is exemplified in Jesus's attitude that He came to serve and not be served, becoming a ransom for many. The Greek word for ransom, *lutron*, means to loosen them from their bonds and set them at liberty. This is the heartbeat of missions.

In his progressive understanding of this new relationship with God, Paul also encouraged believers "not to put an obstacle or a stumbling block in a brother's way" (Romans 14:13). In verse 14, he says that "nothing is unclean in itself," so to enforce any particular requirement or prohibition on others in the name of uncleanness should be avoided.

These actions are not motivated by love but rather by a religious zeal that does not recognize Christ's unlimited atonement. Verses 16–17, "Therefore do not let what is for you a good thing be spoken of as evil; for the kingdom of God is not eating and drinking, but righteousness and peace and joy in the Holy Spirit." The heart of missions does not include requiring any people groups to conform to particular cultural norms, standards, or practices.

Full Commitment

The heart of missions requires total commitment. The missionary recognizes that he is set apart from the world to fulfill God's purposes, particularly spreading the gospel. This effort takes on many forms as God uses each according to his gifts. Still, the missionary spirit is preoccupied with diligence to present oneself as a workman (2 Timothy 2:15) while avoiding worldly influences that might negatively affect those who are the mission's object. Regarding Hudson Taylor, Arthur Glasser said, "He was ambitious without being proud …He was biblical without being bigoted …He was a follower of Jesus, without being superficial …He was charismatic without being selfish." He was promoting the exchanged life.

Taylor's Impact

Hudson Taylor exemplifies Paul's heart. Historian Ruth Tucker summarizes the theme of his life:

> No other missionary in the nineteen centuries since the Apostle Paul has had a wider vision and has carried out a more systematized plan of evangelizing a broad geographical area than Hudson Taylor.

His commitment to the Chinese people included his efforts to preach in several local languages, including Mandarin, Chaozhou, and the Wu dialects of Shanghai and Ningbo. The last of these he knew well enough to help prepare a colloquial edition of the New Testament written in it. The heart of missions is clearly communicating the gospel to any people group, in any language, and in any circumstance.

The biographies of Hudson Taylor inspired generations of Christians to follow his example of service and sacrifice. Notable examples include missionary to India Amy Carmichael, Olympic Gold Medalist Eric Liddell, twentieth-century missionary and martyr Jim Elliot, founder of Bible Study Fellowship Audrey Wetherell Johnson, as well as international evangelists Billy Graham and Luis Palau. Kenneth Scott Latourette said, "Hudson Taylor was …one of the greatest missionaries of all time, and …one of the four or five most influential foreigners who came to China in the nineteenth century for any purpose."

CHAPTER 47: JAMES GARFIELD, MAN OF INTEGRITY

"He stores up sound wisdom for the upright; He is a shield to those who walk in integrity, Guarding the paths of justice, And *He preserves the way of His godly ones*" (Proverbs 2:7) (emphasis added by the author).

When I moved to Northeast Ohio to plant a church in 1998, we ended up locating it at a senior center in Mentor, Ohio. It turns out that building was right around the corner from the presidential library of James Garfield, who lived in Mentor when he was elected the twentieth president of the United States. A few years later, they tore down the senior center building, and we had to move and locate our church at a meeting hall that had been Garfield's church while living in Mentor. He was an impressive man, and the video played at his welcome center suggests that he was the most prepared man we've ever had to be president.

Garfield was born November 19, 1831, in a log cabin near Orange in Cuyahoga County, Ohio. He was the fourth and final child of Abram Garfield and Eliza Ballou Garfield. Garfield's father's ancestors were among the original settlers of the Massachusetts Bay Colony. In 1827 the father carried their pioneering spirit to Ohio, where he worked on an Ohio Canal construction crew. By the time Garfield was born, his father was a struggling farmer and a founding member of the local Disciples of Christ Church. In 1833, when Garfield was just two years old, his father died suddenly, leaving the family in poverty.

At a young age, Garfield became a minister for the Disciples of Christ, where he was lauded for his skill as a preacher, and he learned Greek—the original language of the New Testament. Though it was not his full-time job, he continued to preach and minister for years until his presidency.

"When the Divine Artist would produce a poem, He plants a germ of it in a human soul, and out of that soul the poem springs and grows as from the rose-tree the rose" (James Garfield).

Supporting himself as a part-time teacher, a carpenter, and even a janitor through college, he was an idealistic young man who identified with the antislavery tenets of the new Republican Party. After completing his studies at the local school in Orange and graduating from Williams College, he returned to the Western Reserve Eclectic Institute (later Hiram College) and assumed the duties of teacher and later principal. Garfield studied law on his own and passed the Ohio bar exams in 1861 before throwing himself into politics and winning a seat in the Ohio legislature. Garfield was a loyal Unionist who built a reputation as a Civil War hero and earned him a seat in the House of Representatives without campaigning.

> The people of this country have shown by the highest proofs human nature can give that wherever the path of duty and honor may lead, however steep and rugged it may be, they are ready to walk in it. They summed up and perfected, by one supreme act, the highest virtue of men and citizens. For love of country, they accepted death, and thus re-solved all doubts, and made immortal their patriotism and their virtue.
>
> James Garfield

When he left his position to become president, he said, "I resign the highest office in the land to become President of the United States." However, as Garfield only got to be president for six months before his death (he was assassinated by a religious zealot), there wasn't much time for him to demonstrate divine pursuits while in office.

With his natural speaking ability, Garfield soon found himself in the political arena. In 1859 he was elected to the Ohio state senate. As the United States neared the civil war, Garfield put his speaking abilities to work for the Union, recruiting men and raising troops for battle. He eventually became a brigadier general during the Civil War before being elected in absentia as a US Congressman.

"The men who succeed best in public life are those who take the risk of standing by their own convictions" (James Garfield).

Now faith is the *assurance* [*hupostasis*—that which is the basis of something, hence, assurance, guarantee, confidence] of things hoped for, the *conviction* [*elegchos*—certain persuasion] of things not seen.

Hebrews 11:1
(emphasis added by the author)

Now more than ever before, the people are responsible for the character of their Congress. If that body is ignorant, reckless, and corrupt, it is because the people tolerate ignorance, recklessness, and corruption. If it be intelligent, brave and pure, it is because the people demand these high qualities to represent them in the national legislature ...If the next centennial does not find us a great nation ...it will be because those who represent the enterprise, the culture, and the morality of the nation do not aid in controlling the political forces.

James Garfield

He who walks righteously and *speaks with sincerity*, He who rejects unjust gain And shakes his hands so that they hold no bribe; He who stops his ears from hearing about bloodshed And shuts his eyes from looking upon evil; He will dwell on the heights, His refuge will be the impregnable rock; *His bread will be given him, His water will be sure.*

Isaiah 33:15–16
(emphasis added by the author)

"I never met a ragged boy in the street without feeling that I may owe him a salute, for I know not what possibilities may be buttoned up under his coat" (James Garfield).

"I so despise a man who blows his own horn that I go to the other extreme" (James Garfield).

"If wrinkles must be written upon our brows, let them not be written upon the heart. The spirit should not grow old" (James Garfield).

"Poverty is uncomfortable, but nine times out of ten the best thing that can happen to a young man is to be tossed overboard and compelled to sink or swim" (James Garfield).

"If you are not too large for the place you occupy, you are too small for it" (James Garfield).

"If the power to do hard work is not a skill, it's the best possible substitute for it" (James Garfield).

"If there is one thing upon this earth that mankind love and admire better than another, it is a brave man; it is the man who dares to look the devil in the face and tell him he is a devil" (James Garfield).

> O Lord, who may abide in Your tent? Who may dwell on Your holy hill? He who walks with *integrity* [wholesome, innocent, having integrity], and works righteousness, And speaks truth in his heart. He does not slander with his tongue, Nor does evil to his neighbor, Nor takes up a reproach against his friend; In whose eyes a reprobate is despised, But who honors those who fear the Lord; *He swears to his own hurt and does not change*; He does not put out his money at interest, Nor does he take a bribe against the innocent. *He who does these things will never be shaken.*
>
> Psalm 15
> (emphasis added by the author)

> There are men and women who make the world better just by being the kind of people they are. They have the gift of kindness or courage or loyalty or integrity. It matters very little whether they are behind the wheel of a truck, running a business, or bringing up a family. They teach the truth by living it.
>
> James Garfield

> For the Lord God is a sun and shield; The Lord gives grace and glory; No good thing does He withhold from those who *walk uprightly.* O Lord of hosts, *How blessed is the man who trusts in You*!
>
> Psalm 84:11–12
> (emphasis added by the author)

James Garfield lived and died as a man of integrity who stood by his biblical convictions and treated others with dignity and class. We can learn much today from his life. The dictionary defines integrity as "the quality of being honest and having strong moral principles; moral uprightness." The world needs more men and women who stand for something of value, who live their lives looking above, with accountability to a higher authority. Like Moses, Hebrews 11:27 says (emphasis added by the author), "By faith he left Egypt, not fearing the wrath of the king; for he endured, as seeing Him who is unseen."

Chapter 48: William Tyndale—
A Portrait of Devotion

We laud many heroes throughout human history for their great accomplishments. Whether referring to scientific discovery (Sir Isaac Newton, for example), political conquests (Alexander the Great), social justice reform (Martin Luther King), or religious expression (Moses), there are so many more names that have played an integral part in human achievements whose names we may never know. Throughout the development and maturation of Christianity over the last two millennia, many have contributed immeasurably to the revelation of Jesus Christ throughout the church age, yet many accomplishments may never be remembered. They are the unsung heroes of our faith. Without them, Christianity would be far less than it is today. Just read a few pages of *Foxe's Book of Martyrs* to get a flavor of what I mean. God uses many without fanfare, and they may be as important as or even more important than the ones we know.

I recently read a great book about William Tyndale, one of the incredible Protestant reformers of the sixteenth century, entitled *The Daring Mission of William Tyndale* by Steven Lawson. When you think of the Protestant Reformation, the names that first come to mind are Martin Luther, John Calvin, Ulrich Zwingli, John Knox, etc. Those responsible for translating the Bible into English, including John Wycliffe and William Tyndale, seem to be considered of lesser importance. Yet both of these men had a deep conviction to provide the average person with the truth of God's Word in his English language, and both were willing to pay the ultimate price. This was during times when the Roman Catholic church exercised great authority over society and wished to keep the people in spiritual darkness.

Who Is William Tyndale?

I am particularly impressed by Tyndale's scholarship; a graduate of Oxford and the University of Cambridge and a master of eight languages, including Greek and Hebrew. This gift was used by God not only to translate Scripture but, just as importantly, to help refine the English language from its Anglo-Saxon roots. According to David Rolph Seely,

> His English translations of the Bible provided the basis for the King James Translation, and through his translations, Tyndale became one of the founders of the modern English language. In translating the Bible from Hebrew and Greek into English, Tyndale coined several new English words—transforming older English words or, in some cases, inventing unique and striking new English words—that have since become central terms in religious discourse. From a study of just a few of these words, we can better understand Tyndale's genius for language, his methodology, and his theology. We can also gain insight into the complexity of translation. But, most importantly, we can better appreciate the gift Tyndale gave to English speakers: the word of God in our own language.

In 1523, Tyndale pursued getting approval from an English bishop to translate the Scriptures into English and was summarily turned down. Tyndale had been inspired by Martin Luther's 1522 New Testament translation into German. Knowing that he could not continue his passion in England, Tyndale traveled to Europe, most likely stopping in Wittenberg early on to meet Luther himself. Tyndale had been bitten by the reformation bug and committed himself to his translating work at all costs. He spent the last eleven years of his life remaining incommunicado so his enemies would not derail the divine work. He traveled from city to city throughout Germany and Belgium, not allowing any pictures created of his likeness and using pseudonyms instead of his real name. He was finally arrested in Belgium in 1535 and was executed in the exact location in 1536 by strangulation and burning. William Tyndale is a quintessential unsung hero of the Protestant Reformation.

Integral in the Protestant Reformation

During those years, Tyndale translated into English the New Testament (and revised editions) and large portions of the Old Testament that were published posthumously by others. The impact of his work on the movement of God to bring the Scriptures to the people at large cannot be understated. King Henry VIII authorized that English translations of the Bible written by Tyndale and others be published within ten years of Tyndale's death. The King James (Authorized) Version was published in 1611, and it is estimated that 84 percent of the New Testament and 76 percent of the Old Testament can be attributable to Tyndale's work. These translations were integral in spreading the gospel to America and other parts of the British Empire. Tyndale was not seeking any glory for himself and early understood that it would cost him his life, but he accepted the divine call without reservation.

In Tyndale's day, the Roman Catholic church and the various monarchies ruled with iron fists, not allowing free expression of ideas, particularly those opposing the authorities. Anyone standing against those authorities risked everything. We find that throughout church history, the times of most extraordinary spiritual growth resulted from strong persecution, and the first half of the sixteenth century represented a period of great spiritual awakening. In the twenty-first century, we find increasing public opposition to our Christian heritage; therefore, believers require a deeper commitment to walk in and "publish" the truth. The stronger the opposition, the more faith in God and His plan deepen in the one willing to risk it all. Consider the words of the song "The River," written and performed by Steve Green:

> There's a river ever flowing, widening, never slowing
> And all who wade out in are swept away.
> When it ends, where it's going, like the wind no way of knowing.
> Until we answer the call to risk it all and enter in
>
> The river calls, we can't deny, a step of faith is our reply
> We feel the spirit draw us in, the water's swift, we're forced to swim
> We're out of control, and we go where he flows.

Ezekiel 47 reveals the river that Steve Green speaks of, which flows out from underneath the temple, getting deeper and deeper as one is further away from the temple. In verse 9,

It will come about that every living creature which swarms in every place where the river goes will live. And there will be very many fish, for these waters go there and the others become fresh; so everything will live where the river goes.

This is a picture of the spiritual life the believer experiences when he chooses to follow the Holy Spirit at any cost. Not knowing where the Spirit takes him is not an issue; he has chosen this course out of devotion to a higher purpose. New life experiences are around every bend; as Steve Green continues,

Danger awaits at every turn; we choose a course, we live and learn
As we surrender to His will, we're at peace, but we're seldom still
He is in control, and we go where he flows.

The apostle Paul understood the principle of being an unsung hero. Galatians 6:14, "But may it never be that I would boast, except in the cross of our Lord Jesus Christ, through which has been crucified to me, and I to the world." The spiritual life is not concerned with personal recognition or accolades but exalts the purposes of God without regret. Paul acknowledged his own spiritual bankruptcy, recognizing that the life of Christ was his highest priority, not earned but received by His grace. In 1 Corinthians 15:9–10, he said,

For I am the least of the apostles, and not fit to be called an apostle, because I persecuted the church of God. But by the grace of God I am what I am, and His grace toward me did not prove vain; but I labored even more than all of them, yet not I, but the grace of God with me.

Although we get to read about Paul and his life in the Bible, after his conversion in Acts 9, he did nothing to gain any personal recognition. He called all those individual gifts and accomplishments rubbish (Philippians 3:8).

Publishing the Truth

God is looking for more William Tyndale's who are ready to step up to the unique call of God, believing that God will empower them to fulfill each call through His divine ability. For example, 2 Chronicles 16:9 says, "For the eyes of the Lord move to and fro throughout the earth that He may strongly support those whose heart is completely His." This call includes "publishing" (heralding, declaring) the gospel to a lost and dying world no matter what. We may not be tasked with the challenge of translating Scripture as Tyndale was, but we can be God's communicators of the truth as the church anticipates the return of Christ at any moment.

CHAPTER 49: FILLING MAN'S POVERTY WITH GOD'S RICHES

E. M. Bounds, a nineteenth-century Methodist Episcopal church pastor, wrote several definitive books dealing with the discipline of prayer that are considered classics. Upon his retirement as pastor in 1894, he spent his final seventeen years engaged in intercessory prayer, writing, and itinerant revival ministry. He would typically arise at 4 a.m. to be alone with God in prayer until 7 a.m. and was indefatigable in his study of the Bible. Because Bounds so diligently practiced what he preached, he captured the essence of prayer, and his works live on as a testimony of the importance of prayer in a Christian's life. According to Bounds, "The story of every great Christian achievement is the history of answered prayer."

God's Abundance

Prayer is the contact of a living soul with God. In prayer, God stoops to kiss man, to bless man, and to aid man in everything that God can devise, or man can need. Prayer fills man's emptiness with God's fullness. It fills man's poverty with God's riches. It puts away man's weakness with God's strength. It banishes man's littleness with God's greatness. Prayer is God's plan to supply man's great and continuous need with God's great and continuous abundance.

E. M. Bounds

To receive the full abundance of God's supply, the believer must begin where he believes that God is capable of meeting every need and that He also desires to do it. Jesus said that "with God, all things are possible" (Matthew 19:26) and "apart from Me you can do nothing" (John 15:5). These statements bring us to the understanding that God is capable, and we are not, so we need Him. And how often do we pray, not knowing what we need? Paul tells us that the Holy Spirit helps us by interpreting our groanings on behalf of the Father and the Son (Romans 8:26–27). These realities remove the act of praying from the mundane obligation to appease conscience and bring prayer into a higher experience, an actual communion with the God of all grace (1 Peter 5:10).

Ask

James 1:5, "But if any of you lacks wisdom, let him ask of God, who gives to all generously and without reproach, and it will be given to him." So much of the Christian's shortages come not from his bankruptcy but rather from his unwillingness to ask. A generous God is anxiously waiting to demonstrate His generosity. James 4:2 says you do not have because you do not ask. The New Testament is filled with verses addressing the importance of asking God for the things God desires to give. It starts with our willingness to believe that God wants to give. When the believer asks in prayer and believing, then the answer will follow (Matthew 21:22). Then there is John 14:13 (emphasis added by the author), "Whatever you ask *in My name*, that will I do." In the character and the ability of God, prayer places its faith. The impossible answer can only come from the God of the impossible.

James 5:16 tells us that the effective prayer of a righteous man who lives by faith (Romans 1:17) can accomplish much. This Greek word translated as effective is *energeo*, from which we get the English word energy, which means that this prayer is working and operative. Jesus warns the religious man of the meaningless repetition of prayer and that his repetition of words or phrases will carry no weight with God. They will not work (Matthew 6:7). In the same passage, Jesus teaches that the righteous one who prays is not looking for recognition from others, but the prayer comes from an inner room where no one is watching. Those prayers have rewards attached to them.

Your Father Knows

Jesus also said in Matthew 6:8 that "your Father knows what you need before you ask Him." Prayer is the believer's communion with God around something He already knows. But for what purpose? In Isaiah

65:24, "It will also come to pass that before they call, I will answer; and while they are still speaking, I will hear." It means that God knows what we need before we do, and we can trust Him to solve our situation. Although the context of Isaiah 65 is the millennial kingdom, it also speaks to new covenant believers in the church age. It means that His throne is a throne of grace, so we can have confidence that God's provision is never earned or deserved, but the answer comes in the exact time of need based on His grace and mercy (Hebrews 4:16).

> Prayer is a solemn service due to God, an adoration, a worship, an approach to God for some request, the presenting of some desire, the expression of some need to Him who supplies all need and who satisfies all desires, who, as a Father, finds his greatest pleasure in relieving the wants and granting the desires of his children. Prayer is the child's request, not to the winds nor to the world, but to the Father. Prayer is the outstretched arms of the child for the Father's help. Prayer is the child's cry calling to the Father's ear, the Father's heart, and to the Father's ability, which the Father is to hear, the Father is to feel, and which the Father is to relieve.
>
> E. M. Bounds

Divine Solutions

It took a real commitment to prayer to bring E. M. Bounds to a deeper appreciation of its importance, the intimacy it brings the believer, and the expectation for divine solutions it creates. Depending on the situation, prayer can be a time of meditation, solitude, and, at other times, a wrestling match. In any case, prayer opens access to the riches of heaven like no other activity can afford. It is hard work with an eternal return.

John Newton, who wrote "Amazing Grace," wrote many other poems that became hymns. One of them is below, speaking to God's commitment to answer man's prayers:

> Begone unbelief, my Savior is near.
> And for my relief shall surely appear.
> By prayer let me wrestle, and He will perform.
> With Christ in the vessel, I smile at the storm.
> Though dark be my way since He is my guide,
> 'Tis mine to obey, 'tis His to provide.

Though cisterns be broken, and creatures all fail,
The Word He has spoken shall surely prevail.

Chapter 50: Martin Luther King— The Drum Major Instinct

We have been celebrating the life of Martin Luther King on a national level since Congress passed a bill recognizing his birthday, January 15, as a national holiday in 1983. It is appropriate that America recognize and remember the man and his accomplishments, especially regarding  civil rights. From this celebration, Americans have come to know some of his most famous speeches, many referenced at the Martin Luther King, Jr. Memorial in Washington, DC. In addition, since MLK was also a Baptist minister, many of his sermons have also been memorialized. One of these messages was preached in Atlanta at Ebenezer Baptist Church on February 4, 1968, two months to the day before his death.

King's sermon was an adaptation of the 1952 homily "Drum-Major Instincts" by J. Wallace Hamilton, a well-known, liberal, white Methodist preacher. Both men tell the biblical story of James and John, who ask Jesus for the most prominent seats in heaven in Mark 10:35–45:

> James and John, the two sons of Zebedee, came up to Jesus, saying, "Teacher, we want You to do for us whatever we ask of You." And He said to them, "What do you want Me to do for you?" They said to Him, "Grant that we may sit, one on Your right and one on Your left, in Your glory." But Jesus said to them, "You do not know what you are asking. Are you able to drink the cup that I drink, or to be baptized with the baptism with which I am baptized?" They said to Him, "We are able." And Jesus said to them, "The cup that I drink you shall drink, and you shall be baptized with the baptism with which I

am baptized. But to sit on My right or on My left, this is not Mine to give; but it is for those for whom it has been prepared." Hearing this, the ten began to feel indignant with James and John. Calling them to Himself, Jesus *said to them, "You know that those who are recognized as rulers of the Gentiles lord it over them; and their great men exercise authority over them. But it is not this way among you, but whoever wishes to become great among you shall be your servant, and whoever wishes to be first among you shall be slave of all. *For even the Son of Man did not come to be served, but to serve, and to give His life a ransom for many."*

Mark 10:35–45
(emphasis added by the author)

At the core of their desire was a "drum major instinct—a desire to be out front, a desire to lead the parade." King warns his congregation that this desire for importance can lead to "snobbish exclusivism" and "tragic race prejudice:" "Do you know that a lot of the race problem grows out of the drum major instinct? A need that some people have to feel superior …and to feel that their white skin ordained them to be first." Conversely, King preached that when Jesus responded to the request of James and John, he did not rebuke them for their ambition but taught that greatness comes from humble servitude. As King put it, Jesus "reordered priorities" and told his disciples to "keep feeling the need for being first. But I want you to be first in love."

This message can appropriately apply to each one of us. There is a natural tendency for man to pursue some recognition or fame to find significance. Man needs to recognize that this force exists and should not allow it to take control. According to his message:

> And so, before we condemn them, let us see that we all have the drum major instinct. We all want to be important, surpass others, achieve distinction, and lead the parade. Alfred Adler, the great psychoanalyst, contends this is the dominant impulse. Sigmund Freud used to contend that sex was the dominant impulse, and Adler came up with a new argument saying that this quest for recognition, this desire for attention.

This problem is tied to our human nature. It is confirmed by the apostle Paul in Ephesians 2:1–6 when he states that there is an energy behind it, tied to "the prince of the power of the air" who exercises significant influence over the unregenerate man:

> And you were dead in your trespasses and sins, in which you formerly walked according to the course of this world, according to the prince of the power of the air, of the spirit that is now working in the sons of disobedience. Among them we too all formerly lived in the lusts of our flesh, indulging the desires of the flesh and of the mind, and were by nature children of wrath, even as the rest. *But God*, being rich in mercy, because of His great love with which He loved us, even when we were dead in our transgressions, made us alive together with Christ (by grace you have been saved), and raised us up with Him, and seated us with Him in the heavenly places in Christ Jesus.
>
> Ephesians 2:1–6
(emphasis added by the author)

According to MLK:

> There comes a time that the drum major instinct can become destructive. And that's where I want to move now. I want to move to the point of saying that if this instinct is not harnessed, it becomes a very dangerous, pernicious instinct. For instance, if it isn't harnessed, it causes one's personality to become distorted. I guess that's the most damaging aspect of it: what it does to the personality. If it isn't harnessed, you will end up day in and day out trying to deal with your ego problem by boasting. Have you ever heard people that—you know, and I'm sure you've met them—that really become sickening because they just sit up all the time talking about themselves. And they just boast and boast and boast, and that's the person who has not harnessed the drum major instinct.

The solution is found in the life of Jesus Christ and man's relationship with Him. Paul tells us that the only permanent victory over this power is a living faith in what Jesus accomplished 2,000 years ago. Ephesians 2:8, "For by grace are you saved through faith; and that not of yourselves, it is the gift of God." But this problem is not solved by any membership in the church. The religious man can learn to talk the talk, but walking the walk is a different matter. MLK says:

And you know, that can happen with the church; I know churches get in that bind sometimes. I've been to churches, you know, and they say, "We have so many doctors, and so many schoolteachers, and so many lawyers, and so many businessmen in our church." And that's fine, because doctors need to go to church, and lawyers, and businessmen, teachers—they ought to be in church. But they say that—even the preacher sometimes will go all through that—they say that as if the other people don't count.

And the church is the one place where a doctor ought to forget that he's a doctor. The church is the one place where a Ph.D. ought to forget that he's a Ph.D. The church is the one place that the schoolteacher ought to forget the degree she has behind her name. The church is the one place where the lawyer ought to forget that he's a lawyer. And any church that violates the "whosoever will, let him come" doctrine is a dead, cold church, and nothing but a little social club with a thin veneer of religiosity.

King recognizes this syndrome not only in the church but also prevalent in America in his day.

But God has a way of even putting nations in their place. The God that I worship has a way of saying, "Don't play with me." He has a way of saying, as the God of the Old Testament used to say to the Hebrews, "Don't play with me, Israel. Don't play with me, Babylon. Be still and know that I'm God. And if you don't stop your reckless course, I'll rise up and break the backbone of your power." And that can happen to America. Every now and then, I go back and read Gibbons' *Decline and Fall of the Roman Empire*. And when I come and look at America, I say to myself, the parallels are frightening. And we have perverted the drum major instinct.

This condition of religiosity can only be properly addressed in man's acceptance that the Law cannot bring one to intimacy with Christ since, apart from Christ, it only produces self-righteousness. In Galatians 3:23–29,

But before faith came, we were kept in custody under the law, being shut up to the faith which was later to be revealed. Therefore, the Law has become our tutor to lead us to Christ, so that we may be justified by faith. But now that faith has come, we are no longer under a tutor.

For you are all sons of God through faith in Christ Jesus. *For all of you who were baptized into Christ have clothed yourselves with Christ.* There is neither Jew nor Greek, there is neither slave nor free man, there is neither male nor female; for you are all one in Christ Jesus. And if you belong to Christ, then you are Abraham's descendants, heirs according to promise.

Galatians 3:23–29
(emphasis added by the author)

Jesus taught in the original passage that the key to our victory in Christ is found in our willingness to become a servant. He was teaching a new definition of greatness, according to Dr. King:

And so, Jesus gave us a new norm of greatness. If you want to be important—wonderful. If you want to be recognized—wonderful. If you want to be great—wonderful. But recognize that he who is greatest among you shall be your servant. That's a new definition of greatness.

MLK ends his message by referencing his funeral and how he wished to be remembered. How prophetic were his words:

If any of you are around when I have to meet my day, I don't want a long funeral. And if you get somebody to deliver the eulogy, tell them not to talk too long. And every now and then I wonder what I want them to say. Tell them not to mention that I have a Nobel Peace Prize—that isn't important. Tell them not to mention that I have three or four hundred other awards—that's not important. Tell them not to mention where I went to school. I'd like somebody to mention that day that Martin Luther King, Jr., tried to give his life serving others.

In 1 Corinthians 9:19 (emphasis added by the author), Paul says, "For though I am free from all men, *I have made myself a slave to all, so that I may win more.*" Dr. King closes his message with these words:

Yes, Jesus, I want to be on your right or your left side, not for any selfish reason. I want to be on your right or your left side, not in terms of some political kingdom or ambition. But I just want to be there in love and in justice and in truth and in commitment to others, so that we can make of this old world a new world.

Chapter 51: Practicing the Presence of the Lord

"You will make known to me the path of life; In Your presence is fullness of joy; In Your right hand there are pleasures forever" (Psalm 16:11).

An important book that addresses a Christian's daily relationship with God was written more than 300 years ago by a man we know as Brother Lawrence. The book was written posthumously and captured the essence of his pursuit of a joyous walk with God. That book was *The Practice of the Presence of the Lord – The Best Rule of Holy Life*, and that relationship centered on recognizing God's personal love for him.

He began life as Nicholas Herman, born to peasant parents in Lorraine, France (1611–1691). As a young man, his poverty forced him into joining the Army, and thus he was guaranteed meals and a small stipend. During this period, Herman had an experience that set him on a unique spiritual journey; it wasn't, characteristically, a supernatural vision but a supernatural clarity into a common sight.

In the deep of winter, Herman looked at a barren tree stripped of leaves and fruit, waiting silently and patiently for the sure hope of summer abundance. Gazing at the tree, Herman grasped for the first time the extravagance of God's grace and the unfailing sovereignty of divine providence. Like the tree, he himself was seemingly dead, but God had life waiting for him, and the turn of seasons would bring fullness. At that moment, he said, that leafless tree "first flashed in upon my soul the fact of God" and a love for God that never after ceased to burn. Sometime later, an injury forced his retirement from the Army, and after a stint as a footman, he sought a place where he could suffer for his failures. He thus entered the Discalced Carmelite monastery in Paris as Brother Lawrence.

"I began to live as if there were no one save God and me in the world."

Lawrence cultivated a simple way of communing with God in his everyday duties of cooking, cleaning pots and pans, and whatever else called upon to do, which he termed "practicing the presence of God." Lawrence saw everything he did, whether it was spiritual devotions, church worship, running errands, counseling, and listening to people, no matter how mundane or tedious, as a way of expressing God's love.

> Since then, he had passed his life in perfect liberty and continual joy. That he placed his sins betwixt him and GOD, as it were, to tell Him that he did not deserve His favors, but that GOD still continued to bestow them in abundance.

Fullness of God's Presence

Lawrence began to view every little detail of his life as vitally important in his relationship with God. His exuberance, genuine humility, inner joy, and peace attracted people from near and far. Both church leaders and common folk sought Lawrence for spiritual guidance and prayer. Lawrence understood that the attitude and motivation of the heart were keys to *experiencing the fullness of God's presence at all times.*

> That as he knew his obligation to love GOD in all things, and as he endeavored so to do, he did not need a director to advise him, but he needed much a confessor to absolve him. He was very sensible of his faults but not discouraged by them; he confessed them to GOD and did not plead against Him to excuse them. When he had so done, he peaceably resumed his usual practice of love and adoration.

> He had consulted nobody in his trouble of mind but knowing only by the light of faith that GOD was present, he contented himself with directing all his actions to Him, i.e., doing them with a desire to please Him, let what would come of it.

Hiding from God

Man has a natural tendency to hide from God after failing, as is the testimony of Adam and Eve given in Genesis 3:8 (emphasis added by the author), "They heard the sound of the Lord God walking in the garden in the cool of the day, and the man and his wife *hid from the presence of the Lord God* among the trees of the garden." Their first son, Cain, was banished from the presence of the Lord for his act of murder against his brother (Genesis 4:16). It takes courage to face failure and to trust God for His willingness to accept man despite his weaknesses.

God would address this matter in Numbers 15:37–41 by introducing tassels added to the corners of the peoples' garments as a reminder to keep their focus on God and His Word. In verses 39–40 (emphasis added by the author),

> It shall be a tassel for you to look at and remember all the commandments of the Lord, so as *to do them and not follow after your own heart and your own eyes*, after which you played the harlot, so that you may remember to do all My commandments and be holy to your God.

They were a reminder of both their wicked hearts and the victory that comes from keeping His commandments to *be holy to your God.*

> That useless thoughts spoil all: that the mischief began there; but that we ought to reject them, as soon as we perceived their impertinence to the matter in hand or our salvation; and return to our communion with GOD.

> To form a habit of conversing with GOD continually and referring all we do to Him; we must at first apply to Him with some diligence: but after a little care, we should find His love inwardly excites us to it without any difficulty.

Jesus taught the masses in the Sermon on the Mount that "blessed are the pure in heart, *for they shall see God*" (Matthew 5:8) (emphasis added by the author). This purity of heart is all about honesty and transparency, with nothing withheld. According to Brother Lawrence,

> That we ought to act with GOD in the greatest simplicity, speaking to Him frankly and plainly, and imploring His assistance in our affairs, just as they happen. That GOD never failed to grant it, as he had often experienced.

The Secret Place

King David recognized the value of living in God's presence, in His sanctuary, as a place of worship and sweet fellowship around His Word and wonder. In Psalm 27:4–5 (emphasis added by the author),

One thing I have asked from the Lord, that I shall seek: That I may dwell in the house of the Lord all the days of my life, To behold the beauty of the Lord And to meditate in His temple. For in the day of trouble He will conceal me in His tabernacle; *In the secret place of His tent, He will hide me*; He will lift me up on a rock.

This place is his secret place and his place of protection.

We can do little things for God; I turn the cake that is frying on the pan for love of him, and that done, if there is nothing else to call me, I prostrate myself in worship before him, who has given me the grace to work; afterward, I rise happier than a king. It is enough for me to pick up but a straw from the ground for the love of God.

Men invent means and methods of coming at God's love, they learn rules and set up devices to remind them of that love, and it seems like a world of trouble to bring oneself into the consciousness of God's presence. Yet it might be so simple. Is it not quicker and easier just to do our common business wholly for the love of him?

Tests of Faith

You have tried my heart; You have visited me by night; You have tested me, and You find nothing; *I have purposed* that my mouth will not transgress. As for the deeds of men, by the word of Your lips I have kept from the paths of the violent. My steps have held fast to Your paths. My feet have not slipped. I have called upon You, for You will answer me, O God; incline Your ear to me, hear my speech. Wondrously show Your lovingkindness, O Savior of those who take refuge at Your right hand from those who rise up against them. Keep me as the apple of the eye; *hide me in the shadow of Your wings* from the wicked who despoil me, my deadly enemies who surround me. They have closed their unfeeling heart; with their mouth they speak proudly. They have now surrounded us in our steps; they set their eyes to cast us down to the ground. He is like a lion that is eager to tear, And as a young lion lurking in hiding places. Arise, O Lord, confront him, bring him low; deliver my soul from the wicked with Your sword, from men with Your hand, O Lord, From men of the world, whose portion is in this life, and whose belly You fill with Your treasure; they are satisfied with children, and leave their abundance to their babes. As for me, *I shall behold Your face in righteousness; I will be satisfied with Your likeness when I awake.*

Psalm 17:3–15
(emphasis added by the author)

David uttered this prayer amid some present danger as a means of thankfulness to God's tests to establish and confirm David's integrity. He says his willingness to "purpose" to avoid transgressions and to "hold fast to Your paths" gave him his confidence. When David called upon the Lord, He would answer and show Himself faithful. Practicing the presence of God produced in David the sense that he was the apple of God's eye, and that God hid him in His shadow. Colossians 3:3–4, "For you have died and your life is hidden with Christ in God. When Christ, who is our life, is revealed, then you also will be revealed with Him in glory." As David declares in verse 15 above, "As for me, I shall behold Your face in righteousness; I will be satisfied with Your likeness when I awake."

Chapter 52: Wittenberg—Worms—Wartburg

The story of Martin Luther's importance to the Protestant Reformation can be summed up in three places, representing three significant events in his life. These include Wittenberg, where he nailed his Ninety-five Theses on the door of its church; Worms, where he defended his faith in front of the secular authorities; and Wartburg, where he hid for nearly a year and translated the Bible from Latin to German, the language of the people.

A Catholic priest, Martin Luther became increasingly disenchanted with many practices of the Roman Catholic church. As a professor of theology, he was a trained academic who spent a great deal of time studying the Scriptures and was beginning to question the church's position on salvation. He took a trip to Rome in 1511 when he began to question his spirituality seriously. Luther was bothered by the luxurious living, the loose morals, and the lack of interest in spiritual things among the monks they visited. At the same time, he had a major problem with the church selling indulgences (paying for the absolution of sins) to raise funds for St. Peter's Basilica. As a result of these questions, he wrote his Ninety-five Theses, which challenged the church's practices and spirituality.

Wittenberg

On 31 October 1517, Luther wrote to his bishop, Albrecht von Brandenburg, protesting the sale of indulgences. In his letter, He enclosed a copy of his "Disputation of Martin Luther on the Power and Efficacy of Indulgences," which came to be known as the Ninety-five Theses. Hans Hillerbrand writes that Luther had no intention of confronting the church but saw his disputation as a scholarly objection to church practices. He wanted to challenge the church leadership to change its practices; he was not interested in leaving.

The verse that brought Luther to his knees and to doubt church doctrine on salvation was Romans 1:17, "For in it [the gospel] the righteousness of God is revealed from faith to faith; as it is written, 'BUT THE RIGHTEOUS man SHALL LIVE BY FAITH.'" Paul quoted Habakkuk 2:4, where the contrast is made between the proud one, whose soul is not right, and the righteous man, who lives by his faith. Luther was coming to understand that salvation (and, by extension, righteousness) is a faith decision, made from one decision to believe the gospel and then to another and another. It is a personal decision and has nothing to do with the church.

Worms

The church leadership did not respond well to Luther's challenges. Instead, Pope Leo X issued the Papal bull *Exsurge Domine* ("Arise, O Lord"), outlining forty-one purported errors found in Martin Luther's Ninety-five Theses and other writings related to or written by him. His refusal to renounce all of his writings at the demand of Pope Leo X in 1520 and the Holy Roman Emperor Charles V at the Diet of Worms in 1521 resulted in his excommunication by the Pope and condemnation as an outlaw by the Holy Roman Emperor.

The enforcement of the ban on the Ninety-five Theses fell to the secular authorities. Luther appeared as ordered before the Diet of Worms, a general assembly of the estates of the Holy Roman Empire that took place in Worms with Emperor Charles V presiding in 1521. Luther received a safe conduct passage to and from the meeting. His response to the inquisition was the following:

> Unless I am convinced by the testimony of the Scriptures or by clear reason (for I do not trust either in the pope or in councils alone, since it is well known that they have often erred and contradicted themselves), I am bound by the Scriptures I have quoted, and my conscience is captive to the Word of God. I cannot and will not recant anything since it is neither safe nor right to go against conscience. May God help me. Amen.

Wartburg

Plans were made for Luther's disappearance during his return to Wittenberg. Frederick III had him intercepted on his way home in the forest near Wittenberg by masked horsemen impersonating highway robbers. They escorted Luther to the security of the Wartburg Castle at Eisenach. During his stay at Wartburg, which he referred to as "*my Patmos*," Luther translated the New Testament from Greek into German and created several other doctrinal writings. These included a renewed attack on Archbishop Albrecht of Mainz, whom he shamed into halting the sale of indulgences in his episcopates, and a "Refutation of the Argument of Latomus," in which he expounded the principle of justification. He was a resident of the castle from May 1521 to March 1522.

For many of us, major events have shaped our lives and their directions, and Martin Luther is no different. In his struggle to understand his shortcomings, Luther understood that the Scriptures and not the church had the solution to his dilemma. Once he saw the Scripture expose the church's illegitimate doctrines and actions, he could no longer be silent but expressed them at Wittenburg. The Diet of Worms was his willingness to defend his convictions at all costs, and Wartburg represents the seminal accomplishment of translating the Latin Vulgate into the German language so that the people could study the Scriptures and find the truth, just as he had done.

Beggars

A piece of paper was found after his death containing Luther's last words, ending with, "We are beggars: this is true."

Wittenburg, Worms, & Wartburg represent memorials in Luther's life to the power and presence of God in confronting the effects of hundreds of years of man-made religion. In each instance, God revealed that, despite intense opposition, the believer could rely on the divine ability to accomplish the divine will. It takes the realization that as beggars, we find our true purpose in Christ, as Jesus said in Matthew 5:3, "Blessed are the poor in spirit, for theirs is the kingdom of heaven."

REFERENCES

Ken Johnson, "Ancient Church Fathers; What the Disciples of the Apostles Taught." Copyright 2010.

R.C. Sproul, General Editor, "The Reformation Study Bible." Reformation Trust Publishing, 2016.

Milton Keynes UK
Ingram Content Group UK Ltd.
UKHW020939201123
432909UK00012B/289

John Buchan

THE COMPLETE SHORT STORIES
◆
Volume Two

John Buchan

THE COMPLETE SHORT STORIES

◆

Volume Two

Edited by

ANDREW LOWNIE

THISTLE PUBLISHING

First published in Great Britain in 1997 by
Thistle Publishing
122 Bedford Court Mansions
London WC1B 3AH

A CIP catalogue record for this book is available from the British Library

ISBN 0-9526756-5-X

Designed by Wendy Bann

Typeset by DP Photosetting, Aylesbury, Bucks

Printed and bound in England by Clays Limited, St Ives plc

Contents

Introduction by Andrew Lownie

The success of John Buchan's novels has overshadowed the fact that Buchan's early ambitions were as a short story writer. Three of his first eight books were collections of stories and a 1912 profile in *The Bookman* described him as 'probably the best modern exponent of the short story'. The stories included in this second volume were published between 1899, when Buchan left Oxford, and 1913, when his first 'shocker', *The Power House*, was published in serial form.

These years were among the most active and interesting of Buchan's life and this is apparent in the stories, which are set in such disparate locations as Scotland, the Aegean, Switzerland, Africa and London, and which reflect his interests in, among other things, mountaineering, the classical world, Africa and politics. Three stories are taken from his 1902 collection of short stories, *The Watcher by the Threshold*, eight from his third short story collection, *The Moon Endureth* (1912) and one, 'The Knees of the Gods', appears for the first time in book form.

On coming down from Oxford at the end of 1899 Buchan began to read for the Bar, but his interests remained literary. He had already begun his association with *Blackwood's Magazine* with the publication of his short story 'No-Man's Land' in January 1899, and now in May 1900 he sold his first article – a piece on Rabelais – to the *Spectator* where within a year he was deputising for the editor, J. St Loe Strachey. Both magazines were to be important outlets for his writing.

In spite of being called to the Bar, he remained frustrated by London life and in the summer of 1901 he accepted a job as Private Secretary to Alfred Milner, the High Commissioner for South Africa, to help in the work of reconstruction after the Boer War. His responsibilities, during the two years he spent on Milner's staff, ranged from the resettlement of those herded into the concentration camps to general land settlement, railway financing and acting as Secretary of the Inter-Colonial Council, the first stage in devolving some power to the two recently created colonies of the Transvaal and Orange River Colony.

South Africa was to be a formative influence, not just in his emotional and political maturing but in the inspiration it provided for his writing. Two of the stories in this volume – 'The Kings of Orion' and 'The Grove of Ashtaroth' – are set in South Africa and from the period come his account of the country's political history and geography, *The African Colony* (1903), his philosophical discussion novel about imperialism, *A Lodge in the Wilderness* (1906), and his Boy's Own adventure about Black Nationalism, *Prester John* (1910). His best-known fictional character, Richard Hannay in *The Thirty-Nine Steps* (1915), would be a South African mining engineer.

As a young man Buchan had spent many holidays walking and occasionally climbing in the Scottish hills, especially in Skye, and he had continued to climb while in South Africa. On his return, missing the outdoor life to which he had become so accustomed in South Africa, he joined both the Scottish Mountaineering and Alpine Clubs. Several of his novels have powerful climbing scenes, most notably *Prester John*, *Mr Standfast* (1919) and *The Three Hostages* (1924), and his interest in mountaineering is also reflected in two of the following short stories. 'Space' combines his fascination with the metaphysical teachings of Bergson and Poincaré with the practical difficulties of climbing the Chamonix Aiguilles to produce a haunting story about the nature of reality, while 'The Knees of the Gods' touches on the hallucinatory effects of climbing.

Buchan had met Susan Grosvenor, a relative of the Duke of Westminster, in the summer of 1905 and two years later they married at St George's in Hanover Square. It was to be a happy marriage, producing four children over the next eleven years. At the same time, realising he needed a more stable income than could be provided by the Bar and writing, Buchan took up an invitation to join the publishing firm Thomas Nelson. He also returned to his early love of politics and in March 1911 was adopted as the Prospective Unionist Candidate for Peebleshire and Selkirk, a large seat that stretched from the outskirts of Edinburgh almost to the English border. Two stories set in the area and written while nurturing the seat, 'The Green Glen' and 'The Riding of Ninemileburn', are included in this volume.

Throughout his life Buchan remained fascinated by the 'what-ifs' of history. It was the theme of his 1929 Rede lectures at Cambridge, published as *The Causal and Casual in History* (1929) and is evident in several novels such as *Midwinter* (1923) and *Blanket of the Dark* (1931).

'The Company of the Marjolaine' reveals how a visit to an Italian inn, shortly after American Independence, could have changed the course of American history, while 'The Lemnian' was inspired by a visit to the site of the Battle of Thermopylae in 1910.

Two interesting features of Buchan's short stories are the way he touches on themes and subjects he will later develop in his novels, and the consistency of his world-view. 'The Watcher by the Threshold' and 'The Outgoing of the Tide' are early prototypes of *Witch Wood* (1927); 'Fountainblue' has similarities with *The Half-Hearted* (1900) and looks forward to *Sick Heart River* (1941); while some of the ideas in *The Gap in the Curtain* (1932) can be found in 'Space'.

It is often assumed that Buchan's preoccupation with the fragility of civilisation comes after the First World War or from *The Power House* (1916) with Lumley's famous remark, 'You think that a wall as solid as the earth separates civilisation from barbarism. I tell you the division is a thread, a sheet of glass. A touch here, a push there, and you bring back the reign of Saturn.' In fact Maitland, the central figure in 'Fountainblue', a story writen in 1900, expresses his concern about the 'very narrow line between the warm room and the savage out-of-doors', adding, 'You call it miles of rampart; I call the division a line, a thread, a sheet of glass. But then, you see, you only know one side, and I only know the other.'

This theme of the precarious balance between the civilised and the primitive, already touched on in the early stories, becomes more explicit in this second volume of Buchan's stories. Where in the last volume the contrast has been between England and Scotland, it is now more often to be found between Britain and Africa. Many of his characters exhibit dual personalities, desperate to attune themselves to their primitive sides, especially the more conventionally successful they become. As one character in 'Fountainblue' remarks of Maitland, who turns his back on success to die forgotten in Africa, '. . . he saw our indoor civilisation and his own destiny in so sharp a contrast that he could not choose but make the severance'.

In *A Lodge in the Wilderness* (1906) Buchan had written about a Victorian statesman, Sir Charles Weston, a supporter of good causes and liberal reform who saw himself in his private fantasies as Emperor of Byzantium. Buchan described him as 'an allegory true of us all' and many of his stories are about the underside of our personalities. Ladlaw in 'The Watcher by the Threshold', 'a good landlord and respectable country gentleman, now appeared as a kind of horrible genius, a brilliant and malignant satyr' once possessed by the devil.

It is this dual personality, later to figure so prominently in Buchan's villains, to which one of the characters in 'The Kings of Orion' refers when he says, 'There's our ordinary self, generally rather humdrum; and then there's a bit of something else, good, bad, but never indifferent, – and it is that something else which may make a man a saint or a great villain.' Tommy Lascelles only finds greatness in himself when dealing with a native uprising in Africa; the Establishment in 'A Lucid Interval' are only able to break free of their repressions and hypocrisy under the influence of a truth drug; Maitland in 'Fountainblue' prefers to turn his back on success in this country in search of peace in Africa.

Many of the characters in these and subsequent stories are possessed by powerful atavistic urges as a reaction to the civilised lives they enjoy. Lawson in 'The Grove of Ashtaroth' is drawn to worshipping a primitive African goddess, while Maitland in 'Fountainblue' realises that 'the sad elemental world of wood and mountain was far more truly his own than this cosy and elegant civilisation.'

There is often a sacred place, *temenos*, in Buchan's writing, most obviously in the novels *Witch Wood* and *The Dancing Floor* (1926). It is also to be found in the short stories, either in Scotland as in 'The Green Glen' or in Africa as in 'The Grove of Ashtaroth'. Place is integral to plot and theme in Buchan, often personifying the border between the primitive and the civilised. As a review of *The Watcher by the Threshold* in the *Athenaeum* put it, 'The mountains are no mere piles of rock, they are the abodes of mystery, of romance, of haunting presences and insubstantial forms.' In that story, for example, the dark mysterious Perthshire woods at More are contrasted with the 'green pastoral country with bright streams and valleys' over the hills at Glenaicill.

While many of the stories have an element of mysticism to them, several such as 'The Knees of the Gods' and 'A Lucid Interval' look forward to the Dickson McCunn trilogy in being both light-hearted and satirical. One forgets just how epigrammatic Buchan can be. Lord Mulross in 'A Lucid Interval' felt 'The open season for grouse should be the close season for politicians,' while Hollond in 'Space' 'was the typical Cambridge man, you know – dogmatic about uncertainties, but curiously diffident about the obvious.' There is a certain playfulness about some of the stories here, both in the way he throws around ideas and uses the surnames of close friends, such as Maitland and Wyndham, for his characters.

And it is not only motifs that remain similar in both novels and stories but also characterisation. Linford in 'The Green Glen', like so many Buchan characters, feels, in spite of impeccable Establishment credentials, displaced. He may be 'a magnificent shot, a first-rate horseman, and the best man to sail a boat I have ever met' but he gives 'the impression of having no niche to fit into.' Maitland in 'Fountainblue' rejects fame and fortune in favour of an African Governorship, while Hollond in 'Space' cannot live in this world once he becomes aware of certain scientific knowledge.

Buchan adopts a variety of different narrative techniques in these stories. One is the use of a series of internal narrators, thereby giving greater credibility or bringing out some of the irony of the story. In 'Space' the narrator repeats a story told him by Leithen; in 'The Kings of Orion' the narrator listens to Thirlstone's tale about Tommy Lascelles; while in 'Fountainblue' the first-person narrative is towards the end replaced by a more epistolary approach. There is the sole first-person narrative, thereby investing the story with a certain immediacy as in 'The Grove of Ashtaroth', 'The Company of the Marjolaine' or 'The Green Glen'. Finally, as in 'The Outgoing of the Tide', 'The Lemnian' and 'The Riding of Ninemileburn', there is the distancing effect of the third-person narration.

The prose is unmistakably the Buchan of the subsequent novels, especially in his use of lists of people or exotic places to suggest the cosmopolitanism and importance of his characters. In 'The Kings of Orion' the narrator remembers of another character how 'I had last seen him on the quay at Funchal bargaining with some rascally boatman to take him after mythical wild goats in the Desertas. Before that we had met at an Embassy ball in Vienna, and still earlier at a hill station in Persia to which I had been sent post-haste by an anxious and embarrassed Government.' It is the same technique he will use ten years later in his 'shockers' when he casually mentions an inn on the Achensee in Tyrol, a fur shop in the Galician quarter of Buda, a club in Vienna and a bookshop off the Rackitzstrasse in Leipzig so the reader is immediately made to feel that of course they know these places too. Another technique, which he uses in 'A Lucid Interval', is to suggest the reader is privy to special and secret information by explaining that only a limited number of people actually know the truth of certain events.

A further link between these stories and the novels is the way that Buchan is already creating his own fictional world. Characters are introduced who will reappear in later novels such as the Clanroyden family in 'The Watcher by the Threshold' and 'Fountainblue', the Sempills in 'The Outgoing of the Tide', Lady Amysfort in 'The Green Glen' and the Manorwaters in 'The Company of the Marjolaine'. The same is true of places. Maitland in 'Fountainblue' has rooms in Albany where Lumley will live in *The Power House*; Castle Gay is mentioned in 'The Green Glen'; and Glenaicill makes its first appearance in 'The Watcher by the Threshold' and 'Space'.

Buchan's stories cannot be separated from his novels and are integral to our understanding of his fiction, yet they have received very little critical attention and many are not even recorded in the standard bibliographies. It is to be hoped that the publication of this volume and its two companions will bring his short stories to a wider audience than hitherto. In doing so it should demonstrate just how versatile Buchan is in the short story form. His contemporary reputation as a short story writer was high and though he may not be the equal of Kipling, his stories deserve to survive. The best of the stories in this volume are very good indeed.

The Watcher by the Threshold

'The Watcher by the Threshold' first appeared in *Blackwood's Magazine* and *The Atlantic Monthly* in December 1900 and became the title story of Buchan's second collection of stories, published by *Blackwood's* in 1902. It appeared in various Buchan story collections during his lifetime but its only recent publication has been in Peter Haining's *The Best Supernatural Stories of John Buchan* (1991). The version used here is the much shorter and less well-known one used by *The Atlantic Monthly*. The story may have been partly inspired by Bulwer-Lytton's 'Dweller of the Threshold' in his novel *Zanoni* (1842).

A CHILL EVENING in the early October of the year 189– found me driving in a dogcart through the belts of antique woodland which form the lowland limits of the hilly parish of More. The Highland express, which brought me from the north, took me no farther than Perth. Thence it had been a slow journey in a disjointed local train, till I emerged on the platform at Morefoot, with a bleak prospect of pot stalks, coal heaps, certain sour corn lands, and far to the west a line of moor where the sun was setting. A neat groom and a respectable trap took the edge off my discomfort, and soon I had forgotten my sacrifice and found eyes for the darkening landscape. We were driving through a land of thick woods, cut at rare intervals by old long-frequented highways. The More, which at Morefoot is an open sewer, became a sullen woodland stream, where the brown leaves of the season drifted. At times we would pass an ancient lodge, and through a gap in the trees would come a glimpse of chipped crowstep gable. The names of such houses, as told me by my companion, were all famous. This one had been the home of a drunken Jacobite laird, and a king of north country Medmenham. Unholy revels had waked the old halls, and the devil had been toasted at many a hell-fire dinner. The next was the property of a great Scots law family, and there the old Lord of Session, who built the place, in his frouzy wig and carpet slippers, had laid down the canons of Taste for his day and society. The whole country had the air of faded and bygone gentility. The mossy roadside walls had stood for two hundred years; the few wayside houses were toll bars or defunct hostelries. The names, too, were great: Scots baronial with a smack of France, – Chatelray and Riverslaw, Black Holm and Fountainblue. The place had a cunning charm, mystery dwelt in every cranny, and yet it did not please me. The earth smelt heavy and raw; the roads were red underfoot; all was old, sorrowful, and uncanny. Compared with the fresh Highland glen I had left, where wind and sun and flying showers were never absent, all was chilly and dull and dead. Even when the sun sent a shiver of crimson over the crests of certain firs, I felt no delight in the prospect. I admitted shamefacedly to myself that I was in a very bad temper.

I had been staying at Glenaicill with the Clanroydens, and for a week had found the proper pleasure in life. You know the house with its old rooms and gardens, and the miles of heather which defend it from the world. The shooting had been extraordinary for a wild place late in the season; for there are few partridges, and the woodcock are notoriously late. I had done respectably in my stalking, more than respectably on the river, and creditably on the moors. Moreover, there were pleasant people in the house – and there were the Clanroydens. I had had a hard year's work, sustained to the last moment of term, and a fortnight in Norway had been disastrous. It was therefore with real comfort that I had settled myself down for another ten days in Glenaicill, when all my plans were shattered by Sibyl's letter. Sibyl is my cousin and my very good friend, and in old days when I was briefless I had fallen in love with her many times. But she very sensibly chose otherwise, and married a man Ladlaw – Robert John Ladlaw, who had been at school with me. He was a cheery, good-humoured fellow, a great sportsman, a justice of the peace, and deputy lieutenant for his county, and something of an antiquary in a mild way. He had a box in Leicestershire to which he went in the hunting season, but from February till October he lived in his moorland home. The place was called the House of More, and I had shot at it once or twice in recent years. I remembered its loneliness and its comfort, the charming diffident Sibyl, and Ladlaw's genial welcome. And my recollections set me puzzling again over the letter which that morning had broken into my comfort. 'You promised us a visit this autumn,' Sibyl had written, 'and I wish you would come as soon as you can.' So far common politeness. But she had gone on to reveal the fact that Ladlaw was ill; she did not know how, exactly, but something, she thought, about his heart. Then she had signed herself my affectionate cousin, and then had come a short, violent postscript, in which, as it were, the fences of convention had been laid low. 'For Heaven's sake, come and see us,' she scrawled below. 'Bob is terribly ill, and I am crazy. Come at once.' To cap it she finished with an afterthought: 'Don't bother about bringing doctors. It is not their business.'

She had assumed that I would come, and dutifully I set out. I could not regret my decision, but I took leave to upbraid my luck. The thought of Glenaicill, with the woodcock beginning to arrive and the Clanroydens imploring me to stay, saddened my journey in the morning, and the murky, coaly, midland country of the afternoon completed my depression. The drive through the woodlands of More failed to raise my spirits. I was anxious about Sibyl and Ladlaw, and this accursed country had always given me a certain eeriness on my first approaching it. You may call it silly, but I have no nerves and am little susceptible to vague sentiment. It was sheer physical dislike of the rich deep soil, the woody and antique smells, the melancholy roads and trees, and the flavour of old mystery. I am aggressively healthy and wholly Philistine. I love clear outlines and strong colours, and More with its half tints and hazy distances depressed me miserably. Even when the road crept uphill and the trees ended, I found nothing to hearten me in the moorland which succeeded. It was genuine moorland, close on eight hundred feet above the sea, and through it ran this old grass-grown coach road. Low hills rose to the left, and to the right, after some miles of peat, flared the chimneys of pits and oil works. Straight in front the moor ran out into the horizon, and there in the centre was the last dying spark of the sun. The place was as still as the grave save for the crunch of our wheels on the grassy road, but the flaring lights to the north seemed to endow it with life. I have rarely had so keenly the feeling of movement in the inanimate world. It was an unquiet place, and I shivered nervously. Little gleams of loch came from the hollows, the burns were brown with peat, and every now and then there rose in the moor jags of sickening red stone. I remembered that Ladlaw had talked about the place as the old Manann, the holy land of the ancient races. I had paid little attention at the time, but now it struck me that the old peoples had been wise in their choice. There was something uncanny in this soil and air. Framed in dank mysterious woods and a country of coal and ironstone, at no great distance from the capital city, it was a sullen relic of a lost barbarism. Over the low hills lay a green pastoral country with bright streams and valleys, but here, in this peaty desert, there were few sheep and little cultivation. The House of More was the only dwelling, and, save for the ragged village, the wilderness was given over to the wild things of the hills. The shooting was good, but the best shooting on earth would not persuade me to make my abode in such a place. Ladlaw was ill; well, I did not wonder. You can have uplands without air, moors that are not health-giving, and a country life which is more arduous than a townsman's. I shivered again, for I seemed to have passed in a few hours from the open noon to a kind of dank twilight.

We passed the village and entered the lodge gates. Here there were trees again – little innocent new-planted firs, which flourished ill. Some large plane trees grew near the house, and there were thickets upon thickets of the ugly elderberry. Even in the half darkness I could see that the lawns were trim and the flower beds respectable for the season; doubtless Sibyl looked after the gardeners. The oblong whitewashed house, more like a barrack than ever, opened suddenly on my sight, and I experienced my first sense of comfort since I left Glenaicill. Here I should find warmth and company; and sure enough, the hall door was wide open, and in the great flood of light which poured from it Sibyl stood to welcome me.

She ran down the steps as I dismounted, and, with a word to the groom, caught my arm and drew me into the shadow. 'Oh, Henry, it was so good of you to come. You mustn't let Bob think that you know he is ill. We don't talk about it. I'll tell you afterwards. I want you to cheer him up. Now we must go in, for he is in the hall expecting you.'

While I stood blinking in the light, Ladlaw came forward with outstretched hand and his usual cheery greeting. I looked at him and saw nothing unusual in his appearance; a little drawn at the lips, perhaps, and heavy below the eyes, but still fresh-coloured and healthy. It was Sibyl who showed change. She was very pale, her pretty eyes were deplorably mournful, and in place of her delightful shyness there were the self-confidence and composure of pain. I was honestly shocked, and as I dressed my heart was full of hard thoughts about Ladlaw. What could his illness mean? He seemed well and cheerful, while Sibyl was pale; and yet it was Sibyl who had written the postscript. As I warmed myself by the fire, I resolved that this particular family difficulty was my proper business.

The Ladlaws were waiting for me in the drawing-room. I noticed something new and strange in Sibyl's demeanour. She looked to her husband with a motherly, protective air, while Ladlaw, who had been the extreme of masculine independence, seemed to cling to his wife with a curious appealing fidelity. In conversation he did little more than echo her words. Till dinner was announced he spoke of the weather, the shooting, and Mabel Clanroyden. Then he did a queer thing; for when I was about to offer my arm to Sibyl he forestalled me, and clutching her right arm with his left hand led the way to the dining room, leaving me to follow in some bewilderment.

I have rarely taken part in a more dismal meal. The House of More has a pretty Georgian panelling through most of the rooms, but in the dining room the walls are level and painted a dull stone colour. Abraham offered up Isaac in a ghastly picture in front of me. Some photographs of the Quorn hung over the mantelpiece, and five or six drab ancestors filled up the remaining space. But one thing was new and startling. A great marble bust, a genuine antique, frowned on me from a pedestal. The head was in the late Roman style, clearly of some emperor, and in its commonplace environment the great brows, the massive neck, and the mysterious solemn lips had a surprising effect. I nodded toward the thing, and asked what it represented.

Ladlaw grunted something which I took for 'Justinian', but he never raised his eyes from his plate. By accident I caught Sibyl's glance. She looked toward the bust, and laid a finger on her lips.

The meal grew more doleful as it advanced. Sibyl scarcely touched a dish, but her husband ate ravenously of everything. He was a strong, thickset man, with a square kindly face burned brown by the sun. Now he seemed to have suddenly coarsened. He gobbled with undignified haste, and his eye was extraordinarily vacant. A question made him start, and he would turn on me a face so strange and inert that I repented the interruption.

I asked him about the autumn's sport. He collected his wits with difficulty. He thought it had been good, on the whole, but he had shot badly. He had not been quite so fit as usual. No, he had had nobody staying with him. Sibyl had wanted to be alone. He was afraid the moor might have been undershot, but he would make a big day with keepers and farmers before the winter.

'Bob has done pretty well,' Sibyl said. 'He hasn't been out often, for the weather has been very bad here. You can have no idea, Henry, how horrible this moorland place of ours can be when it tries. It is one great sponge sometimes, with ugly red burns and mud to the ankles.'

'I don't think it's healthy,' said I.

Ladlaw lifted his face. 'Nor do I. I think it's intolerable, but I am so busy I can't get away.'

Once again I caught Sibyl's warning eye as I was about to question him on his business.

Clearly the man's brain had received a shock, and he was beginning to suffer from hallucinations. This could be the only explanation, for he had always led a temperate life. The distrait, wandering manner was the only sign of his malady, for otherwise he seemed normal and mediocre as ever. My heart grieved for Sibyl, alone with him in this wilderness.

Then he broke the silence. He lifted his head and looked nervously around till his eye fell on the Roman bust.

'Do you know that this countryside is the old Manann?' he said.

It was an odd turn to the conversation, but I was glad of a sign of intelligence. I answered that I had heard so.

'It's a queer name,' he said oracularly, 'but the thing it stood for was queerer, Manann, Manaw,' he repeated, rolling the words on his tongue. As he spoke, he glanced sharply, and, as it seemed to me, fearfully, at his left side.

The movement of his body made his napkin slip from his left knee and fall on the floor. It leaned against his leg, and he started from its touch as if he had been bitten by a snake. I have never seen a more sheer and transparent terror on a man's face. He got to his feet, his strong frame shaking like a rush. Sibyl ran round to his side, picked up the napkin and flung it on a sideboard. Then she stroked his hair as one would stroke a frightened horse. She called him by his old boy's name of Robin, and at her touch and voice he became quiet. But the particular course then in progress was removed, untasted.

In a few minutes he seemed to have forgotten his behaviour, for he took up the former conversation. For a time he spoke well and briskly. 'You lawyers,' he said, 'understand only the dry framework of the past. You cannot conceive the rapture, which only the antiquary can feel, of constructing in every detail an old culture. Take this Manann. If I could explore the secret of these moors, I would write the world's greatest book. I would write of that prehistoric life when man was knit close to nature. I would describe the people who were brothers of the red earth and the red rock and the red streams of the hills. Oh, it would be horrible, but superb, tremendous! It would be more than a piece of history; it would be a new gospel, a new theory of life. It would kill materialism once and for all. Why, man, all the poets who have deified and personified nature would not do an eighth part of my work. I would show you the unknown, the hideous, shrieking mystery at the back of this simple nature. Men would see the profundity of the old crude faiths which they affect to despise. I would make a picture of our shaggy, sombre-eyed forefather, who heard strange things in the hill silences. I would show him brutal and terror-stricken, but wise, wise, God alone knows how wise! The Romans knew it, and they learned what they could from him, though he did not tell them much. But we have some of his blood in us, and we may go deeper. Manann! A queer land nowadays! I sometimes love it and sometimes hate it, but I always fear it. It is like that statue, inscrutable.'

I would have told him that he was talking mystical nonsense, but I had looked toward the bust, and my rudeness was checked on my lips. The moor might be a common piece of ugly waste land, but the statue was inscrutable, – of that there was no doubt. I hate your cruel heavy-mouthed Roman busts; to me they have none of the beauty of life, and little of the interest of art. But my eyes were fastened on this as they had never before looked on marble. The oppression of the heavy woodlands, the mystery of the silent moor, seemed to be caught and held in this face. It was the intangible mystery of culture on the verge of savagery – a cruel, lustful wisdom, and yet a kind of bitter austerity which laughed at the game of life and stood aloof. There was no weakness in the heavy-veined brow and slumbrous eyelids. It was the face of one who had conquered the world, and found it dust and ashes; one who had eaten of the tree of the knowledge of good and evil, and scorned human wisdom. And at the same time, it was the face of one who knew uncanny things, a man who was the intimate of the half-world and the dim background of life. Why on earth I should connect the Roman grandee* with the moorland parish of More I cannot say, but the fact remains that there was that in the face which I knew had haunted me through the woodlands and bogs of the place – a sleepless, dismal, incoherent melancholy.

'I bought that at Colenzo's,' Ladlaw said, 'because it took my fancy. It matches well with this place?'

I thought it matched very ill with his drab walls and Quorn photographs, but I held my peace.

'Do you know who it is?' he asked. 'It is the head of the greatest man the world has ever seen. You are a lawyer and know your Justinian.'

The Pandects are scarcely part of the daily work of a common-law barrister. I had not looked into them since I left college.

'I know that he married an actress,' I said, 'and was a sort of all-round genius. He made law, and fought battles, and had rows with the Church. A curious man! And wasn't there some story about his selling his soul to the devil, and getting law in exchange? Rather a poor bargain!'

I chattered away, sillily enough, to dispel the gloom of that dinner table. The result of my words was unhappy. Ladlaw gasped and caught at his left side, as if in pain. Sibyl, with tragic eyes, had been making signs to me to hold my peace. Now she ran round to her husband's side and comforted him like a child. As she passed me, she managed to whisper in my ear to talk to her only, and let her husband alone.

For the rest of dinner I obeyed my orders to the letter. Ladlaw ate his food in gloomy silence, while I spoke to Sibyl of our relatives and friends, of London, Glenaicill, and any random subject. The poor girl was dismally forgetful, and her eye would wander to her husband with wifely anxiety. I remember being suddenly overcome by the comic aspect of it all. Here were we three fools alone in the dank upland: one of us sick and nervous, talking out-of-the-way nonsense about Mann and Justinian, gobbling his food and getting scared at his napkin; another gravely anxious; and myself at my wits' end for a solution. It was a Mad Tea-Party with a vengeance: Sibyl the melancholy little

* I have identified the bust, which, when seen under other circumstances, had little power to affect me. It was a copy of the head of Justinian in the Tesci Museum at Venice, and several duplicates exist, dating apparently from the seventh century, and showing traces of Byzantine decadence in the scroll work on the hair. It is engraved in M. Delacroix's Byzantium, and, I think, in Windscheid's Pandektenlehrbuch.

Dormouse, and Ladlaw the incomprehensible Hatter. I laughed aloud, but checked myself when I caught my cousin's eye. It was really no case for finding humour. Ladlaw was very ill, and Sibyl's face was getting deplorably thin.

I welcomed the end of that meal with unmannerly joy, for I wanted to speak seriously with my host. Sibyl told the butler to have the lamps lighted in the library. Then she leaned over toward me and spoke low and rapidly: 'I want you to talk with Bob. I'm sure you can do him good. You'll have to be very patient with him, and very gentle. Oh, please try to find out what is wrong with him. He won't tell me, and I can only guess.'

The butler returned with word that the library was ready to receive us, and Sibyl rose to go. Ladlaw half rose, protesting, making the most curious feeble clutches to his side. His wife quieted him. 'Henry will look after you, dear,' she said. 'You are going into the library to smoke.' Then she slipped from the room, and we were left alone.

He caught my arm fiercely with his left hand, and his grip nearly made me cry out. As we walked down the hall, I could feel his arm twitching from the elbow to the shoulder. Clearly he was in pain, and I set it down to some form of cardiac affection, which might possibly issue in paralysis.

I settled him in the biggest armchair, and took one of his cigars. The library is the pleasantest room in the house, and at night, when a peat fire burned on the old hearth and the great red curtains were drawn, it used to be the place for comfort and good talk. Now I noticed changes. Ladlaw's bookshelves had been filled with the Pro-ceedings of antiquarian societies and many light-hearted works on sport. But now the Badminton library had been cleared out of a shelf where it stood most convenient to the hand, and its place taken by an old Leyden reprint of Justinian. There were books on Byzantine subjects of which I never dreamed he had heard the names; there were volumes of history and speculation, all of a slightly bizarre kind; and to crown everything, there were several bulky medical works with gaudily coloured plates. The old atmosphere of sport and travel had gone from the room with the medley of rods, whips, and gun cases which used to cumber the tables. Now the place was moderately tidy and somewhat learned, and I did not like it.

Ladlaw refused to smoke, and sat for a little while in silence. Then of his own accord he broke the tension.

'It was devilish good of you to come, Harry. This is a lonely place for a man who is a bit seedy.'

'I thought you might be alone,' I said, 'so looked you up on my way down from Glenaicill. I'm sorry to find you feeling ill.'

'Do you notice it?' he asked sharply.

'It's tolerably patent,' I said. 'Have you seen a doctor?'

He said something uncomplimentary about doctors, and kept looking at me with his curious dull eyes.

I remarked the strange posture in which he sat, his head screwed round to his right shoulder, and his whole body a protest against something at his left hand.

'It looks like a heart,' I said. 'You seem to have pains in your left side.'

Again a spasm of fear. I went over to him and stood at the back of his chair.

'Now for goodness' sake, my dear fellow, tell me what is wrong. You're scaring Sibyl to death. It's lonely work for the poor girl, and I wish you would let me help you.'

He was lying back in his chair now, with his eyes half shut, and shivering like a frightened colt. The extraordinary change in one who had been the strongest of the strong kept me from realising his gravity. I put a hand on his shoulder, but he flung it off.

'For God's sake, sit down!' he said hoarsely. 'I'm going to tell you, but I'll never make you understand.'

I sat down promptly opposite him.

'It's the devil,' he said very solemnly.

I am afraid that I was rude enough to laugh. He took no notice, but sat, with the same tense, miserable air, staring over my head.

'Right,' said I. 'Then it is the devil. It's a new complaint, so it's as well I did not bring a doctor. How does it affect you?'

He made the old impotent clutch at the air with his left hand. I had the sense to become grave at once. Clearly this was some serious mental affection, some hallucination born of physical pain.

Then he began to talk in a low voice, very rapidly, with his head bent forward like a hunted animal's. I am not going to set down what he told me in his own words, for they were incoherent often, and there was much repetition. But I am going to write the gist of the odd story which took my sleep away on that autumn night, with such explanations and additions I think needful. The fire died down, the wind arose, the hour grew late, and still he went on in his mumbling recitative. I forgot to smoke, forgot my comfort – everything but the odd figure of my friend and his inconceivable romance. And the night before I had been in cheerful Glenaicill!

He had returned to the House of More, he said, in the latter part of May, and shortly after he fell ill. It was a trifling sickness, – influenza or something, – but he had never quite recovered. The rainy weather of June depressed him, and the extreme heat of July made him listless and weary. A kind of insistent sleepiness hung over him, and he suffered much from nightmare. Toward the end of July his former health returned, but he was haunted with a curious oppression. He seemed to himself to have lost the art of being alone. There was a perpetual sound in his left ear, a kind of moving and rustling at his left side, which never left him by night or day. In addition, he had become the prey of nerves and an insensate dread of the unknown.

Ladlaw, as I have explained, was a commonplace man, with fair talents, a mediocre culture, honest instincts, and the beliefs and incredulities of his class. On abstract grounds, I should have declared him an unlikely man to be the victim of an hallucination. He had a kind of dull bourgeois rationalism, which used to find reasons for all things in heaven and earth. At first he controlled his dread with proverbs. He told himself it was the sequel of his illness or the light-headedness of summer heat on the moors. But it soon outgrew his comfort. It became a living second presence, an *alter ego* which dogged his footsteps. He grew acutely afraid of it. He dared not be alone for a moment, and clung to Sibyl's company despairingly. She went off for a week's visit in the beginning of August, and he endured for seven days the tortures of the lost. The malady advanced upon him with swift steps. The presence became more real daily. In the early dawning, in the twilight, and in the first hour of the morning it seemed at times to take a visible bodily form. A kind of amorphous featureless shadow would run from his side into the darkness, and he would sit palsied with terror. Sometimes, in lonely places, his footsteps sounded double, and something would brush elbows with him. Human society alone exorcised it. With Sibyl at his side he was happy; but as soon as she left him, the thing came slinking back from the unknown to watch by him. Company might have saved him, but joined to his affliction was a crazy dread of his fellows. He would not leave his moorland home, but must bear his burden alone among the wild streams and mosses of that dismal place.

The 12th came, and he shot wretchedly, for his nerve had gone to pieces. He stood exhaustion badly, and became a dweller about the doors. But with this bodily inertness came an extraordinary intellectual revival. He read widely in a blundering way, and he speculated unceasingly. It was characteristic of the man that as soon as he left the paths of the prosaic he should seek his supernatural in a very concrete form. He assumed that he was haunted by the devil – the visible personal devil in whom our fathers believed. He waited hourly for the shape at his side to speak, but no words came. The Accuser of the Brethren in all but tangible form was his ever present companion. He felt, he declared, the spirit of old evil entering subtly into his blood. He sold his soul many times over, and yet there was no possibility of resistance. It was a Visitation more undeserved than Job's, and a thousandfold more awful.

For a week or more he was tortured with a kind of religious mania. When a man of a healthy secular mind finds himself adrift on the terrible ocean of religious troubles he is peculiarly helpless, for he has not the most rudimentary knowledge of the winds and tides. It was useless to call up his old carelessness; he had suddenly dropped into a new world where old proverbs did not apply. And all the while, mind you, there was the shrinking terror of it – an intellect all alive to the torture and the most unceasing physical fear. For a little he was on the far edge of idiocy.

Then by accident it took a new form. While sitting with Sibyl one day in the library, he began listlessly to turn over the leaves of an old book. He read a few pages, and found the hint to a story like his own. It was some French Life of Justinian, one of the unscholarly productions of last century, made up of stories from Procopius and tags of Roman law. Here was his own case written down in black and white; and the man had been a king of kings. This was a new comfort, and for a little – strange though it may seem – he took a sort of pride in his affliction. He worshiped the great Emperor, and read every scrap he could find on him, not excepting the Pandects and the Digest. He sent for the bust in the dining room, paying a fabulous price. Then he settled himself to study his imperial prototype, and the study became an idolatry. As I have said, Ladlaw was a man of ordinary talents, and certainly of meagre imaginative power. And yet from the lies of the Secret History and the crudities of German legalists he had constructed a marvellous portrait of a man. Sitting there in the half-lighted room, he drew the picture: the quiet cold man with his inheritance of Dacian mysticism, holding the great world in fee, giving it law and religion, fighting its wars, building its churches, and yet all the while intent upon his own private work of making his peace with his soul – the churchman and warrior whom all the world worshipped, and yet one going through life with his lip quivering. He Watched by the Threshold ever at the left side. Sometimes at night, in the great Brazen Palace, warders heard the Emperor walking in the dark corridors, alone, and yet not alone; for once, when a servant entered with a lamp, he saw his master with a face as of another world, and something beside him which had no face or shape, but which he knew to be that hoary Evil which is older than the stars.

Crazy nonsense! I had to rub my eyes to assure myself that I was not sleeping. No! There was my friend with his suffering face, and it was the library of More.

And then he spoke of Theodora, – actress, harlot, *dévote*, empress. For him the lady was but another part of the uttermost horror, a form of the shapeless thing at his side. I felt myself falling under the fascination. I have no nerves and little imagination, but in a flash I seemed to realise something of that awful featureless face, crouching ever at a man's hand, till darkness and loneliness come, and it rises to its mastery. I shivered as I looked at the man in the chair before me. These dull eyes of his were looking upon things I could not see, and I saw their terror. I realised that it was grim earnest for him. Nonsense or no, some devilish fancy had usurped the place of his sanity, and he was being slowly broken upon the wheel. And then, when his left hand twitched, I almost cried out. I had thought it comic before; now it seemed the last proof of tragedy.

He stopped, and I got up with loose knees and went to the window. Better the black night than the intangible horror within. I flung up the sash and looked out across the moor. There was no light; nothing but an inky darkness and the uncanny rustle of elder bushes. The sound chilled me, and I closed the window.

'The land is the old Mannann,' Ladlaw was saying. 'We are beyond the pale here. Do you hear the wind?'

I forced myself back into sanity and looked at my watch. It was nearly one o'clock.

'What ghastly idiots we are!' I said. 'I am off to bed.'

Ladlaw looked at me helplessly. 'For God's sake, don't leave me alone!' he moaned. 'Get Sibyl.'

We went together back to the hall, while he kept the same feverish grasp on my arm. Some one was sleeping in a chair by the hall fire, and to my distress I recognised my hostess. The poor child must have been sadly wearied. She came forward with her anxious face.

'I'm afraid Bob has kept you very late, Henry,' she said. 'I hope you will sleep well. Breakfast at nine, you know.' And then I left them.

Over my bed there was a little picture, a reproduction of some Italian work, of Christ and the Demoniac. Some impulse made me hold my candle up to it. The madman's face was torn with passion and suffering, and his eye had the pained furtive expression which I had come to know. And by his left side there was a dim shape crouching.

I got into bed hastily, but not to sleep. I felt that my reason must be going. I had been pitchforked from our clear and cheerful modern life into the mists of old superstition. Old tragic stories of my Calvinist upbringing returned to haunt me. The man dwelt in by a devil was no new fancy, but I believed that science had docketed and analysed and explained the devil out of the world. I remembered my dabblings in the occult before I settled down to law – the story of Donisarius, the monk of Padua, the unholy legend of the Face of Proserpine, the tales of *succubi* and *incubi*, the Leannain Sith and the Hidden Presence. But here was something stranger still. I had stumbled upon that very possession which fifteen hundred years ago had made the monks of New Rome tremble and cross themselves. Some devilish occult force, lingering through the ages, had come to life after a long sleep. God knows what earthly connection there was between the splendid Emperor of the World and my prosaic friend, or between the glittering shores of the Bosporus and this moorland parish! But the land was the old Manann! The spirit may have lingered in the earth and air, a deadly legacy from Pict and Roman. I had felt the uncanniness of the place; I had augured ill of it from the first. And then in sheer disgust I rose and splashed my face with cold water.

I lay down again, laughing miserably at my credulity. That I, the sober and rational, should believe in this crazy fable was too palpably absurd. I would steel my mind resolutely against such harebrained theories. It was a mere bodily ailment – liver out of order, weak heart, bad circulation, or something of that sort. At the worst it might be some affection of the brain, to be treated by a specialist. I vowed to myself that next morning the best doctor in Edinburgh should be brought to More.

The worst of it was that my duty compelled me to stand my ground. I foresaw the few remaining weeks of my holiday blighted. I should be tied to this moorland prison, a sort of keeper and nurse in one, tormented by silly fancies. It was a charming prospect, and the thought of Glenaicill and the woodcock made me bitter against Ladlaw. But there was no way out of it. I might do Ladlaw good, and I could not have Sibyl worn to death by his vagaries.

My ill nature comforted me, and I forgot the horror of the thing in its vexation. After that I think I fell asleep and dozed uneasily till morning. When I woke I was in a better frame of mind. The early sun had worked wonders with the moorland. The low hills stood out fresh-coloured and clear against a pale October sky; the elders sparkled with frost; the raw film of morn was rising from the little loch in tiny clouds. It was a cold, rousing day, and I dressed in good spirits and went down to breakfast.

I found Ladlaw looking ruddy and well; very different from the broken man I remembered of the night before. We were alone, for Sibyl was breakfasting in bed. I remarked on his ravenous appetite, and he smiled cheerily. He made two jokes during the meal; he laughed often, and I began to forget the events of the previous day. It seemed to me that I might still flee from More with a clear conscience. He had forgotten about his illness. When I touched distantly upon the matter he showed a blank face.

It might be that the affection had passed; on the other hand, it might return to him at the darkening. I had no means to decide. His manner was still a trifle distrait and peculiar, and I did not like the dullness in his eye. At any rate, I should spend the day in his company, and the evening would decide the question.

I proposed shooting, which he promptly vetoed. He was no good at walking, he said, and the birds were wild. This seriously limited the possible occupations. Fishing there was none, and hill-climbing was out of the question. He proposed a game at billiards, and I pointed to the glory of the morning. It would have been sacrilege to waste such

[21]

sunshine in knocking balls about. Finally we agreed to drive somewhere and have lunch, and he ordered the dogcart.

In spite of all forebodings I enjoyed the day. We drove in the
opposite direction from the woodland parts, right away across the
moor to the coal country beyond. We lunched at the little mining
town of Borrowmuir, in a small and noisy public house. The roads
made bad going, the country was far from pretty, and yet the drive
did not bore me. Ladlaw talked incessantly – talked as I had never
heard man talk before. There was something indescribable in all he
said, a different point of view, a lost groove of thought, a kind of
innocence and archaic shrewdness in one. I can only give you a hint
of it, by saying that it was like the mind of an early ancestor placed
suddenly among modern surroundings. It was wise with a remote
wisdom, and silly (now and then) with a quite antique and distant
silliness.

I will give instances of both. He provided me with a theory of
certain early fortifications, which must be true, which commends itself
to the mind with overwhelming conviction, and yet which is so out of
the way of common speculation that no man could have guessed it. I
do not propose to set down the details, for I am working at it on my
own account. Again, he told me the story of an old marriage custom,
which till recently survived in this district – told it with full circumstantial detail and constant allusions to other customs which he
could not possibly have known of. Now for the other side. He
explained why well water is in winter warmer than a running stream,
and this was his explanation: at the antipodes our winter is summer,
consequently, the water of a well which comes through from the other
side of the earth must be warm in winter and cold in summer, since in
our summer it is winter there. You perceive what this is. It is no mere
silliness, but a genuine effort of an early mind, which had just grasped
the fact of the antipodes, to use it in explanation.

Gradually I was forced to the belief that it was not Ladlaw who was
talking to me, but something speaking through him, something at
once wiser and simpler. My old fear of the devil began to depart. This
spirit, the exhalation, whatever it was, was ingenuous in its way, at
least in its daylight aspect. For a moment I had an idea that it was a
real reflex of Byzantine thought, and that by cross-examining I might
make marvellous discoveries. The ardour of the scholar began to rise in
me, and I asked a question about that much-debated point, the legal

status of the *apocrisiarii*. To my vexation he gave no response. Clearly the intelligence of this familiar had its limits.

It was about three in the afternoon, and we had gone half of our homeward journey, when signs of the old terror began to appear. I was driving, and Ladlaw sat on my left. I noticed him growing nervous and silent, shivering at the flick of the whip, and turning halfway round toward me. Then he asked me to change places, and I had the unpleasant work of driving from the wrong side. After that I do not think he spoke once till we arrived at More, but sat huddled together, with the driving rug almost up to his chin – an eccentric figure of a man.

I foresaw another such night as the last, and I confess my heart sank. I had no stomach for more mysteries, and somehow with the approach of twilight the confidence of the day departed. The thing appeared in darker colours, and I found it in my mind to turn coward. Sibyl alone deterred me. I could not bear to think of her alone with this demented being. I remembered her shy timidity, her innocence. It was monstrous that the poor thing should be called on thus to fight alone with phantoms.

When we came to the House it was almost sunset. Ladlaw got out very carefully on the right side, and for a second stood by the horse. The sun was making our shadows long, and as I stood beyond him it seemed for a moment that his shadow was double. It may have been mere fancy, for I had not time to look twice. He was standing, as I have said, with his left side next the horse. Suddenly the harmless elderly cob fell into a very panic of fright, reared upright, and all but succeeded in killing its master. I was in time to pluck Ladlaw from under its feet, but the beast had become perfectly unmanageable, and we left a groom struggling to quiet it.

In the hall the butler gave me a telegram. It was from my clerk, summoning me back at once to an important consultation.

Here was a prompt removal of my scruples. There could be no question of my remaining, for the case was one of the first importance, which I had feared might break off my holiday. The consultation fell in vacation time to meet the convenience of certain people who were going abroad, and there was the most instant demand for my presence. I must go, and at once; and, as I hunted in the time-table, I found that in three hours' time a night train for the south would pass Borrowmuir which might be stopped by special wire.

But I had no pleasure in my freedom. I was in despair about Sibyl, and I hated myself for my cowardly relief. The dreary dining room, the sinister bust, and Ladlaw crouching and quivering – the recollection, now that escape was before me, came back on my mind with the terror of a nightmare. My first thought was to persuade the Ladlaws to come away with me. I found them both in the drawing-room – Sibyl very fragile and pale, and her husband sitting as usual like a frightened child in the shadow of her skirts. A sight of him was enough to dispel my hope. The man was fatally ill, mentally, bodily; and who was I to attempt to minister to a mind diseased?

But Sibyl – she might be saved from the martyrdom. The servants would take care of him, and, if need be, a doctor might be got from Edinburgh to live in the house. So while he sat with vacant eyes staring into the twilight, I tried to persuade Sibyl to think of herself. I am frankly a sun worshipper. I have no taste for arduous duty, and the quixotic is my abhorrence. I laboured to bring my cousin to this frame of mind. I told her that her first duty was to herself, and that this vigil of hers was beyond human endurance. But she had no ears for my arguments.

'While Bob is ill I must stay with him,' she said always in answer, and then she thanked me for my visit, till I felt a brute and a coward. I strove to quiet my conscience, but it told me always that I was fleeing from my duty; and then, when I was on the brink of a nobler resolution, a sudden overmastering terror would take hold of me, and I would listen hysterically for the sound of the dogcart on the gravel.

At last it came, and in a sort of fever I tried to say the conventional farewells. I shook hands with Ladlaw, and when I dropped his hand it fell numbly on his knee. Then I took my leave, muttering hoarse nonsense about having had a 'charming visit', and 'hoping soon to see them both in town'. As I backed to the door, I knocked over a lamp on a small table. It crashed on the floor and went out, and at the sound Ladlaw gave a curious childish cry. I turned like a coward, and ran across the hall to the front door, and scrambled into the dogcart.

The groom would have driven me sedately through the park, but I must have speed or go mad. I took the reins from him and put the horse into a canter. We swung through the gates and out into the moor road, for I could have no peace till the ghoulish elder world was exchanged for the homely ugliness of civilisation. Once only I looked back, and there against the sky line, with a solitary lit window, the House of More stood lonely in the red desert.

Fountainblue

'Fountainblue' is another story from *The Watcher by the Threshold* (1902) and was first published in *Blackwood's Magazine* in August 1901. It subsequently appeared in the American edition of Buchan's third story collection, *The Moon Endureth* (1912), and was sold to various magazines such as *Argosy* during the 1920s and 1930s.

The adventurer who devoted himself to the service of Britain but was not able to live there was a familiar theme in the fiction of the period, most notably demonstrated in Somerset Maugham's *The Explorer* (1907).

I

ONCE UPON A time, as the story-books say, a boy came over a ridge of hill, from which a shallow vale ran out into the sunset. It was a high, wind-blown country, where the pines had a crook in their backs and the rocks were scarred and bitten with winter storms. But below was the beginning of pastoral. Soft birch-woods, shady beeches, meadows where cattle had browsed for generations, fringed the little brown river as it twined to the sea. Farther, and the waves broke on white sands, the wonderful billows of the West which cannot bear to be silent. And between, in a garden wilderness, with the evening flaming in its windows, stood Fountainblue, my little four-square castle which guards the valley and the beaches.

The boy had torn his clothes, scratched his face, cut one finger deeply, and soaked himself with bog-water, but he whistled cheerfully and his eyes were happy. He had had an afternoon of adventure, startling emprises achieved in solitude; assuredly a day to remember and mark with a white stone. And the beginning had been most unpromising. After lunch he had been attired in his best raiment, and, in the misery of a broad white collar, despatched with his cousins to

[25]

take tea with the small lady who domineered in Fountainblue. The prospect had pleased him greatly, the gardens fed his fancy, the hostess was an old confederate, and there were sure to be excellent things to eat. But his curious temper had arisen to torment him. On the way he quarrelled with his party, and in a moment found himself out of sympathy with the future. The enjoyment crept out of the prospect. He knew that he did not shine in society, he foresaw an afternoon when he would be left out in the cold and his hilarious cousins treated as the favoured guests. He reflected that tea was a short meal at the best, and that games on a lawn were a poor form of sport. Above all, he felt the torture of his collar and the straitness of his clothes. He pictured the dreary return in the twilight, when the afternoon, which had proved, after all, such a dismal failure, had come to a weary end. So, being a person of impulses, he mutinied at the gates of Fountainblue and made for the hills. He knew he should get into trouble, but trouble, he had long ago found out, was his destiny, and he scorned to avoid it. And now, having cast off the fear of God and man, he would for some short hours do exactly as he pleased.

Half-crying with regret for the delights he had forsworn, he ran over the moor to the craggy hills which had always been forbidden him. When he had climbed among the rocks awe fell upon the desolate little adventurer, and he bewailed his choice. But soon he found a blue hawk's nest, and the possession of a coveted egg inspired him to advance. By-and-by he had climbed so high that he could not return, but must needs scale Stob Ghabhar itself. With a quaking heart he achieved it, and then, in the pride of his heroism, he must venture down the Grey Correi where the wild goats lived. He saw a bearded ruffian, and pursued him with stones, stalking him cunningly till he was out of breath. Then he found odd little spleenwort ferns, which he pocketed, and high up in the rocks a friendly raven croaked his encouragement. And then, when the shadows lengthened, he set off cheerily homewards, hungry, triumphant, and very weary.

All the way home he flattered his soul. In one afternoon he had been hunter and trapper, and what to him were girls' games and pleasant things to eat? He pictured himself the hardy outlaw, feeding on oatmeal and goat's-flesh, the terror and pride of his neighbourhood. Could the little mistress of Fountainblue but see him now, how she would despise his prosaic cousins! And then, as he descended on the highway, he fell in with his forsaken party.

For a wonder they were in good spirits – so good that they forgot to remind him, in their usual way, of the domestic terrors awaiting him. A man had been there who had told them stories and shown them tricks, and there had been coconut cake, and Sylvia had a new pony on which they had ridden races. The children were breathless with excitement, very much in love with each other as common sharers in past joys. And as they talked all the colour went out of his afternoon. The blue hawk's egg was cracked, and it looked a stupid, dingy object as it lay in his cap. His rare ferns were crumpled and withered, and who was to believe his stories of Stob Ghabhar and the Grey Correi? He had been a fool to barter ponies and tea and a man who knew tricks for the barren glories of following his own fancy. But at any rate he would show no sign. If he was to be an outlaw, he would carry his outlawry well; so with a catch in his voice and tears in his eyes he jeered at his inattentive companions, upbraiding himself all the while for his folly.

II

The sun was dipping behind Stob Ghabhar when Maitland drove over the ridge of hill, whence the moor-road dips to Fountainblue. Twenty long miles from the last outpost of railway to the western sea-loch, and twenty of the barest, steepest miles in the bleak north. And all the way he had been puzzling himself with the half-painful, half-pleasing memories of a childhood which to the lonely man still overtopped the present. Every wayside bush was the home of recollection. In every burn he had paddled and fished; here he had found the jack-snipe's nest, there he had hidden when the shepherds sought him for burning the heather in May. He lost for a little the burden of his years and cares, and lived again in that old fresh world which had no boundaries, where sleep and food were all his thought at night, and adventure the sole outlook of the morning. The western sea lay like a thin line of gold beyond the moorland, and down in the valley in a bower of trees lights began to twinkle from the little castle. The remote mountains, hiding deep corries and woods in their bosom, were blurred by twilight to a single wall of hazy purple, which shut off this fairy glen impenetrably from the world. Fountainblue – the name rang witchingly in his ears. Fountainblue, the last home of the Good Folk, the last hold of the vanished kings, where the last wolf in Scotland was

slain, and, as stories go, the last saint of the Great Ages taught the
people – what had Fountainblue to do with his hard world of facts and
figures? The thought woke him to a sense of the present, and for a
little he relished the paradox. He had left it long ago, an adventurous
child; now he was returning with success behind him and a portion of
life's good things his own. He was rich, very rich and famous. Few men
of forty had his power, and he had won it all in fair struggle with
enemies and rivals and a niggardly world. He had been feared and
hated, as he had been extravagantly admired; he had been rudely
buffeted by fortune, and had met the blows with a fighter's joy. And
out of it all something hard and austere had shaped itself, something
very much a man, but a man with little heart and a lack of kindly
human failings. He was master of himself in a curious degree, but the
mastery absorbed his interests. Nor had he ever regretted it, when
suddenly in this outlandish place the past swept over him, and he had
a vision of a long avenue of vanished hopes. It pleased and disquieted
him, and as the road dipped into the valley he remembered the prime
cause of this mood of vagaries.

He had come up into the north with one purpose in view, he frankly
told himself. The Etheridges were in Fountainblue, and ever since,
eight months before, he had met Clara Etheridge, he had forgotten his
ambitions. A casual neighbour at a dinner-party, a chance partner at a
ball – and then he had to confess that this slim, dark, bright-eyed girl
had broken in irrevocably upon his contentment. At first he hated it
for a weakness, then he welcomed the weakness with feverish ecstasy.
He did nothing by halves, so he sought her company eagerly, and,
being a great man in his way, found things made easy for him. But the
girl remained shy and distant, flattered doubtless by his attention, but
watching him curiously as an intruder from an alien world. It was
characteristic of the man that he never thought of a rival. His whole
aim was to win her love; for rivalry with other men he had the con-
tempt of a habitual conqueror. And so the uneasy wooing went on till
the Etheridges left town, and he found himself a fortnight later with
his work done and a visit before him to which he looked forward with
all the vehemence of a nature whose strong point had always been its
hope. As the road wound among the fir-trees, he tried to forecast the
life at Fountainblue, and map out the future in his usual business-like
way. But now the future refused to be thus shorn and parcelled: there
was an unknown quantity in it which defied his efforts.

The house-party were sitting round the hall-fire when he entered. The high-roofed place, the flagged floor strewn with rugs, and the walls bright with the glow of fire on armour, gave him a boyish sense of comfort. Two men in knickerbockers were lounging on a settle, and at his entrance came forward to greet him. One was Sir Hugh Clanroyden, a follower of his own; the other he recognised as a lawyer named Durward. From the circle of women Miss Etheridge rose and welcomed him. Her mother was out, but would be back for dinner; meantime he should be shown his room. He noticed that her face was browner, her hair a little less neat, and there seemed something franker and kindlier in her smile. So in a very good humour he went to rid himself of the dust of the roads.

Durward watched him curiously, and then turned, laughing, to his companion, as the girl came back to her friends with a heightened colour in her cheeks.

'Romeo the second,' he said. 'We are going to be spectators of a comedy. And yet, heaven knows! Maitland is not cast for comedy.'

The other shook his head. 'It will never come off. I've known Clara Etheridge most of my life, and I would as soon think of marrying a dancing-girl to a bishop. She is a delightful person, and my very good friend, but how on earth is she ever to understand Maitland? And how on earth can he see anything in her? Besides, there's another man.'

Durward laughed. 'Despencer! I suppose he will be a serious rival with a woman; but imagine him Maitland's rival in anything else! He'd break him like a rotten stick in half an hour. I like little Despencer, and I don't care about Maitland; but all the same it is absurd to compare the two, except in love-making.'

'Lord, it will be comic,' and Clanroyden stretched his long legs and lay back on a cushion. The girls were still chattering beside the fire, and the twilight was fast darkening into evening.

'You dislike Maitland?' he asked, looking up. 'Now, I wonder why?'

Durward smiled comically at the ceiling. 'Oh, I know I oughtn't to. I know he's supposed to be a man's man, and that it's bad form for a man to say he dislikes him. But I'm honest enough to own to detesting him. I suppose he's great, but he's not great enough yet to compel one to fall down and worship him, and I hate greatness in the making. He goes through the world with his infernal arrogance and expects everybody to clear out of his way. I am told we live in an age of reason, but that fellow has burked reason. He never gives a reason for a thing he does, and if you try to argue he crushes you. He has killed good talk for ever with his confounded rudeness. All the little sophistries and conventions which make life tolerable are so much rubbish to him, and he shows it. The plague of him is that he can never make-believe. He is as hard as iron, and as fierce as the devil, and about as unpleasant. You may respect the sledge-hammer type, but it's confoundedly dull. Why, the man has not the imagination of a rabbit, except in his description of people he dislikes. I liked him when he said that Layden reminded him of a dissipated dove, because I disliked Layden; but when Freddy Alton played the fool and people forgave him, because he was a good sort, Maitland sent him about his business, saying he had no further use for weaklings. He is so abominably cold-blooded and implacable that everyone must fear him, and yet most people can afford to despise him. All the kind simple things of life are shut out of his knowledge. He has no nature, only a heart of stone and an iron will and a terribly subtle brain. Of course he is a great man – in a way, but at the best he is only half a man. And to think that he should have fallen in love, and be in danger of losing to Despencer! It's enough to make one forgive him.'

Clanroyden laughed. 'I can't think of Despencer. It's too absurd. But, seriously, I wish I saw Maitland well rid of this mood, married or cured. That sort of man doesn't take things easily.'

'It reminds one of Theocritus and the Cyclops in love. Who would have thought to see him up in this moorland place, running after a girl? He doesn't care for sport.'

'Do you know that he spent most of his childhood in this glen, and that he *is* keen about sport? He is too busy for many holidays, but he once went with Burton to the Caucasus, and Burton said the experience nearly killed him. He said that the fellow was tireless, and as mad and reckless as a boy with nothing to lose.'

'Well, that simply bears out what I say of him. He does not understand the meaning of sport. When he gets keen about anything he pursues it as carefully and relentlessly as if it were something on the Stock Exchange. Now little Despencer is a genuine sportsman in his canary-like way. He loves the art of the thing and the being out of doors. Maitland, I don't suppose, ever thinks whether it is a ceiling or the sky above his august head. Despencer—'

But at the moment Clanroyden uncrossed his legs, bringing his right foot down heavily upon his companion's left. Durward looked up and saw a young man coming towards him, smiling.

The newcomer turned aside to say something to the girls round the fire, and then came and sat on an arm of the settle. He was a straight, elegant person, with a well-tanned, regular face, and very pleasant brown eyes.

'I've had such an afternoon,' he said. 'You never saw a place like Cairnlora. It's quite a little stone tower all alone in a fir-wood, and nothing else between the moor and the sea. It is furnished as barely as a prison, except for the chairs, which are priceless old Dutch things. Oh, and the silver at tea was the sort of thing that only Americans can buy nowadays. Mrs Etheridge is devoured with envy. But the wonder of the house is old Miss Elphinstone. She must be nearly seventy, and she looks forty-five, except for her hair. She speaks broad Scots, and she has the manners of a *marquise*. I would give a lot to have had Raeburn paint her. She reminded me of nothing so much as a hill-wind with her keen high-coloured old face. Yes, I have enjoyed the afternoon.'

'Jack has got a new enthusiasm,' said Durward. 'I wish I were like you to have a new one once a week. By the way, Maitland has arrived at last.'

'Really!' said Despencer. 'Oh, I forgot to tell you something which you would never have guessed. Miss Elphinstone is Maitland's aunt, and he was brought up a good deal at Cairnlora. He doesn't take his manners from her, but I suppose he gets his cleverness from that side of the family. She disapproves of him strongly, so of course I had to defend him. And what do you think she said? "He has betrayed his tradition. He has sold his birthright for a mess of pottage and I wish him joy of his bargain!" Nice one for your party, Hugh.'

Miss Etheridge had left the group at the fire and was standing at Despencer's side. She listened to him with a curious air of solicitude, like an affectionate sister. At the mention of Maitland's name Clan-royden had watched her narrowly, but her face did not change. And when Despencer asked, 'Where is the new arrival?' she talked of him with the utmost nonchalance.

Maitland came down to dinner, ravenously hungry and in high spirits. Nothing was changed in this house since he had stared at the pictures and imagined terrible things about the armour and broken teacups with childish impartiality. His own favourite seat was still there, where, hidden by a tapestry screen, he had quarrelled with Sylvia while their elders gossiped. This sudden flood of memories mellowed him towards the world. He was cordial to Despencer, forbore to think Durward a fool, and answered every one of Mr Etheridge's many questions. For the first time he felt the success of his life. The old house recalled his childhood, and the sight of Clanroyden, his devoted follower, reminded him of his power. Somehow the weariful crying for the moon, which had always tortured him, was exchanged for a glow of comfort, a shade of complacency in his haggard soul ... And then the sight of Clara dispelled his satisfaction.

Here in this cheerful homely party of friends he found himself out of place. On state occasions he could acquit himself with credit, for the man had a mind. He could make the world listen to him when he chose, and the choice was habitual. But now his loneliness claimed its lawful consequences, and he longed for the little friendly graces which he had so often despised. Despencer talked of scenery and weather with a tenderness to which this man, who loved nature as he loved little else, was an utter stranger. This elegant and appropriate sentiment would have worried him past endurance, if Miss Clara had not shared it. It was she who told some folk-tale about the Grey Correi with the prettiest hesitancy which showed her feeling. And then the talk drifted to books and people, flitting airily about their petty world. Maitland felt himself choked by their accomplishments. Most of the subjects were ones no sane man would trouble to think of, and yet here were men talking keenly about trifles and disputing with nimble-witted cleverness on the niceties of the trivial. Feeling miserably that he was the only silent one, he plunged desperately into the stream, found himself pulled up by Despencer and deftly turned. The event gave him the feeling of having been foiled by a kitten.

Angry with the world, angrier with his own angularity, he waited for the end of the meal. Times had not changed in this house since he had been saved by Sylvia from social disgrace. But when the women left the room he found life easier. His host talked of sport, and he could tell him more about Stob Ghabhar than any keeper. Despencer, victorious at dinner, now listened like a docile pupil. Durward asked a political question, and the answer came sharp and definite. Despencer demurred gently, after his fashion. 'Well, but surely—' and a grimly smiling 'What do you know about it?' closed the discussion. The old Maitland had returned for the moment.

The night was mild and impenetrably dark, and the fall of waters close at hand sounded like a remote echo. An open hall-door showed that some of the party had gone out to the garden, and the men followed at random. A glimmer of white frocks betrayed the women on the lawn, standing by the little river which slipped by cascade and glide from the glen to the low pasture-lands. In the featureless dark there was no clue to locality. The place might have been Berkshire or a suburban garden.

Suddenly the scream of some animal came from the near thicket. The women started and asked what it was.

'It was a hill-fox,' said Maitland to Clara. 'They used to keep me awake at nights on the hill. They come and bark close to your ear and give you nightmare.'

The lady shivered. 'Thank Heaven for the indoors,' she said. 'Now, if I had been the daughter of one of your old Donalds of the Isles, I should have known that cry only too well. Wild nature is an excellent background, but give me civilisation in front.'

Maitland was looking into the wood. 'You will find it creeps far into civilisation if you look for it. There is a very narrow line between the warm room and the savage out-of-doors.'

'There are miles of luxuries,' the girl cried, laughing. 'People who are born in the wrong country have to hunt over half the world before they find their savagery. It is all very tame, but I love the tameness. You may call yourself primitive, Mr Maitland, but you are the most complex and modern of us all. What would Donald of the Isles have said to politics and the Stock Exchange?'

They had strolled back to the house. 'Nevertheless I maintain my belief,' said the man. 'You call it miles of rampart; I call the division a line, a thread, a sheet of glass. But then, you see, you only know one side, and I only know the other.'

'What preposterous affectation!' the girl said, as with a pretty shiver she ran indoors. Maitland stood for a moment looking back at the darkness. Within the firelit hall, with its rugs and little tables and soft chairs, he had caught a glimpse of Despencer smoking a cigarette. As he looked towards the hills he heard the fox's bark a second time, and then somewhere from the black distance came a hawk's scream, hoarse, lonely, and pitiless. The thought struck him that the sad elemental world of wood and mountain was far more truly his own than this cosy and elegant civilisation. And, oddly enough, the thought pained him.

III

The day following was wet and windy, when a fire was grateful, and the hills, shrouded in grey mist, had no attractions. The party read idly in armchairs during the morning, and in the afternoon Maitland and Clanroyden went down to the stream-mouth after sea-trout. So Despencer remained to talk to Clara, and, having played many games of picquet and grown heartily tired of each other, as tea-time approached they fell to desultory comments on their friends. Maitland was beginning to interest the girl in a new way. Formerly he had been a great person who was sensible enough to admire her, but something remote and unattractive, for whom friendship (much less love) was impossible. But now she had begun to feel his power, his manhood. The way in which other men spoke of him impressed her unconsciously, and she began to ask Despencer questions which were gall and wormwood to that young man. But he answered honestly, after his fashion.

'Isn't he very rich?' she asked. 'And I suppose he lives very plainly?'

'Rich as Crœsus, and he sticks in his ugly rooms in the Albany because he never thinks enough about the thing to change. I've been in them once, and you never saw such a place. He's a maniac for fresh air, so they're large enough, but they're littered like a stable with odds and ends of belongings. He must have several thousand books, and yet he hasn't a decent binding among them. He hasn't a photograph of a single soul, and only one picture, which, I believe, was his father. But you never saw such a collection of whips and spurs and bits. It smells like a harness-room, and there you find Maitland, when by any chance he is at home, working half the night and up to the eyes in papers. I don't think the man has any expenses except food and rent, for he wears the same clothes for years. And he has given up horses.'

'Was he fond of horses?' Miss Clara asked.

'Oh, you had better ask him. I really can't tell you any more about him.'

'But how do his friends get on with him?'

'He has hardly any, but his acquaintances, who are all the world, say he is the one great man of the future. If you want to read what people think of him, you had better look at the "Monthly".'

Under cover of this one ungenerous word Despencer made his escape, for he hated the business, but made it the rule of his life 'never to crab a fellow'. Miss Clara promptly sought out the 'Monthly', and found twenty pages of super-fine analysis and bitter, grudging praise. She read it with interest, and then lay back in her chair and tried to fix her thoughts. It is only your unhealthy young woman who worships strength in the abstract, and the girl tried to determine whether she admired the man as a power or disliked him as a brute. She chose a compromise, and the feeling which survived was chiefly curiosity.

The result of the afternoon was that when the fishermen returned, and Maitland, in dry clothes, appeared for tea, she settled herself beside him and prepared to talk. Maitland, being healthily tired, was in an excellent temper, and he found himself enticed into what for him was a rare performance – talk about himself. They were sitting apart from the others, and, ere ever he knew, he was answering the girl's questions with an absent-minded frankness. In a little she had drawn from him the curious history of his life, which most men knew, but never from his own lips.

'I was at school for a year,' he said, 'and then my father died and our affairs went to pieces. I had to come back and go into an office, a sort of bank. I hated it, but it was good for me, for it taught me something, and my discontent made me ambitious. I had about eighty pounds a year, and I saved from that. I worked too at books incessantly, and by-and-by I got an Oxford scholarship, at an obscure college. I went up there, and found myself in a place where everyone seemed well-off, while I was a pauper. However, it didn't trouble me much, for I had no ambition to play the fool. I only cared about two things – horses and metaphysics. I hated all games, which I thought only fit for children. I daresay it was foolish, but then you see I had had a queer upbringing. I managed to save a little money, and one vacation when I was wandering about in Norfolk, sleeping under haystacks and working in harvest-fields when my supplies ran down, I came across a farmer. He was a good fellow and a sort of sportsman, and I took a fancy to him. He had a colt to sell which I fancied more, for I saw it had blood in it. So I bought it for what seemed a huge sum to me in those days, but I kept it at his farm and I superintended its education. I broke it myself and taught it to jump, and by-and-by in my third year I brought it to Oxford and entered for the Grind on it. People laughed at me, but I knew my own business. The little boys who rode in the thing knew nothing about horses, and not one in ten could ride; so I entered and won. It was all I wanted, for I could sell my horse then, and the fellow who rode second bought it. It was decent of him, for I asked a big figure, and I think he had an idea of doing me a kindness. I made him my private secretary the other day.'

'You mean Lord Drapier?' she asked.

'Yes – Drapier. That gave me money to finish off and begin in town. Oh, and I had got a first in my schools. I knew very little about anything except metaphysics, and I never went to tutors. I suppose I knew a good deal more than the examiners in my own subject, and anyhow they felt obliged to give me my first after some grumbling. Then I came up to town with just sixty pounds in my pocket, but I had had the education of a gentleman.'

Maitland looked out of the window, and the sight of the mist-clad hills recalled him to himself. He wondered why he was telling the girl this story, and he stopped suddenly.

'And what did you do in town?' she asked, with interest.

'I hung round and kept my eyes open. I nearly starved, for I put half my capital on a horse which I thought was safe, and lost it. By-and-by, quite by accident, I came across a curious fellow, Ransome – you probably have heard his name. I met him in some stables where he was buying a mare, and he took a liking to me. He made me his secretary, and then, because I liked hard work, he let me see his business. It was enormous, for the man was a genius after a fashion; and I slaved away in his office and down at the docks for about three years. He paid me just enough to keep body and soul together and cover them with clothes; but I didn't grumble, for I had a sort of idea that I was on my probation. And then my apprenticeship came to an end.'

'Yes,' said the girl.

'Yes; for you see Ransome was an odd character. He had a sort of genius for finance, and within his limits he was even a great administrator. But in everything else he was as simple as a child. His soul was idyllic: he loved green fields and Herrick and sheep. So it had always been his fancy to back out some day and retire with his huge fortune to some country place and live as he pleased. It seemed that he had been training me from the first day I went into the business, and now he cut the rope and left the whole enormous concern in my hands. I needed every atom of my wits, and the first years were a hard struggle. I became of course very rich; but I had to do more, I had to keep the thing at its old level. I had no natural turn for the work, and I had to acquire capacity by sheer grind. However, I managed it, and then, when I felt my position sure, I indulged myself with a hobby and went into politics.'

'You call it a hobby?'

'Certainly. The ordinary political career is simply a form of trifling. There's no trade on earth where a man has to fear so few able competitors. Of course it's very public and honourable and that sort of thing, and I like it; but sometimes it wearies me to death.'

The girl was looking at him with curious interest. 'Do you always get what you want?' she asked.

'Never,' he said.

'Then is your success all disappointment?'

'Oh, I generally get a bit of my ambitions, which is all one can hope for in this world.'

'I suppose your ambitions are not idyllic, like Mr Ransome's?'

He laughed. 'No, I suppose not. I never could stand your Corot meadows and ivied cottages and village church bells. But I am at home in this glen, or used to be.'

'You said that last night, and I thought it was affectation,' said the girl; 'but perhaps you are right. I'm not at home in this scenery, at any rate in this weather. Ugh, look at that mist driving and that spur of Stob Ghabhar! I really must go and sit by the fire.'

IV

The next day dawned clear and chill, with a little frost to whiten the heather; but by midday the sun had turned August to June, and sea and land drowsed in a mellow heat. Maitland was roused from his meditations with a pipe on a garden-seat by the appearance of Miss Clara, her eyes bright with news. He had taken her in to dinner the night before, and for the first time in his life had found himself talking easily to a woman. Her interest of the afternoon had not departed; and Despencer in futile disgust shunned the drawing-room, his particular paradise, and played billiards with Clanroyden in the spirit of an unwilling martyr.

'We are going out in the yacht,' Miss Clara cried, as she emerged from the shadow of a fuchsia-hedge, 'to the Isles of the Waves, away beyond the Seal's Headland. Do you know the place, Mr Maitland?'

'Eilean na Cille? Yes. It used to be dangerous for currents, but a steam-yacht does not require to fear them.'

'Well, we'll be ready to start at twelve, and I must go in to give orders about lunch.'

A little later she came out with a bundle of letters in her hands. 'Here are your letters, Mr Maitland; but you mustn't try to answer them, or you'll be late.' He put the lot in his jacket pocket and looked up at the laughing girl. 'My work is six hundred miles behind me,' he said, 'and today I have only the Eilean na Cille to think of.' And, as she passed by, another name took the place of the Eilean, and it seemed to him that at last he had found the link which was to bind together the two natures – his boyhood and his prime.

Out on the loch the sun was beating with that steady August blaze which is more torrid than midsummer. But as the yacht slipped between the horns of the land, it came into a broken green sea with rollers to the north where the tireless Atlantic fretted on the reefs. In a world of cool salt winds and the golden weather of afternoon, with the cries of tern and gull about the bows and the foam and ripple of green water in the wake, the party fell into a mood of supreme contentment. The restless Miss Clara was stricken into a figure of contemplation, which sat in the bows and watched the hazy blue horizon and the craggy mainland hills in silent delight. Maitland was revelling in the loss of his isolation. He had ceased to be alone, a leader, and for the moment felt himself one of the herd, a devotee of humble pleasures. His mind was blank, his eyes filled only with the sea, and the lady of his devotion, in that happy moment of romance, seemed to have come at last within the compass of his hopes.

The Islands of the Waves are low green ridges which rise little above the highest tide-mark. The grass is stiff with salt, the sparse heather and rushes are crooked with the winds, but there are innumerable little dells where a light wild scrub flourishes, and in one a spring of sweet water sends a tiny stream to the sea. The yacht's company came ashore in boats, and tea was made with a great bustle beside the well, while the men lay idly in the bent and smoked. All wind seemed to have died down, a soft, cool, airless peace like a June evening was abroad, and the heavy surging of the tides had sunk to a distant whisper. Maitland lifted his head, sniffed the air, and looked uneasily to the west, meeting the eye of one of the sailors engaged in the same scrutiny. He beckoned the man to him.

'What do you make of the weather?' he asked.

The sailor, an East-coast man from Arbroath, shook his head. 'It's owner lown a' of a sudden,' he said. 'It looks like mair wind nor we want, but I think it'll haud till the morn.'

Maitland nodded and lay down again. He smiled at the return of his old sea craft and weather-lore, on which he had prided himself in his boyhood; and when Miss Clara came up to him with tea she found him grinning vacantly at the sky.

'What a wonderful lull in the wind,' she said. 'When I was here last these were real isles of the waves, with spray flying over them and a great business to land. But now they might be the island in Fountainblue lake.'

'Did you ever hear of the Ocean Quiet?' he asked. 'I believe it to be a translation of a Gaelic word which is a synonym for death, but it is also a kind of natural phenomenon. Old people at Cairnlora used to talk of it. They said that sometimes fishermen far out at sea in blowing weather came into a place of extraordinary peace, where the whole world was utterly still and they could hear their own hearts beating.'

'What a pretty fancy!' said the girl.

'Yes; but it had its other side. The fishermen rarely came home alive, and if they did they were queer to the end of their days. Another name for the thing was the Breathing of God. It is an odd idea, the passing from the wholesome turmoil of nature to the uncanny place where God crushes you by His silence.'

'All the things to eat are down by the fire,' she said, laughing. 'Do you know, if you weren't what you are, people might think you a poet, Mr Maitland. I thought you cared for none of these things.'

'What things?' he asked. 'I don't care for poetry. I am merely repeating the nonsense I was brought up on. Shall I talk to you about politics?'

'Heaven forbid! And now I will tell you my own story about these isles. There is a hermit's cell on one of them and crosses, like Iona. The hermit lived alone all winter, and was fed by boats from the shore when the weather was calm. When one hermit died another took his place, and no one knew where he came from. Now one day a great lord in Scotland disappeared from his castle. He was the King's Warden of the Marches and the greatest soldier of his day, but he disappeared utterly out of men's sight, and people forgot about him. Long years after the Northmen in a great fleet came down upon these isles, and the little chiefs fled before them. But suddenly among them there appeared an old man, the hermit of the Wave Islands, who organised resistance and gathered a strong army. No one dared oppose him, and the quarrelsome petty chiefs forgot their quarrels under his banner, for he had the air of one born to command. At last he met the invaders in the valley of Fountainblue, and beat them so utterly that few escaped to their ships. He fell himself in the first charge, but not before his followers had heard his battle-cry of "Saint Bride", and known the Hermit of the Isles and the great King's Warden were the same.'

'That was a common enough thing in wild times. Men grew tired of murder and glory and waving banners, and wanted quiet to make their peace with their own souls. I should have thought the craving scarcely extinct yet.'

'Then here is your chance, Mr Maitland,' said the girl, laughing. 'A little trouble would make the hut habitable, and you could simply disappear, leaving no address to forward your letters to. Think of the sensation, "Disappearance of a Secretary of State", and the wild theories and the obituaries. Then some day when the land question became urgent on the mainland, you would turn up suddenly, settle it with extraordinary wisdom, and die after confiding your life-story to some country reporter. But I am afraid it would scarcely do, for you would be discovered by Scotland Yard, which would be ignominious.'

'It is a sound idea, but the old device is too crude. However, it could be managed differently. Some day, when civilisation grows oppressive, Miss Clara, I will remember your advice.'

The afternoon shadows were beginning to lengthen, and from the west a light sharp wind was crisping the sea. The yacht was getting up steam, and boats were coming ashore for the party. The deep blue waters were flushing rose-pink as the level westering sun smote them from the summit of a cloudbank. The stillness had gone, and the air was now full of sounds and colour. Miss Clara, with an eye on the trim yacht, declared her disapproval. 'It is an evening for the cutter,' she cried, and in spite of Mrs Etheridge's protests she gave orders for it to be made ready. Then the self-willed young woman looked round for company. 'Will you come, Mr Maitland?' she said. 'You can sail a boat, can't you? And Mr Despencer, I shall want you to talk to me when Mr Maitland is busy. We shall race the yacht, for we ought to be able to get through the Scart's Neck with this wind.'

'I am not sure if you are wise, Miss Clara,' and Maitland pulled down his brows as he looked to the west. 'It will be wind – in a very little, and you stand the chance of a wetting.'

'I don't mind. I want to get the full good of such an evening. You want to be near the water to understand one of our sunsets. I can be a barbarian too, you know.'

It was not for Maitland to grumble at this friendliness; so he followed her into the cutter with Despencer, who had no love for the orders but much for her who gave them. He took the helm and steered, with directions from the lady, from his memory of the intricate coast. Despencer with many rugs looked to Miss Clara's comfort, and, having assured his own, was instantly entranced with the glories of the evening.

The boat tripped along for a little in a dazzle of light into the silvery grey of the open water. Far in front lay the narrow gut called the Scart's Neck, which was the by-way to the loch of Fountainblue. Then Maitland at the helm felt the sheets suddenly begin to strain, and, looking behind, saw that the Isles of the Waves were almost lost in the gloom, and that the roseate heavens were quickly darkening behind. The wind which he had feared was upon them; a few seconds more and it was sending the cutter staggering among billows. He could hardly make himself heard in the din, as he roared directions to Despencer about disposing of his person in another part of the boat. The girl with flushed face was laughing in pure joy of the storm. She caught a glimpse of Maitland's serious eye and looked over the gunwale at the threatening west. Then she too became quiet, and meekly sat down on the thwart to which he motioned her.

The gale made the Scart's Neck impossible, and the murky sky seemed to promise greater fury ere the morning. Twilight was falling, and the other entrance to the quiet loch meant the rounding of a headland and a difficult course through a little archipelago. It was the only way, for return was out of the question, and it seemed vain to risk the narrow chances of the short-cut. Maitland looked down at his two companions, and reflected with pleasure that he was the controller of their fates. He had sailed much as a boy, and he found in this moment of necessity that his old lore returned to him. He felt no mistrust of his powers: whatever the gale he could land them at Fountainblue, though it might take hours and involve much discomfort. He remembered the coast like his own name; he relished the grim rage of the elements, and he kept the cutter's head out to sea with a delight in the primeval conflict.

The last flickering rays of light, coming from the screen of cloud, illumined the girl's pale face, and the sight disquieted him. There was a hint of tragedy in this game. Despencer, nervously self-controlled, was reassuring Clara. Ploughing onward in the blackening night in a frail boat on a wind-threshed sea was no work for a girl. But it was Despencer who was comforting her! Well, it was his proper work. He was made for the business of talking soft things to women. Maitland, his face hard with spray, looked into the darkness with a kind of humour in his heart. And then, as the boat shore and dipped into the storm, its human occupants seemed to pass out of the picture, and it was only a shell tossed on great waters in the unfathomable night. The evening had come, moonless and starless, and Maitland steered as best he could by the deeper blackness which was the configuration of the shore. Something loomed up that he knew for the headland, and they were drifting in a quieter stretch of sea, with the breakers grumbling ahead from the little tangle of islands.

Suddenly he fell into one of the abstractions which had always dogged him through his strenuous life. His mind was clear, he chose his course with a certain precision, but the winds and waves had become to him echoes of echoes. Wet with spray and shifting his body constantly with the movement of the boat, it yet was all a phantasmal existence, while his thoughts were following an airy morrice in a fairyland world. The motto of his house, the canting motto of old reivers, danced in his brain – '*Parmi ceu haut bois conduyrai m'amie*' – 'Through the high wood I will conduct my love' – and in a land of green forests, dragon-haunted, he was piloting Clara robed in a quaint medieval gown, himself in speckless plate-armour. His fancy fled through a score of scenes, sometimes on a dark heath, or by a lonely river, or among great mountains, but always the lady and her protector. Clara, looking up from Despencer's side, saw his lips moving, noted that his eyes were glad, and for a moment hoped better things of their chances.

Then suddenly she was dumb with alarm, for the cutter heeled over, and but that Maitland woke to clear consciousness and swung the sheet loose, all would have been past. The adventure nerved him

[42]

and quickened his senses. The boat seemed to move more violently than the wind drove her, and in the utter blackness he felt for the first time the grip of the waters. The ugly cruel monster had wakened, and was about to wreak its anger on the toy. And then he remembered the currents which raced round Eilean Righ and the scattered isles. Dim shapes loomed up, shapes strange and unfriendly, and he felt miserably that he was as helpless now as Despencer. To the left night had wholly shut out the coast; his one chance was to run for one of the isles and risk a landing. It would be a dreary waiting for the dawn, but safety had come before any comfort. And yet, he remembered, the little islands were rock-bound and unfriendly, and he was hurrying forward in the grip of a black current with a gale behind and unknown reefs before.

And then he seemed to remember something of this current which swept along the isles. In a little – so he recalled a boyish voyage in clear weather – they would come to a place where the sea ran swift and dark beside a kind of natural wharf. Here he had landed once upon a time, but it was a difficult enterprise, needing a quick and a far leap at the proper moment, for the stream ran very fast. But if this leap were missed there was still a chance. The isle was the great Eilean Righ, and the current swung round its southern end, and then, joining with another stream, turned up its far side, and for a moment washed the shore. But if this second chance were missed, then nothing remained but to fall into the great sea-going stream and be carried out to death in the wide Atlantic. He strained his eyes to the right for Eilean Righ. Something seemed to approach, as they bent under an access of the gale. They bore down upon it, and he struggled to keep the boat's head away, for at this pace to grate upon rock would mean upsetting. The sail was down, fluttering amidships like a captive bird, and the gaunt mast bowed with the wind. A horrible fascination, the inertia of nightmare, seized him. The motion was so swift and beautiful; why not go on and onward, listlessly? And then, conquering the weakness, he leaned forward and called to Clara. She caught his arm like a child, and he pulled her up beside him. Then he beckoned Despencer, and, shrieking against the din, told him to follow him when he jumped. Despencer nodded, his teeth chattering with cold and the novel business. Suddenly out of the darkness, a yard on their right, loomed a great flat rock along which the current raced like a mill-lade. The boat made to strike, but Maitland forced her nose out to sea, and then as the stern swung round he seized his chance. Holding Clara with his left arm he stood up, balanced himself for a moment on the gunwale, and jumped. He landed sprawling on his side on some wet seaweed, over which the sea was lipping, but undeniably on land. As he pulled himself up he had a vision of the cutter, dancing like a cork, vanishing down the current into the darkness.

Holding the girl in his arms he picked his way across the rock pools to the edge of the island heather. For a moment he thought Clara had fainted. She lay still and inert, her eyes shut, her hair falling foolishly over her brow. He sprinkled some water on her face, and she revived sufficiently to ask her whereabouts. He was crossing the island to find Despencer, but he did not tell her. 'You are safe,' he said, and he carried her over the rough ground as lightly as a child. An intense exhilaration had seized him. He ran over the flats and strode up the low hillocks with one thought possessing his brain. To save Despencer, that of course was the far-off aim on his mind's horizon, but all the foreground was filled with the lady. '*Parmi ceu haut bois*' – the old poetry of the world had penetrated to his heart. The black night and the wild wind and the sea were the ministrants of love. The hollow shams of life with their mincing conventions had departed, and in this savage out-world a man stood for a man. The girl's light tweed jacket was no match for this chill gale, so he stopped for a moment, took off his own shooting-coat and put it round her. And then, as he came over a little ridge, he was aware of a grumbling of waters and the sea.

The beach was hidden in a veil of surf which sprinkled the very edge of the bracken. Beyond, the dark waters were boiling like a caldron, for the tides in this little bay ran with the fury of a river in spate. A moon was beginning to struggle through the windy clouds, and surf, rock, and wave began to shape themselves out of the night. Clara stood on the sand, a slim, desolate figure, and clung to Maitland's arm. She was still dazed with the storm and the baffling suddenness of change. Maitland, straining his eyes out to sea, was in a waking dream. With the lady no toil was too great, no darkness terrible; for her he would scale the blue air and plough the hills and do all the lover's feats of romance. And then suddenly he shook her hand roughly from his arm and ran forward, for he saw something coming down the tide.

Before he left the boat he had lowered the sail, and the cutter swung to the current, an odd amorphous thing, now heeling over with a sudden gust and now pulled back to balance by the strong grip of the water. A figure seemed to sit in the stern, making feeble efforts to steer. Maitland knew the coast and the ways of the sea. He ran through the surf-ring into the oily-black eddies, shouting to Despencer to come overboard. Soon he was not ten yards from the cutter's line, where the current made a turn towards the shore before it washed the iron rocks to the right. He found deep water, and in two strokes was in the grip of the tides and borne wildly towards the reef. He prepared himself for what was coming, raising his feet and turning his right shoulder to the front. And then with a shock he was pinned against the rock-wall, with the tides tugging at his legs, while his hands clung desperately to a shelf. Here he remained, yelling directions to the coming boat. Surf was in his eyes, so that at first he could not see, but at last in a dip of the waves he saw the cutter, a man's form in the stern, plunging not twenty yards away. Now was his chance or never, for while the tide would take a boat far from his present place of vantage, it would carry a lighter thing, such as a man's body, in a circle nearer to the shore. He yelled again, and the world seemed to him quiet for a moment, while his voice echoed eerily in the void. Despencer must have heard it, for the next moment he saw him slip pluckily overboard, making the cutter heel desperately with his weight. And then – it seemed an age – a man, choking and struggling weakly, came down the current, and, pushing his right arm out against the rush of water, he had caught the swimmer by the collar and drawn him in to the side of the rock.

Then came the harder struggle. Maitland's left hand was numbing, and though he had a foothold, it was too slight to lean on with full weight. A second lassitude oppressed him, a supreme desire to slip into those racing tides and rest. He was in no panic about death, but he had the practical man's love of an accomplished task, and it nerved him to the extreme toil. Slowly by inches he drew himself up the edge of the reef, cherishing jealously each grip and foothold, with Despencer, half-choked and all but fainting, hanging heavily on his right arm. Blind with spray, sick with sea-water, and aching with his labours, he gripped at last the tangles of seaweed, which meant the flat surface, and with one final effort raised himself and Despencer to the top. There he lay for a few minutes with his head in a rock-pool till the first weariness had passed.

He staggered with his burden in his arms along the ragged reef to the strip of sand where Clara was weeping hysterically. The sight of her restored Maitland to vigour, the appeal of her lonely figure there in the wet brackens. She must think them all dead, he reflected, and herself desolate, for she could not have interpreted rightly his own wild rush into the waves. When she heard his voice she started, as if at a ghost, and then seeing his burden, ran towards him. 'Oh, he is dead!' she cried. 'Tell me! tell me!' and she clasped the inert figure so that her arm crossed Maitland's. Despencer, stupefied and faint, was roused to consciousness by a woman's kisses on his cheek, and still more by his bearer abruptly laying him on the heather. Clara hung over him like a mother, calling him by soft names, pushing his hair from his brow, forgetful of her own wet and sorry plight. And meanwhile Maitland stood watching, while his palace of glass was being shivered about his ears.

Aforetime his arrogance had kept him from any thought of jealousy; now the time and place were too solemn for trifling, and facts were laid bare before him. Sentiment does not bloom readily in a hard nature, but if it once comes to flower it does not die without tears and agonies. The wearied man, who stood quietly beside the hysterical pair, had a moment of peculiar anguish. Then he conquered sentiment, as he had conquered all other feelings of whose vanity he was assured. He was now, as he was used to be, a man among children; and as a man he had his work. He bent over Clara. 'I know a hollow in the middle of the island,' he said, 'where we can camp the night. I'll carry Despencer, for his ankle is twisted. Do you think you could try to walk?'

The girl followed obediently, her eyes only on her lover. Her trust in the other was infinite, her indifference to him impenetrable; while he, hopelessly conscious of his fate, saw in the slim dishevelled figure at his side the lost lady, the mistress for him of all romance and generous ambitions. The new springs in his life were choked; he had still his work, his power, and, thank God, his courage; but the career which ran out to the horizon of his vision was black and loveless. And he held in his arms the thing which had frustrated him, the thing he had pulled out of the deep in peril of his body; and at the thought life for a moment seemed to be only a comic opera with tragedy to shift the scenes.

He found a cleft between two rocks with a soft floor of heather. There had been no rain, so the bracken was dry, and he gathered great armfuls and driftwood logs from the shore. Soon he had a respectable pile of timber, and then in the nick of the cleft he built a fire. His matches, being in his jacket pocket, had escaped the drenchings of salt water, and soon with a smoke and crackling and sweet scent of burning wood, a fire was going cheerily in the darkness. Then he made a couch of bracken, and laid there the still feeble Despencer. The man was more weak than ill; but for his ankle he was unhurt; and a little brandy would have brought him to himself. But this could not be provided, and Clara saw in his condition only the sign of mortal sickness. With haggard eyes she watched by him, easing his head, speaking soft kind words, forgetful of her own cold and soaking clothes. Maitland drew her gently to the fire, shook down the bracken to make a rest for her head, and left a pile of logs ready for use. 'I am going to the end of the island,' he said, 'to light a fire for a signal. It is the only part which they can see on the mainland, and if they see the blaze they will come off for us as soon as it is light.' The pale girl listened obediently. This man was the master, and in his charge was the safety of her lover and herself.

Maitland turned his back upon the warm nook, and stumbled along the ridge to the northern extremity of the isle. It was not a quarter of a mile away, but the land was so rough with gullies and crags that the journey took him nearly an hour. Just off the extreme point was a flat rock, sloping northward to a considerable height, a place from which a beacon could penetrate far over the mainland. He gathered brackens for kindling, and driftwood which former tides had heaped on the beach; and then with an armful he splashed through the shallow surf to the rock. Scrambling to the top, he found a corner where a fire might be lit, a place conspicuous and yet sheltered. Here he laid his kindling, and then in many wet journeys he carried his stores of firewood from the mainland to the rock. The lighting was nervous work, for he had few matches; but at last the dampish wood had caught, and tongues of flame shot up out of the smoke. Meantime the wind had sunk lower, the breakers seemed to have been left behind, and the eternal surge of the tides became the dominant sound to the watcher by the beacon.

And then, it seemed to him, the great convulsions of the night died away, and a curious peace came down upon the waters. The fire leaped in the air, the one living thing in a hushed and expectant world. It was not the quiet of sleep but of a sudden cessation, like the lull after a

[47]

great flood or a snowslip. The tides still eddied and swayed, but it was noiselessly; the world moved, yet without sound or friction. The bitter wind which chilled his face and stirred up the red embers was like a phantom blast, without the roughness of a common gale. For a moment he seemed to be set upon a high mountain with the world infinitely remote beneath his feet. To all men there come moments of loneliness of body, and to some few the mingled ecstasy and grief of loneliness of soul. The child-tale of the Ocean Quiet came back to him, the hour of the Breathing of God. Surely the great silence was now upon the world. But it was an evil presage, for all who sailed into it were homeless wanderers for ever after. Ah well! he had always been a wanderer, and the last gleam of home had been left behind, where by the firelight in the cold cranny a girl was crooning over her lover.

His past, his monotonous, brilliant past, slipped by with the knotless speed of a vision. He saw a boy, haunted with dreams, chafing at present delights, clutching evermore at the faint things of fancy. He saw a man, playing with the counters which others played with, fighting at first for bare existence and then for power and the pride of life. Success came over his path like a false dawn, but he knew in his heart that he had never sought it. What was that remote ineffable thing he had followed? Here in the quiet of the shadowy waters he had the moment of self-revelation which comes to all, and hopes and dim desires seemed to stand out with the clearness of accomplished facts. There had always been something elect and secret at the back of his fiercest ambitions. The ordinary cares of men had been to him but little things to be played with; he had won by despising them; casting them from him, they had fallen into the hollow of his hand. And he had held them at little, finding his reward in his work, and in a certain alertness and freshness of spirit which he had always cherished. There is a story of island-born men who carry into inland places and the streets of cities the noise of sea-water in their ears, and hear continually the tern crying and the surf falling. So from his romantic boyhood this man had borne an arrogance towards the things of the world which had given him a contemptuous empire over a share of them. As he saw the panorama of his life no place or riches entered into it, but only himself, the haggard, striving soul, growing in power, losing, perhaps, in wisdom. And then, at the end of the way, Death, to shrivel the power to dust, and with the might of his sunbeam to waken to life the forgotten world of the spirit.

In the hush he seemed to feel the wheel and the drift of things, the cosmic order of nature. He forgot his weariness and his plashing clothes as he put more wood on the beacon and dreamed into the night. The pitiless sea, infinite, untamable, washing the Poles and hiding Earth's secrets in her breast, spoke to him with a far-remembered voice. The romance of the remote isles, the homes of his people, floating still in a twilight of old story, rose out of the darkness. His life, with its routine and success, seemed in a moment hollow, a child's game, unworthy of a man. The little social round, the manipulation of half-truths, the easy victories over fools – surely this was not the task for him. He was a dreamer, but a dreamer with an iron hand; he was scarcely in the prime of life; the world was wide and his chances limitless. One castle of cards had already been overthrown; the Ocean Quiet was undermining another. He was sick of domesticity of every sort – of town, of home, of civilisation. The sad elemental world was his, the fury and the tenderness of nature, the peace of the wilds which old folk had called the Breathing of God. '*Parmi ceu haut bois conduyrai m'amie*' – this was still his motto, to carry untarnished to the end an austere and beautiful dream. His little ambitions had been but shreds and echoes and shadows of this supreme reality. And his love had been but another such simulacrum; for what he had sought was no foolish, laughing girl, but the Immortal Shepherdess, who, singing the old songs of youth, drives her flocks to the hill in the first dewy dawn of the world.

Suddenly he started and turned his head. Day was breaking in a red windy sky, and somewhere a boat's oars were plashing in the sea. And then he realised for the first time that he was cold and starving and soaked to the bone.

V

Mr Henry Durward to Lady Claudia Etheridge

'... Things have happened, my dear Clo, since I last wrote; time has passed; tomorrow I leave this place and go to stalk with Drapier; and yet in the stress of departure I take time to answer the host of questions with which you assailed me. I am able to give you the best of news. You have won your bet. Your prophecy about the conduct of the "other Etheridge girl" has come out right. They are both here, as it happens, having come on from Fountainblue, – both the hero and the heroine, I mean, of this most reasonable romance. You know Jack Despencer, one of the best people in the world, though a trifle given to chirping. But I don't think the grasshopper will become a burden to Miss Clara, for she likes that sort of thing. She must, for there is reason to believe that she refused for its sake the greatest match – I speak with all reverence – which this happy country could offer. I know you like Maitland as little as I do, but we agree in admiring the Colossus from a distance. Well, the Colossus has, so to speak, been laid low by a frivolous member of your sex. It is all a most romantic tale. Probably you have heard the gist of it, but here is the full and circumstantial account.

'We found Maitland beside the fire he had been feeding all night, and I shall never forget his figure alone in the dawn on that rock, drenched and dishevelled, but with his haggard white face set like a Crusader's. He took us to a kind of dell in the centre of the island, where we found Clara and Despencer shivering beside a dying fire. He had a twisted ankle and had got a bad scare, while she was perfectly composed, though she broke down when we got home. It must have been an awful business for both, but Maitland never seems to have turned a hair. I want to know two things. First, how in the presence of great danger he managed to get his dismissal from the lady? – for get it he assuredly did, and Despencer at once appeared in the part of the successful lover; second, what part he played in the night's events? Clara remembered little, Despencer only knew that he had been pulled out of the sea, but over all Maitland seems to have brooded like a fate. As usual he told us nothing. It was always his way to give the world results and leave it to find out his methods for itself . . .

'Despencer overwhelmed him with gratitude. His new happiness made him in love with life, and he included Maitland in the general affection. The night's events seemed to have left their mark on the great man also. He was very quiet, forgot to be rude to anybody, and was kind to both Clara and Despencer. It is his way of acknowledging defeat, the great gentleman's way, for, say what we like about him, he is a tremendous gentleman, one of the last of the breed . . .

'And then he went away – two days later. Just before he went Hugh Clanroyden and myself were talking in the library, which has a window opening on a flower-garden. Despencer was lying in an invalid's chair under a tree and Clara was reading to him. Maitland was saying goodbye, and he asked for Despencer. We told him that he was with Clara in the garden. He smiled one of those odd scarce smiles of his, and went out to them. When I saw his broad shoulders bending over the chair and the strong face looking down at the radiant Jack with his amiable good looks, confound it, Clo, I had to contrast the pair, and admit with Shakespeare the excellent foppery of the world. Well-a-day! "Smooth Jacob still robs homely Esau." And perhaps it is a good thing, for we are most of us Jacobs, and Esau is an uncomfortable fellow in our midst.

'A week later came the surprising, the astounding news that he had taken the African Governorship. A career ruined, everyone said, the finest chance in the world flung away; and then people speculated, and the story came out in bits, and there was only one explanation. It is the right one, as I think you will agree, but it points to some hidden weakness in that iron soul that he could be moved to fling over the ambitions of years because of a girl's choice. He will go and bury himself in the wilds, and our party will have to find another leader. Of course he will do his work well, but it is just as if I were to give up my chances of the Woolsack for a county-court judgeship. He will probably be killed, for he has a million enemies; he is perfectly fearless, and he does not understand the arts of compromise. It was a privilege, I shall always feel, to have known him. He was a great man, and yet – intellect, power, character, were at the mercy of a girl's caprice. As I write, I hear Clara's happy laugh below in the garden, probably at some witticism of the fortunate Jack's. Upon which, with my usual pride in the obvious, I am driven to reflect that the weak things in life may confound the strong, and that, after all, the world is to the young...'

VI
Sir Hugh Clanroyden to Mr Henry Durward
some years later

'... I am writing this on board ship, as you will see from the heading, and shall post it when I get to the Cape. You have heard of my appointment, and I need not tell you how deep were my searchings of heart before I found courage to accept. Partly I felt that I had got my chance; partly I thought – an inconsequent feeling – that Maitland, if he had lived, would have been glad to see me in the place. But I am going to wear the Giant's Robe, and Heaven knows I have not the shoulders to fill it. Yet I am happy in thinking that I am in a small sense faithful to his memory.

'No further news, I suppose, has come of the manner of his death? Perhaps we shall never know, for it was on one of those Northern expeditions with a few men by which he held the frontier. I wonder if anyone will ever write fully the history of all that he did? It must have been a titanic work, but his methods were always so quiet that people accepted his results like a gift from Providence. He was given, one gathers, a practically free hand, and he made the country – four years' work of a man of genius. They wished to bring his body home, but he made them bury him where he fell – a characteristic last testament. And so he has gone out of the world into the world's history.

'I am still broken by his death, but, now that he is away, I begin to see him more clearly. Most people, I think, misunderstood him. I was one of his nearest friends, and I only knew bits of the man. For one thing – and I hate to use the vulgar word – he was the only aristocrat I ever heard of. Our classes are three-fourths of them of yesterday's growth, without the tradition, character, manner, or any trait of an aristocracy. And the few, who are nominally of the blood, have gone to seed in mind, or are spoilt by coarse marriages, or, worst of all, have the little trifling superior airs of incompetence. But he, he had the most transcendent breeding in mind and spirit. He had no need for self-assertion, for his most casual acquaintances put him at once in a different class from all other men. He had never a trace of a vulgar ideal; men's opinions, worldly honour, the common pleasures of life, were merely degrees of the infinitely small. And yet he was no bloodless mystic. If race means anything, he had it to perfection. Dreams and fancies to him were the realities, while facts were the shadows which he made dance as it pleased him.

'The truth is, that he was that rarest of mortals, the iron dreamer. He thought in æons and cosmic cycles, and because of it he could do what he pleased in life. We call a man practical if he is struggling in the crowd with no knowledge of his whereabouts, and yet in our folly we deny the name to the clear-sighted man who can rule the crowd from above. And here I join issue with you and everybody else. You thought it was Miss Clara's refusal which sent him abroad and interrupted his career. I read the thing otherwise. His love for the girl was a mere accident, a survival of the domestic in an austere spirit.

Something, I do not know what, showed him his true desires. She may have rejected him; he may never have spoken to her; in any case the renunciation had to come. You must remember that that visit to Fountainblue was the first that he had paid since his boyhood to his boyhood's home. Those revisitings have often a strange trick of self-revelation. I believe that in that night on the island he saw our indoor civilisation and his own destiny in so sharp a contrast that he could not choose but make the severance. He found work where there could be small hope of honour or reward, but many a chance for a hero. And I am sure that he was happy, and that it was the longed-for illumination that dawned on him with the bullet which pierced his heart.

'But, you will say, the fact remains that he was once in love with Miss Clara, and that she would have none of him. I do not deny it. He was never a favourite with women; but, thank heaven, I have better things to do than study their peculiarities . . .'

The Outgoing of the Tide*

'The Outgoing of the Tide' was probably written in 1898 while Buchan was still at Oxford – it appears in a notebook of that date – but was not published until the January 1902 issue of *The Atlantic Monthly*. It was one of the five long stories in *The Watcher by the Threshold* (1902) and has been included in several anthologies, including *Scottish Short Stories* (1948).

'Between the hours of twelve and one, even at the turning of the tide.'

MEN COME FROM distant parts to admire the tides of Solway, which race in at flood and retreat at ebb with a greater speed than a horse can follow. But nowhere are there queerer waters than in our own parish of Caulds, at the place called the Sker Bay, where between two horns of land a shallow estuary receives the stream of the Sker. I never daunder by its shores and see the waters hurrying like messengers from the great deep without solemn thoughts, and a memory of Scripture words on the terror of the sea. The vast Atlantic may be fearful in its wrath, but with us it is no clean open rage, but the deceit of the creature, the unholy ways of quicksands when the waters are gone, and their stealthy return like a thief in the night watches. But in times of which I write there were more awful fears than any from the violence of nature. It was before the day of my ministry in Caulds, for then I was a tot callant in short clothes in my native parish of Lesmahagow; but the worthy Dr Chrystal, who had charge of spiritual things, had told me often of the power of Satan and his emissaries in that lonely place. It was the day of warlocks and apparitions, now

---

*From the unpublished Remains of the Reverend John Dennistoun: Sometime Minister of the Gospel in the Parish of Caulds, and Author of Satan's Artifices against the Elect.

[54]

happily driven out by the zeal of the General Assembly. Witches pursued their wanchancy calling, bairns were spirited away, young lassies selled their souls to the Evil One, and the Accuser of the Brethren, in the shape of a black tyke, was seen about cottage doors in the gloaming. Many and earnest were the prayers of good Dr Chrystal, but the evil thing, in spite of his wrestling, grew and flourished in his midst. The parish stank of idolatry, abominable rites were practised in secret, and in all the bounds there was no one had a more evil name for the black traffic than one Alison Sempill, who bode at the Sker-burnfoot.

The cottage stood nigh the burn, in a little garden, with lilyoaks and grosart bushes lining the pathway. The Sker ran by in a line among rowand trees, and the noise of its waters was ever about the place. The highroad on the other side was frequented by few, for a nearer-hand way to the west had been made through the lower Moss. Sometimes a herd from the hills would pass by with sheep, sometimes a tinkler or a wandering merchant, and once in a long while the laird of Heriotside on his grey horse riding to Gledsmuir. And they who passed would see Alion trupling in her garden, speaking to herself like the ill wife she was, or sitting on a cutty-stool by the doorside, with her eyes on other than mortal sights. Where she came from no man could tell. There were some said she was no woman, but a ghost haunting some mortal tenement. Others would threep she was gentrice, come of a persecuting family in the west, who had been ruined in the Revolution wars. She never seemed to want for siller; the house was as bright as a new preen, the yaird better delved than the manse garden; and there was routh of fowls and doos about the small steading, forbye a whee sheep and milk-kye in the fields. No man ever saw Alison at any market in the countryside, and yet the Skerburnfoot was plenished yearly in all proper order. One man only worked on the place, a doited lad who had long been a charge to the parish, and who had not the sense to fear danger or the wit to understand it. Upon all others the sight of Alison, were it but for a moment, cast a cold grue, not to be remembered without terror. It seems she was not ordinarily ill-famed, as men use the word. She was maybe sixty years in age, small and trig, with her grey hair folded neatly under her mutch. But the sight of her eyes was not a thing to forget. John Dodds said they were the een of a deer with the Devil ahint them; and indeed, they would so appal an onlooker that a sudden unreasoning terror came into his heart, while his feet would impel him to flight. Once John, being overtaken in drink on the roadside by the cottage, and dreaming that he was burning in hell, awoke and saw the old wife hobbling toward him. Thereupon he fled soberly to the hills, and from that day became a quiet-living, humble-minded Christian. She moved about the country like a ghost, gathering herbs in dark loanings, lingering in kirkyairds, and casting a blight on innocent bairns. Once Robert Smellie found her in a ruinous kirk on the Lang Muir, where of old the idolatrous rites of Rome were practised. It was a hot day, and in the quiet place the flies buzzed in clouds, and he noted that she sat clothed in them as with a garment, yet suffering no discomfort. Then he, having mind of Beelzebub, the god of flies, fled without a halt homewards; but, falling in the coo's loan, broke two ribs and a collar bone, the whilk misfortune was much blessed to his soul. And there were darker tales in the countryside, of weans stolen, of lassies misguided, of innocent beasts cruelly tortured, and in one and all there came in the name of the wife of the Skerburnfoot. It was noted by them that kenned best that her cantrips were at their worst when the tides in the Sker Bay ebbed between the hours of twelve and one. At this season of the night the tides of mortality run lowest, and when the outgoing of these unco waters fell in with the setting of the current of life, then indeed was the hour for unholy revels. While honest men slept in their beds, the auld rudas carlines took their pleasure. That there is a delight in sin no man denies, but to most it is but a broken glint in the pauses of their conscience. But what must be the hellish joy of those lost beings who have forsworn God, and trysted with the Prince of Darkness, it is not for a Christian to say. Certain it is that it must be great, though their master waits at the end of the road to claim the wizened things they call their souls. Serious men – notably Gidden Scott in the Bach of the Hill, and Simon Wanch in the Sheilin of Chasehope – have seen Alison wandering on the wet sands, dancing to no earthy musick, while the heavens, they said, were full of lights and sounds which betokened the presence of the Prince of the Powers of the Air. It was a season of heart-searching for God's saints in Caulds, and the dispensation was blessed to not a few.

It will seem strange that in all this time the Presbytery was idle, and no effort was made to rid the place of so fell an influence. But there was a reason, and the reason, as in most like cases, was a lassie. Forbye Alison there lived at the Skerburnfoot a young maid, Ailie Sempill, who by all accounts was as good and bonnie as the other was evil. She passed for a daughter of Alison's – whether born in wedlock or not I cannot tell; but there were some said she was no kin to the auld witch wife, but some bairn spirited away from honest parents. She was young and blithe, with a face like an April morning, and a voice in her that put the laverocks to shame. When she sang in the kirk, folk have told me that they had a foretaste of the musick of the New Jerusalem, and when she came in by the village of Caulds old men stottered to their doors to look at her. Moreover, from her earliest days the bairn had some glimmerings of grace. Though no minister would visit the Skerburnfoot, or, if he went, departed quicker than he came, the girl Ailie attended regular at the catechising at the mains of Sker. It may be that Alison thought she would be a better offering for the Devil if she were given the chance of forswearing God, or it may be that she was so occupied in her own dark business that she had no care of the bairn. Meanwhile, the lass grew up in the nurture and admonition of the Lord. I have heard Dr Chrystal say that he never had a communicant more full of the things of the Spirit. From the day when she first declared her wish to come forward to the hour when she broke bread at the table, she walked like one in a dream. The lads of the parish might cast admiring eyes on her bright cheeks and yellow hair, as she sat in her white gown in the kirk, but well they knew she was not for them. To be the bride of Christ was the thought that filled her heart; and when, at the fencing of the table, Dr Chrystal preached from Matthew nine and fifteen, 'Can the children of the bridechamber mourn as long as the bridegroom is with them?' it was remarked by sundry that Ailie's face was liker the countenance of an angel than of a mortal lass.

It is with the day of her first communion that this narrative of mine begins. As she walked home, after the morning table, she communed in secret, and her heart sang within her. She had mind of God's mercies in the past; how he had kept her feet from the snares of evil doers which had been spread around her youth. She had been told unholy charms like the Seven South Streams and the Nine Rowand Berries, and it was noted, when she went first to the catechising, that she prayed, 'Our Father which wert in heaven,' the prayer which the ill wife Alison had taught her; meaning by it Lucifer, who had been in heaven, and had been cast out therefrom. But when she had come to years of discretion, she had freely chosen the better part, and evil had

ever been repelled from her soul like gled water from the stones of
Gled brig. Now she was in a rapture of holy content. The Druchen
Bell – for the ungodly fashion lingered in Caulds – was ringing in her
ears as she left the village, but to her it was but a kirk bell and a goodly
sound. As she went through the woods where the primroses and the
whitethorn were blossoming, the place seemed as the land of Elim,
wherein there were twelve wells and threescore and ten palm trees.
And then, as it might be, another thought came into her head, for it is
ordained that frail mortality cannot long continue in holy joy. In the
kirk she had been only the bride of Christ, but as she came through the
wood, with the birds lilting and the winds of the world blowing, she
had mind of another lover; for this lass, though so cold to men, had
not escaped the common fate. It seems that the young Heriotside,
riding by one day, stopped to speir something or other, and got a glisk
of Ailie's face which caught his fancy. He passed the road again many
times, and then he would meet her in the gloaming, or of a morning in
the field as she went to fetch the kye. 'Blue are the hills that are far
away,' is an owercome in the countryside, and while at first on his side
it may have been but a young man's fancy, to her he was like the god
Apollo descending from the skies. He was good to look on, brawly
dressed, and with a tongue in his head that would have wiled the bird
from the tree. Moreover, he was of gentle kin, and she was a poor lass
biding in a cot house with an ill-reputed mother. It seems that in time
the young man, who had begun the affair with no good intentions, fell
honestly in love, while she went singing about the doors as innocent as
a bairn, thinking of him when her thoughts were not on higher things.
So it came about that long ere Ailie reached home it was on young
Heriotside that her mind dwelled, and it was the love of him that
made her eyes glow and her cheeks redden.

Now it chanced that at that very hour her master had been with
Alison, and the pair of them were preparing a deadly pit. Let no man
say that the Devil is not a cruel tyrant. He may give his folk some
scrapings of unhallowed pleasure, but he will exact tithes, yea, of anise
and cummin, in return, and there is aye the reckoning to pay at the
hinder end. It seems that now he was driving Alison hard. She had
been remiss of late – fewer souls sent to hell, less zeal in quenching the
Spirit, and, above all, the crowning offence that her bairn had communicated in Christ's kirk. She had waited overlong, and now it was
like that Ailie would escape her toils. I have no skill of fancy to tell of

that dark collogue, but the upshot was that Alison swore by her lost soul and the pride of sin to bring the lass into thrall to her master. The fiend had bare departed when Ailie came over the threshold to find the auld carline glunching over the fire.

It was plain she was in the worst of tempers. She flyted on the lass till the poor thing's cheek paled. 'There you gang,' she cries, 'broking wi' thae wearifu' Pharisees o' Caulds, whae daurna darken your mither's door! A bonnie dutiful child, quotha! Wumman, hae ye nae pride, or even the excuse o' a tinkler-lass?' And then she changed her voice and would be as saft as honey: 'My puir wee Ailie, was I thrawn till ye? Never mind, my bonnie. You and me are a' that's left, and we maunna be ill to ither.' And then the two had their dinner, and all the while the auld wife was crooning over the lass. 'We maun 'gree weel,' she says, 'for we 're like to be our lee-lane for the rest o' our days. They tell me Heriotside is seeking Joan o' the Croft, and they're sune to be cried in Gledsmuir's kirk.'

It was the first the lass had heard of it, and you may fancy she was struck dumb. And so with one thing and other the auld witch raised the fiends of jealousy in that innocent heart. She would cry out that Heriotside was an ill-doing wastrel, and had no business to come and flatter honest lassies. And then she would speak of his gentle birth and his leddy mother, and say it was indeed presumption to hope that so great a gentleman could mean all that he said. Before long Ailie was silent and white, while her mother rimed on about men and their ways. And then she could thole it no longer, but must go out and walk by the burn to cool her hot brow and calm her thoughts, while the witch indoors laughed to herself at her devices.

For days Ailie had an absent eye and a sad face, and it so fell out that in all that time young Heriotside, who had scarce missed a day, was laid up with a broken arm and never came near her. So in a week's time she was beginning to hearken to her mother when she spoke of incantations and charms for restoring love. She kenned it was sin, but though not seven days syne she had sat at the Lord's table, so strong is love in a young heart that she was on the very brink of it. But the grace of God was stronger than her weak will. She would have none of her mother's runes and philters, though her soul cried out for them. Always when she was most disposed to listen some merciful power stayed her consent. Alison grew thrawner as the hours passed. She kenned of Heriotside's broken arm, and she feared that any day he might recover and put her stratagems to shame. And then it seems that she collogued with her master and heard word of a subtler device. For it was approaching that uncanny time of year, the festival of Beltane, when the auld pagans were wont to sacrifice to their god Baal. In this season warlocks and carlines have a special dispensation to do evil, and Alison waited on its coming with graceless joy. As it happened, the tides in the Sker Bay ebbed at this time between the hours of twelve and one, and, as I have said, this was the hour above all others when the Powers of Darkness were most potent. Would the lass but consent to go abroad in the unhallowed place at this awful season and hour of the night, she was as firmly handfasted to the Devil as if she had signed a bond with her own blood; for then, it seemed, the forces of good fled far away, the world for one hour was given over to its ancient prince, and the man or woman who willingly sought the spot was his bondservant forever. There are deadly sins from which God's people may recover. A man may even communicate unworthily, and yet, so be it he sin not against the Holy Ghost, he may find forgiveness. But it seems that for the Beltane sin there could be no pardon, and I can testify from my own knowledge that they who once committed it became lost souls from that day. James Denchar, once a promising professor, fell thus out of sinful bravery and died blaspheming; and of Kate Mallison, who went the same road, no man can tell. Here indeed was the witch wife's chance; and she was the more keen, for her master had warned her that this was her last chance. Either Ailie's soul would be his, or her auld wrunkled body and black heart would be flung from this pleasant world to their apportioned place.

Some days later it happened that young Heriotside was stepping home over the Lang Muir about ten at night, it being his first jaunt from home since his arm had mended. He had been to the supper of the Forest Club at the Cross Keys in Gledsmuir, a clamjamphry of wild young blades who passed the wine and played at cartes once a fortnight. It seems he had drunk well, so that the world ran round about and he was in the best of tempers. The moon came down and bowed to him, and he took off his hat to it. For every step he travelled miles, so that in a little he was beyond Scotland altogether and pacing the Arabian desert. He thought he was the Pope of Rome, so he held out his foot to be kissed, and rolled twenty yards to the bottom of a small brae. Syne he was the king of France, and fought hard with a whin bush till he had banged it to pieces. After that nothing would content him but he must be a bogle, for he found his head dunting on the stars and his legs were knocking the hills together. He thought of the mischief he was doing to the auld earth, and sat down and cried at his wickedness. Then he went on, and maybe the steep road to the Moss Rig helped him, for he began to get soberer and ken his whereabouts.

On a sudden he was aware of a man linking along at his side. He cried a fine night, and the man replied. Syne, being merry from his cups, he tried to slap him on the back. The next he kenned he was rolling on the grass, for his hand had gone clean through the body and found nothing but air.

His head was so thick with wine that he found nothing droll in this. 'Faith, friend,' he says, 'that was a nasty fall for a fellow that has supped weel. Where might your road be gaun to?'

'To the World's End,' said the man, 'but I stop at the Skerburn-foot.'

'Bide the night at Heriotside,' says he. 'It's a thought out of your way, but it's a comfortable bit.'

'There's mair comfort at the Skerburnfoot,' said the dark man.

Now the mention of the Skerburnfoot brought back to him only the thought of Ailie, and not of the witch wife, her mother. So he jaloused no ill, for at the best he was slow in the uptake.

The two of them went on together for a while, Heriotside's fool head filled with the thought of the lass. Then the dark man broke silence. 'Ye 're thinkin' o' the maid Ailie Sempill,' says he.

'How ken ye that?' asked Heriotside.

'It is my business to read the hearts o' men,' said the other.

'And who may ye be?' said Heriotside, growing eerie.

'Just an auld packman,' says he, 'nae name ye wad ken, but kin to mony gentle houses.'

'And what about Ailie, you that ken sae muckle?' asked the young man.

'Naething,' was the answer, – 'naething that concerns you, for ye'll never get the lass.'

'By God and I will!' says Heriotside, for he was a profane swearer.

'That's the wrong name to seek her in, ony way,' said the man.

At this the young laird struck a great blow at him with his stick, but found nothing to resist him but the hill wind.

When they had gone on a bit the dark man spoke again. 'The lassie is thirled to holy things,' says he; 'she has nae care for flesh and blood, – only for devout contemplation.'

'She loves me,' says Heriotside.

'Not you,' says the other, 'but a shadow in your stead.'

At this the young man's heart began to tremble, for it seemed that there was truth in what his companion said, and he was owerdrunk to think gravely.

'I kenna whatna man ye are,' he says, 'but ye have the skill of lassies' hearts. Tell me truly, is there no way to win her to common love?'

'One way there is,' said the man, 'and for our friendship's sake I will tell you it. If ye can ever tryst wi' her on Beltane's E'en on the Sker sands, at the green link o' the burn where the sands begin, on the ebb o' the tide when the midnight is by, but afore cockcrow, she'll be yours, body and soul, for this world and forever.'

And then it appeared to the young man that he was walking his love up the grass walk of Heriotside, with the house close by him. He thought no more of the stranger he had met, but the word stuck in his heart.

It seems that about this very time Alison was telling the same tale to poor Ailie. She cast up to her every idle gossip she could think of. 'It's Joan o' the Croft,' was aye her owercome, and she would threep that they were to be cried in kirk on the first Sabbath of May. And then she would rime on about the black cruelty of it, and cry down curses on the lover, so that her daughter's heart grew cauld with fear. It is terrible to think of the power of the world even in a redeemed soul. Here was a maid who had drunk of the well of grace and tasted of God's mercies, and yet there were moments when she was ready to renounce her hope. At those awful seasons God seemed far off and the world very nigh, and to sell her soul for love looked a fair bargain; at other times she would resist the Devil and comfort herself with prayer; but aye when she awoke there was the sore heart, and when she went to sleep there were the weary eyes. There was no comfort in the goodliness of spring or the bright sunshine weather, and she who had been wont to go about the doors lightfoot and blithe was now as dowie as a widow woman.

And then one afternoon in the hinder end of April came young Heriotside riding to the Skerburnfoot. His arm was healed, he had got him a fine new suit of green, and his horse was a mettle beast that well set off his figure. Ailie was standing by the doorstep as he came down the road, and her heart stood still with joy. But a second thought gave her anguish. This man, so gallant and braw, would never be for her; doubtless the fine suit and the capering horse were for Joan o' the Croft's pleasure. And he, in turn, when he remarked her wan cheeks and dowie eyes, had mind to what the dark man said on the muir, and saw in her a maid sworn to no mortal love. Yet his passion for her had grown fiercer than ever, and he swore to himself that he would win her back from her phantasies. She, one may believe, was ready enough to listen. As she walked with him by the Sker water his words were like musick to her ears, and Alison within doors laughed to herself and saw her devices prosper.

He spoke to her of love and his own heart, and the girl hearkened gladly. Syne he rebuked her coldness and cast scorn upon her piety, and so far was she beguiled that she had no answer. Then from one thing and another he spoke of some true token of their love. He said he was jealous, and craved something to ease his care. 'It's but a small thing I ask,' says he, 'but it will make me a happy man, and nothing ever shall come atween us. Tryst wi' me for Beltane's E'en on the Sker sands, at the green link o' the burn where the sands begin, on the ebb o' the tide when midnight is by, but afore cockcrow. For,' said he, 'that was our forbears' tryst for true lovers, and wherefore no for you and me?'

The lassie had grace given her to refuse, but with a woeful heart, and Heriotside rode off in black discontent, leaving poor Ailie to sigh her love. He came back the next day and the next, but aye he got the same answer. A season of great doubt fell upon her soul. She had no clearness in her hope, nor any sense of God's promises. The Scriptures were an idle tale to her, prayer brought her no refreshment, and she was convicted in her conscience of the unpardonable sin. Had she been less full of pride, she would have taken her troubles to good Dr Chrystal and got comfort; but her grief made her silent and timorous, and she found no help anywhere. Her mother was ever at her side, seeking with coaxings and evil advice to drive her to the irrevocable step. And all the while there was her love for the man riving in her bosom, and giving her no ease by night or day. She believed she had driven him away, and repented her denial. Only her pride held her back from going to Heriotside and seeking him herself. She watched the road hourly for a sight of his face, and when the darkness came she would sit in a corner brooding over her sorrows.

At last he came, speiring the old question. He sought the same tryst, but now he had a further tale. It seemed he was eager to get her away from the Skerburnside and auld Alison. His aunt, Lady Balerynie, would receive her gladly at his request till the day of their marriage; let her but tryst with him at the hour and place he named, and he would carry her straight to Balerynie, where she would be safe and happy. He named that hour, he said, to escape men's observation, for the sake of her own good name. He named that place, for it was near her dwelling, and on the road between Balerynie and Heriotside, which fords the Sker Burn. The temptation was more than mortal heart could resist. She gave him the promise he sought, stifling the voice of conscience; and as she clung to his neck it seemed to her that heaven was a poor thing compared with a man's love.

Three days remained till Beltane's E'en, and throughout this time it was noted that Heriotside behaved like one possessed. It may be that his conscience pricked him, or that he had a glimpse of his sin and its coming punishment. Certain it is that if he had been daft before, he now ran wild in his pranks, and an evil report of him was in every mouth. He drank deep at the Cross Keys, and fought two battles with young lads that had angered him. One he let off with a touch on the shoulder; the other goes lame to this day from a wound he got in the groin. There was word of the procurator fiscal taking note of his doings, and troth, if they had continued long he must have fled the country. For a wager he rode his horse down the Dow Craig, wherefore the name of the place has been the Horseman's Craig ever since. He laid a hundred guineas with the laird of Slofferfield that he would drive four horses through the Slofferfield loch, and in the prank he had his bit chariot dung to pieces and a good mare killed. And all men observed that his eyes were wild and the face grey and thin, and that his hand would twitch, as he held the glass, like one with the palsy.

The Eve of Beltane was lower and hot in the low country, with fire hanging in the clouds and thunder grumbling about the heavens. It seems that up in the hills it had been an awesome deluge of rain, but on the coast it was still dry and lowering. It is a long road from Heriotside to the Skerburnfoot. First you go down the Heriot water, and syne over the Lang Muir to the edge of Mucklewhan. When you pass the steadings of Mirehope and Cockmalane, you turn to the right and ford the Mire Burn. That brings you on to the turnpike road, which you will ride till it bends inland, while you keep on straight over the Whinny Knowes to the Sker Bay. There, if you are in luck, you will find the tide out and the place fordable dryshod for a man on a horse. But if the tide runs, you will do well to sit down on the sands and content yourself till it turn, or it will be the solans and scarts of the Solway that will be seeing the next of you. On this Beltane's E'en, the young man, after supping with some wild young blades, bade his horse be saddled about ten o'clock. The company were eager to ken his errand, but he waved them back. 'Bide here,' he says, 'and boil the wine till I return. This is a ploy of my own on which no man follows me.' And there was that in his face, as he spoke, which chilled the wildest, and left them well content to keep to the good claret and the saft seat, and let the daft laird go his own ways.

Well and on he rode down the bridle path in the wood, along the top of the Heriot glen, and as he rode he was aware of a great noise beneath him. It was not wind, for there was none, and it was not the sound of thunder; and aye as he speired at himself what it was it grew the louder, till he came to a break in the trees. And then he saw the cause, for Heriot was coming down in a furious flood, sixty yards wide, tearing at the roots of the aiks and flinging red waves against the drystone dykes. It was a sight and sound to solemnise a man's mind, deep calling unto deep, the great waters of the hills running to meet with the great waters of the sea. But Heriotside recked nothing of it, for his heart had but one thought and the eye of his fancy one figure. Never had he been so filled with love of the lass; and yet it was not happiness, but a deadly, secret fear.

As he came to the Lang Muir it was gey and dark, though there was a moon somewhere behind the clouds. It was little he could see of the road, and ere long he had tried many moss pools and sloughs, as his braw new coat bare witness. Aye in front of him was the great hill of Mucklewhan, where the road turned down by the Mire. The noise of the Heriot had not long fallen behind him ere another began, the same eerie sound of burns crying to ither in the darkness. It seemed that the whole earth was overrun with waters. Every little runnel in the bay was astir, and yet the land around him was as dry as flax, and no drop of rain had fallen. As he rode on the din grew louder, and as he came over the top of Mirehope he kenned by the mighty rushing noise that something uncommon was happening with the Mire Burn. The light from Mirehope Sheilin twinkled on his left, and had the man not been dozened with his fancies he might have observed that the steading was deserted and men were crying below in the fields. But he rode on, thinking of but one thing, till he came to the cot house of Cockmalane, which is nigh the fords of the Mire.

John Dodds, the herd who bode in the place, was standing at the door, and he looked to see who was on the road so late.

'Stop!' says he – 'stop, Laird Heriotside! I kenna what your errand is, but it is to no holy purpose that ye're out on Beltane E'en. D' ye no hear the warring o' the waters?'

And then in the still night came the sound of Mire like the clash of armies.

'I must win over the ford,' says the laird quickly, thinking of another thing.

'Ford!' cried John, in scorn. 'There'll be nae ford for you the nicht unless it was the ford o' the river Jordan. The burns are up and bigger than man ever saw them. It'll be a Beltane's E'en that a' folk will remember. They tell me that Gled valley is like a loch, and that there's an awesome heap o' folk drouned in the hills. Gin ye were ower the Mire, what about crossin' the Caulds and the Sker?' says he, for he jaloused he was going to Gledsmuir.

And then it seemed that that word brought the laird to his senses. He looked the airt the rain was coming from, and he saw it was the airt the Sker flowed. In a second, he has told me, the works of the Devil were revealed to him. He saw himself a tool in Satan's hands; he saw his tryst a device for the destruction of the body as it was assuredly meant for the destruction of the soul; and there came black on his mind the picture of an innocent lass borne down by the waters, with no place for repentance. His heart grew cold in his breast. He had but one thought, – a sinful and reckless one: to get to her side, that the two might go together to their account. He heard the roar of the Mire as in a dream, and when John Dodds laid hands on his bridle he felled him to the earth. And the next seen of it was the laird riding the floods like a man possessed.

The horse was the grey stallion he aye rode, the very beast he had ridden for many a wager with the wild lads of the Cross Keys. No man but himself durst back it, and it had lamed many a hostler lad and broke two necks in its day. But it seems it had the mettle for any flood, and took the Mire with little spurring. The herds on the hillside looked to see man and steed swept into eternity; but though the red waves were breaking about his shoulders, and he was swept far down, he aye held on for the shore. The next thing the watchers saw was the laird struggling up the far bank and casting his coat from him, so that he rode in his sark. And then he set off like a wildfire across the muir toward their turnpike road. Two men saw him on the road, and have recorded their experience. One was a gangrel, by name McNab, who was travelling from Gledsmuir to Allerkirk with a heavy pack on his back and a bowed head. He heard a sound like wind afore him, and, looking up, saw coming down the road a grey horse stretched out to a wild gallop, and a man on its back with a face like a soul in torment. He kenned not whether it was devil or mortal, but flung himself on the roadside and lay like a corp for an hour or more, till the rain aroused him. The other was one Sim Doolittle, the fish hawker from Allerfoot, jogging home in his fish cart from Gledsmuir fair. He had drunk more than was fit for him, and he was singing some light song, when he saw approaching, as he said, the pale horse mentioned in the Revelation, with Death seated as the rider. Thought of his sins came on him like a thunderclap; fear loosened his knees. He leaped from the cart to the road, and from the road to the back of a dyke; thence he flew to the hills, and was found the next morning far up among the Mire Craigs, while his horse and cart were gotten on the Aller sands, the horse lamed and the cart without the wheels.

At the tollhouse the road turns inland to Gledsmuir, and he who goes to the Sker Bay must leave it and cross the wild land called Whinny Knowes, a place rough with bracken and foxes' holes and old stone cairns. The toll-man, John Gilzean, was opening the window to get a breath of air in the lower night, when he heard or saw the approaching horse. He kenned the beast for Heriotside's, and, being a friend of the laird's, he ran down in all haste to open the yett, wondering to himself about the laird's errand on this night. A voice came down the road to him bidding him hurry; but John's old fingers were slow with the keys, and so it happened that the horse had to stop, and John had time to look up at the gast and woeful face.

'Where away the nicht sae late, laird?' says John.

'I go to save a soul from hell,' was the answer.

And then it seems that through the open door there came the chapping of a clock.

'Whatna hour is that?' asks Heriotside.

'Midnicht,' says John, trembling, for he did not like the look of things.

There was no answer but a groan, and horse and man went racing down the dark hollows of the Whinny Knowes.

How he escaped a broken neck in that dreadful place no human being will ever ken. The sweat, he has told me, stood in cold drops upon his forehead; he scarcely was aware of the saddle in which he sat, and his eyes were stelled in his head so that he saw nothing but the sky ayont him. The night was growing colder, and there was a small sharp wind stirring from the east. But hot or cold, it was all one to him, who was already cold as death. He heard not the sound of the sea nor the peeseweeps startled by his horse, for the sound that ran in his ears was the roaring Sker water and a girl's cry. The thought kept goading him, and he spurred the grey horse till the creature was madder than himself. It leaped the hole which they call the Devil's Mull as I would step over a thristle, and the next he kenned he was on the edge of the Sker Bay.

It lay before him white and ghaistly, with mist blowing in wafts across it and a slow swaying of the tides. It was the better part of a mile wide, but save for some fathoms in the middle, where the Sker current ran, it was no deeper even at flood than a horse's fetlocks. It looks eerie at bright midday, when the sun is shining and whaups are crying among the seaweeds; but think what it was on that awesome night, with the Powers of Darkness brooding over it like a cloud! The rider's heart quailed for a moment in natural fear. He stepped his beast a few feet in, still staring afore him like a daft man. And then something in the sound or the feel of the waters made him look down, and he perceived that the ebb had begun and the tide was flowing out to sea.

He kenned that all was lost, and the knowledge drove him to stark despair. His sins came in his face like birds of night, and his heart shrunk like a pea. He knew himself for a lost soul, and all that he loved in the world was out in the tides. There, at any rate, he could go, too, and give back that gift of life he had so blackly misused. He cried small and saft like a bairn, and drove the grey out into the water. And aye as he spurred it the foam should have been flying as high as his head, but in that uncanny hour there was no foam; only the waves running sleek like oil. It was not long ere he had come to the Sker channel, where the red moss waters were roaring to the sea, – an ill place to ford in midsummer heat, and certain death, as folk reputed it, at the smallest spate. The grey was swimming; but it seemed the Lord had other purposes for him than death, for neither man nor horse could droun. He tried to leave the saddle, but he could not; he flung the bridle from him, but the grey held on as if some strong hand were guiding. He cried out upon the Devil to help his own; he renounced his Maker and his God: but whatever his punishment, he was not to be drouned. And then he was silent, for something was coming down the tide.

It came down as quiet as a sleeping bairn, straight for him as he sat with his horse breasting the waters; and as it came the moon crept out of a cloud, and he saw a glint of yellow hair. And then his madness died away, and he was himself again, a weary and stricken man. He hung down over the tide and caught the body in his arms, and then let the grey make for the shallows. He cared no more for the Devil and all his myrmidons, for he kenned brawly he was damned. It seemed to him that his soul had gone from him, and he was as toom as a hazel shell. His breath rattled in his throat, the tears were dried up in his head, his body had lost its strength, and yet he clung to the drouned maid as to a hope of salvation. And then he noted something at which he marvelled dumbly. Her hair was drookit back from her clay-cold brow, her eyes were shut, but in her face there was the peace of a child; it seemed even that her lips were smiling. Here, certes, was no lost soul, but one who had gone joyfully to meet her Lord. It may be in that dark hour at the burn-foot, before the spate caught her, she had been given grace to resist her adversary and fling herself upon God's mercy. And it would seem that it had been granted; for when he came to the Skerbumfoot, there in the corner sat the weird wife Alison, dead as a stone.

For days Heriotside wandered the country, or sat in his own house with vacant eye and trembling hands. Conviction of sin held him like a vice: he saw the lassie's death laid at his door; her face haunted him by day and night, and the word of the Lord dirled in his ears, telling of wrath and punishment. The greatness of his anguish wore him to a shadow, and at last he was stretched on his bed and like to perish. In his extremity worthy Dr Chrystal went to him unasked, and strove to comfort him. Long, long the good man wrestled, but it seemed as if his ministrations were to be of no avail. The fever left his body, and he rose to stotter about the doors; but he was still in his torments, and the mercy-seat was far from him. At last in the back end of the year came Mungo Muirhead to Caulds to the autumn communion, and nothing would serve him but he must try his hand at the storm-tossed soul. He spoke with power and unction, and a blessing came with his words: the black cloud lifted and showed a glimpse of grace, and in a little the man had some assurance of salvation. He became a pillar of Christ's kirk, prompt to check abominations, notably the sin of witchcraft; foremost in good works, but with it all a humble man who walked contritely till his death. When I came first to Caulds I sought to prevail upon him to accept the eldership, but he aye put me by, and when I heard his tale I saw that he had done wisely. I mind him well as he sat in his chair or daundered through Caulds, a kind word for every one and sage counsel in time of distress, but withal a severe man to himself and a crucifier of the body. It seems that this severity weakened his frame, for three years syne come Martinmas he was taken ill with a fever of the bowels, and after a week's sickness he went to his account, where I trust he is accepted.

The Kings of Orion

Written in 1905 and first published in *Blackwood's Magazine* in January 1906, 'The Kings of Orion' appeared in Buchan's third collection of stories — almost all of them from *Blackwood's* — *The Moon Endureth* (1912). Apart from extracts in South African and Australian papers in 1936, it has not been reprinted in book form for over eighty years.

An ape and a lion lie side by side in the heart of a man.
Persian Proverb

SPRING-FISHING IN the North is a cold game for a man whose blood has become thin in gentler climates. All afternoon I had failed to stir a fish, and the wan streams of the Laver, swirling between bare grey banks, were as icy to the eye as the sharp gusts of hail from the north-east were to the fingers. I cast mechanically till I grew weary, and then with an empty creel and a villainous temper set myself to trudge the two miles of bent to the inn. Some distant ridges of hill stood out snow-clad against the dun sky, and half in anger, half in a dismal satisfaction, I told myself that fishing to-morrow would be as barren as to-day.

At the inn door a tall man was stamping his feet and watching a servant lifting rod-cases from a dog-cart. Hooded and wrapped though he was, my friend Thirlstone was an unmistakable figure in any landscape. The long, haggard, brown face, with the skin drawn tightly over the cheek-bones, the keen blue eyes finely wrinkled round the corners with staring at many suns, the scar which gave his mouth a humorous droop to the right, made up a whole which was not easily forgotten. I had last seen him on the quay at Funchal bargaining with some rascally boatman to take him after mythical wild goats in the Desertas. Before that we had met at an embassy ball in Vienna, and still earlier at a hill station in Persia to which I had been sent post-haste by an anxious and embarrassed Government. Also I had been at school with him, in those faraway days when we rode nine stone and dreamed of cricket averages. He was a soldier of note, who had taken part in two little wars and one big one; had himself conducted a political mission through a hard country with some success, and was habitually chosen by his superiors to keep his eyes open as a foreign attaché in our neighbours' wars. But his fame as a hunter had gone abroad into places where even the name of the British army is unknown. He was the hungriest shikari I have ever seen, and I have seen many. If you are wise you will go forthwith to some library and procure a little book entitled *Three Hunting Expeditions*, by A.W.T. It is a modest work, and the style is that of a leading article, but all the lore and passion of the Red Gods are in its pages.

The sitting-room at the inn is a place of comfort, and while Thirlstone warmed his long back at the fire I sank contentedly into one of the well-rubbed leather arm-chairs. The company of a friend made the weather and the scarcity of salmon less the intolerable grievance they had seemed an hour ago than a joke to be laughed at. The landlord came in with whisky, and banked up the peats till they glowed beneath a pall of blue smoke.

'I hope to goodness we are alone,' said Thirlstone, and he turned to the retreating landlord and asked the question.

'There's naebody bidin' the nicht forbye yoursels,' he said, 'but the morn there's a gentleman comin'. I got a letter frae him the day. Maister Wiston, they ca' him. Maybe ye ken him?'

I started at the name, which I knew very well. Thirlstone, who knew it better, stopped warming himself and walked to the window, where he stood pulling his moustache and staring at the snow. When the man had left the room, he turned to me with the face of one whose mind is made up on a course but uncertain of the best method.

'Do you know this sort of weather looks infernally unpromising? I've half a mind to chuck it and go back to town.'

I gave him no encouragement, finding amusement in his difficulties.

'Oh, it's not so bad,' I said, 'and it won't last. To-morrow we may have the day of our lives.'

He was silent for a little, staring at the fire. 'Anyhow,' he said at last, 'we were fools to be so far up the valley. Why shouldn't we go down to the Forest Lodge? They'll take us in, and we should be deucedly comfortable, and the water's better.'

'There's not a pool on the river to touch the stretch here,' I said. 'I know, for I've fished every inch of it.'

He had no reply to this, so he lit a pipe and held his peace for a time. Then, with some embarrassment but the air of having made a discovery, he announced that his conscience was troubling him about his work, and he thought he ought to get back to it at once. 'There are several things I have forgotten to see to, and they're rather important. I feel a beast behaving like this, but you won't mind, will you?'

'My dear Thirlstone,' I said, 'what is the good of hedging? Why can't you say you won't meet Wiston?'

His face cleared. 'Well, that's the fact – I won't. It would be too infernally unpleasant. You see, I was once by way of being his friend, and he was in my regiment. I couldn't do it.'

The landlord came in at the moment with a basket of peats. 'How long is Capt— Mr Wiston staying here?' I asked.

'He's no bidin' ony time. He's just comin' here in the middle o' the day for his denner, and then drivin' up the water to Altbreac. He has the fishin' there.'

Thirlstone's face showed profound relief. 'Thank God!' I heard him mutter under his breath, and when the landlord had gone he fell to talking of salmon with enthusiasm. 'We must make a big day of it tomorrow, dark to dark, you know. Thank Heaven, our beat's downstream, too.' And thereafter he made frequent excursions to the door, and bulletins on the weather were issued regularly.

Dinner over, we drew our chairs to the hearth, and fell to talk and the slow consumption of tobacco. When two men from the ends of the earth meet by a winter fire, their thoughts are certain to drift overseas. We spoke of the racing tides off Vancouver, and the lonely pine-clad ridges running up to the snow peaks of the Selkirks, to which we had both travelled once upon a time in search of sport. Thirlstone on his own account had gone wandering to Alaska, and brought back some bear skins and a frost-bitten toe as trophies, and from his tales had consorted with the finest band of rogues which survived unhanged on this planet. Then some casual word took our thoughts to the south, and our memories dallied with Africa. Thirlstone had hunted in Somaliland and done mighty slaughter; while I had spent some never-to-be-forgotten weeks long ago in the hinterland of Zanzibar, in the days before railways and game preserves. I had gone through life with a keen eye for the discovery of earthly paradises, to which I intend to retire when my work is over, and the fairest I thought I had found above the Rift valley, where you have a hundred miles of blue horizon and the weather of Scotland. Thirlstone, not having been there, naturally differed, and urged the claim of a certain glen in Kashmir, where you may hunt two varieties of bear and three of buck in thickets of rhododendron, and see the mightiest mountain-wall on earth from your tent door. The mention of the Indian frontier brought us back to our professions, and for a little we talked 'shop', with the unblushing confidence of those who know each other's work and approve it. As a very young soldier Thirlstone had gone shooting in the Pamirs, and had blundered into a Russian party of exploration which contained Kuropatkin. He had in consequence grossly outstayed his leave, having been detained for a fortnight by an arbitrary hospitality; but he had learned many things, and the experience had given him strong views on frontier questions. Half an hour was devoted to a masterly survey of the East, until a word pulled us up.

'I went there in '99,' Thirlstone was saying, – 'the time Wiston and I were sent—' and then he stopped, and his eager face clouded. Wiston's name cast a shadow over our reminiscences.

'What did he actually do?' I asked after a short silence.

'Pretty bad! He seemed a commonplace, good sort of fellow, popular, fairly competent, a little bad-tempered perhaps. And then suddenly he did something so extremely blackguardly that everything was at an end. It's no good repeating details, and I hate to think about it. We know little about our neighbours, and I'm not sure that we know much about ourselves. There may be appalling depths of iniquity in every one of us, only most people are fortunate enough to go through the world without meeting anything to wake the devil in them. I don't believe Wiston was bad in the ordinary sense. Only there was something else in him – *somebody else*, if you like – and in a moment it came uppermost, and he was a branded man. Ugh! it's a gruesome thought.'

Thirlstone had let his pipe go out, and was staring moodily into the fire.

'How do you explain things like that?' he asked. 'I have an idea of my own about them. We talk glibly of ourselves and our personality and our conscience, as if every man's nature were a smooth, round, white thing, like a chuckie-stone. But I believe there are two men – perhaps more – in every one of us. There's our ordinary self, generally rather humdrum; and then there's a bit of something else, good, bad, but never indifferent, – and it is that something else which may make a man a saint or a great villain.'

' "The Kings of Orion have come to earth," ' I quoted.

Something in the words struck Thirlstone, and he asked me what was the yarn I spoke of.

'It's an old legend,' I explained. 'When the kings were driven out of Orion, they were sent to this planet and given each his habitation in some mortal soul. There were differences of character in that royal family, and so the *alter ego* which dwells alongside of us may be virtuous or very much the reverse. But the point is that he is always greater than ourselves, for he has been a king. It's a foolish story, but very widely believed. There is something of the sort in Celtic folk-lore, and there's a reference to it in Ausonius. Also the bandits in the Bakhtiari have a version of it in a very excellent ballad.'

'Kings of Orion,' said Thirlstone musingly. 'I like that idea. Good or bad, but always great! After all, we show a kind of belief in it in our daily practice. Every man is always making fancies about himself; but it is never his workaday self, but something else. The bank clerk who pictures himself as a financial Napoleon knows that his own thin little soul is incapable of it; but he knows, too, that it is possible enough for that other bigger thing which is not his soul, but yet in some odd way is bound up with it. I fancy myself a field-marshal in a European war; but I know perfectly well that if the job were offered me, I should realise my incompetence and decline. I expect you rather picture yourself now and then as a sort of Julius Cæsar and empire-maker, and yet, with all respect, my dear chap, I think it would be rather too much for you.'

'There was once a man,' I said, 'an early Victorian Whig, whose chief ambitions were to reform the criminal law and abolish slavery. Well, this dull, estimable man in his leisure moments was Emperor of Byzantium. He fought great wars and built palaces, and then, when the time for fancy was past, went into the House of Commons and railed against militarism and Tory extravagance. That particular king from Orion had a rather odd sort of earthly tenement.'

Thirlstone was all interest. 'A philosophic Whig and the throne of Byzantium. A pretty rum mixture! And yet – yet,' and his eyes became abstracted. 'Did you ever know Tommy Lacelles?'

'The man who once governed Deira? Retired now, and lives somewhere in Kent? Yes, I've met him once or twice. But why?'

'Because,' said Thirlstone solemnly, 'unless I'm greatly mistaken, Tommy was another such case, though no man ever guessed it except myself. I don't mind telling you the story, now that he is retired and vegetating in his ancestral pastures. Besides, the facts are all to his credit, and the explanation is our own business ...

'His wife was my cousin, and when she died Tommy was left a very withered, disconsolate man, with no particular object in life. We all thought he would give up the service, for he was hideously well off; and then one fine day, to our amazement, he was offered Deira, and accepted it. I was short of a job at the time, for my battalion was at home, and there was nothing going on anywhere, so I thought I should like to see what the East Coast of Africa was like, and wrote to Tommy about it. He jumped at me, cabled offering me what he called his Military Secretaryship, and I got seconded, and set off. I had never known him very well, but what I had seen I had liked; and I suppose he was glad to have one of Maggie's family with him, for he was still very low about her loss. I was in pretty good spirits, for it meant new experiences, and I had hopes of big game.

'You've never been to Deira? Well, there's no good trying to describe it, for it's the only place in the world like itself. God made it and left it to its own devices. The town is pretty enough, with its palms and green headland, and little scrubby islands in the river's mouth. It has the usual half-Arab, half-Portugee look – white green-shuttered houses, flat roofs, sallow little men in duck, and every type of nigger from the Somali to the Shangaan. There are some good buildings, and Government House was the mansion of some old Portugee seigneur, and was built when people in Africa were not in such a hurry as to-day. Inland there's a rolling forest country, beginning with decent trees and ending in mimosa-thorn, when the land begins to rise to the stony hills of the interior; and that poisonous yellow river rolls through it all, with a denser native population along its banks than you will find anywhere else north of the Zambesi. For about two months in the year the climate is Paradise, and for the rest you live in a Turkish bath, with every known kind of fever hanging about. We cleaned out the town and improved the sanitation, so there were few epidemics, but there was enough ordinary malaria to sicken a crocodile.

'The place was no special use to us. It had been annexed in spite of a tremendous Radical outcry, and, upon my soul, it was one of the few cases where the Radicals had something to say for themselves. All we got by it was half a dozen of the nastiest problems an unfortunate governor can have to face. Ten years before it had been a decaying strip of coast, with a few trading firms in the town, and a small export of ivory and timber. But some years before Tommy took it up there had been a huge discovery of copper in the hills inland, a railway had been built, and there were several biggish mining settlements at the end of it. Deira itself was filled with offices of European firms, it had got a Stock Exchange of its own, and it was becoming the usual cosmopolitan playground. It had a knack, too, of getting the very worst breed of adventurer. I know something of your South African and Australian mining towns, and with all their faults they are run by white men. If they haven't much morals, they have a kind of decency which keeps them fairly straight. But for our sins we got a brand of Levantine Jew who was fit for nothing but making money and making trouble. They were always defying the law, and then, when they got into a hole, they squealed to Government for help, and started a racket in the home papers about the weakness of the Imperial power. The crux of the whole difficulty was the natives, who lived along the river and in the foot-hills. They were a hardy race of Kaffirs, sort of far-away cousins to the Zulu, and till the mines were opened they had behaved well enough. They had arms, which we had never dared to take away, but they kept quiet and paid their hut-taxes like men. I got to know many of the chiefs, and liked them, for they were upstanding fellows to look at and heaven-born shikaris. However, when the Jews came along they wanted labour, and, since we did not see our way to allow them to add to the imported coolie population, they had to fall back upon the Labonga. At first things went smoothly. The chiefs were willing to let their men work for good wages, and for a time there was enough labour for everybody. But as the mines extended, and the natives, after making a few pounds, wanted to get back to their kraals, there came a shortage; and since the work could not be allowed to slacken, the owners tried other methods. They made promises which they never intended to keep, and they stood on the letter of a law which the natives did not understand, and they employed touts who were little better than slave-dealers. They got the labour, of course, but soon they had put the Labonga into a state of unrest which a very little would turn into a rising.

'Into this kettle of fish Tommy was pitchforked, and when I arrived he was just beginning to understand how unpleasant it was. As I said before, I did not know him very well, and I was amazed to find how bad he was at his job. A more curiously incompetent person I never met. He was a long, thin man, with a grizzled moustache, and a mild sleepy eye – not an impressive figure, except on a horse; and he had an odd lisp which made even a shrewd remark sound foolish. He was the most industrious creature in the world, and a model of official decorum. His papers were always in order, his dispatches always neat and correct, and I don't believe any one ever caught him tripping in office work. But he had no more conception than a child of the kind of trouble that was brewing. He never knew an honest man from a rogue, and the result was that he received all unofficial communications with a polite disbelief. I used to force him to see people – miners, prospectors, traders, any one who had something to say worth listening to, but it all glided smoothly off his mind. He was simply the most incompetent being ever created, living in the world as not being of it, or rather creating a little official world of his own, where all events happened on lines laid down by the Colonial Office, and men were like papers, to be rolled into packets and properly docketed. He had an Executive Council of people like himself, competent officials and blind bats at anything else. Then there was a precious Legislative Council, intended to represent the different classes of the population. There were several good men on it – one old trader called Mackay, for instance, who had been thirty years in the country – but most were nominees of the mining firms, and very seedy rascals at that. They were always talking about the rights of the white man, and demanding popular control of the Government, and similar twaddle. The leader was a man who hailed from Hamburg, and called himself Le Foy – descended from a Crusader of the name of Levi – who was a jackal of one of the chief copper firms. He overflowed with Imperialist sentiment, and when he was not waving the flag he used to gush about the beauties of English country life and the grandeur of the English tradition. He hated me from the start, for when he talked of going 'home' I thought he meant Hamburg, and said so; and then a thing happened which made him hate me worse. He was infernally rude to Tommy, who, like the dear sheep he was, never saw it, and, if he had, wouldn't have minded. But one day I chanced to overhear some of his impertinences, so I hunted out my biggest sjambok and lay in wait for Mr Le Foy. I told him that he was a representative of the sovereign people, that I was a member of an effete bureaucracy, and that it would be most painful if unpleasantness arose between us. But, I added, I was prepared, if necessary, to sacrifice my official career to my private feelings, and if he dared to use such language again to his Majesty's representative I would give him a hiding he would remember till he found himself in Abraham's bosom. Not liking my sjambok, he became soap and butter at once, and held his tongue for a month or two.

'But though Tommy was no good at his job, he was a tremendous swell at other things. He was an uncommonly good linguist, and had always about a dozen hobbies which he slaved at; and when he found himself at Deira with a good deal of leisure, he became a bigger crank than ever. He had a lot of books which used to follow him about the world in zinc-lined boxes – your big paper-backed German books which mean research – and he was a Fellow of the Royal Society, and corresponded with half a dozen foreign shows. India was his great subject, but he had been in the Sudan and knew a good deal about African races. When I went out to him, his pet hobby was the Bantu, and he had acquired an amazing amount of miscellaneous learning. He knew all about their immigration from the North, and the Arab and Phœnician trade-routes, and the Portuguese occupation, and the rest of the history of that unpromising seaboard. The way he behaved in his researches showed the man. He worked hard at the Labonga language – which, I believe, is a linguistic curiosity of the first water – from missionary books and the conversation of tame Kaffirs. But he never thought of paying them a visit in their native haunts. I was constantly begging him to do it, but it was not Tommy's way. He did not care a straw about political expedience, and he liked to look at things through the medium of paper and ink. Then there were the Phœnician remains in the foot-hills where the copper was mined – old workings, and things which might have been forts or temples. He knew all that was to be known about them, but he had never seen them, and never wanted to. Once only he went to the hills, to open some new reservoirs and make the ordinary Governor's speech; but he went in a special train and stayed two hours, most of which was spent in lunching and being played to by brass bands.

'But, oddly enough, there was one thing which stirred him with an interest that was not academic. I discovered it by accident one day when I went into his study and found him struggling with a map of Central Asia. Instead of the mild, benevolent smile with which he usually greeted my interruptions, he looked positively furtive, and, I could have sworn, tried to shuffle the map under some papers. Now it happens that Central Asia is the part of the globe that I know better than most men, and I could not help picking up the map and looking at it. It was a wretched thing, and had got the Oxus two hundred miles out of its course. I pointed this out to Tommy, and to my amazement he became quite excited. "Nonsense," he said. "You don't mean to say it goes south of that desert. Why, I meant to—" and then he stammered and stopped. I wondered what on earth he had meant to do, but I merely observed that I had been there, and knew. That brought Tommy out of his chair in real excitement. "What!" he cried, "you! You never told me," and he started to fire off a round of questions, which showed that if he knew very little about the place, he had it a good deal in his mind. I drew some sketch-plans for him, and left him brooding over them.

'That was the first hint I got. The second was a few nights later, when we were smoking in the billiard-room. I had been reading Marco Polo, and the talk got on to Persia and drifted all over the north side of the Himalaya. Tommy, with an abstracted eye, talked of Alexander and Timour and Genghis Khan, and particularly of Prester John, who was a character that took his fancy. I had told him that the natives in the Pamirs were true Persian stock, and this interested him greatly. "Why was there never a great state built up in those valleys?" he asked. "You get nothing but a few wild conquerors rushing east and west, and then some squalid khanates. And yet all the materials were there – the stuff for a strong race, a rich land, the traditions of an old civilisation, and natural barriers against invasion."

' "I suppose they never found the man," I said.

'He agreed. "Their princes were sots, or they were barbarians of genius who could devastate to the gates of Peking or Constantinople, but could never build. They did not recognise their limits, and so they went out in a whirlwind. But if there had been a man of solid genius he might have built up the strongest nation on the globe. In time he could have annexed Persia and nibbled at China. He would have been rich, for he could tap all the inland trade-routes of Asia. He would have had to be a conqueror, for his people would be a race of warriors, but first and foremost he must have been a statesman. Think of such a civilisation, *the* Asian civilisation, growing up mysteriously behind the deserts and the ranges! That's my idea of Prester John. Russia would have been confined to the line of the Urals. China would have been absorbed. There would have been no Japan. The whole history of the world for the last few hundred years would have been different. It is the greatest of all the lost chances in history." Tommy waxed pathetic over the loss.

'I was a little surprised at his eloquence, especially when he seemed to remember himself and stopped all of a sudden. But for the next week I got no peace with his questions. I told him all I knew of Bokhara, and Samarkand, and Tashkend, and Yarkand. I showed him the passes in the Pamirs and the Hindu Kush. I traced out the rivers, and I calculated distances; we talked over imaginary campaigns, and set up fanciful constitutions. It was a childish game, but I found it interesting enough. He spoke of it all with a curious personal tone which puzzled me, till one day when we were amusing ourselves with a fight on the Zarafshan, and I put in a modest claim to be allowed to win once in a while. For a second he looked at me in blank surprise. "You can't," he said; "I've got to enter Samarkand before I can ..." and he stopped again, with a glimmering sense in his face that he was giving himself away. And then I knew that I had surprised Tommy's secret. While he was muddling his own job, he was salving his pride with fancies of some wild career in Asia, where Tommy, disguised as the lord knows what Mussulman grandee, was hammering the little states into an empire.

'I did not think then as I think now, and I was amused to find so odd a trait in a dull man. I had known something of the kind before. I had met fellows who after their tenth peg would begin to swagger about some ridiculous fancy of their own – their little private corner of soul showing for a moment when the drink had blown aside their common sense. True, I had never known the thing appear in cold blood and everyday life, but I assumed the case to be the same. I thought of it only as a harmless fancy, never imagining that it had anything to do with character. I put it down to that kindly imagination which is the old opiate for failures. So I played up to Tommy with all my might, and though he became very discreet after the first betrayal, having hit upon the clue, I knew what to look for, and I found it. When I told him that the Labonga were in a devil of a mess, he would look at me with an empty face and change the subject; but once among the Turcomans his eye would kindle, and he would slave at his confounded folly with sufficient energy to reform the whole East Coast. It was the spark that kept the man alive. Otherwise he would have been as limp as a rag, but this craziness put life into him, and made him carry his head in the air and walk like a free man. I remember he was very keen about any kind of martial poetry. He used to go about crooning Scott and Macaulay to himself, and when we went for a walk or a ride he wouldn't speak for miles, but keep smiling to himself and humming bits of songs. I daresay he was very happy – far happier than your stolid, competent man, who sees only the one thing to do, and does it. Tommy was muddling his particular duty, but building glorious palaces in the air.

'One day Mackay, the old trader, came to me after a sitting of the precious Legislative Council. We were very friendly, and I had done all I could to get the Government to listen to his views. He was a dour, ill-tempered Scotsman, very anxious for the safety of his property, but perfectly careless about any danger to himself.

'"Captain Thirlstone," he said, "that Governor of yours is a damned fool."

'Of course I shut him up very brusquely, but he paid no attention. "He just sits and grins, and lets yon Pentecostal crowd we've gotten here as a judgment for our sins do what they like wi' him. God kens what'll happen. I would go home to-morrow, if I could realise without an immoderate loss. For the day of reckoning is at hand. Maark my words, Captain – at hand."

'I said I agreed with him about the approach of trouble, but that the Governor would rise to the occasion. I told him that people like Tommy were only seen at their best in a crisis, and that he might be perfectly confident that when it arrived he would get a new idea of the man. I said this, but of course I did not believe a word of it. I thought Tommy was only a dreamer, who had rotted any grit he ever possessed by his mental opiates. At that time I did not understand about the kings from Orion.

'And then came the thing we had all been waiting for – a Labonga rising. A week before I had got leave and had gone up country, partly to shoot, but mainly to see for myself what trouble was brewing. I kept away from the river, and therefore missed the main native

centres, but such kraals as I passed had a look I did not like. The chiefs
were almost always invisible, and the young bloods were swaggering
about and bukking to each other, while the women were grinding
maize as if for some big festival. However, after a bit the country
seemed to grow more normal, and I went into the foot-hills to shoot,
fairly easy in my mind. I had got up to a place called Shimonwe, on the
Pathi river, where I had ordered letters to be sent, and one night
coming in from a hard day after kudu I found a post-runner half-dead
of fatigue with a chit from Utterson, who commanded a police district
twenty miles nearer the coast. It said simply that all the young men
round about him had cleared out and appeared to be moving towards
Deira, that he was in a devil of a quandary, and that, since the police
were under the Governor, he would take his orders from me.

'It looked as if the heather were fairly on fire at last, so I set off early
next morning to trek back. About midday I met Utterson, a very
badly scared little man, who had come to look for me. It seemed that
his policemen had bolted in the night and gone to join the rising,
leaving him with two white sergeants, barely fifty rounds of ammu-
nition, and no neighbour for a hundred miles. He said that the
Labonga chiefs were not marching to the coast, as he had thought, but
north along the eastern foot-hills in the direction of the mines. This
was better news, for it meant that in all probability the railway would
remain open. It was my business to get somehow to my chief, and I
was in the deuce of a stew how to manage it. It was no good following
the line of the natives' march, for they would have been between me
and my goal, and the only way was to try and outflank them by going
due east, in the Deira direction, and then turning north, so as to strike
the railway about half-way to the mines. I told Utterson we had better
scatter, otherwise we should have no chance of getting through a
densely populated native country. So, about five in the afternoon, I set
off with my chief shikari, who, by good luck, was not a Labonga, and
dived into the jungly bush which skirts the hills.

'For three days I had a baddish time. We steered by the stars,
travelling chiefly by night, and we showed extraordinary skill in
missing the water-holes. I had a touch of fever and got light-headed,
and it was all I could do to struggle through the thick grass and wait-
a-bit thorns. My clothes were torn to rags, and I grew so footsore that
it was agony to move. All the same we travelled fast, and there was no
chance of our missing the road, for any route due north was bound to

cut the railway. I had the most sickening uncertainty about what was to come next. Hely, who was in command at Deira, was a good enough man, but he had only three companies of white troops, and the black troops were as likely as not to be on their way to join the rebels. It looked as if we should have a Cawnpore business on a small scale, though I thanked Heaven there were no women in the case. As for Tommy, he would probably be repeating platitudes in Deira and composing an intelligent dispatch on the whole subject.

'About four in the afternoon of the third day I struck the line near a little station called Palala. I saw by the look of the rails that trains were still running, and my hopes revived. At Palala there was a coolie stationmaster, who gave me a drink and a little food, after which I slept heavily in his office till wakened by the arrival of an up train. It contained one of the white companies and a man Davidson, of the 101st, who was Hely's second in command. From him I had news that took away my breath. The Governor had gone up the line two days before with an ADC and old Mackay. "The sportsman has got a move on him at last," said Davidson, "but what he means to do Heaven only knows. The Labonga are at the mines, and a kind of mine-guard has been formed for defence. The joke of it is that most of the magnates are treed up there, for the railway is cut and they can't get away. I don't envy your chief the job of schooling that nervous crowd."

'I went on with Davidson, and very early next morning we came to a broken culvert and had to stop. There we stuck for three hours till the down train arrived, and with it Hely. He was for ordinary a stolid soul, but I never saw a man in such a fever of excitement. He gripped me by the arm and fairly shook me. "That old man of yours is a hero," he cried. "The Lord forgive me! and I have always crabbed him."

'I implored him in Heaven's name to tell me what was up, but he would say nothing till he had had his pow-wow with Davidson. It seemed that he was bringing all his white troops up the line for some great demonstration that Tommy had conceived. Davidson went back to Deira, while we mended the culvert and got the men transferred to the other train. Then I screwed the truth out of Hely. Tommy had got up to the mines before the rebels arrived, and had found as fine a chaos as can be imagined. He did not seem to have had any doubts what to do. There were a certain number of white workmen, hard fellows from Cornwall mostly, with a few Australians, and these he got together with Mackay's help and organised into a pretty useful corps. He set them to guard the offices, and gave them strict orders to shoot at sight any one attempting to leave. Then he collected the bosses and talked to them like a father. What he said Hely did not know, except that he had damned their eyes pretty heartily, and told them what a set of swine they were, making trouble which they had not the pluck to face. Whether from Mackay, or from his own intelligence, or from a memory of my neglected warnings, he seemed to have got a tight grip on the facts at last. Meanwhile, the Labonga were at the doors, chanting their battle-songs half a mile away, and shots were heard from the far pickets. If they had tried to rush the place then, all would have been over, but, luckily, that was never their way of fighting. They sat down in camp to make their sacrifices and consult their witch-doctors, and presently Hely arrived with the first troops, having come in on the northern flank when he found the line cut. He had been in time to hear the tail-end of Tommy's final address to the mine-owners. He told them, in words which Hely said he could never have imagined coming from his lips, that they would be well served if the Labonga cleaned the whole place out. Only, he said, that would be against the will of Britain, and it was his business, as a loyal servant, to prevent it. Then, after giving Hely his instructions, he had put on his uniform, gold lace and all, and every scrap of bunting he possessed – all the orders and "Golden Stars" of half a dozen Oriental States where he had served. He made Ashurst, the ADC, put on his best Hussar's kit, and Mackay rigged himself out in a frock coat and a topper; and the three set out on horseback for the Labonga. "I believe he'll bring it off," said Hely, with wild eyes, "and, by Heaven, if he does, it'll be the best thing since John Nicholson!"

'For the rest of the way I sat hugging myself with excitement. The miracle of miracles seemed to have come. The old, slack, incompetent soul in Tommy seemed to have been driven out by that other spirit, which had hitherto been content to dream of crazy victories on the Oxus. I cursed my folly in having missed it all, for I would have given my right hand to be with him among the Labonga. I envied that young fool Ashurst his luck in being present at that queer transformation scene. I had not a doubt that Tommy would bring it off all right. The kings from Orion don't go into action without coming out on top. As we got near the mines I kept my ears open for the sound of shots; but all was still – not even the kind of hubbub a native force makes when it is on the move. Something had happened, but what it was no man could guess. When we got to where the line was up, we made very good time over the five miles to the mines. No one interfered with us, and the nearer we got the greater grew my certainty. Soon we were at the pickets, who had nothing to tell us; and then we were racing up the long sandy street to the offices, and there, sitting smoking on the doorstep of the hotel, surrounded by everybody who was not on duty, were Mackay and Ashurst.

'They were an odd pair. Ashurst still wore his uniform; but he seemed to have been rolling about in it on the ground; his sleek hair was wildly ruffled, and he was poking holes in the dust with his sword. Mackay had lost his topper, and wore a disreputable cap, his ancient frock coat was without buttons, and his tie had worked itself up behind his ears. They talked excitedly to each other, now and then vouchsafing a scrap of information to an equally excited audience. When they saw me they rose and rushed for me, and dragged me between them up the street, while the crowd tailed at our heels.

' "Ye're a true prophet, Captain Thirlstone," Mackay began, "and I ask your pardon for doubting you. Ye said the Governor only needed a crisis to behave like a man. Well, the crisis has come; and if there's a man alive in this sinful world, it's that chief o' yours." And then his emotion overcame him, and, hard-bitten devil as he was, he sat down on the ground and gasped with hysterical laughter, while Ashurst, with a very red face, kept putting the wrong end of a cigarette in his mouth and swearing profanely.

'I never remember a madder sight. There was the brassy blue sky and reddish granite rock and acres of thick red dust. The scrub had that metallic greenness which you find in all copper places. Pretty unwholesome it looked, and the crowd, which had got round us again, was more unwholesome still. Fat Jew boys, with diamond rings on dirty fingers and greasy linen cuffs, kept staring at us with twitching lips; and one or two smarter fellows in riding-breeches, mine managers and suchlike, tried to show their pluck by nervous jokes. And in the middle was Mackay, with his damaged frocker, drawling out his story in broad Scots.

' "He made this laddie put on his braws, and he commandeered this iniquitous garment for me. I've raxed its seams, and it'll never look again on the man that owns it. Syne he arrayed himself in purple and fine linen till he was like the king's daughter, all glorious without; and says he to me, 'Mackay,' he says, 'we'll go and talk to these uncovenanted deevils in their own tongue. We'll visit them at home, Mackay,' he says. 'They're none such bad fellows, but they want a little humouring from men like you and me.' So we got on our horses and started the procession – the Governor with his head in the air, and the laddie endeavouring to look calm and collected, and me praying to the God of Israel and trying to keep my breeks from working up above my knees. I've been in Kaffir wars afore, but I never thought I would ride without weapon of any kind into such a black Armageddon. I am a peaceable man for ordinar', and a canny one, but I wasna myself in that hour. Man, Thirlstone, I was that overcome by the spirit of your chief, that if he had bidden me gang alone on the same errand, I wouldna say but what I would have gone.

'"We hadna ridden half a mile before we saw the indunas and their men, ten thousand if there was one, and terrible as an army with banners. I speak feeguratively, for they hadna the scrap of a flag among them. They were beating the war-drums, and the young men were dancing with their big skin shields and wagging their ostrich feathers, so I saw they were out for business. I'll no' say but what my blood ran cold, but the Governor's eye got brighter and his back stiffer. 'Kings may be blest,' I says to myself, 'but thou art glorious.'

'"We rode straight for the centre of the crowd, where the young men were thickest and the big war-drums lay. As soon as they saw us a dozen lifted their spears and ran out to meet us. But they stopped after six steps. The sun glinted on the Governor's gold lace and my lum hat, and no doubt they thought we were heathen deities descended from the heavens. Down they went on their faces, and then back like rabbits to the rest, while the drums stopped, and the whole body awaited our coming in a silence like the tomb.

'"Never a word we spoke, but just jogged on with our chins cocked up till we were forenent the big drum, where yon old scoundrel Umgazi was standing with his young men looking as black as sin. For a moment their spears were shaking in their hands, and I heard the click of a breech-bolt. If we had winked an eye we would have become pincushions that instant. But some unearthly power upheld us. Even the laddie kept a stiff face, and for me I forgot my breeks in watching the Governor. He looked as solemn as an archangel, and comes to a halt opposite Umgazi, where he glowers at the old man for maybe three minutes, while we formed up behind him. Their eyes fell before his, and by and by their spears dropped to their sides. 'The father has come to his children,' says he in their own tongue. 'What do the children seek from their father?'

' "Ye see the cleverness of the thing. The man's past folly came to help him. The natives had never seen the Governor before till they beheld him in gold lace and a cocked hat on a muckle horse, speaking their own tongue and looking like a destroying angel. I tell you the Labonga's knees were loosed under them. They durstna speak a word until the Governor repeated the question in the same quiet, steely voice. 'You seek something,' he said, 'else you had not come out to meet me in your numbers. The father waits to hear the children's desires.'

' "Then Umgazi found his tongue and began an uneasy speech. The mines, he said, truly enough, were the abode of devils, who compelled the people to work under the ground. The crops were unreaped and the buck went unspeared, because there were no young men left to him. Their father had been away or asleep, they thought, for no help had come from him; therefore it had seemed good to them, being freemen and warriors, to seek help for themselves.

' "The Governor listened to it all with a set face. Then he smiled at them with supernatural assurance. They were fools, he said, and people of little wit, and he flung the better part of the Book of Job at their heads. The Lord kens where the man got his uncanny knowledge of the Labonga. He had all their heathen customs by heart, and he played with them like a cat with a mouse. He told them they were damned rascals to make such a stramash, and damned fools to think they could frighten the white man by their demonstrations. There was no brag about his words, just a calm statement of fact. At the same time, he said, he had no mind to let any one wrong his children, and if any wrong had been done it should be righted. It was not meet, he said, that the young men should be taken from the villages unless by their own consent, though it was his desire that such young men as could be spared should have a chance of earning an honest penny. And then he fired at them some stuff about the British Empire and the King, and you could see the Labonga imbibing it like water. The man in a cocked hat might have told them that the sky was yellow, and they would have swallowed it.

' " 'I have spoken,' he says at last, and there was a great shout from the young men, and old Umgazi looked pretty foolish. They were coming round our horses to touch our stirrups with their noses, but the Governor stopped them.

' " 'My children will pile their weapons in front of me,' says he, 'to show me how they have armed themselves, and likewise to prove that their folly is at an end. All except a dozen,' says he, 'whom I select as a bodyguard.' And there and then he picked twelve lusty savages for his guard, while the rest without a cheep stacked their spears and guns forenent the big drum.

' "Then he turned to us and spoke in English. 'Get back to the mines hell-for-leather, and tell them what's happening, and see that you get up some kind of a show for to-morrow at noon. I will bring the chiefs, and we'll feast them. Get all the bands you can, and let them play me in. Tell the mines fellows to look active, for it's the chance of their lives.' Then he says to the Labonga, 'My men will return,' he says, 'but as for me I will spend the night with my children. Make ready food, but let no beer be made, for it is a solemn occasion.'

' "And so we left him. I will not describe how I spent last night mysel', but I have something to say about this remarkable phenomenon. I could enlarge on the triumph of mind over matter . . .'

'Mackay did not enlarge. He stopped, cocked his ears, and looked down the road, from which came the strains of "Annie Laurie", played with much spirit but grievously out of tune. Followed "The British Grenadiers", and then an attempt at "The March of the Priests". Mackay rose in excitement and began to crane his disreputable neck, while the band – a fine scratch collection of instruments – took up their stand at the end of the street, flanked by a piper in khaki who performed when their breath failed. Mackay chuckled with satisfaction. "The deevils have entered into the spirit of my instructions," he said. "In a wee bit the place will be like Falkirk Tryst for din."

'Punctually at twelve there came a great hullabaloo up the road, the beating of drums and the yelling of natives, and presently the procession hove in sight. There was Tommy on his horse, and on each side of him six savages with feather head-dress, and shields and war-paint complete. After him trooped about thirty of the great chiefs, walking two by two, for all the world like an Aldershot parade. They carried no arms, but the bodyguard shook their spears, and let yells out of them that would have scared Julius Cæsar. Then the band started in, and the piper blew up, and the mines people commenced to cheer, and I thought the heavens would fall. Long before Tommy came abreast of me I knew what I should see. His uniform looked as if it had been slept in, and his orders were all awry. But he had his head flung back, and his eyes very bright, and his jaw set square. He never looked to right or left, never recognised me or anybody, for he was seeing something quite different from the red road and the white shanties and the hot sky.'

The fire had almost died out. Thirlstone stooped for a moment and stirred the peats.

'Yes,' he said, 'I knew that in his fool's ear the trumpets of all Asia were ringing, and the King of Bokhara was entering Samarkand.'

The Knees of the Gods

This hitherto uncollected Buchan story first appeared in *The Scottish Mountaineering Club Journal* in January 1907 and shows certain similarities with a later mountaineering story, 'Space' (*see* p. 182).

THIS STORY WAS told to me by a friend whom I shall call Smith, a man of limited imagination and unswerving veracity. He prefaced his narrative by declaring that never in his life had he dreamed before or at any rate remembered the details in the morning, and that in any other case and to any other man he would have been ashamed to repeat the nonsense. From which I argued that my friend had been more than a little scared.

It seemed that Smith had gone to Chamonix in the end of May for a rest. He had had no thought of climbing, for at that season it is only by the merest chance that serious ascents are possible. As it fell out, however, the chance was given him. A fortnight of uninterrupted sunshine stripped the snow from the Aiguilles, and Smith, forgetful of the work he was writing on 'The Metaphysics of the Impossible', was tempted and fell. He began with the Charmoz; he then did the Blaitière by the northern ridge; and, fired now with intolerable pride, attempted and achieved the Grèpon. It was on the night following this last ascent that he dreamed the dream I am about to relate. As I have said, his pride had become overweening, and he had gone to bed with his head full of presumptuous plans. He would do the Dent de Requin; then he might have a try at the Aiguille de la Republique; after that, perhaps, at the virgin Capuchin. He would return to England with a record of achievements, done out of due season, which would make his mountaineering friends blaspheme.

The slumbers of a climber are usually dreamless. No sooner has tattered cheek been laid to cool pillow than there comes that hammering of the infamous boots on the door which announces three o'clock and time to get up. But on this night Smith had scarcely closed his eyes when he began to dream.

He found himself, he said, in what seemed to be the smoking-room of an hotel. It was winter time, for a large fire was burning on the hearth, and on closer inspection he noticed that the fuel was peat. Clearly this was not Switzerland. And then something about the room struck him as familiar. He went to the window, drew up the blind a little and looked out. Snow lay deep on the ground, and a moon in a patch of open sky showed a line of jagged white hills. The sight brought him at once to his bearings. The ancient barn-like shape had been changed. The well-worn sofa had gone; gone, too, the moth-eaten deer's horn above the fireplace, the rickety writing-tables, the few well-thumbed books. There were some good Della Robbia imitations on the mantelpiece. A Chippendale bureau stood in a corner, and some pretty Turcoman rugs lay on the floor. The place was furnished like a sitting-room at the Ritz, but it was none the less the smoking-room of the Sligachan Inn.

While Smith sat on a spindle-legged chair, wondering what had become of his pipe, and wondering still more how on earth he had got there, a party of men entered, dressed as if for some climbing expedition. It seemed an odd thing to be starting at dead of night in mid-winter for the Coolins, but somehow when he looked at the climbers he did not think their conduct ridiculous. They were all long men and incredibly lean, and about their movement was a nervous strength which Smith remembered to have noticed in one or two great guides of his acquaintance. With them came a man whom he thought he recognised. He rubbed his eyes and stared at him, and then a nod from the other convinced him. It was his friend Brown, a Chancery barrister, longer and thinner than he remembered him, but undoubtedly Brown.

The party talked for a few minutes and drank minute tumblers of milk. Then they departed, leaving Brown behind them. Smith had by this time found his pipe, and walked to the fireplace to get a light.

'My dear good fellow,' said Brown, 'for Heaven's sake throw away that poison!' and he looked darkly at the pipe.

Now Brown had been accustomed to smoke cigars of a peculiar rankness, and Smith was therefore surprised at his tone.

'What do you mean?' he asked. 'You know you smoke like a chimney yourself.'

'I!' cried Brown in horror, 'I never touched the stuff in my life. No one does nowadays, except a few obese Germans.'

Smith would have liked to contradict him, but he had so many questions to ask that he forbore.

'Where are those fellows going?' he said. 'They must be maniacs to set out at this time of night. I suppose they are walking to Glenbrittle or Camasunary?'

Brown stared. 'My dear man, they are not trippers. They are going to do the traverse of the Coolins – Sgurr-nan Gillean to Garsbheinn. They will breakfast at Glenbrittle about nine o'clock.'

'Now, look here, Brown,' said Smith, 'what is the good of talking rot to me? That traverse has never been done in the longest summer's day, and in a winter night it is unthinkable—'

He stopped, for it seemed to him that everything about his present position was unthinkable. How had he come there, what had happened to the Sligachan Inn, what above all things had happened to Brown, who used to be a tubby little man tired out by a day's grouse shooting? Had he, Smith, gone to sleep like Rip Van Winkle and awakened in a new century? The odd thing was that he felt no alarm, only an insatiable curiosity. He wanted to cross-examine Brown, but he did not know how to begin, for his ignorance would seem to the other to call for an explanation he was unable to give.

'You have been away from mountaineering for some years,' said Brown politely. 'I don't wonder that it all seems odd to you.'

'I wish you'd explain things a bit,' said Smith. 'What do people do nowadays? As you say, I have been out of the world for some time. About Chamonix, for instance?'

'Ah, there you touch upon a sore subject. There has been a great row, but happily it is now settled. There are railways, of course, up Mont Blanc and the Verte and the Grandes Jorasses, but these we did not mind. But last year they proposed to put electric lifts on the Aiguilles, and then we had to draw the line. There are five ex-presidents of the Alpine Club in the Cabinet, including the Foreign Secretary, so we brought pressure to bear on France, and after a little fuss she climbed down. There is not much good climbing left at Chamonix, but the Aiguilles still make a pleasant day.'

'How do you mean?' said Smith. 'A pleasant *day!*'

'Oh, yes. One of the most popular scrambles in Europe is to start from the Montanvert and run over the Charmoz, Grèpon, Blaitière, Plan, and Midi. The best time is nine and a half hours.'

'That,' said Smith excitedly, 'is an infernal lie.'

Brown coloured. 'I beg your pardon,' he said stiffly. 'Do you doubt my word?'

Smith saw that he had made a mistake. 'Forgive me, old man, but it seems so strange to me. I am sorry for being rude, but I feel exactly like some kind of Rip Van Winkle awakening to a more strenuous world. What about Zermatt?'

'Alas,' said Brown, restored to good temper, 'that is a sad tale. No mountaineer goes there now except for exercise. The Dent Blanche still offers interesting snow work for beginners. But the other peaks are festooned with railways, and the Matterhorn, as you have probably heard, is covered in.'

'Covered in,' said Smith in amazement. 'What are you saying?'

'Oh, you go to the Schwarzsee or the Zmutt, and you find a door where you take a ticket – 10 francs it costs. Then you are conducted by housemaids up carpeted stairs heated by electricity. At every third landing or so there is a restaurant where you can lunch, and there are balconies for the view. In the end you come to a little glass cupola, and you raise a skylight and climb out on the top. Or if you like you can do the whole thing in a lift. The summit is a sort of German beer-garden.'

'Then where do people climb nowadays – serious climbers, I mean?' asked Smith with a doleful sinking of heart.

'Mainly in the Himalaya and the Karakoram. Everest and the other great peaks are a little hackneyed, but there are still a good many summits unclimbed. There are one or two places also in the Kuen-lun and the Bolivian Andes where I am told you have a chance of first ascents. Ruwenzori, too, has a good reputation because of the difficulty of equatorial snow.'

'And what about Scotland?' said Smith, looking sadly around the room, filled for him with so many memories of wearied and contented evenings.

'Scotland is still fairly good, given the right kind of weather, but the Coolins are almost the only hills which are worth doing. You see all the other places like Coire Mhic Fhearchair and Ben Nevis and the Sutherland hills are a little too much scrambled about on. But some of us combined and had the Coolins made a climbing reserve, and we don't allow fancy railways on the peaks. Of course they are useless in summer, only fit for tourists and artists and people out of training. But given a really good snow-storm or a pitch-dark night, and you may get some very fair scrambling. I had quite a hard time last Christmas Eve in a blizzard doing the traverse of the range. We nearly got hung up at the Alasdair-Dubh Gap. The best thing here, I think, is the Waterpipe Gully, when there is a real torrent coming down it, provided you keep to the gully all the time, and don't go out on the face. You're half drowned before you finish, but it's excellent fun.'

Smith, having no comment to make adequate to his surprise, disregarded Brown's disapproval and lit his pipe.

'Have some Talisker,' he said hospitably to his companion.

'Good Lord!' said Brown in consternation. 'What are you saying? The thing's forbidden as a beverage, and there's a tremendous penalty on its sale. Unless you're ill, and have a doctor's certificate, you can't get it . . . You were asking about Ben Nevis. The last time I was there was when my battalion of the Scottish Mountain Rifles went into camp on the top in December. We had some good practice with ice-axes among the gullies.'

'What in the name of wonder are the Scottish Mountain Rifles?' asked Smith, and then he repented of his question, fearing that Brown might think him a maniac and tell him no more. But Brown seemed to have a love for explaining what to him must have been the obvious, and continued without a sign of surprise.

'In old days they were called the Scottish Horse. But when motors displaced horses in war it was thought best to utilise the advantage Scotland offered, and turn them into a mountain corps. About the same time the deer-forests were made national manœuvre grounds, so they had every chance in training. They are a very fit lot of men, and all of them can climb rocks with heavy baggage, and handle an ice-axe. The officers are *ex-officio* members of the Alpine Club. I should like to have shown you the way the sergeants took their men up the Ben Nevis buttresses.'

A question had long been hovering on Smith's lips. 'But what started all this colossal revolution?' he asked.

Brown stared. 'This is schoolboy history with a vengeance. Every one knows that it began years ago when the Labour Party first came into power, and introduced *geist* into our national life. The first Haldane Ministry nationalised the great landed estates, introduced conscription, made the phonetic spelling of Gaelic names compulsory, and united the Empire. After that, of course, it was a short step to physical training and the reform of diet and the reconstruction of the individual life. Now, thank Heaven, we are on the road to national health – some way off it yet, but still on the road.'

'What the devil do you mean by *geist?*' asked Smith testily, darkly suspicious of something which stood between him and his Talisker.

'Reason,' said Brown, 'reason – science – intelligence – all the things that used to be at a discount in politics, and are now the only things that matter. We have got rid of feudalism and clericalism and prejudice on the one hand, and doctrinairedom on the other.'

'And has all the world got *geist* like you?'

Brown laughed. 'Oh no! We have it in the Empire – at least the rudiments of it. The other peoples, except Japan, refused it, and have suffered accordingly. To-day we divide the world between us. Japan has China and the American continent. Europe is a collection of small republics under our suzerainty, all except France, which we have neutralised, and keep as an independent centre of art and culture.'

'Give me some dates,' said Smith plaintively; 'my memory is so bad nowadays.'

'You seem to have become very stupid, old man,' said Brown. 'It's all due to that infamous tobacco of yours. I oughtn't to have to instruct you in these rudiments. The beginning was in 1911, the date of the first Haldane Ministry. In 1915 we fought the Triple Alliance. In 1916 Japan conquered and annexed the United States, and in 1920 there was the famous Conference of Ecclefechan between the Mikado and our Emperor. In 1921 the last Liberal died, and was preserved in the British Museum. In 1923—'

But at this moment Smith unfortunately chose to knock the ashes out of his pipe. As a Gladstonian of the old school, Brown's last remark had annoyed him greatly, and he was about to declare that the new régime, for all its mountaineering pride, was one from which beer and skittles, not to mention tobacco and Talisker, were deplorably absent. But the sound of his pipe-bowl, hammered against the mantelpiece, seemed to echo and reverberate with uncanny persistence...

And then he suddenly awoke to the fact that he was not in the Sligachan smoking-room, but in his bedroom at Chamonix, and that the boots was beating at his door, and striving in broken English to tell him that it was two o'clock in the morning.

Smith got up in a daze and struggled into his clothes. As a sign of his preoccupation he told me that he was half-way to the Blaitière chalet before it occurred to him to notice the state of the weather.

The Company of the Marjolaine

This, one of Buchan's most anthologised stories, was written in 1908 and appeared simultaneously in *Blackwood's Magazine* and *The Atlantic Monthly* in February 1909, and in *The Living Age* the following month. Its first book appearance was in *The Moon Endureth* (1912) and it has appeared in such collections as Hutchinson's *Standard Stories* (1926) and Oxford University Press's *Scottish Short Stories* (1963). In a letter to Buchan in 1912, Arthur Conan Doyle, commenting on the story, wrote, 'I don't think the eighteenth century was ever better caught.'

Qu'est-c' qui passe ici si tard,
Compagnons de la Marjolaine?
Chansons de France

[This extract from the unpublished papers of the Manorwater family has seemed to the Editor worth printing for its historical interest. The famous Lady Molly Carteron became Countess of Manorwater by her second marriage. She was a wit and a friend of wits, and her nephew, the Honourable Charles Hervey-Townshend (afterwards our Ambassador at The Hague), addressed to her a series of amusing letters while making, after the fashion of his contemporaries, the Grand Tour of Europe. Three letters, written at various places in the Eastern Alps and dispatched from Venice, contain the following short narrative. (JB)]

I

... I CAME DOWN from the mountains and into the pleasing valley of the Adige in as pelting a heat as ever mortal suffered under. The way underfoot was parched and white; I had newly come out of a wilderness of white limestone crags, and a sun of Italy blazed blindingly in an azure Italian sky. You are to suppose, my dear Aunt, that I had had enough and something more of my craze for foot-marching. A fortnight ago I had gone to Belluno in a post-chaise, dismissed my fellow to carry my baggage by way of Verona, and with no more than a valise on my back plunged into the fastnesses of those mountains. I had a fancy to see the little sculptured hills which made backgrounds for Gianbellin, and there were rumours of great mountains built wholly of marble which shone like the battlements of the Celestial City. So at any rate reported young Mr Wyndham, who had travelled with me from Milan to Venice. I lay the first night at Piave, where Titian had the fortune to be born, and the landlord at the inn displayed a set of villainous daubs which he swore were the early works of that master. Thence up a toilsome valley I journeyed to the Ampezzan country, where indeed I saw my white mountains, but, alas! no longer Celestial. For it rained like Westmoreland for five endless days, while I kicked my heels in an inn and turned a canto of Ariosto into halting English couplets. By and by it cleared, and I headed westward towards Bozen, among the tangle of wild rocks where the Dwarf King had once his rose garden. The first night I had no inn, but slept in the vile cabin of a forester, who spoke a tongue half Latin, half Dutch, which I could not master. The next day was a blaze of heat, the mountain paths lay thick with dust, and I had no wine from sunrise to sunset. Can you wonder that, when the following noon I saw Santa Chiara sleeping in its green circlet of meadows, my thought was only of a deep draught and a cool chamber? I protest that I am a great lover of natural beauty, of rock and cascade, and all the properties of the poet; but the enthusiasm of M. Rousseau himself would sink from the stars to earth if he had marched since breakfast in a cloud of dust with a throat like the nether millstone.

Yet I had not entered the place before Romance revived. The little town – a mere wayside halting-place on the great mountain road to the North – had the air of mystery which foretells adventure. Why is it that a dwelling or a countenance catches the fancy with the promise of some strange destiny? I have houses in my mind which I know will some day and somehow be intertwined oddly with my life; and I have faces in memory of which I know nothing save that I shall undoubtedly cast my eyes again upon them. My first glimpses of Sant

Chiara gave me this earnest of romance. It was walled and fortified, the streets were narrow pits of shade, old tenements with bent fronts swayed to meet each other. Melons lay drying on flat roofs, and yet now and then would come a high-pitched northern gable. Latin and Teuton met and mingled in the place, and, as Mr Gibbon has taught us, the offspring of this admixture is something fantastic and unpredictable. I forgot my grievous thirst and my tired feet in admiration and a certain vague expectation of wonders. Here, ran my thought, it is fated, maybe, that Romance and I shall at last compass a meeting. Perchance some princess is in need of my arm, or some affair of high policy is afoot in this jumble of old masonry. You will laugh at my folly, but I had an excuse for it. A fortnight in strange mountains disposes a man to look for something at his next encounter with his kind, and the sight of Sant Chiara would have fired the imagination of a judge in Chancery.

I strode happily into the courtyard of the Tre Croci, and presently had my expectation confirmed. For I found my fellow, Gianbattista – a faithful rogue I got in Rome on a Cardinal's recommendation – hot in pursuit with a lady's maid. The woman was old, harsh-featured – no Italian clearly, though she spoke fluently in the tongue. She rated my man like a pick-pocket, and the dispute was over a room.

'The signor will bear me out,' said Gianbattista. 'Was not I sent to Verona with his baggage, and thence to this place of ill manners? Was I not bidden engage for him a suite of apartments? Did I not duly choose these fronting on the gallery, and dispose therein the signor's baggage? And lo! an hour ago I found it all turned into the yard and this woman installed in its place. It is monstrous, unbearable! Is this an inn for travellers, or haply the private mansion of these Magnificences?'

'My servant speaks truly,' I said, firmly yet with courtesy, having had no mind to spoil adventure by urging rights. 'He had orders to take these rooms for me, and I know not what higher power can countermand me.'

The woman had been staring at me scornfully, for no doubt in my dusty habit I was a figure of small count; but at the sound of my voice she started, and cried out, 'You are English, signor?'

I bowed an admission.

'Then my mistress shall speak with you,' she said, and dived into the inn like an elderly rabbit.

Gianbattista was for sending for the landlord and making a riot in that hostelry; but I stayed him, and bidding him fetch me a flask of white wine, three lemons, and a glass of *eau de vie*, I sat down peaceably at one of the little tables in the courtyard and prepared for the quenching of my thirst. Presently, as I sat drinking that excellent compound which was my own invention, my shoulder was touched, and I turned to find the maid and her mistress. Alas for my hopes of a glorious being, young and lissom and bright with the warm riches of the south! She had plump red cheeks, and fair hair dressed indifferently in the Roman fashion. Two candid blue eyes redeemed her plainness, and a certain grave and gentle dignity. She was notably a gentlewoman, so I got up, doffed my hat, and awaited her commands.

She spoke in Italian. 'Your pardon, signor, but I fear my good Cristine has done you unwittingly a wrong.'

Cristine snorted at this premature plea of guilty, while I hastened to assure the fair apologist that any rooms I might have taken were freely at her service.

I spoke unconsciously in English, and she replied in a halting parody of that tongue. 'I understand him,' she said, 'but I do not speak him happily. I will discourse, if the signor pleases, in our first speech.'

She and her father, it appeared, had come over the Brenner, and arrived that morning at the Tre Croci, where they purposed to lie for some days. He was an old man, very feeble, and much depending upon her constant care. Wherefore it was necessary that the rooms of all the party should adjoin, and there was no suite of the size in the inn save that which I had taken. Would I therefore consent to forgo my right, and place her under an eternal debt?

I agreed most readily, being at all times careless where I sleep, so the bed be clean, or where I eat, so the meal be good. I bade my servant see the landlord and have my belongings carried to other rooms. Madame thanked me sweetly, and would have gone, when a thought detained her.

'It is but courteous,' she said, 'that you should know the names of those whom you have befriended. My father is called the Count d'Albani, and I am his only daughter. We travel to Florence, where we have a villa in the environs.'

'My name,' said I, 'is Hervey-Townshend, an Englishman travelling abroad for his entertainment.'

'Hervey?' she repeated. 'Are you one of the family of Miladi Hervey?'

'My worthy aunt,' I replied, with a tender recollection of that preposterous woman.

Madame turned to Cristine, and spoke rapidly in a whisper.

'My father, sir,' she said, addressing me, 'is an old frail man, little used to the company of strangers; but in former days he has had kindness from members of your house, and it would be a satisfaction to him, I think, to have the privilege of your acquaintance.'

She spoke with the air of a vizier who promises a traveller a sight of the Grand Turk. I murmured my gratitude, and hastened after Gianbattista. In an hour I had bathed, rid myself of my beard, and arrayed myself in decent clothing. Then I strolled out to inspect the little city, admired an altar-piece, chaffered with a Jew for a cameo, purchased some small necessaries, and returned early in the afternoon with a noble appetite for dinner.

The Tre Croci had been in happier days a bishop's lodging, and possessed a dining-hall ceiled with black oak and adorned with frescoes. It was used as a general *salle à manger* for all dwellers in the inn, and there accordingly I sat down to my long-deferred meal. At first there were no other diners, and I had two maids as well as Gianbattista, to attend on my wants. Presently Madame d'Albani entered, escorted by Cristine and by a tall gaunt serving-man, who seemed no part of the hostelry. The landlord followed, bowing civilly, and the two women seated themselves at the little table at the farther end. 'Il Signor Conte dines in his room,' said Madame to the host, who withdrew to see to that gentleman's needs.

I found my eyes straying often to the little party in the cool twilight of that refectory. The man-servant was so old and battered, and yet of such a dignity, that he lent a touch of intrigue to the thing. He stood stiffly behind Madame's chair, handing dishes with an air of silent reverence – the lackey of a great noble, if ever I had seen the type. Madame never glanced towards me, but conversed sparingly with Cristine, while she pecked delicately at her food. Her name ran in my head with a tantalising flavour of the familiar. Albani! D'Albani! It was a name not uncommon in the Roman States, but I had never heard it linked to a noble family. And yet I had – somehow, somewhere; and in the vain effort at recollection I had almost forgotten my hunger. There was nothing bourgeois in the little lady. The austere servants, the high manner of condescension, spake of a stock used to deference, though, maybe, pitifully decayed in its fortunes. There was a mystery in these quiet folk which tickled my curiosity. Romance after all was not destined to fail me at Santa Chiara.

My doings of the afternoon were of interest to myself alone. Suffice it to say that when I returned at nightfall I found Gianbattista the trustee of a letter. It was from Madame, written in a fine thin hand on a delicate paper, and it invited me to wait upon the signor, her father, that evening at eight o'clock. What caught my eye was a coronet stamped in a corner. A coronet, I say, but in truth it was a crown, the same as surmounts the Arms Royal of England on the signboard of a Court tradesman. I marvelled at the ways of foreign heraldry. Either this family of d'Albani had higher pretensions than I had given it credit for, or it employed an unlearned and imaginative stationer. I scribbled a line of acceptance and went to dress.

The hour of eight found me knocking at the Count's door. The grim serving-man admitted me to the pleasant chamber which should have been mine own. A dozen wax candles burned in sconces, and on the table, among fruits and the remains of supper, stood a handsome candelabra of silver. A small fire of logs had been lit on the hearth, and before it in an armchair sat a strange figure of a man. He seemed not so much old as aged. I should have put him at sixty, but the marks he bore were clearly less those of Time than of Life. There sprawled before me the relics of noble looks. The fleshy nose, the pendulous cheek, the drooping mouth, had once been cast in the lines of manly beauty. Heavy eyebrows above and heavy bags beneath spoiled the effect of a choleric blue eye, which age had not dimmed. The man was gross and yet haggard; it was not the padding of good living which clothed his bones, but a heaviness as of some dropsical malady. I could picture him in health a gaunt loose-limbed being, high-featured and swift and eager. He was dressed wholly in black velvet, with fresh ruffles and wristbands, and he wore heeled shoes with antique silver buckles. It was a figure of an older age which rose slowly to greet me, in one hand a snuff-box and a purple handkerchief, and in the other a book with finger marking place. He made me a great bow as Madame uttered my name, and held out a hand with a kindly smile.

'Mr Hervey-Townshend,' he said, 'we will speak English, if you please. I am fain to hear it again, for 'tis a tongue I love. I make you welcome, sir, for your own sake and for the sake of your kin. How is her honourable ladyship, your aunt? A week ago she sent me a letter.'

I answered that she did famously, and wondered what cause of correspondence my worthy aunt could have with wandering nobles of Italy.

He motioned me to a chair between Madame and himself, while a servant set a candle on a shelf behind him. Then he proceeded to catechise me in excellent English, with now and then a phrase of French, as to the doings in my own land. Admirably informed this Italian gentleman proved himself. I defy you to find in Almack's more intelligent gossip. He inquired as to the chances of my Lord North and the mind of my Lord Rockingham. He had my Lord Shelburne's foibles at his fingers' ends. The habits of the Prince, the aims of their ladyships of Dorset and Buckingham, the extravagance of this noble Duke and that right honourable gentleman were not hid from him. I answered discreetly yet frankly, for there was no ill-breeding in his curiosity. Rather it seemed like the inquiries of some fine lady, now buried deep in the country, as to the doings of a forsaken Mayfair. There was humour in it and something of pathos.

'My aunt must have been a voluminous correspondent, sir,' I said.

He laughed. 'I have many friends in England who write to me, but I have seen none of them for so long, and I doubt I may never see them again. Also in my youth I have been in England.' And he sighed as at a sorrowful recollection.

Then he showed the book in his hand. 'See,' he said, 'here is one of your English writings, the greatest book I have ever happened on.' It was a volume of Mr Fielding.

For a little he talked of books and poets. He admired Mr Fielding profoundly, Dr Smollett somewhat less, Mr Richardson not at all. But he was clear that England had a monopoly of good writers, saving only my friend M. Rousseau, whom he valued, yet with reservations. Of the Italians he had no opinion. I instanced against him the plays of Signor Alfieri. He groaned, shook his head, and grew moody.

'Know you Scotland?' he asked suddenly.

I replied that I had visited Scotch cousins, but had no great estimation for the country. 'It is too poor and jagged,' I said, 'for the taste of one who loves colour and sunshine and suave outlines.'

He sighed. 'It is indeed a bleak land, but a kindly. When the sun shines at all he shines on the truest hearts in the world. I love its bleakness too. There is a spirit in the misty hills, and the harsh sea-wind which inspires men to great deeds. Poverty and courage go often together, and my Scots, if they are poor, are as untameable as their mountains.'

'You know the land, sir?' I asked.

'I have seen it, and I have known many Scots. You will find them in Paris and Avignon and Rome, with never a plack in their pockets. I have a feeling for exiles, sir, and I have pitied these poor people. They gave their all for the cause they followed.'

Clearly the Count shared my aunt's views of history – those views which have made such sport for us often at Carteron. Stalwart Whig as I am, there was something in the tone of the old gentleman which made me feel a certain majesty in the lost cause.

'I am a Whig in blood and Whig in principle,' I said, 'but I have never denied that those Scots who followed the Chevalier were too good to waste on so trumpery a leader.'

I had no sooner spoken the words than I felt that somehow I had been guilty of a *bêtise*.

'It may be so,' said the Count. 'I did not bid you here, sir, to argue on politics, on which I am assured we should differ. But I will ask you one question. The King of England is a stout upholder of the right of kings. How does he face the defection of his American possessions?'

'The nation takes it well enough, and as for His Majesty's feelings, there is small inclination to inquire into them. I conceive of the whole war as a blunder out of which we have come as we deserved. The day is gone by for the assertion of monarchic rights against the will of a people.'

'May be. But take note that the King of England is suffering today as – how do you call him? – the Chevalier suffered forty years ago. "The wheel has come full circle", as your Shakespeare says. Time has wrought his revenge.'

He was staring into a fire, which burned small and smokily.

'You think the days for kings is ended. I read it differently. The world will ever have the need of kings. If a nation cast out one it will have to find another. And mark you, those later kings, created by the people, will bear a harsher hand than the old race who ruled as of right. Some day the world will regret having destroyed the kindly and legitimate line of monarchs and put in their place tyrants who govern by the sword or by flattering an idle mob.'

This belated dogma would at other times have set me laughing, but the strange figure before me gave no impulse to merriment. I glanced at Madame, and saw her face grave and perplexed, and I thought I read a warning gleam in her eye. There was a mystery about the party which irritated me, but good breeding forbade me to seek a clue.

'You will permit me to retire, sir,' I said. 'I have but this morning come down from a long march among the mountains east of this valley. Sleeping in wayside huts and tramping those sultry paths make a man think pleasantly of bed.'

The Count seemed to brighten at my words. 'You are a marcher, sir, and love the mountains? Once I would gladly have joined you, for in my youth I was a great walker in hilly places. Tell me, now, how many miles will you cover in a day?'

I told him thirty at a stretch.

'Ah,' he said, 'I have done fifty, without food, over the roughest and mossiest mountains. I lived on what I shot, and for drink I had spring water. Nay, I am forgetting. There was another beverage, which I wager you have never tasted. Heard you ever, sir, of that *eau de vie* which the Scots call *usquebagh*? It will comfort a traveller as no thin Italian wine will comfort him. By my soul, you shall taste it. Charlotte, my dear, bid Oliphant fetch glasses and hot water and lemons. I will give Mr Hervey-Townshend a sample of the brew. You English are all *têtes-de-fer*, sir, and are worthy of it.'

The old man's face had lighted up, and for the moment his air had the jollity of youth. I would have accepted the entertainment had I not again caught Madame's eye. It said, unmistakably and with serious pleading, 'Decline.' I therefore made my excuses, urged fatigue, drowsiness, and a delicate stomach, bade my host goodnight, and in deep mystification left the room.

Enlightenment came upon me as the door closed. There on the threshold stood the man-servant whom they called Oliphant, erect as a sentry on guard. The sight reminded me of what I had once seen at Basle when by chance a Rhenish Grand Duke had shared the inn with me. Of a sudden a dozen clues linked together – the crowned note-paper, Scotland, my aunt Hervey's politics, the tale of old wanderings.

'Tell me,' I said in a whisper. 'Who is the Count d'Albani, your master?' and I whistled softly a bar of 'Charlie is my darling'.

'Ay,' said the man, without relaxing a muscle of his grim face. 'It is the King of England – my king and yours.'

II

In the small hours of the next morning I was awoke by a most unearthly sound. It was as if all the cats on all the roofs of Santa Chiara were sharpening their claws and wailing their battle-cries. Presently out of the noise came a kind of music – very slow, solemn, and melancholy. The notes ran up in great flights of ecstasy, and sunk anon to the tragic deeps. In spite of my sleepiness I was held spellbound, and the musician had concluded with certain barbaric grunts before I had the curiosity to rise. It came from somewhere in the gallery of the inn, and as I stuck my head out of my door I had a glimpse of Oliphant, nightcap on head and a great bagpipe below his arm, stalking down the corridor.

The incident, for all the gravity of the music, seemed to give a touch of farce to my interview of the past evening. I had gone to bed with my mind full of sad stories of the deaths of kings. Magnificent in tatters has always affected my pity more deeply than tatters with no such antecedent, and a monarch out at elbows stood for me as the last irony of our mortal life. Here was a king whose misfortunes could find no parallel. He had been in his youth the hero of a high adventure, and his middle age had been spent in fleeting among the courts of Europe, and waiting as pensioner on the whims of his foolish but regnant brethren. I had heard tales of a growing sottishness, a decline in spirit, a squalid taste in pleasures. Small blame, I had always thought, to so ill-fated a princeling. And now I had chanced upon the gentleman in his dotage, travelling with a barren effort at mystery, attended by a sad-faced daughter and two ancient domestics. It was a lesson in the vanity of human wishes which the shallowest moralist would have noted. Nay, I felt more than the moral. Something human and kindly in the old fellow had caught my fancy. The decadence was too tragic to prose about, the decadent too human to moralise on. I had left the chamber of the – shall I say *de jure* King of England? – a sentimental adherent of the cause. But this business of the bagpipes touched the comic. To harry an old valet out of bed and set him droning on pipes in the small hours smacked of a theatrical taste, or at least of an undignified fancy. Kings in exile, if they wish to keep the tragic air, should not indulge in such fantastic serenades.

My mind changed again when after breakfast I fell in with Madame on the stair. She drew aside to let me pass, and then made as if she would speak to me. I gave her good-morning, and, my mind being full of her story, addressed her as 'Excellency'.

'I see, sir,' she said, 'that you know the truth. I have to ask your forbearance for the concealment I practised yesterday. It was a poor requital for your generosity, but it is one of the shifts of our sad fortune. An uncrowned king must go in disguise or risk the laughter of every stable-boy. Besides, we are too poor to travel in state, even if we desired it.'

Honestly, I knew not what to say. I was not asked to sympathise, having already revealed my politics, and yet the case cried out for sympathy. You remember, my dear aunt, the good Lady Culham, who was our Dorsetshire neighbour, and tried hard to mend my ways at Carteron? This poor Duchess – for so she called herself – was just such another. A woman made for comfort, housewifery, and motherhood, and by no means of racing about Europe in charge of a disreputable parent. I could picture her settled equably on a garden seat with a lapdog and needlework, blinking happily over green lawns and mildly rating an errant gardener. I could fancy her sitting in a summer parlour, very orderly and dainty, writing lengthy epistles to a tribe of nieces. I could see her marshalling a household in the family pew, or riding serenely in the family coach behind fat bay horses. But here, on an inn staircase, with a false name and a sad air of mystery, she was woefully out of place. I noted little wrinkles forming in the corners of her eyes, and the ravages of care beginning in the plump rosiness of her face. Be sure there was nothing appealing in her mien. She spoke with the air of a great lady, to whom the world is matter only for an afterthought. It was the facts that appealed and grew poignant from her courage.

'There is another claim upon your good nature,' she said. 'Doubtless you were awoke last night by Oliphant's playing upon the pipes. I rebuked the landlord for his insolence in protesting, but to you, a gentleman and a friend, an explanation is due. My father sleeps ill, and your conversation seems to have cast him into a train of sad memories. It has been his habit on such occasions to have the pipes played to him, since they remind him of friends and happier days. It is a small privilege for an old man, and he does not claim it often.'

I declared that the music had only pleased, and that I would welcome its repetition. Whereupon she left me with a little bow and an invitation to join them that day at dinner, while I departed into the town on my own errands. I returned before midday, and was seated at an arbour in the garden, busy with letters, when there hove in sight the gaunt figure of Oliphant. He hovered around me, if such a figure can be said to hover, with the obvious intention of addressing me. The fellow had caught my fancy, and I was willing to see more of him. His face might have been hacked out of grey granite, his clothes hung loosely on his spare bones, and his stockinged shanks would have done no discredit to Don Quixote. There was no dignity in his air, only a steady and enduring sadness. Here, thought I, is the one of the establishment who most commonly meets the shock of the world's buffets. I called him by name and asked him his desires.

It appeared that he took me for a Jacobite, for he began a rigmorale about loyalty and hard fortune. I hastened to correct him, and he took the correction with the same patient despair with which he took all things. 'Twas but another of the blows of Fate.

'At any rate,' he said in a broad Scotch accent, 'ye come of kin that has helpit my maister afore this. I've many times heard tell o' Herveys and Townshends in England, and a' folk said they were on the richt side. Ye're maybe no a freend, but ye're a freend's freend, or I wadna be speirin' at ye.'

I was amused at the prologue, and waited on the tale. It soon came. Oliphant, it appeared, was the purse-bearer of the household, and woeful straits that poor purse-bearer must have been often put to. I questioned him as to his master's revenues, but could get no clear answer. There were payments due next month in Florence which would solve the difficulties for the winter, but in the meantime expenditure had beaten income. Travelling had cost much, and the Count must have his small comforts. The result, in plain words, was that Oliphant had not the wherewithal to frank the company to Florence; indeed, I doubted if he could have paid the reckoning in Santa Chiara. A loan was therefore sought from a friend's friend, meaning myself.

I was very really embarrassed. Not that I would not have given willingly, for I had ample resources at the moment and was mightily concerned about the sad household. But I knew that the little Duchess would take Oliphant's ears from his head if she guessed that he had dared to borrow from me, and that, if I lent, her back would for ever be turned against me. And yet, what would follow on my refusal? In a day or two there would be a pitiful scene with mine host, and as like as not some of their baggage detained as security for payment. I did not love the task of conspiring behind the lady's back, but if it could be contrived 'twas indubitably the kindest course. I glared sternly at Oliphant, who met me with his pathetic, dog-like eyes.

'You know that your mistress would never consent to the request you have made of me?'

'I ken,' he said humbly. 'But payin' is *my* job, and I simply havena the siller. It's no' the first time it has happened, and it's a sair trial for them both to be flung out o' doors by a foreign hostler because they canna meet his charges. But, sir, if ye can lend to me, ye may be certain that her leddyship will never hear a word o't. Puir thing, she takes nae thocht o' where the siller comes frae, ony mair than the lilies o' the field.'

I became a conspirator. 'You swear, Oliphant, by all you hold sacred, to breathe nothing of this to your mistress, and if she should suspect, to lie like a Privy Councillor?'

A flicker of a smile crossed his face. 'I'll lee like a Scots packman, and the Father o' lees could do nae mair. You need have no fear for your siller, sir. I've aye repaid when I borrowed, though you may have to wait a bittock.' And the strange fellow strolled off.

At dinner no Duchess appeared till long after the appointed hour, nor was there any sign of Oliphant. When she came at last with Cristine, her eyes looked as if she had been crying, and she greeted me with remote courtesy. My first thought was that Oliphant had revealed the matter of the loan, but presently I found that the lady's trouble was far different. Her father, it seemed, was ill again with his old complaint. What that was I did not ask, nor did the Duchess reveal it.

We spoke in French, for I had discovered that this was her favourite speech. There was no Oliphant to wait on us, and the inn servants were always about, so it was well to have a tongue they did not comprehend. The lady was distracted and sad. When I inquired feelingly as to the general condition of her father's health she parried the question, and when I offered my services she disregarded my words. It was in truth a doleful meal, while the faded Cristine sat like a sphinx staring into vacancy. I spoke of England and of her friends, of Paris and Versailles, of Avignon where she had spent some years, and of the amenities of Florence, which she considered her home. But it was like talking to a nunnery door. I got nothing but 'It is indeed true, sir,' or 'Do you say so, sir?' till my energy began to sink. Madame perceived my discomfort, and, as she rose, murmured an apology. 'Pray forgive my distraction, but I am poor company when my father is ill. I have a foolish mind, easily frightened. Nay, nay!' she went on when I again offered help, 'the illness is trifling. It will pass off by tomorrow, or at the latest the next day. Only I had looked forward to some ease at Santa Chiara, and the promise is belied.'

As it chanced that evening, returning to the inn, I passed by the north side where the windows of the Count's room looked over a little flower garden abutting on the courtyard. The dusk was falling, and a lamp had been lit which gave a glimpse into the interior. The sick man was standing by the window, his figure flung into relief by the lamplight. If he was sick, his sickness was of a curious type. His face was ruddy, his eye wild, and, his wig being off, his scanty hair stood up oddly round his head. He seemed to be singing, but I could not catch the sound through the shut casement. Another figure in the room, probably Oliphant, laid a hand on the Count's shoulder, drew him from the window, and closed the shutter.

It needed only the recollection of stories which were the property of all Europe to reach a conclusion on the gentleman's illness. The legitimate King of England was very drunk.

As I went to my room that night I passed the Count's door. There stood Oliphant as sentry, more grim and haggard than ever, and I thought that his eye met mine with a certain intelligence. From inside the room came a great racket. There was the sound of glasses falling, then a string of oaths, English, French, and for all I knew, Irish, rapped out in a loud drunken voice. A pause, and then came the sound of maudlin singing. It pursued me along the gallery, an old childish song, delivered as if 'twere a pot-house catch—

> *Qu'est-c' qui passe ici si tard*
> *Compagnons de la Marjolaine—*

One of the late-going company of the Marjolaine hastened to bed. This king in exile, with his melancholy daughter, was becoming too much for him.

III

It was just before noon next day that the travellers arrived. I was sitting in the shady loggia of the inn, reading a volume of De Thou, when there drove up to the door two coaches. Out of the first descended very slowly and stiffly four gentlemen; out of the second four servants and a quantity of baggage. As it chanced there was no one about, the courtyard slept its sunny noontide sleep, and the only movement was a lizard on the wall and a buzz of flies by the fountain. Seeing no sign of the landlord, one of the travellers approached me with a grave inclination.

'This is the inn called the Tre Croci, sir?' he asked.

I said it was, and shouted on my own account for the host. Presently that personage arrived with a red face and a short wind, having descended rapidly from his own cellar. He was awed by the dignity of the travellers, and made none of his usual protests of incapacity. The servants filed off solemnly with the baggage, and the four gentlemen set themselves down beside me in the loggia and ordered each a modest flask of wine.

At first I look them for our countrymen, but as I watched them the conviction vanished. All four were tall and lean beyond the average of mankind. They wore suits of black, with antique starched frills to their shirts; their hair was their own and unpowdered. Massive buckles of an ancient pattern adorned their square-toed shoes, and the canes they carried were like the yards of a small vessel. They were four merchants, I had guessed, of Scotland, maybe, or of Newcastle, but their voices were not Scotch, and their air had no touch of commerce. Take the heavy-browed preoccupation of a Secretary of State, add the dignity of a bishop, the sunburn of a fox-hunter, and something of the disciplined erectness of a soldier, and you may perceive the manner of these four gentlemen. By the side of them my assurance vanished. Compared with their Olympian serenity my person seemed fussy and servile. Even so, I mused, must Mr Franklin have looked when baited in Parliament by the Tory pack. The reflection gave me the cue. Presently I caught from their conversation the word 'Washington', and the truth flashed upon me. I was in the presence of four of Mr Franklin's countrymen. Having never seen an American in the flesh, I rejoiced at the chance of enlarging my acquaintance.

They brought me into the circle by a polite question as to the length of road to Verona. Soon introductions followed. My name intrigued them, and they were eager to learn of my kinship to Uncle Charles. The eldest of the four, it appeared, was Mr Galloway out of Maryland. Then came two brothers, Sylvester by name, of Pennsylvania, and last Mr Fish, a lawyer of New York. All four had campaigned in the late war, and all four were members of the Convention, or whatever they call their rough-and-ready Parliament. They were modest in their behaviour, much disinclined to speak of their past, as great men might be whose reputation was world-wide. Somehow the names stuck in my memory. I was certain that I had heard them linked with some stalwart fight or some moving civil deed or some defiant manifesto. The making of history was in their steadfast eye and the grave lines of the mouth. Our friendship flourished mightily in a brief hour, and brought me the invitation, willingly accepted, to sit with them at dinner.

There was no sign of the Duchess or Cristine or Oliphant. Whatever had happened, that household today required all hands on deck, and I was left alone with the Americans. In my day I have supped with the Macaronies, I have held up my head at the Cocoa Tree, I have avoided the floor at hunt dinners, I have drunk glass to glass with Tom Carteron. But never before have I seen such noble consumers of good liquor as those four gentlemen from beyond the Atlantic. They drank the strong red Cyprus as if it had been spring water. 'The dust of your Italian roads takes some cleansing, Mr Townshend,' was their only excuse, but in truth none was needed. The wine seemed only to thaw their iron decorum. Without any surcease of dignity they grew communicative, and passed from lands to peoples and from peoples to constitutions. Before we knew it we were embarked upon high politics.

Naturally we did not differ on the war. Like me, they held it to have been a grievous necessity. They had no bitterness against England, only regret for her blunders. Of His Majesty they spoke with respect, of His Majesty's advisers with dignified condemnation. They thought highly of our troops in America; less highly of our generals.

'Look you, sir,' said Mr Galloway, 'in a war such as we have witnessed the Almighty is the only strategist. You fight against the forces of Nature, and a newcomer little knows that the success or failure of every operation he can conceive depends not upon generalship, but upon the conformation of a vast country. Our generals, with this in mind and with fewer men, could make all your schemes miscarry. Had the English soldiery not been of such stubborn stuff, we should have been victors from the first. Our leader was not General Washington, but General America, and his brigadiers were forests, swamps, lakes, rivers, and high mountains.'

'And now,' I said, 'having won, you have the greatest of human experiments before you. Your business is to show that the Saxon stock is adaptable to a republic.'

It seemed to me that they exchanged glances.

'We are not pedants,' said Mr Fish, 'and have no desire to dispute about the form of a constitution. A people may be as free under a king as under a senate. Liberty is not the lackey of any type of government.'

These were strange words from a member of a race whom I had thought wedded to the republicanism of Helvidius Priscus.

'As a loyal subject of a monarchy,' I said, 'I must agree with you. But your hands are tied, for I cannot picture the establishment of a House of Washington, and – if not, where are you to turn for your sovereign?'

Again a smile seemed to pass among the four.

'We are experimenters, as you say, sir, and must go slowly. In the meantime, we have an authority which keeps peace and property safe. We are at leisure to cast our eyes round and meditate on the future.'

'Then, gentlemen,' said I, 'you take an excellent way of meditation in visiting this museum of old sovereignties. Here you have the relics of any government you please – a dozen republics, tyrannies, theo-cracies, merchant confederations, kingdoms, and more than one empire. You have your choice. I am tolerably familiar with the land, and if I can assist you I am at your service.'

They thanked me gravely. 'We have letters,' said Mr Galloway; 'one in especial is to a gentleman whom we hope to meet in this place. Have you heard in your travels of the Count of Albany?'

'He has arrived,' said I, 'two days ago. Even now he is in the chamber above us at dinner.'

The news interested them hugely.

'You have seen him?' they cried. 'What is he like?'

'An elderly gentleman in poor health, a man who has travelled much, and, I judge, has suffered something from fortune. He has a fondness for the English, so you will be welcome, sirs; but he was indisposed yesterday, and may still be unable to receive you. His daughter travels with him and tends his old age.'

'And you – you have spoken with him?'

'The night before last I was in his company. We talked of many things, including the late war. He is somewhat of your opinion on matters of government.'

The four looked at each other, and then Mr Galloway rose.

'I ask your permission, Mr Townshend, to consult for a moment with my friends. The matter is of some importance, and I would beg you to await us.' So saying, he led the others out of doors, and I heard them withdraw to a corner of the loggia. Now, thought I, there is something afoot, and my long-sought romance approaches fruition. The company of the Marjolaine, whom the Count had sung of, have arrived at last.

Presently they returned and seated themselves at the table.

'You can be of great assistance to us, Mr Townshend, and we would fain take you into our confidence. Are you aware who is this Count of Albany?'

I nodded. 'It is a thin disguise to one familiar with history.'

'Have you reached any estimate of his character or capabilities? You speak to friends, and, let me tell you, it is a matter which deeply concerns the Count's interests.'

'I think him a kindly and pathetic old gentleman. He naturally bears the mark of forty years' sojourn in the wilderness.'

Mr Galloway took snuff.

'We have business with him, but it is business which stands in need of an agent. There is no one in the Count's suite with whom we could discuss affairs?'

'There is his daughter.'

'Ah, but she would scarcely suit the case. Is there no man – a friend, and yet not a member of the family, who can treat with us?'

I replied that I thought I was the only one in Santa Chiara who answered the description.

'If you will accept the task, Mr Townshend, you are amply qualified. We will be frank with you and reveal our business. We are on no less an errand than to offer the Count of Albany a crown.'

I suppose I must have had some suspicion of their purpose, and yet the revelation of it fell on me like a thunderclap. I could only stare owlishly at my four grave gentlemen.

Mr Galloway went on unperturbed. 'I have told you that in America we are not yet republicans. There are those among us who favour a republic, but they are by no means a majority. We have got rid of a king who misgoverned us, but we have no wish to get rid of kingship. We want a king of our own choosing, and we would get with him all the ancient sanctions of monarchy. The Count of Albany is of the most illustrious stock in Europe – he is, if legitimacy goes for anything, the rightful King of Britain. Now, if the republican party among us is to be worsted, we must come before the nation with a powerful candidate for its favour. You perceive my drift? What more potent appeal to American pride than to say: "We have got rid of King George; we choose of own free will the older line and King Charles"?'

I said foolishly that I thought monarchy had had its day, and that 'twas idle to revive it.

'That is a sentiment well enough under a monarchical government; but we, with a clean page to write upon, do not share it. You know your ancient historians. Has not the repository of the chief power always been the rock on which republicanism has shipwrecked? If that power is given to the chief citizen, the way is prepared for the tyrant. If it abides peacefully in a royal house, it abides with cyphers who dignify, without obstructing, a popular constitution. Do not mistake me, Mr Townshend. This is no whim of a sentimental girl, but the reasoned conclusion of the men who achieved our liberty. There is every reason to believe that General Washington shares our views, and Mr Hamilton, whose name you may know, is the inspirer of our mission.'

'But the Count is an old man,' I urged; for I knew not where to begin in my exposition of the hopelessness of their errand.

'By so much the better. We do not wish a young king who may be fractious. An old man tempered by misfortune is what our purpose demands.'

'He has also his failings. A man cannot lead his life for forty years and retain all the virtues.'

At that one of the Sylvesters spoke sharply. 'I have heard such gossip, but I do not credit it. I have not forgotten Preston and Derby.'

I made my last objection. 'He has no posterity – legitimate posterity – to carry on his line.'

The four gentlemen smiled. 'That happens to be his chiefest recommendation,' said Mr Galloway. 'It enables us to take the House of Stuart on trial. We need a breathing-space and leisure to look around; but unless we establish the principle of monarchy at once the republicans will forestall us. Let us get our king at all costs, and during the remaining years of his life we shall have time to settle the succession problem. We have no wish to saddle ourselves for good with a race who might prove burdensome. If King Charles fails he has no son, and we can look elsewhere for a better monarch. You perceive the reason of my view?'

I did, and I also perceived the colossal absurdity of the whole business. But I could not convince them of it, for they met my objections with excellent arguments. Nothing save a sight of the Count would, I feared, disillusion them.

'You wish me to make this proposal on your behalf?' I asked.

'We shall make the proposal ourselves, but we desire you to prepare the way for us. He is an elderly man, and should first be informed of our purpose.'

'There is one person whom I beg leave to consult – the Duchess, his daughter. It may be that the present is an ill moment for approaching the Count, and the affair requires her sanction.'

They agreed, and with a very perplexed mind I went forth to seek the lady. The irony of the thing was too cruel, and my heart ached for her. In the gallery I found Oliphant packing some very shabby trunks, and when I questioned him he told me that the family were to leave Santa Chiara on the morrow. Perchance the Duchess had awakened to the true state of their exchequer, or perchance she thought it well to get her father on the road again as a cure for his ailment.

I discovered Cristine, and begged for an interview with her mistress on an urgent matter. She led me to the Duchess's room, and there the evidence of poverty greeted me openly. All the little luxuries of the menage had gone to the Count. The poor lady's room was no better than a servant's garret, and the lady herself sat stitching a rent in a travelling cloak. She rose to greet me with alarm in her eyes.

As briefly as I could I set out the facts of my amazing mission. At first she seemed scarcely to hear me. 'What do they want with him?' she asked. 'He can give them nothing. He is no friend to the Americans or to any people who have deposed their sovereign.' Then, as she grasped my meaning, her face flushed.

'It is a heartless trick, Mr Townshend. I would fain think you no party to it.'

'Believe me, dear madame, it is no trick. The men below are in sober earnest. You have but to see their faces to know that theirs is no wild adventure. I believe sincerely that they have the power to implement their promise.'

'But it is madness. He is old and worn and sick. His day is long past for winning a crown.'

'All this I have said, but it does not move them.' And I told her rapidly Mr Galloway's argument.

She fell into a muse. 'At the eleventh hour! Nay, too late, too late. Had he been twenty years younger, what a stroke of fortune! Fate bears too hard on us, too hard!'

Then she turned to me fiercely. 'You have no doubt heard, sir, the gossip about my father, which is on the lips of every fool in Europe. Let us have done with this pitiful make-believe. My father is a sot. Nay, I do not blame him. I blame his enemies and his miserable destiny. But there is the fact. Were he not old, he would still be unfit to grasp a crown and rule over a turbulent people. He flees from one city to another, but he cannot flee from himself. That is his illness on which you condoled with me yesterday.'

The lady's control was at breaking-point. Another moment and I expected a torrent of tears. But they did not come. With a great effort she regained her composure.

'Well, the gentlemen must have an answer. You will tell them that the Count, my father – nay, give him his true title if you care – is vastly obliged to them for the honour they have done him, but would decline on account of his age and infirmities. You know how to phrase a decent refusal.'

'Pardon me,' said I, 'but I might give them that answer till doomsday and never content them. They have not travelled many thousand miles to be put off by hearsay evidence. Nothing will satisfy them but an interview with your father himself.'

'It is impossible,' she said sharply.

'Then we must expect the renewed attentions of our American friends. They will wait till they see him.'

She rose and paced the room.

'They must go,' she repeated many times. 'If they see him sober he will accept with joy, and we shall be the laughing-stock of the world. I tell you it cannot be. I alone know how immense is the impossibility. He cannot afford to lose the last rags of his dignity, the last dregs of his ease. They must not see him. I will speak with them myself.'

'They will be honoured, madame, but I do not think they will be convinced. They are what we call in my land "men of business". They will not be content till they get the Count's reply from his own lips.'

A new Duchess seemed to have arisen, a woman of quick action and sharp words.

'So be it. They shall see him. Oh, I am sick to death of fine sentiments and high loyalty and all the vapouring stuff I have lived among for years. All I ask for myself and my father is a little peace, and, by Heaven! I shall secure it. If nothing will kill your gentlemen's folly but truth, why, truth they shall have. They shall see my father, and this very minute. Bring them up, Mr Townshend, and usher them into the presence of the rightful King of England. You will find him alone.' She stopped her walk and looked out of the window.

I went back in a hurry to the Americans. 'I am bidden to bring you to the Count's chamber. He is alone and will see you. These are the commands of madame his daughter.'

'Good!' said Mr Galloway, and all four, grave gentlemen as they were, seemed to brace themselves to a special dignity as befitted ambassadors to a king. I led them upstairs, tapped at the Count's door, and, getting no answer, opened it and admitted them.

And this was what we saw. The furniture was in disorder, and on a couch lay an old man sleeping a heavy drunken sleep. His mouth was open and his breath came stertorously. The face was purple, and large purple veins stood out on the mottled forehead. His scanty white hair was draggled over his cheek. On the floor was a broken glass, wet stains still lay on the boards, and the place reeked of spirits.

The four looked for a second – I do not think longer – at him whom they would have made their king. They did not look at each other. With one accord they moved out, and Mr Fish, who was last, closed the door very gently behind him.

In the hall below Mr Galloway turned to me. 'Our mission is ended, Mr Townshend. I have to thank you for your courtesy.' Then to the others, 'If we order the coaches now, we may get well on the way to Verona ere sundown.'

An hour later two coaches rolled out of the courtyard of the Tre Croci. As they passed, a window was half-opened on the upper floor, and a head looked out. A line of a song came down, a song sung in a strange quavering voice. It was the catch I had heard the night before:

JOHN BUCHAN

Qu'est-c' qui passe ici si tard,
Compagnons de la Marjolaine–e?

It was true. The company came late indeed – too late by forty
years . . .

A Lucid Interval

'A Lucid Interval' was written in 1909 and first published in *Blackwood's Magazine* in February 1910 and simultaneously under the title 'God's Providence' in *The Atlantic Monthly*. It was one of the stories in *The Moon Endureth* (1912) and marks the first appearance of Tommy Deloraine, who would appear in *The Power House* (1916).

TO ADOPT THE opening words of a more famous tale, 'The truth of this strange matter is what the world has long been looking for.' The events which I propose to chronicle were known to perhaps a hundred people in London whose fate brings them into contact with politics. The consequences were apparent to all the world, and for one hectic fortnight tinged the soberest newspapers with saffron, drove more than one worthy election agent to an asylum, and sent whole batches of legislators to Continental 'cures'. But no reasonable explanation of the mystery has been forthcoming until now, when a series of chances gave the key into my hands.

Lady Caerlaverock is my aunt, and I was present at the two remarkable dinner-parties which form the main events in this tale. I was also taken into her confidence during the terrible fortnight which intervened between them. Like everybody else, I was hopelessly in the dark, and could only accept what happened as a divine interposition. My first clue came when James, the Caerlaverocks' second footman, entered my service as valet, and, being a cheerful youth, chose to gossip while he shaved me. I checked him, but he babbled on, and I could not choose but learn something about the disposition of the Caerlaverock household below-stairs. I learned – what I knew before – that his lordship had an inordinate love for curries, a taste acquired during some troubled years as Indian Viceroy. I had often eaten that admirable dish at his table, and had heard him boast of the skill of the Indian cook who prepared it. James, it appeared, did not hold with the

Orient in the kitchen. He described the said Indian gentleman as a 'nigger', and expressed profound distrust of his ways. He referred darkly to the events of the year before, which in some distorted way had reached the servants' ears. 'We always thought as 'ow it was them niggers as done it,' he declared; and when I questioned him on his use of the plural, admitted that at the time in question 'there 'ad been more nor one nigger 'anging about the kitchen.'

Pondering on these sayings, I asked myself if it were not possible that the behaviour of certain eminent statesmen was due to some strange devilry of the East, and I made a vow to abstain in future from the Caerlaverock curries. But last month my brother returned from India, and I got the whole truth. He was staying with me in Scotland, and in the smoking-room the talk turned on occultism in the East. I declared myself a sceptic, and George was stirred. He asked me rudely what I knew about it, and proceeded to make a startling confession of faith. He was cross-examined by the others, and retorted with some of his experiences. Finding an incredulous audience, his tales became more defiant, until he capped them all with one monstrous yarn. He maintained that in a Hindu family of his acquaintance there had been transmitted the secret of a drug, capable of altering a man's whole temperament until the antidote was administered. It would turn a coward into a bravo, a miser into a spendthrift, a rake into a fakir. Then, having delivered his manifesto, he got up abruptly and went to bed.

I followed him to his room, for something in the story had revived a memory. By dint of much persuasion I dragged from the somnolent George various details. The family in question were Beharis, large landholders dwelling near the Nepal border. He had known old Ram Singh for years, and had seen him twice since his return from England. He got the story from him, under no promise of secrecy, for the family drug was as well known in the neighbourhood as the nine incarnations of Krishna. He had no doubt about the truth of it, for he had positive proof. 'And others besides me,' said George. 'Do you remember when Vennard had a lucid interval a couple of years ago and talked sense for once? That was old Ram Singh's doing, for he told me about it.'

Three years ago, it seems, the Government of India saw fit to appoint a commission to inquire into land tenure on the Nepal border. Some of the feudal Rajahs had been 'birsing yont', like the Breadalbanes, and the smaller zemindars were gravely disquieted. The result of the commission was that Ram Singh had his boundaries rectified, and lost a mile or two of country which his hard-fisted fathers had won. I know nothing of the rights of the matter, but there can be no doubt about Ram Singh's dissatisfaction. He appealed to the law courts, but failed to upset the commission's finding, and the Privy Council upheld the Indian judgement. Thereupon in a flowery and eloquent document he laid his case before the Viceroy, and was told that the matter was closed. Now Ram Singh came of fighting stock, so he straightway took ship to England to petition the Crown. He petitioned Parliament, but his petition went into the bag behind the Speaker's chair, from which there is no return. He petitioned the King, but was courteously informed that he must approach the Department concerned. He tried the Secretary of State for India, and had an interview with Abinger Vennard, who was very rude to him, and succeeded in mortally insulting the feudal aristocrat. He appealed to the Prime Minister, and was warned off by a harassed private secretary. The handful of members of Parliament who make Indian grievances their stock-in-trade fought shy of him, for indeed Ram Singh's case had no sort of platform appeal in it, and his arguments were flagrantly undemocratic. But they sent him to Lord Caerlaverock, for the ex-viceroy loved to be treated as a kind of consul-general for India. But this Protector of the Poor proved a broken reed. He told Ram Singh flatly that he was a belated feudalist, which was true; and implied that he was a land-grabber, which was not true, Ram Singh having only enjoyed the fruits of his forbears' enterprise. Deeply incensed, the appellant shook the dust of Caerlaverock House from his feet, and sat down to plan a revenge upon the Government which had wronged him. And in his wrath he thought of the heirloom of his race, the drug which could change men's souls.

It happened that Lord Caerlaverock's cook came from the same neighbourhood as Ram Singh. This cook, Lal Muhammad by name, was one of a large poor family, hangers-on of Ram Singh's house. The aggrieved landowner summoned him, and demanded as of right his humble services. Lal Muhammad, who found his berth to his liking, hesitated, quibbled, but was finally overborne. He suggested a fee for his services, but hastily withdrew when Ram Singh sketched a few of the steps he proposed to take on his return by way of punishing Lal Muhammad's insolence on Lal Muhammad's household. Then he got to business. There was a great dinner next week – so he had learned from Jephson, the butler – and more than one member of the Government would honour Caerlaverock House by his presence. With deference he suggested this as a fitting occasion for the experiment, and Ram Singh was pleased to assent.

I can picture these two holding their meetings in the South Kensington lodgings where Ram Singh dwelt. We know from James, the second footman, that they met also at Caerlaverock House, no doubt that Ram Singh might make certain that his orders were duly obeyed. I can see the little packet of clear grains – I picture them like small granulated sugar – added to the condiments, and soon dissolved out of sight. The deed was done; the cook returned to Bloomsbury and Ram Singh to Gloucester Road, to await with the patient certainty of the East the consummation of a great vengeance.

II

My wife was at Kissingen and I was dining with the Caerlaverocks *en garçon*. When I have not to wait upon the adornment of the female person I am a man of punctual habits, and I reached the house as the hall clock chimed the quarter-past. My poor friend, Tommy Deloraine, arrived along with me, and we ascended the staircase together. I call him 'my poor friend', for at the moment Tommy was under the weather. He had the misfortune to be a marquis, and a very rich one, and at the same time to be in love with Claudia Barriton. Neither circumstance was in itself an evil, but the combination made for tragedy. For Tommy's twenty-five years of healthy manhood, his cleanly made up-standing figure, his fresh countenance and cheerful laugh, were of no avail in the lady's eyes when set against the fact that he was an idle peer. Miss Claudia was a charming girl, with a notable bee in her bonnet. She was burdened with the cares of the State, and had no patience with anyone who took them lightly. To her mind the social fabric was rotten beyond repair, and her purpose was frankly destructive. I remember some of her phrases: 'A bold and generous policy of social amelioration'; 'The development of a civic conscience'; 'A strong hand to lop off decaying branches from the trunk of the State'. I have no fault to find with her creed, but I objected to its practical working when it took the shape of an inhuman hostility to that devout lover, Tommy Deloraine. She had refused him, I believe, three times, with every circumstance of scorn. The first time she had analysed his character, and described him as a bundle of attractive weaknesses. 'The only forces I recognise are those of intellect and conscience,' she had said, 'and you have neither.' The second time – it was after he had been to Canada on the staff – she spoke of the irreconcilability of their political ideals. 'You are an Imperialist,' she said, 'and believe in an empire of conquest for the benefit of the few. I want a little island with a rich life for all.' Tommy declared that he would become a Doukhobor to please her, but she said something about the inability of Ethiopians to change their skin. The third time she hinted vaguely that there was 'another'. The star of Abinger Vennard was now blazing in the firmament, and she had conceived a platonic admiration for him. The truth is that Miss Claudia, with all her cleverness, was very young and – dare I say it? – rather silly.

Caerlaverock was stroking his beard, his legs astraddle on the hearthrug, with something appallingly viceregal in his air, when Mr and Mrs Alexander Cargill were announced. The Home Secretary was a joy to behold. He had the face of an elderly and pious bookmaker, and a voice in which lurked the indescribable Scotch quality of 'unction'. When he was talking you had only to shut your eyes to imagine yourself in some lowland kirk on a hot Sabbath morning. He had been a distinguished advocate before he left the law for politics, and had swayed juries of his countrymen at his will. The man was extraordinarily efficient on a platform. There were unplumbed depths of emotion in his eye, a juicy sentiment in his voice, an overpowering tenderness in his manner, which gave to politics the glamour of a revival meeting. He wallowed in obvious pathos, and his hearers, often unwillingly, wallowed with him. I have never listened to any orator at once so offensive and so horribly effective. There was no appeal too base for him, and none too august: by some subtle alchemy he blended the arts of the prophet and the fishwife. He had discovered a new kind of language. Instead of 'the hungry millions', or 'the toilers', or any of the numerous synonyms for our masters, he invented the phrase, 'Goad's people'. 'I shall never rest,' so ran his great declaration, 'till Goad's green fields and Goad's clear waters are free to Goad's people.' I remember how on this occasion he pressed my hand with his famous cordiality, looked gravely and earnestly into my face, and then gazed sternly into vacancy. It was a fine picture of genius descending for a moment from its hill-top to show how close it was to poor humanity.

Then came Lord Mulross, a respectable troglodytic peer, who

represented the one sluggish element in a swiftly progressing Government. He was an oldish man with bushy whiskers and a reputed mastery of the French tongue. A Whig, who had never changed his creed one iota, he was highly valued by the country as a sober element in the nation's councils, and endured by the Cabinet as necessary ballast. He did not conceal his dislike for certain of his colleagues, notably Mr Vennard and Mr Cargill.

When Miss Barriton arrived with her stepmother the party was almost complete. She entered with an air of apologising for her prettiness. Her manner with old men was delightful, and I watched with interest the unbending of Caerlaverock and the simplifying of Mr Cargill in her presence. Deloraine, who was talking feverishly to Mrs Cargill, started as if to go and greet her, thought better of it, and continued his conversation. The lady swept the room with her eye, but did not acknowledge his presence. She floated off with Mr Cargill to a window-corner, and metaphorically sat at his feet. I saw Deloraine saying things behind his moustache, while he listened to Mrs Cargill's new cure for dyspepsia.

Last of all, twenty minutes late, came Abinger Vennard. He made a fine stage entrance, walking swiftly with a lowering bow to his hostess, and then glaring fiercely round the room as if to challenge criticism. I have heard Deloraine, in a moment of irritation, describe him as a 'Pre-Raphaelite attorney', but there could be no denying his good looks. He had a bad, loose figure, and a quantity of studiously neglected hair, but his face was the face of a young Greek. A certain kind of political success gives a man the manners of an actor, and both Vennard and Cargill bristled with self-consciousness. You could see it in the way they patted their hair, squared their shoulders, and shifted their feet to positions loved by sculptors.

'Well, Vennard, what's the news from the House?' Caerlaverock asked.

'Simpson is talking,' said Vennard wearily. 'He attacks me, of course. He says he has lived forty years in India – as if that mattered! When will people recognise that the truths of democratic policy are independent of time and space? Liberalism is a category, an eternal mode of thought, which cannot be overthrown by any trivial happenings. I am sick of the word 'facts'. I long for truths.'

Miss Barriton's eyes brightened, and Cargill said, 'Excellent.' Lord Mulross, who was a little deaf, and in any case did not understand the language, said loudly to my aunt that he wished there was a close time for legislation. 'The open season for grouse should be the close season for politicians.'

And then we went down to dinner.

Miss Barriton sat on my left hand, between Deloraine and me, and it was clear she was discontented with her position. Her eyes wandered down the table to Vennard, who had taken in an American duchess, and seemed to be amused at her prattle. She looked with complete disfavour at Deloraine, and turned to me as the lesser of two evils.

I was tactless enough to say that I thought there was a good deal in Lord Mulross's view.

'Oh, how can you?' she cried. 'Is there a close season for the wants of the people? It sounds to me perfectly horrible the way you talk of government, as if it were a game for idle men of the upper classes. I want professional politicians, men who give their whole heart and soul to the service of the State. I know the kind of member you and Lord Deloraine like – a rich young man who eats and drinks too much, and thinks the real business of life is killing little birds. He travels abroad and shoots some big game, and then comes home and rants about the Empire. He knows nothing about realities, and will go down before the men who take the world seriously.'

I am afraid I laughed, but Deloraine, who had been listening, was in no mood to be amused.

'I don't think you are quite fair to us, Miss Claudia,' he said slowly. 'We take things seriously enough, the things we know about. We can't be expected to know about everything, and the misfortune is that the things I care about don't interest you. But they are important enough for all that.'

'Hush,' said the lady rudely. 'I want to hear what Mr Vennard is saying.'

Mr Vennard was addressing the dinner table as if it were a large public meeting. It was a habit he had, for he had no mind to confine the pearls of his wisdom to his immediate neighbours. His words were directed to Caerlaverock at the far end.

'In my opinion this craze for the scientific standpoint is not merely overdone – it is radically vicious. Human destinies cannot be treated as if they were inert objects under the microscope. The cold-blooded logical way of treating a problem is in almost every case the wrong way. Heart and imagination to me are more vital than intellect. I have

[127]

the courage to be illogical, to defy facts for the sake of an ideal, in the certainty that in time facts will fall into conformity. My creed may be put in the words of Newman's favourite quotation: *Non in dialectica complacuit Deo salvum facere populum suum* – Not in cold logic is it God's will that His people should find salvation.'

'It is profoundly true,' sighed Mr Cargill, and Miss Claudia's beaming eyes proved her assent.

The moment of destiny, though I did not know it, had arrived. The *entrée* course had begun, and of the two *entrées* one was the famous Caerlaverock curry. Now on a hot July evening in London there are more attractive foods than curry seven times heated, *more Indico*. I doubt if any guest would have touched it, had not our host in his viceregal voice called the attention of the three Ministers to its merits, while explaining that under doctor's orders he was compelled to refrain for a season. The result was that Mulross, Cargill, and Vennard alone of the men partook of it. Miss Claudia, alone of the women, followed suit in the fervour of her hero-worship. She ate a mouthful, and then drank rapidly two glasses of water.

My narrative of the events which followed is based rather on what I should have seen than on what I saw. I had not the key, and missed much which otherwise would have been plain to me. For example, if I had known the secret, I must have seen Miss Claudia's gaze cease to rest upon Vennard and the adoration die out of her eyes. I must have noticed her face soften to the unhappy Deloraine. As it was, I did not remark her behaviour, till I heard her say to her neighbour, – 'Can't you get hold of Mr Vennard and forcibly cut his hair?'

Deloraine looked round with a start. Miss Barriton's tone was intimate and her face friendly.

'Some people think it picturesque,' he said in serious bewilderment.

'Oh yes, picturesque – like a hairdresser's young man!' She shrugged her shoulders. 'He looks as if he had never been out of doors in his life.'

Now, whatever the faults of Tommy's appearance, he had a wholesome sunburnt face, and he knew it. This speech of Miss Barriton's cheered him enormously, for he argued that if she had fallen out of love with Vennard's looks she might fall in love with his own. Being a philosopher in his way, he was content to take what the gods gave, and ask for no explanations.

I do not know how their conversation prospered, for my attention was distracted by the extraordinary behaviour of the Home Secretary. Mr Cargill had made himself notorious by his treatment of 'political' prisoners. It was sufficient in his eyes for a criminal to confess to political convictions to secure the most lenient treatment and a speedy release. The Irish patriot who cracked skulls in the Scotland Division of Liverpool, the Suffragist who broke windows and the noses of the police, the Social Democrat whose antipathy to the Tsar revealed itself in assaults upon the Russian Embassy, the 'hunger-marchers' who had designs on the British Museum – all were sure of respectful and tender handling. He had announced, more than once, amid tumultuous cheering, that he would never be the means of branding earnestness, however mistaken, with the badge of the felon.

He was talking, as I recall the scene, to Lady Lavinia Dobson, renowned in two hemispheres for her advocacy of women's rights. And this was what I heard him say. His face had grown suddenly flushed and his eye bright, so that he looked liker than ever to a bookmaker who had had a good meeting. 'No, no, my dear lady, I have been a lawyer, and it is my duty in office to see that the law, the palladium of British liberties, is kept sacrosanct. The law is no respecter of persons, and I intend that it shall be no respecter of creeds. If men or women break the laws, to jail they shall go, though their intentions were those of the Apostle Paul. We don't punish them for being Socialists or Suffragists, but for breaking the peace. Why, goodness me, if we didn't, we should have every malefactor in Britain claiming preferential treatment because he was a Christian Scientist or a Pentecostal Dancer.'

'Mr Cargill, do you realise what you are saying?' said Lady Lavinia with a scared face.

'Of course I do. I am a lawyer, and may be presumed to know the law. If any other doctrine were admitted, the Empire would burst up in a fortnight.'

'That I should live to hear you name that accursed name!' cried the outraged lady. 'You are denying your gods, Mr Cargill. You are forgetting the principles of a lifetime.'

Mr Cargill was becoming excited, and exchanging his ordinary Edinburgh-English for a broader and more effective dialect.

'Tut, tut, my good wumman, I may be allowed to know my own principles best. I tell ye I've always maintained these views from the day when I first walked the floor of the Parliament House. Besides, even if I hadn't, I'm surely at liberty to change if I get more light. Whoever makes a fetich of consistency is a trumpery body and little use to God or man. What ails ye at the Empire, too? Is it not better to have a big country than a kailyard, or a house in Grosvenor Square than a but-and-ben in Balham?'

Lady Lavinia folded her hands. 'We slaughter our black fellow-citizens, we fill South Africa with yellow slaves, we crowd the Indian prisons with the noblest and most enlightened of the Indian race, and we call it Empire-building!'

'No, we don't,' said Mr Cargill stoutly, 'we call it common sense. That is the penal and repressive side of any great activity. D'ye mean to tell me that you never give your maid a good hearing? But would you like it to be said that you spent the whole of your days swearing at the wumman?'

'I never swore in my life,' said Lady Lavinia.

'I spoke metaphorically,' said Mr Cargill. 'If ye cannot understand a simple metaphor, ye cannot understand the rudiments of politics.'

Picture to yourself a prophet who suddenly discovers that his God is laughing at him, a devotee whose saint winks and tells him that the devotion of years has been a farce, and you will get some idea of Lady Lavinia's frame of mind. Her sallow face flushed, her lip trembled, and she slewed round as far as her chair would permit her. Meanwhile Mr Cargill, redder than before, went on contentedly with his dinner.

I was glad when my aunt gave the signal to rise. The atmosphere was electric, and all were conscious of it save the three Ministers, Deloraine, and Miss Claudia. Vennard seemed to be behaving very badly. He was arguing with Caerlaverock down the table, and the ex-Viceroy's face was slowly getting purple. When the ladies had gone, we remained oblivious to wine and cigarettes, listening to this heated controversy which threatened any minute to end in a quarrel.

The subject was India, and Vennard was discoursing on the follies of all Viceroys.

'Take this idiot we've got now,' he declared. 'He expects me to be a sort of wet-nurse to the Government of India and do all their dirty work for them. They know local conditions, and they have ample powers if they would only use them, but they won't take an atom of responsibility. How the deuce am I to decide for them, when in the nature of things I can't be half as well informed about the facts!'

'Do you maintain,' said Caerlaverock, stuttering in his wrath, 'that the British Government should divest itself of responsibility for the government of our great Indian Dependency?'

'Not a bit,' said Vennard impatiently; 'of course we are responsible, but that is all the more reason why the fellows who know the business at first hand should do their duty. If I am the head of a bank I am responsible for its policy, but that doesn't mean that every local bank manager should consult me about the solvency of clients I never heard of. Faversham keeps bleating to me that the state of India is dangerous. Well, for God's sake let him suppress every native paper, shut up the schools, and send every agitator to the Andamans. I'll back him up all right. But don't let him ask me what to do, for I don't know.'

'You think such a course would be popular?' asked a large, grave man, a newspaper editor.

'Of course it would,' said Vennard cheerily. 'The British public hates the idea of letting India get out of hand. But they want a lead. They can't be expected to start the show any more than I can.'

Lord Caerlaverock rose to join the ladies with an air of outraged dignity. Vennard pulled out his watch and announced that he must get back to the House.

'Do you know what I am going to do?' he asked. 'I am going down to tell Simpson what I think of him. He gets up and prates of having been forty years in India. Well, I am going to tell him that it is to him and his forty-year lot that all this muddle is due. Oh, I assure you, there's going to be a row,' said Vennard, as he struggled into his coat.

Mulross had been sitting next to me, and I asked him if he was leaving town. 'I wish I could,' he said, 'but I fear I must stick on over the Twelfth. I don't like the way that fellow von Kladow has been talking. He's up to no good, and he's going to get a flea in his ear before he is very much older.'

Cheerfully, almost hilariously, the three Ministers departed, Vennard and Cargill in a hansom, and Mulross on foot. I can only describe the condition of those left behind as nervous prostration. We looked furtively at each other, each afraid to hint his suspicions, but all convinced that a surprising judgement had befallen at least two members of His Majesty's Government. For myself I put the number at three, for I did not like to hear a respected Whig Foreign Secretary talk about giving the Chancellor of a friendly but jealous Power a flea in his ear.

The only unperplexed face was Deloraine's. He whispered to me that Miss Barriton was going on to the Alvanleys' ball, and had warned him to be there. 'She hasn't been to a dance for months, you know,' he said. 'I really think things are beginning to go a little better, old man.'

III

When I opened my paper next morning I read two startling pieces of news. Lord Mulross had been knocked down by a taxi-cab on his way home the night before, and was now in bed suffering from a bad shock and a bruised ankle. There was no cause for anxiety, said the report, but his lordship must keep his room for a week or two.

The second item, which filled leading articles and overflowed into 'Political Notes', was Mr Vennard's speech. The Secretary for India had gone down about eleven o'clock to the House, where an Indian debate was dragging out its slow length. He sat himself on the Treasury Bench and took notes, and the House soon filled in antici-pation of his reply. His 'tail' – progressive young men like himself – were there in full strength, ready to cheer every syllable which fell from their idol. Somewhere about half-past twelve he rose to wind up the debate, and the House was treated to an unparalleled sensation. He began with his critics, notably the unfortunate Simpson, and, pretty much in Westbury's language to the herald, called them silly old men who did not understand their silly old business. But it was the reasons he gave for this abuse which left his followers aghast. He attacked his critics not for being satraps and reactionaries, but because they had dared to talk second-rate Western politics in connection with India. 'Have you lived for forty years with your eyes shut,' he cried, 'that you cannot see the differences between a Bengali, married at fifteen and worshipping a pantheon of savage gods, and the university-extension young Radical at home? There is a thousand years between them, and you dream of annihilating the centuries with a little dubious popular science!' Then he turned to the other critics of Indian administration – his quondam supporters. He analysed the character of these 'members for India' with a vigour and acumen which deprived them of speech. The East, he said, had had its revenge upon the West by making certain Englishmen babus. His honourable friends had the same slipshod minds, and they talked the same pigeon-English, as the patriots of Bengal. Then his mood changed, and he delivered a solemn warning against what he called 'the treason begotten of restless vanity and proved incompetence'. He sat down, leaving a House deeply impressed and horribly mystified.

The Times did not know what to make of it at all. In a weighty leader it welcomed Mr Vennard's conversion, but hinted that with a convert's zeal he had slightly overstated his case. The *Daily Chronicle* talked of 'nervous breakdown', and suggested 'kindly forgetfulness' as the best treatment. The *Daily News*, in a spirited article called 'The Great Betrayal', washed its hands of Mr Vennard unless he donned the white sheet of the penitent. Later in the day I got the *Westminster Gazette*, and found an ingenious leader which proved that the speech in no way conflicted with Liberal principles, and was capable of a quite ordinary explanation. Then I went to see Lady Caerlaverock.

I found my aunt almost in tears.

'What has happened?' she cried. 'What have we done that we should be punished in this awful way? And to think that the blow fell in this house? Caerlaverock – we all – thought Mr Vennard so strange last night, and Lady Lavinia told me that Mr Cargill was perfectly horrible. I suppose it must be the heat and the strain of the session. And that poor Lord Mulross, who was always so wise, should be stricken down at this crisis!'

I did not say that I thought Mulross's accident a merciful dispensation. I was far more afraid of him than of all the others, for if with his reputation for sanity he chose to run amok, he would be taken seriously. He was better in bed than affixing a flea to von Kladow's ear.

'Caerlaverock was with the Prime Minister this morning,' my aunt went on. 'He is going to make a statement in the Lords tomorrow to try to cover Mr Vennard's folly. They are very anxious about what Mr Cargill will do today. He is addressing the National Convention of Young Liberals at Oldham this afternoon, and though they have sent him a dozen telegrams they can get no answer. Caerlaverock went to Downing Street an hour ago to get news.'

There was the sound of an electric brougham stopping in the square below, and we both listened with a premonition of disaster. A minute later Caerlaverock entered the room, and with him the Prime Minister. The cheerful, eupeptic countenance of the latter was clouded with care. He shook hands dismally with my aunt, nodded to me, and flung himself down on a sofa.

'The worst has happened,' Caerlaverock boomed solemnly. 'Cargill has been incredibly and infamously silly.' He tossed me an evening paper.

One glance convinced me that the Convention of Young Liberals had had a waking-up. Cargill had addressed them on what he called the true view of citizenship. He had dismissed manhood suffrage as an obsolete folly. The franchise, he maintained, should be narrowed and given only to citizens, and his definition of citizenship was military training combined with a fairly high standard of rates and taxes. I do not know how the Young Liberals received this creed, but it had no sort of success with the Prime Minister.

'We must disavow him,' said Caerlaverock.

'He is too valuable a man to lose,' said the Prime Minister. 'We must hope that it is only a temporary aberration. I simply cannot spare him in the House.'

'But this is flat treason.'

'I know, I know. It is all too horrible, and utterly unexpected. But the situation wants delicate handling, my dear Caerlaverock. I see nothing for it but to give out that he was ill.'

'Or drunk?' I suggested.

The Prime Minister shook his head sadly. 'I fear it will be the same thing. What we call illness the ordinary man will interpret as intoxication. It is a most regrettable necessity, but we must face it.'

The harassed leader rose, seized the evening paper, and departed as swiftly as he had come. 'Remember, illness,' were his parting words. 'An old heart trouble, which is apt to affect his brain. His friends have always known about it.'

I walked home, and looked in at the Club on my way. There I found Deloraine devouring a hearty tea and looking the picture of virtuous happiness.

'Well, this is tremendous news,' I said, as I sat down beside him.

'What news?' he asked with a start.

'This row over Vennard and Cargill.'

'Oh, that! I haven't seen the papers today. What's it all about?' His tone was devoid of interest.

Then I knew that something of great private moment had happened to Tommy.

'I hope I may congratulate you,' I said.

Deloraine beamed on me affectionately. 'Thanks very much, old man. Things came all right, quite suddenly, you know. We spent most of the time at the Alvanleys' together, and this morning in the Park she accepted me. It will be in the papers next week, but we mean to keep it quiet for a day or two. However, it was your right to be told – and besides, you guessed.'

I remember wondering, as I finished my walk home, whether there could not be some connection between the stroke of Providence which had driven three Cabinet Ministers demented and that gentler touch which had restored Miss Claudia Barriton to good sense and a reasonable marriage.

IV

The next week was an epoch in my life. I seemed to live in the centre of a Mad Tea-party, where every one was convinced of the madness, and yet resolutely protested that nothing had happened. The public events of those days were simple enough. While Lord Mulross's ankle approached convalescence, the hives of politics were humming with rumours. Vennard's speech had dissolved his party into its parent elements, and the Opposition, as nonplussed as the Government, did not dare as yet to claim the recruit. Consequently he was left alone till he should see fit to take a further step. He refused to be interviewed, using blasphemous language about our free Press; and mercifully he showed no desire to make speeches. He went down to golf at Littlestone, and rarely showed himself in the House. The earnest young reformer seemed to have adopted not only the creed but the habits of his enemies.

Mr Cargill's was a hard case. He returned from Oldham, delighted with himself and full of fight, to find awaiting him an urgent message from the Prime Minister. His chief was sympathetic and kindly. He had long noticed that the Home Secretary looked fagged and ill. There was no Home Office Bill very pressing, and his assistance in general debate could be dispensed with for a little. Let him take a fortnight's holiday – fish, golf, yacht – the Prime Minister was airily suggestive. In vain Mr Cargill declared he was perfectly well. His chief gently but firmly overbore him, and insisted on sending him his own doctor. That eminent specialist, having been well coached, was vaguely alarming, and advised a change. Then Mr Cargill began to suspect, and asked the Prime Minister point-blank if he objected to his

Oldham speech. He was told that there was no objection – a little strong meat, perhaps, for Young Liberals, a little daring, but full of Mr Cargill's old intellectual power. Mollified and reassured, the Home Secretary agreed to a week's absence, and departed for a little salmon fishing in Scotland. His wife had meantime been taken into the affair, and privately assured by the Prime Minister that she would greatly ease the mind of the Cabinet if she could induce her husband to take a longer holiday – say three weeks. She promised to do her best and to keep her instructions secret, and the Cargills duly departed for the North. 'In a fortnight,' said the Prime Minister to my aunt, 'he will have forgotten all this nonsense; but of course we shall have to watch him very carefully in the future.'

The Press was given its cue, and announced that Mr Cargill had spoken at Oldham while suffering from severe nervous breakdown, and that the remarkable doctrines of that speech need not be taken seriously. As I had expected, the public put its own interpretation upon this tale. Men took each other aside in clubs, women gossiped in drawing-rooms, and in a week the Cargill scandal had assumed amazing proportions. The popular version was that the Home Secretary had got very drunk at Caerlaverock House, and still under the influence of liquor had addressed the Young Liberals at Oldham. He was now in an Inebriates' Home, and would not return to the House that session. I confess I trembled when I heard this story, for it was altogether too libellous to pass unnoticed. I believed that soon it would reach the ear of Cargill, fishing quietly at Tomandhoul, and that then there would be the deuce to pay.

Nor was I wrong. A few days later I went to see my aunt to find out how the land lay. She was very bitter, I remember, about Claudia Barriton. 'I expected sympathy and help from her, and she never comes near me. I can understand her being absorbed in her engagement, but I cannot understand the frivolous way she spoke when I saw her yesterday. She had the audacity to say that both Mr Vennard and Mr Cargill had gone up in her estimation. Young people can be so heartless.'

I would have defended Miss Barriton, but at this moment an astonishing figure was announced. It was Mrs Cargill in travelling dress, with a purple bonnet and a green motor veil. Her face was scarlet, whether from excitement or the winds of Tomandhoul, and she charged down on us like a young bull.

'We have come back,' she said, 'to meet our accusers.'

'Accusers!' cried my aunt.

'Yes, accusers!' said the lady. 'The abominable rumour about Alexander has reached our ears. At this moment he is with the Prime Minister, demanding an official denial. I have come to you, because it was here, at your table, that Alexander is said to have fallen.'

'I really don't know what you mean, Mrs Cargill.'

'I mean that Alexander is said to have become drunk while dining here, to have been drunk when he spoke at Oldham, and to be now in a Drunkards' Home.' The poor lady broke down. 'Alexander,' she cried, 'who has been a teetotaller from his youth, and for thirty years an elder in the UP Church! No form of intoxicant has ever been permitted at our table. Even in illness the thing has never passed our lips.'

My aunt by this time had pulled herself together. 'If this outrageous story is current, Mrs Cargill, there was nothing for it but to come back. Your friends know that it is a gross libel. The only denial necessary is for Mr Cargill to resume his work. I trust his health is better.'

'He is well, but heartbroken. His is a sensitive nature, Lady Caerlaverock, and he feels a stain like a wound.'

'There is no stain,' said my aunt briskly. 'Every public man is a target for scandals, but no one but a fool believes them. They will die a natural death when he returns to work. An official denial would make everybody look ridiculous, and encourage the ordinary person to think that there may have been something in them. Believe me, dear Mrs Cargill, there is nothing to be anxious about now that you are back in London again.'

On the contrary, I thought, there was more cause for anxiety than ever. Cargill was back in the House, and the illness game could not be played a second time. I went home that night acutely sympathetic towards the worries of the Prime Minister. Mulross would be abroad in a day or two, and Vennard and Cargill were volcanoes in eruption. The Government was in a parlous state, with three demented Ministers on the loose.

The same night I first heard the story of *the* Bill. Vennard had done more than play golf at Littlestone. His active mind – for his bitterest enemies never denied his intellectual energy – had been busy on a great scheme. At that time, it will be remembered, a serious shrinkage of unskilled labour existed not only in the Transvaal, but in the new copper fields of East Africa. Simultaneously a famine was scourging Behar, and Vennard, to do him justice, had made manful efforts to cope with it. He had gone fully into the question, and had been slowly coming to the conclusion that Behar was hopelessly overcrowded. In his new frame of mind – unswervingly logical, utterly unemotional, and wholly unbound by tradition – he had come to connect the African and Indian troubles, and to see in one the relief of the other. The first fruit of his meditations was a letter to *The Times*. In it he laid down a new theory of emigration. The peoples of the Empire, he said, must be mobile, shifting about to suit economic conditions. But if this was true for the white man, it was equally true for the dark races under our tutelage. He referred to the famine, and argued that the recurrence of such disasters was inevitable, unless we assisted the poverty-stricken ryot to emigrate and sell his labour to advantage. He proposed indentures and terminable contracts, for he declared he had no wish to transplant for good. All that was needed was a short season of wage-earning abroad, that the labourer might return home with savings which would set him for the future on a higher economic plane. The letter was temperate and academic in phrasing, the speculation of a publicist rather than the declaration of a Minister. But in Liberals, who remembered the pandemonium raised over the Chinese in South Africa, it stirred up the gloomiest forebodings.

Then, whispered from mouth to mouth, came the news of the Great Bill. Vennard, it was said, intended to bring in a measure at the earliest possible date to authorise a scheme of enforced and State-aided emigration to the African mines. It would apply at first only to the famine districts, but power would be given to extend its working by proclamation to other areas. Such was the rumour, and I need not say it was soon magnified. Questions were asked in the House which the Speaker ruled out of order. Furious articles, inviting denial, appeared in the Liberal press; but Vennard took not the slightest notice. He spent his time between his office in Whitehall and the links at Littlestone, dropping into the House once or twice for half an hour's slumber while a colleague was speaking. His Under Secretary in the Lords – a young gentleman who had joined the party for a bet, and to his immense disgust had been immediately rewarded with office – lost his temper under cross-examination, and swore audibly at the Opposition. In a day or two the story universally believed was that the Secretary for India was about to transfer the bulk of the Indian people to work as indentured labourers for South African Jews.

It was this popular version, I fancy, which reached the ears of Ram Singh, and the news came on him like a thunderclap. He thought that what Vennard proposed Vennard could do. He saw his native province stripped of its people, his fields left unploughed, and his cattle untended; nay, it was possible, his own worthy and honourable self sent to a far country to dig in a hole. It was a grievous and intolerable prospect. He walked home to Gloucester Road in heavy preoccupation, and the first thing he did was to get out the mysterious brass box in which he kept his valuables. From a pocket-book he took a small silk packet, opened it, and spilled a few clear grains on his hand. It was the antidote.

He waited two days, while on all sides the rumour of the Bill grew stronger and its provisions more stringent. Then he hesitated no longer, but sent for Lord Caerlaverock's cook.

V

I conceive that the drug did not create new opinions, but elicited those which had hitherto lain dormant. Every man has a creed, but in his soul he knows that that creed has another side, possibly not less logical, which it does not suit him to produce. Our most honest convictions are not the children of pure reason, but of temperament, environment, necessity, and interest. Most of us take sides in life and forget the one we reject. But our conscience tells us it is there, and we can on occasion state it with a fairness and fullness which proves that it is not wholly repellent to our reason. During the crisis I write of, the attitude of Cargill and Vennard was not that of roysterers out for irresponsible mischief. They were eminently reasonable and wonderfully logical, and in private conversation they gave their opponents a very bad time. Cargill, who had hitherto been the hope of the extreme Free-traders, wrote an article for the *Quarterly* on Tariff Reform. It was set up, but long before it could be used it was cancelled and the type scattered. I have seen a proof of it, however, and I confess I have never read a more brilliant defence of a doctrine which the author had hitherto described as a childish heresy. Which proves my contention – that Cargill all along knew that there was a case against Free Trade, but naturally did not choose to admit it, his allegiance being vowed elsewhere. The drug altered temperament, and with it the creed which is based mainly on temperament. It scattered current convictions, roused dormant speculations, and without damaging the reason switched it on to a new track.

I can see all this now, but at the time I saw only stark madness and the horrible ingenuity of the lunatic. While Vennard was ruminating on his Bill, Cargill was going about London arguing like a Scotch undergraduate. The Prime Minister had seen from the start that the Home Secretary was the worse danger. Vennard might talk of his preposterous Bill, but the Cabinet would have something to say before its introduction, and he was mercifully disinclined to go near St Stephen's. But Cargill was assiduous in his attendance at the House, and at any moment might blow the Government sky-high. His colleagues were detailed in relays to watch him. One would hale him to luncheon, and keep him till question time was over. Another would insist on taking him for a motor ride, which would end in a breakdown about Brentford. Invitations to dinner were showered upon him, and Cargill, who had been unknown in society, found the whole social machinery of his party set at work to make him a lion. The result was that he was prevented from speaking in public, but given far too much encouragement to talk in private. He talked incessantly, before, at, and after dinner, and he did enormous harm. He was horribly clever, too, and usually got the best of an argument, so that various eminent private Liberals had their tempers ruined by his dialectic. In his rich and unabashed accent – he had long discarded his Edinburgh-English – he dissected their arguments and ridiculed their character. He had once been famous for his soapy manners: now he was as rough as a Highland stot.

Things could not go on in this fashion: the risk was too great. It was just a fortnight, I think, after the Caerlaverock dinner-party, when the Prime Minister resolved to bring matters to a head. He could not afford to wait for ever on a return of sanity. He consulted Caerlaverock, and it was agreed that Vennard and Cargill should be asked, or rather commanded, to dine on the following evening at Caerlaverock House. Mulross, whose sanity was not suspected, and whose ankle was now well again, was also invited, as were three other members of the Cabinet, and myself as *amicus curiæ*. It was understood that after dinner there would be a settling-up with the two rebels. Either they should recant and come to heel, or they should depart from the fold to swell the wolf-pack of the Opposition. The Prime Minister did not conceal the loss which his party would suffer, but he argued very sensibly that anything was better than a brace of vipers in its bosom.

I have never attended a more lugubrious function. When I arrived I found Caerlaverock, the Prime Minister, and the three other members of the Cabinet standing round a small fire in attitudes of nervous dejection. I remember it was a raw, wet evening, but the gloom out of doors was sunshine compared to the gloom within. Caerlaverock's viceregal air had sadly altered. The Prime Minister, once famous for his genial manners, was pallid and preoccupied. We exchanged remarks about the weather and the duration of the session. Then we fell silent till Mulross arrived.

He did not look as if he had come from a sick bed. He came in as jaunty as a boy, limping just a little from his accident. He was greeted by his colleagues with tender solicitude – solicitude, I fear, completely wasted on him.

'Devilish silly thing to do to get run over,' he said. 'I was in a brown study when a cab came round a corner. But I don't regret it, you know. During the past fortnight I have had leisure to go into this Bosnian Succession business, and I see now that Von Kladow has been playing one big game of bluff. Very well; it has got to stop. I am going to prick the bubble before I am many days older.'

The Prime Minister looked anxious. 'Our policy towards Bosnia has been one of non-interference. It is not for us, I should have thought, to read Germany a lesson.'

'Oh, come now,' Mulross said, slapping – yes, actually slapping – his leader on the back; 'we may drop that nonsense when we are alone. You know very well that there are limits to our game of non-inter-ference. If we don't read Germany a lesson, she will read us one – and a damned long unpleasant one too. The sooner we give up all this milk-blooded, blue-spectacled, pacificist talk the better. However, you will see what I have got to say tomorrow in the House.'

The Prime Minister's face lengthened. Mulross was not the pillar he had thought him, but a splintering reed. I saw that he agreed with me that this was the most dangerous of the lot.

Then Cargill and Vennard came in together. Both looked uncommonly fit, younger, trimmer, cleaner. Vennard, instead of his sloppy clothes and shaggy hair, was groomed like a guardsman; had a large pearl-and-diamond solitaire in his shirt, and a white waistcoat with jewelled buttons. He had lost all his self-consciousness, grinned cheerfully at the others, warmed his hands at the fire, and cursed the weather. Cargill, too, had lost his sanctimonious look. There was a bloom of rustic health on his cheek, and a sparkle in his eye, so that he had the appearance of some rosy Scotch laird of Raeburn's painting. Both men wore an air of purpose and contentment.

Vennard turned at once on the Prime Minister. 'Did you get my letter?' he asked. 'No? Well, you'll find it waiting when you get home. We're all friends here, so I can tell you its contents. We *must* get rid of this ridiculous Radical 'tail'. They think they have the whip-hand of us; well, we have got to prove that we can do very well without them. They are a collection of confounded, treacherous, complacent prigs, but they have no grit in them, and will come to heel if we tackle them firmly. I respect an honest fanatic, but I do not respect those senti-ment-mongers. They have the impudence to say that the country is with them. I tell you it is rank nonsense. If you take a strong hand with them, you'll double your popularity, and we'll come back next year with an increased majority. Cargill agrees with me.'

The Prime Minister looked grave. 'I am not prepared to discuss any policy of ostracism. What you call our 'tail' is a vital section of our party. Their creed may be one-sided, but it is none the less part of our mandate from the people.'

'I want a leader who governs as well as reigns,' said Vennard. 'I believe in discipline, and you know as well as I do that the Rump is infernally out of hand.'

'They are not the only members who fail in discipline.'

Vennard grinned. 'I suppose you mean Cargill and myself. But we are following the central lines of British policy. We are on your side, and we want to make your task easier.'

Cargill suddenly began to laugh. 'I don't want any ostracism. Leave them alone, and Vennard and I will undertake to give them such a time in the House that they will wish they had never been born. We'll make them resign in batches.'

Dinner was announced, and, laughing uproariously, the two rebels went arm-in-arm into the dining-room.

Cargill was in tremendous form. He began to tell Scotch stories, memories of his old Parliament House days. He told them admirably, with a raciness of idiom which I had thought beyond him. They were long tales, and some were as broad as they were long, but Mr Cargill disarmed criticism. His audience, rather scandalised at the start, were soon captured, and political troubles were forgotten in old-fashioned laughter. Even the Prime Minister's anxious face relaxed.

This lasted till the *entrée*, the famous Caerlaverock curry.

As I have said, I was not in the secret, and did not detect the transition. As I partook of the dish, I remember feeling a sudden giddiness and a slight nausea. The antidote, to those who had not taken the drug, must have been, I suppose, in the nature of a mild emetic. A mist seemed to obscure the faces of my fellow-guests, and slowly the tide of conversation ebbed away. First Vennard, then Cargill, became silent. I was feeling rather sick, and I noticed with some satisfaction that all our faces were a little green. I wondered casually if I had been poisoned.

The sensation passed, but the party had changed. More especially I was soon conscious that something had happened to the three Ministers. I noticed Mulross particularly, for he was my neighbour. The look of keenness and vitality had died out of him, and suddenly he seemed a rather old, rather tired man, very weary about the eyes.

I asked him if he felt seedy.

'No, not specially,' he replied, 'but that accident gave me a nasty shock.'

'You should go off for a change,' I said.

'I almost think I will,' was the answer. 'I had not meant to leave town till just before the Twelfth, but I think I had better get away to Marienbad for a fortnight. There is nothing doing in the House, and work at the Office is at a standstill. Yes, I fancy I'll go abroad before the end of the week.'

I caught the Prime Minister's eye and saw that he had forgotten the purpose of the dinner, being dimly conscious that that purpose was now idle. Cargill and Vennard had ceased to talk like rebels. The Home Secretary had subsided into his old suave, phrasing self. The humour had gone out of his eye, and the looseness had returned to his lips. He was an older and more commonplace man, and harmless, quite harmless. Vennard, too, wore a new air, or rather had recaptured his old one. He was saying little, but his voice had lost its crispness and recovered its half-plaintive unction; his shoulders had a droop in them; once more he bristled with self-consciousness.

We others were still shaky from that detestable curry, and were so puzzled as to be acutely uncomfortable. Relief would come later, no doubt; for the present we were uneasy at this weird transformation. I saw the Prime Minister examining the two faces intently, and the result seemed to satisfy him. He sighed and looked at Caerlaverock, who smiled and nodded.

'What about that Bill of yours, Vennard?' he asked. 'There have been a lot of stupid rumours.'

'Bill?' Vennard said. 'I know of no Bill. Now that my departmental work is over, I can give my whole soul to Cargill's Small Holdings. Do you mean that?'

'Yes, of course. There was some confusion in the popular mind, but the old arrangement holds. You and Cargill will put it through between you.'

They began to talk about those weariful small holdings, and I ceased to listen. We left the dining-room and drifted to the library, where a fire tried to dispel the gloom of the weather. There was a feeling of deadly depression abroad, so that, for all its awkwardness, I would really have preferred the former Caerlaverock dinner. The Prime Minister was whispering to his host. I heard him say something about there being 'the devil of a lot of explaining' before him.

Vennard and Cargill came last to the library, arm-in-arm as before.

'I should count it a greater honour,' Vennard was saying, 'to sweeten the lot of one toiler in England than to add a million miles to our territory. While one English household falls below the minimum scale of civic wellbeing, all talk of Empire is sin and folly.'

'Excellent!' said Mr Cargill.

Then I knew for certain that at last peace had descended upon the vexed tents of Israel.

The Grove of Ashtaroth

The first of Buchan's stories to draw on his South African experiences, 'The Grove of Ashtaroth' first appeared in *Blackwood's Magazine* in June 1910 during the magazine serialisation of his South African novel *Prester John* (1910), and was collected in *The Moon Endureth* (1912). It was published by the magazine *Argosy* during the 1930s and later appeared beside stories by R.L. Stevenson, Rudyard Kipling and Joseph Conrad in *Four Long Short Stories* (1960).

Ashtaroth, the Hebrew word for wife, was a fertility-goddess worshipped by all Semitic nations in ancient times and is mentioned in the Bible. Kore Arabin in *The Dancing Floor* (1926) is a further exploration of the type.

C'est enfin que dans leurs prunelles
Rit et pleure – fastidieux –
L'amour des choses éternelles,
Des vieux morts et des anciens dieux!
PAUL VERLAINE

WE WERE SITTING around the camp fire, some thirty miles north of a place called Taqui, when Lawson announced his intention of finding a home. He had spoken little the last day or two, and I had guessed that he had struck a vein of private reflection. I thought it might be a new mine or irrigation scheme, and I was surprised to find that it was a country house.

'I don't think I shall go back to England,' he said, kicking a sputtering log into place. 'I don't see why I should. For business purposes I am far more useful to the firm in South Africa than in Throgmorton Street. I have no relations left except a third cousin, and I have never cared a rush for living in town. That beastly house of mine in Hill Street will fetch what I gave for it, – Isaacson cabled about it the other day, offering for furniture and all. I don't want to go into Parliament, and I hate shooting little birds and tame deer. I am one of those fellows who are born Colonial at heart, and I don't see why I shouldn't arrange my life as I please. Besides, for ten years I have been falling in love with this country, and now I am up to the neck.'

He flung himself back in the camp-chair till the canvas creaked, and looked at me below his eyelids. I remember glancing at the lines of him, and thinking what a fine make of a man he was. In his untanned, field-boots, breeches, and grey shirt he looked the born wilderness-hunter, though less than two months before he had been driving down to the City every morning in the sombre regimentals of his class. Being a fair man, he was gloriously tanned, and there was a clear line at his shirt-collar to mark the limits of his sunburn. I had first known him years ago, when he was a broker's clerk working on half commission. Then he had gone to South Africa, and soon I heard he was a partner in a mining house which was doing wonders with some gold areas in the North. The next step was his return to London as the new millionaire – young, good-looking, wholesome in mind and body, and much sought after by the mothers of marriageable girls. We played polo together, and hunted a little in the season, but there were signs that he did not propose to become the conventional English gentleman. He refused to buy a place in the country, though half the Homes of England were at his disposal. He was a very busy man, he declared, and had not time to be a squire. Besides, every few months he used to rush out to South Africa. I saw that he was restless, for he was always badgering me to go big-game hunting with him in some remote part of the earth. There was that in his eyes, too, which marked him out from the ordinary blonde type of our countrymen. They were large and brown and mysterious, and the light of another race was in their odd depths.

To hint such a thing would have meant a breach of friendship, for Lawson was very proud of his birth. When he first made his fortune he had gone to the Heralds to discover his family, and those obliging gentlemen had provided a pedigree. It appeared that he was a scion of the house of Lowson or Lowieson, an ancient and rather disreputable clan on the Scottish side of the Border. He took a shooting in Teviotdale on the strength of it, and used to commit lengthy Border ballads to memory. But I had known his father, a financial journalist who never quite succeeded, and I had heard of a grandfather who sold antiques in a back street at Brighton. The latter, I think, had not changed his name, and still frequented the synagogue. The father was a progressive Christian, and the mother had been a blonde Saxon from the Midlands. In my mind there was no doubt, as I caught Lawson's heavy-lidded eyes fixed on me. My friend was of a more ancient race than the Lowsons of the Border.

'Where are you thinking of looking for your house?' I asked. 'In Natal or in the Cape Peninsula? You might get the Fishers' place if you paid a price.'

'The Fishers' place be hanged!' he said crossly. 'I don't want any stuccoed overgrown Dutch farm. I might as well be at Roehampton as in the Cape.'

He got up and walked to the far side of the fire, where a lane ran down through thornscrub to a gully of the hills. The moon was silvering the bush of the plains, forty miles off and three thousand feet below us.

'I am going to live somewhere hereabouts,' he answered at last.

I whistled. 'Then you've got to put your hand in your pocket, old man. You'll have to make everything, including a map of the countryside.'

'I know,' he said; 'that's where the fun comes in. Hang it all, why shouldn't I indulge my fancy? I'm uncommonly well off, and I haven't chick or child to leave it to. Supposing I'm a hundred miles from a railhead, what about it? I'll make a motor-road and fix up a telephone. I'll grow most of my supplies, and start a colony to provide labour. When you come and stay with me, you'll get the best food and drink on earth, and sport that will make your mouth water. I'll put Lochleven trout in these streams – at 6000 feet you can do anything. We'll have a pack of hounds, too, and we can drive pig in the woods, and if we want big game there are the Mangwe flats at our feet. I tell you I'll make such a country-house as nobody ever dreamed of. A man will come plumb out of stark savagery into lawns and rose-gardens.' Lawson flung himself into his chair again and smiled dreamily at the fire.

'But why here, of all places?' I persisted. I was not feeling very well and did not care for the country.

'I can't quite explain. I think it's the sort of land I have always been looking for. I always fancied a house on a green plateau in a decent climate looking down on the tropics. I like heat and colour, you know, but I like hills too, and greenery, and the things that bring back Scotland. Give me a cross between Teviotdale and the Orinoco, and, by Gad! I think I've got it here.'

I watched my friend curiously, as with bright eyes and eager voice he talked of his new fad. The two races were very clear in him – the one desiring gorgeousness, the other athirst for the soothing spaces of the North. He began to plan out the house. He would get Adamson to design it, and it was to grow out of the landscape like a stone on the hillside. There would be wide verandahs and cool halls, but great fireplaces against winter time. It would all be very simple and fresh – 'clean as morning' was his odd phrase; but then another idea super-vened, and he talked of bringing the Tintorets from Hill Street. 'I want it to be a civilised house, you know. No silly luxury, but the best pictures and china and books . . . I'll have all the furniture made after the old plain English models out of native woods. I don't want second-hand sticks in a new country. Yes, by Jove, the Tintorets are a great idea, and all those Ming pots I bought. I had meant to sell them, but I'll have them out here.'

He talked for a good hour of what he would do, and his dream grew richer as he talked, till by the time we went to bed he had sketched something liker a palace than a country-house. Lawson was by no means a luxurious man. At present he was well content with a Wolseley valise, and shaved cheerfully out of a tin mug. It struck me as odd that a man so simple in his habits should have so sumptuous a taste in bric-à-brac. I told myself, as I turned in, that the Saxon mother from the Midlands had done little to dilute the strong wine of the East.

It drizzled next morning when we inspanned, and I mounted my horse in a bad temper. I had some fever on me, I think, and I hated this lush yet frigid table-land, where all the winds on earth lay in wait for one's marrow. Lawson was, as usual, in great spirits. We were not hunting, but shifting our hunting-ground, so all morning we travelled fast to the north along the rim of the uplands.

At midday it cleared, and the afternoon was a pageant of pure colour. The wind sank to a low breeze; the sun lit the infinite green spaces, and kindled the wet forest to a jewelled coronal. Lawson gaspingly admired it all, as he cantered bareheaded up a bracken-clad slope. 'God's country,' he said twenty times. 'I've found it.' Take a piece of Saxon downland; put a stream in every hollow and a patch of wood; and at the edge, where the cliffs at home would fall to the sea, put a cloak of forest muffling the scarp and dropping thousands of feet to the blue plains. Take the diamond air of the Görnergrat, and the riot of colour which you get by a West Highland lochside in late September. Put flowers everywhere, the things we grow in hothouses, geraniums like sun-shades and arums like trumpets. That will give you a notion of the countryside we were in. I began to see that after all it was out of the common.

And just before sunset we came over a ridge and found something better. It was a shallow glen, half a mile wide, down which ran a blue-grey stream in linns like the Spean, till at the edge of the plateau it leaped into the dim forest in a snowy cascade. The opposite side ran up in gentle slopes to a rocky knoll, from which the eye had a noble prospect of the plains. All down the glen were little copses, half moons of green edging some silvery shore of the burn, or delicate clusters of tall trees nodding on the hill brow. The place so satisfied the eye that for the sheer wonder of its perfection we stopped and stared in silence for many minutes.

Then 'The House,' I said, and Lawson replied softly, 'The House!'

We rode slowly into the glen in the mulberry gloaming. Our transport waggons were half an hour behind, so we had time to explore. Lawson dismounted and plucked handfuls of flowers from the water-meadows. He was singing to himself all the time – an old French catch about *Cadet Rousselle* and his *trois maisons*.

'Who owns it?' I asked.

'My firm, as like as not. We have miles of land about here. But whoever the man is, he has got to sell. Here I build my tabernacle, old man. Here, and nowhere else!'

In the very centre of the glen, in a loop of the stream, was one copse which even in that half light struck me as different from the others. It was of tall, slim, fairy-like trees, the kind of wood the monks painted in old missals. No, I rejected the thought. It was no Christian wood. It was not a copse, but a 'grove', – one such as Diana may have flitted through in the moonlight. It was small, forty or fifty yards in diameter, and there was a dark something at the heart of it which for a second I thought was a house.

We turned between the slender trees, and – was it fancy? – an odd tremor went through me. I felt as if I were penetrating the *temenos* of some strange and lovely divinity, the goddess of this pleasant vale. There was a spell in the air, it seemed, and an odd dead silence.

Suddenly my horse started at a flutter of light wings. A flock of doves rose from the branches, and I saw the burnished green of their plumes against the opal sky. Lawson did not seem to notice them. I saw his keen eyes staring at the centre of the grove and what stood there.

It was a little conical tower, ancient and lichened, but, so far as I could judge, quite flawless. You know the famous, Conical Temple at Zimbabwe, of which prints are in every guide-book. This was of the same type, but a thousand-fold more perfect. It stood about thirty feet high, of solid masonry, without door or window or cranny, as shapely as when it first came from the hands of the old builders. Again I had the sense of breaking in on a sanctuary. What right had I, a common vulgar modern, to be looking at this fair thing, among these delicate trees, which some white goddess had once taken for her shrine?

Lawson broke in on my absorption. 'Let's get out of this,' he said hoarsely, and he took my horse's bridle (he had left his own beast at the edge) and led him back to the open. But I noticed that his eyes were always turning back, and that his hand trembled.

'That settles it,' I said after supper. 'What do you want with your mediaeval Venetians and your Chinese pots now? You will have the finest antique in the world in your garden – a temple as old as time, and in a land which they say has no history. You had the right inspiration this time.'

I think I have said that Lawson had hungry eyes. In his enthusiasm they used to glow and brighten; but now, as he sat looking down at the olive shades of the glen, they seemed ravenous in their fire. He had hardly spoken a word since we left the wood.

'Where can I read about those things?' he asked, and I gave him the names of books.

Then, an hour later, he asked me who were the builders. I told him the little I knew about Phoenician and Sabaean wanderings, and the ritual of Sidon and Tyre. He repeated some names to himself and went soon to bed.

As I turned in, I had one last look over the glen, which lay ivory and black in the moon. I seemed to hear a faint echo of wings, and to see over the little grove a cloud of light visitants. 'The Doves of Ashtaroth have come back,' I said to myself. 'It is a good omen. They accept the new tenant.' But as I fell asleep I had a sudden thought that I was saying something rather terrible.

Three years later, pretty nearly to a day, I came back to see what Lawson had made of his hobby. He had bidden me often to Welge-vonden, as he chose to call it – though I do not know why he should have fixed a Dutch name to a countryside where Boer never trod. At the last there had been some confusion about dates, and I wired the time of my arrival, and set off without an answer. A motor met me at the queer little wayside station of Taqui, and after many miles on a doubtful highway I came to the gates of the park, and a road on which it was a delight to move. Three years had wrought little difference in the landscape. Lawson had done some planting, – conifers and flowering shrubs and such-like – but wisely he had resolved that Nature had for the most part forestalled him. All the same, he must have spent a mint of money. The drive could not have been beaten in England, and fringes of mown turf on either hand had been pared out of the lush meadows. When we came over the edge of the hill and looked down on the secret glen, I could not repress a cry of pleasure. The house stood on the farther ridge, the view-point of the whole neighbourhood; and its brown timbers and white rough-cast walls melted into the hillside as if it had been there from the beginning of things. The vale below was ordered in lawns and gardens. A blue lake received the rapids of the stream, and its banks were a maze of green shades and glorious masses of blossom. I noticed, too, that the little grove we had explored on our first visit stood alone in a big stretch of lawn, so that its perfection might be clearly seen. Lawson had excellent taste, or he had had the best advice.

The butler told me that his master was expected home shortly, and took me into the library for tea. Lawson had left his Tintorets and Ming pots at home after all. It was a long, low room, panelled in teak half-way up the walls, and the shelves held a multitude of fine bindings. There were good rugs on the parquet floor, but no orna-ments anywhere, save three. On the carved mantelpiece stood two of the old soapstone birds which they used to find at Zimbabwe, and between, on an ebony stand, a half moon of alabaster, curiously carved with zodiacal figures. My host had altered his scheme of furnishing, but I approved the change.

He came in about half-past six, after I had consumed two cigars and all but fallen asleep. Three years make a difference in most men, but I was not prepared for the change in Lawson. For one thing, he had grown fat. In place of the lean young man I had known, I saw a heavy, flaccid being, who shuffled in his gait, and seemed tired and listless. His sunburn had gone, and his face was as pasty as a city clerk's. He had been walking, and wore shapeless flannel clothes, which hung loose even on his enlarged figure. And the worst of it was, that he did not seem over-pleased to see me. He murmured something about my journey, and then flung himself into an arm-chair and looked out of the window.

I asked him if he had been ill.

'Ill! No!' he said crossly. 'Nothing of the kind. I'm perfectly well.'

'You don't look as fit as this place should make you. What do you do with yourself? Is the shooting as good as you hoped?'

He did not answer, but I thought I heard him mutter something like 'shooting be damned.'

Then I tried the subject of the house. I praised it extravagantly, but with conviction. 'There can be no place like it in the world,' I said.

He turned his eyes on me at last, and I saw that they were as deep and restless as ever. With his pallid face they made him look curiously Semitic. I had been right in my theory about his ancestry.

'Yes,' he said slowly, 'there is no place like it – in the world.'

Then he pulled himself to his feet. 'I'm going to change,' he said. 'Dinner is at eight. Ring for Travers, and he'll show you your room.'

I dressed in a noble bedroom, with an outlook over the garden-vale and the escarpment to the far line of the plains, now blue and saffron in the sunset. I dressed in an ill temper, for I was seriously offended with Lawson, and also seriously alarmed. He was either very unwell or going out of his mind, and it was clear, too, that he would resent any anxiety on his account. I ransacked my memory for rumours, but found none. I had heard nothing of him except that he had been extraordinarily successful in his speculations, and that from his hill-top he directed his firm's operations with uncommon skill. If Lawson was sick or mad, nobody knew of it.

Dinner was a trying ceremony. Lawson, who used to be rather particular in his dress, appeared in a kind of smoking suit with a flannel collar. He spoke scarcely a word to me, but cursed the servants with a brutality which left me aghast. A wretched footman in his nervousness spilt some sauce over his sleeve. Lawson dashed the dish from his hand, and volleyed abuse with a sort of epileptic fury. Also he, who had been the most abstemious of men, swallowed disgusting quantities of champagne and old brandy.

He had given up smoking, and half an hour after we left the dining-room he announced his intention of going to bed. I watched him as he waddled upstairs with a feeling of angry bewilderment. Then I went to the library and lit a pipe. I would leave first thing in the morning – on that I was determined. But as I sat gazing at the moon of alabaster and the soapstone birds my anger evaporated, and concern took its place. I remembered what a fine fellow Lawson had been, what good times we had had together. I remembered especially that evening when we had found this valley and given rein to our fancies. What horrid alchemy in the place had turned a gentleman into a brute? I thought of drink and drugs and madness and insomnia, but I could fit none of them into my conception of my friend. I did not consciously rescind my resolve to depart, but I had a notion that I would not act on it.

The sleepy butler met me as I went to bed. 'Mr Lawson's room is at the end of your corridor, sir,' he said. 'He don't sleep over well, so you may hear him stirring in the night. At what hour would you like breakfast, sir? Mr Lawson mostly has his in bed.'

My room opened from the great corridor, which ran the full length of the front of the house. So far as I could make out, Lawson was three rooms off, a vacant bedroom and his servant's room being between us. I felt tired and cross, and tumbled into bed as fast as possible. Usually I sleep well, but now I was soon conscious that my drowsiness was wearing off and that I was in for a restless night. I got up and laved my face, turned the pillows, thought of sheep coming over a hill and clouds crossing the sky; but none of the old devices were any use. After about an hour of make-believe I surrendered myself to facts, and, lying on my back, stared at the white ceiling and the patches of moonshine on the walls.

It certainly was an amazing night. I got up, put on a dressing-gown, and drew a chair to the window. The moon was almost at its full, and the whole plateau swam in a radiance of ivory and silver. The banks of the stream were black, but the lake had a great belt of light athwart it, which made it seem like a horizon, and the rim of land beyond it like a contorted cloud. Far to the right I saw the delicate outlines of the little wood which I had come to think of as the Grove of

Ashtaroth. I listened. There was not a sound in the air. The land seemed to sleep peacefully beneath the moon, and yet I had a sense that the peace was an illusion. The place was feverishly restless.

I could have given no reason for my impression, but there it was. Something was stirring in the wide moonlit landscape under its deep mask of silence. I felt as I had felt on the evening three years ago when I had ridden into the grove. I did not think that the influence, whatever it was, was maleficent. I only knew that it was very strange, and kept me wakeful.

By-and-by I bethought me of a book. There was no lamp in the corridor save the moon, but the whole house was bright as I slipped down the great staircase and over the hall to the library. I switched on the lights and then switched them off. They seemed a profanation, and I did not need them.

I found a French novel, but the place held me and I stayed. I sat down in an arm-chair before the fireplace and the stone birds. Very odd those gawky things, like prehistoric Great Auks, looked in the moonlight. I remember that the alabaster moon shimmered like translucent pearl, and I fell to wondering about its history. Had the old Sabaeans used such a jewel in their rites in the Grove of Ashtaroth?

Then I heard footsteps pass the window. A great house like this would have a watchman, but these quick shuffling footsteps were surely not the dull plod of a servant. They passed on to the grass and died away. I began to think of getting back to my room.

In the corridor I noticed that Lawson's door was ajar, and that a light had been left burning. I had the unpardonable curiosity to peep in. The room was empty, and the bed had not been slept in. Now I knew whose were the footsteps outside the library window.

I lit a reading-lamp and tried to interest myself in *La Cruelle Enigme*. But my wits were restless, and I could not keep my eyes on the page. I flung the book aside and sat down again by the window. The feeling came over me that I was sitting in a box at some play. The glen was a huge stage, and at any moment the players might appear on it. My attention was strung as high as if I had been waiting for the advent of some world-famous actress. But nothing came. Only the shadows shifted and lengthened as the moon moved across the sky.

Then quite suddenly the restlessness left me, and at the same moment the silence was broken by the crow of a cock and the rustling of trees in a light wind. I felt very sleepy, and was turning to bed when again I heard footsteps without. From the window I could see a figure moving across the garden towards the house. It was Lawson, got up in the sort of towel dressing-gown that one wears on board ship. He was walking slowly and painfully, as if very weary. I did not see his face, but the man's whole air was that of extreme fatigue and dejection.

I tumbled into bed and slept profoundly till long after daylight.

The man who valeted me was Lawson's own servant. As he was laying out my clothes I asked after the health of his master, and was told that he had slept ill and would not rise till late. Then the man, an anxious-faced Englishman, gave me some information on his own account. Mr Lawson was having one of his bad turns. It would pass away in a day or two, but till it had gone he was fit for nothing. He advised me to see Mr Jobson, the factor, who would look to my entertainment in his master's absence.

Jobson arrived before luncheon, and the sight of him was the first satisfactory thing about Welgevonden. He was a big, gruff Scot from Roxburghshire, engaged, no doubt, by Lawson as a duty to his Border ancestry. He had short grizzled whiskers, a weatherworn face, and a shrewd, calm blue eye. I knew now why the place was in such perfect order.

We began with sport, and Jobson explained what I could have in the way of fishing and shooting. His exposition was brief and business-like, and all the while I could see his eye searching me. It was clear that he had much to say on other matters than sport.

I told him that I had come here with Lawson three years before, when he chose the site. Jobson continued to regard me curiously. 'I've heard tell of ye from Mr Lawson. Ye're an old friend of his, I understand.'

'The oldest,' I said. 'And I am sorry to find that the place does not agree with him. Why it doesn't I cannot imagine, for you look fit enough. Has he been seedy for long?'

'It comes and goes,' said Mr Jobson. 'Maybe once a month he has a bad turn. But on the whole it agrees with him badly. He's no' the man he was when I first came here.'

Jobson was looking at me very seriously and frankly. I risked a question.

'What do you suppose is the matter?'

He did not reply at once, but leaned forward and tapped my knee.

'I think it's something that doctors canna cure. Look at me, sir. I've always been counted a sensible man, but if I told you what was in my head you would think me daft. But I have one word for you. Bide till to-night is past and then speir your question. Maybe you and me will be agreed.'

The factor rose to go. As he left the room he flung me back a remark over his shoulder – 'Read the eleventh chapter of the First Book of Kings.'

After luncheon I went for a walk. First I mounted to the crown of the hill and feasted my eyes on the unequalled loveliness of the view. I saw the far hills in Portuguese territory, a hundred miles away, lifting up thin blue fingers into the sky. The wind blew light and fresh, and the place was fragrant with a thousand delicate scents. Then I descended to the vale, and followed the stream up through the garden. Poinsettias and oleanders were blazing in coverts, and there was a paradise of tinted water-lilies in the slacker reaches. I saw good trout rise at the fly, but I did not think about fishing. I was searching my memory for a recollection which would not come. By-and-by I found myself beyond the garden, where the lawns ran to the fringe of Ashtaroth's Grove.

It was like something I remembered in an old Italian picture. Only, as my memory drew it, it should have been peopled with strange figures – nymphs dancing on the sward, and a prick-eared faun peeping from the covert. In the warm afternoon sunlight it stood, ineffably gracious and beautiful, tantalising with a sense of some deep hidden loveliness. Very reverently I walked between the slim trees, to where the little conical tower stood half in sun and half in shadow. Then I noticed something new. Round the tower ran a narrow path, worn in the grass by human feet. There had been no such path on my first visit, for I remembered the grass growing tall to the edge of the stone. Had the Kaffirs made a shrine of it, or were there other and stranger votaries?

When I returned to the house I found Travers with a message for me. Mr Lawson was still in bed, but he would like me to go to him. I found my friend sitting up and drinking strong tea – a bad thing, I should have thought, for a man in his condition. I remember that I looked over the room for some sign of the pernicious habit of which I believed him a victim. But the place was fresh and clean, with the windows wide open, and, though I could not have given my reasons,

I was convinced that drugs or drink had nothing to do with the sickness.

He received me more civilly, but I was shocked by his looks. There were great bags below his eyes, and his skin had the wrinkled puffy appearance of a man in dropsy. His voice, too, was reedy and thin. Only his great eyes burned with some feverish life.

'I am a shocking bad host,' he said, 'but I'm going to be still more inhospitable. I want you to go away. I hate anybody here when I'm off colour.'

'Nonsense,' I said; 'you want looking after. I want to know about this sickness. Have you had a doctor?'

He smiled wearily. 'Doctors are no earthly use to me. There's nothing much the matter, I tell you. I'll be all right in a day or two, and then you can come back. I want you to go off with Jobson and hunt in the plains till the end of the week. It will be better fun for you, and I'll feel less guilty.'

Of course I pooh-poohed the idea, and Lawson got angry. 'Damn it, man,' he cried, 'why do you force yourself on me when I don't want you? I tell you your presence here makes me worse. In a week I'll be as right as the mail, and then I'll be thankful for you. But get away now; get away, I tell you.'

I saw that he was fretting himself into a passion. 'All right,' I said soothingly; 'Jobson and I will go off hunting. But I am horribly anxious about you, old man.'

He lay back on his pillows. 'You needn't trouble. I only want a little rest. Jobson will make all arrangements, and Travers will get you anything you want. Good-bye.'

I saw it was useless to stay longer, so I left the room. Outside I found the anxious-faced servant. 'Look here,' I said, 'Mr Lawson thinks I ought to go, but I mean to stay. Tell him I'm gone if he asks you. And for Heaven's sake keep him in bed.'

The man promised, and I thought I saw some relief in his face.

I went to the library, and on the way remembered Jobson's remark about 1st Kings. With some searching I found a Bible and turned up the passage. It was a long screed about the misdeeds of Solomon, and I read it through without enlightenment. I began to re-read it, and a word suddenly caught my attention—

For Solomon went after Ashtaroth, the goddess of the Zidonians.

That was all, but it was like a key to a cipher. Instantly there flashed over my mind all that I had heard or read of that strange ritual which seduced Israel to sin. I saw a sunburnt land and a people vowed to the stern service of Jehovah. But I saw, too, eyes turning from the austere sacrifice to lonely hill-top groves and towers and images, where dwelt some subtle and evil mystery. I saw the fierce prophets, scourging the votaries with rods, and a nation penitent before the Lord; but always the backsliding again, and the hankering after forbidden joys. Ashtaroth was the old goddess of the East. Was it not possible that in all Semitic blood there remained, transmitted through the dim generations, some craving for her spell? I thought of the grandfather in the back street at Brighton and of those burning eyes upstairs.

As I sat and mused my glance fell on the inscrutable stone birds. They knew all those old secrets of joy and terror. And that moon of alabaster! Some dark priest had worn it on his forehead when he worshipped, like Ahab, 'all the host of Heaven'. And then I honestly began to be afraid. I a prosaic, modern Christian gentleman, a half-believer in casual faiths, was in the presence of some hoary mystery of sin far older than creeds or Christendom. There was fear in my heart, – a kind of uneasy disgust, and above all a nervous eerie disquiet. Now I wanted to go away, and yet I was ashamed of the cowardly thought. I pictured Ashtaroth's Grove with sheer horror. What tragedy was in the air? what secret awaited twilight? For the night was coming, the night of the Full Moon, the season of ecstasy and sacrifice.

I do not know how I got through that evening. I was disinclined for dinner, so I had a cutlet in the library and sat smoking till my tongue ached. But as the hours passed a more manly resolution grew up in my mind. I owed it to old friendship to stand by Lawson in this extremity. I could not interfere, – God knows, his reason seemed already rocking, – but I could be at hand in case my chance came. I determined not to undress, but to watch through the night. I had a bath, and changed into light flannels and slippers. Then I took up my position in a corner of the library close to the window, so that I could not fail to hear Lawson's footsteps if he passed.

Fortunately I left the lights unlit, for as I waited I grew drowsy, and fell asleep. When I woke the moon had risen, and I knew from the feel of the air that the hour was late. I sat very still, straining my ears, and as I listened I caught the sound of steps. They were crossing the hall stealthily, and nearing the library door. I huddled into my corner as Lawson entered.

He wore the same towel dressing-gown, and he moved swiftly and silently as if in a trance. I watched him take the alabaster moon from the mantelpiece and drop it in his pocket. A glimpse of white skin showed that the gown was his only clothing. Then he moved past me to the window, opened it, and went out.

Without any conscious purpose I rose and followed, kicking off my slippers that I might go quietly. He was running, running fast, across the lawns in the direction of the grove – an odd shapeless antic in the moonlight. I stopped, for there was no cover, and I feared for his reason if he saw me. When I looked again he had disappeared among the trees.

I saw nothing for it but to crawl, so on my belly I wormed my way over the dripping sward. There was a ridiculous suggestion of deer-stalking about the game which tickled me and dispelled my uneasiness. Almost I persuaded myself I was tracking an ordinary sleep-walker. The lawns were broader than I imagined, and it seemed an age before I reached the edge of the grove. The world was so still that I appeared to be making a most ghastly amount of noise. I remember that once I heard a rustling in the air, and looked up to see the green doves circling about the treetops.

There was no sign of Lawson. On the edge of the grove I think that all my assurance vanished. I could see between the trunks to the little tower, but it was quiet as the grave, save for the wings above. Once more there came over me the unbearable sense of anticipation I had felt the night before. My nerves tingled with mingled expectation and dread. I did not think that any harm would come to me, for the powers of the air seemed not malignant. But I knew them for powers, and felt awed and abased. I was in the presence of the 'host of Heaven', and I was no stern Israelitish prophet to prevail against them.

I must have lain for hours waiting in that spectral place, my eyes riveted on the tower and its golden cap of moonshine. I remember that my head felt void and light, as if my spirit were becoming disembodied and leaving its dew-drenched sheath far below. But the most curious sensation was of something drawing me to the tower, something mild and kindly and rather feeble, for there was some other and stronger force keeping me back. I yearned to move nearer, but I could not drag my limbs an inch. There was a spell somewhere which

I could not break. I do not think I was in any way frightened now. The starry influence was playing tricks with me, but my mind was half asleep. Only I never took my eyes from the little tower. I think I could not, if I had wanted to.

Then suddenly from the shadows came Lawson. He was stark-naked, and he wore, bound across his brow, the half moon of alabaster. He had something, too, in his hand – something which glittered.

He ran round the tower, crooning to himself, and flinging wild arms to the skies. Sometimes the crooning changed to a shrill cry of passion, such as a maenad may have uttered in the train of Bacchus. I could make out no words, but the sound told its own tale. He was absorbed in some infernal ecstasy. And as he ran, he drew his right hand across his breast and arms, and I saw that it held a knife.

I grew sick with disgust – not terror, but honest physical loathing. Lawson, gashing his fat body, affected me with an overpowering repugnance. I wanted to go forward and stop him, and I wanted, too, to be a hundred miles away. And the result was that I stayed still. I believe my own will held me there, but I doubt if in any case I could have moved my legs.

The dance grew swifter and fiercer. I saw the blood dripping from Lawson's body, and his face ghastly white above his scarred breast. And then suddenly the horror left me; my head swam; and for one second – one brief second – I seemed to peer into a new world. A strange passion surged up in my heart. I seemed to see the earth peopled with forms – not human, scarcely divine, but more desirable than man or god. The calm face of Nature broke up for me into wrinkles of wild knowledge. I saw the things which brush against the soul in dreams, and found them lovely. There seemed no cruelty in the knife or the blood. It was a delicate mystery of worship, as wholesome as the morning song of birds. I do not know how the Semites found Ashtaroth's ritual; to them it may well have been more rapt and passionate than it seemed to me. For I saw in it only the sweet simplicity of Nature, and all riddles of lust and terror soothed away as a child's nightmares are calmed by a mother. I found my legs able to move, and I think I took two steps through the dusk towards the tower.

And then it all ended. A cock crew, and the homely noises of earth were renewed. While I stood dazed and shivering, Lawson plunged through the Grove towards me. The impetus carried him to the edge, and he fell fainting just outside the shade.

My wits and common-sense came back to me with my bodily strength. I got my friend on my back, and staggered with him towards the house. I was afraid in real earnest now, and what frightened me most was the thought that I had not been afraid sooner. I had come very near the 'abomination of the Zidonians'.

At the door I found the scared valet waiting. He had apparently done this sort of thing before.

'Your master has been sleep-walking, and has had a fall,' I said. 'We must get him to bed at once.'

We bathed the wounds as he lay in a deep stupor, and I dressed them as well as I could. The only danger lay in his utter exhaustion, for happily the gashes were not serious, and no artery had been touched. Sleep and rest would make him well, for he had the constitution of a strong man. I was leaving the room when he opened his eyes and spoke. He did not recognise me, but I noticed that his face had lost its strangeness, and was once more that of the friend I had known. Then I suddenly bethought me of an old hunting remedy which he and I always carried on our expeditions. It is a pill made up from an ancient Portuguese prescription. One is an excellent specific for fever. Two are invaluable if you are lost in the bush, for they send a man for many hours into a deep sleep, which prevents suffering and madness, till help comes. Three give a painless death. I went to my room and found the little box in my jewel-case. Lawson swallowed two, and turned wearily on his side. I bade his man let him sleep till he woke, and went off in search of food.

I had business on hand which would not wait. By seven, Jobson, who had been sent for, was waiting for me in the library. I knew by his grim face that here I had a very good substitute for a prophet of the Lord.

'You were right,' I said. 'I have read the 11th chapter of 1st Kings, and I have spent such a night as I pray God I shall never spend again.'

'I thought you would,' he replied. 'I've had the same experience myself.'

'The Grove?' I said.

'Ay, the wud,' was the answer in broad Scots.

I wanted to see how much he understood.

'Mr Lawson's family is from the Scotch Border?'

'Ay. I understand they come off Borthwick Water side,' he replied, but I saw by his eyes that he knew what I meant.

'Mr Lawson is my oldest friend,' I went on, 'and I am going to take measures to cure him. For what I am going to do I take the sole responsibility. I will make that plain to your master. But if I am to succeed I want your help. Will you give it to me? It sounds like madness, and you are a sensible man and may like to keep out of it. I leave it to your discretion.'

Jobson looked me straight in the face. 'Have no fear for me,' he said; 'there is an unholy thing in that place, and if I have the strength in me I will destroy it. He has been a good master to me, and forbye, I am a believing Christian. So say on, sir.'

There was no mistaking the air. I had found my Tishbite.

'I want men,' I said, – 'as many as we can get.'

Jobson mused. 'The Kaffirs will no' gang near the place, but there's some thirty white men on the tobacco farm. They'll do your will, if you give them an indemnity in writing.'

'Good,' said I. 'Then we will take our instructions from the only authority which meets the case. We will follow the example of King Josiah.' I turned up the 23rd Chapter of 2nd Kings, and read;

> And the high places that were before Jerusalem, which were on the right hand of the Mount of Corruption, which Solomon the king of Israel had builded for Ashtaroth the abomination of the Zidonians ... did the king defile.
>
> And he brake in pieces the images, and cut down the groves, and filled their places with the bones of men.
>
> Moreover the altar that was at Beth-el, and the high place which Jeroboam the son of Nebat, who made Israel to sin, had made, both that altar and the high place he brake down, and burned the high place, and stamped it small to powder, and burned the grove.

Jobson nodded. 'It'll need dinnymite. But I've plenty of yon down at the workshops. I'll be off to collect the lads.'

Before nine the men had assembled at Jobson's house. They were a hardy lot of young farmers from home, who took their instructions docilely from the masterful factor. On my orders they had brought their shot-guns. We armed them with spades and woodmen's axes, and one man wheeled some coils of rope in a hand-cart.

In the clear, windless air of morning the Grove, set amid its lawns, looked too innocent and exquisite for ill. I had a pang of regret that a thing so fair should suffer; nay, if I had come alone, I think I might have repented. But the men were there, and the grim-faced Jobson was waiting for orders. I placed the guns, and sent beaters to the far side. I told them that every dove must be shot.

It was only a small flock, and we killed fifteen at the first drive. The poor birds flew over the glen to another spinney, but we brought them back over the guns and seven fell. Four more were got in the trees, and the last I killed myself with a long shot. In half an hour there was a pile of little green bodies on the sward.

Then we went to work to cut down the trees. The slim stems were an easy task to a good woodman, and one after another they toppled to the ground. And meantime, as I watched, I became conscious of a strange emotion.

It was as if someone were pleading with me. A gentle voice, not threatening, but pleading – something too fine for the sensual ear, but touching inner chords of the spirit. So tenuous it was and distant that I could think of no personality behind it. Rather it was the viewless, bodiless grace of this delectable vale, some old exquisite divinity of the groves. There was the heart of all sorrow in it, and the soul of all loveliness. It seemed a woman's voice, some lost lady who had brought nothing but goodness unrepaid to the world. And what the voice told me was that I was destroying her last shelter.

That was the pathos of it – the voice was homeless. As the axes flashed in the sunlight and the wood grew thin, that gentle spirit was pleading with me for mercy and a brief respite. It seemed to be telling of a world for centuries grown coarse and pitiless, of long sad wanderings, of hardly won shelter, and a peace which was the little all she sought from men. There was nothing terrible in it, no thought of wrongdoing. The spell which to Semitic blood held the mystery of evil, was to me, of the Northern race, only delicate and rare and beautiful. Jobson and the rest did not feel it, I with my finer senses caught nothing but the hopeless sadness of it. That which had stirred the passion in Lawson was only wringing my heart. It was almost too pitiful to bear. As the trees crashed down and the men wiped the sweat from their brows, I seemed to myself like the murderer of fair women and innocent children. I remember that the tears were running over my cheeks. More than once I opened my mouth to countermand the work, but the face of Jobson, that grim Tishbite, held me back. I knew now what gave the Prophets of the Lord their mastery, and I knew also why the people sometimes stoned them.

The last tree fell, and the little tower stood like a ravished shrine, stripped of all defence against the world. I heard Jobson's voice speaking. 'We'd better blast that stane thing now. We'll trench on four sides and lay the dinnymite. Ye're no' looking weel, sir. Ye'd better go and sit down on the brae-face.'

I went up the hillside and lay down. Below me, in the waste of shorn trunks, men were running about, and I saw the mining begin. It all seemed like an aimless dream in which I had no part. The voice of that homeless goddess was still pleading. It was the innocence of it that tortured me. Even so must a merciful Inquisitor have suffered from the plea of some fair girl with the aureole of death on her hair. I knew I was killing rare and unrecoverable beauty. As I sat dazed and heartsick, the whole loveliness of Nature seemed to plead for its divinity. The sun in the heavens, the mellow lines of upland, the blue mystery of the far plains, were all part of that soft voice. I felt bitter scorn for myself. I was guilty of blood; nay, I was guilty of the sin against light which knows no forgiveness. I was murdering innocent gentleness, and there would be no peace on earth for me. Yet I sat helpless. The power of a sterner will constrained me. And all the while the voice was growing fainter and dying away into unutterable sorrow.

Suddenly a great flame sprang to heaven, and a pall of smoke. I heard men crying out, and fragments of stone fell around the ruins of the grove. When the air cleared, the little tower had gone out of sight.

The voice had ceased and there seemed to me to be a bereaved silence in the world. The shock moved me to my feet, and I ran down the slope to where Jobson stood rubbing his eyes.

'That's done the job. Now we maun get up the tree-roots. We've no time to howk. We'll just dinnymite the feck o' them.'

The work of destruction went on, but I was coming back to my senses. I forced myself to be practical and reasonable. I thought of the night's experience and Lawson's haggard eyes, and I screwed myself into a determination to see the thing through. I had done the deed; it was my business to make it complete. A text in Jeremiah came into my head: *'Their children remember their altars and their groves by the green trees upon the high hills.'* I would see to it that this grove should be utterly forgotten.

We blasted the tree roots, and, yoking oxen, dragged the *débris* into a great heap. Then the men set to work with their spades, and roughly levelled the ground. I was getting back to my old self, and Jobson's spirit was becoming mine.

'There is one thing more,' I told him. 'Get ready a couple of ploughs. We will improve upon King Josiah.' My brain was a medley of Scripture precedents, and I was determined that no safeguard should be wanting.

We yoked the oxen again and drove the ploughs over the site of the grove. It was rough ploughing, for the place was thick with bits of stone from the tower, but the slow Afrikander oxen plodded on, and sometime in the afternoon the work was finished. Then I sent down to the farm for bags of rock-salt, such as they use for cattle. Jobson and I took a sack apiece, and walked up and down the furrows, sowing them with salt.

The last act was to set fire to the pile of tree-trunks. They burned well, and on the top we flung the bodies of the green doves. The birds of Ashtaroth had an honourable pyre.

Then I dismissed the much-perplexed men, and gravely shook hands with Jobson. Black with dust and smoke I went back to the house, where I bade Travers pack my bags and order the motor. I found Lawson's servant, and heard from him that his master was sleeping peacefully. I gave some directions, and then went to wash and change.

Before I left I wrote a line to Lawson. I began by transcribing the verses from the 23rd Chapter of 2nd Kings. I told him what I had done, and my reason. 'I take the whole responsibility upon myself,' I wrote. 'No man in the place had anything to do with it but me. I acted as I did for the sake of our old friendship, and you will believe it was no easy task for me. I hope you will understand. Whenever you are able to see me send me word, and I will come back and settle with you. But I think you will realise that I have saved your soul.'

The afternoon was merging into twilight as I left the house on the road to Taqui. The great fire, where the grove had been, was still blazing fiercely, and the smoke made a cloud over the upper glen, and filled all the air with a soft violet haze. I knew that I had done well for my friend, and that he would come to his senses and be grateful. My mind was at ease on that score, and in something like comfort I faced the future. But as the car reached the ridge I looked back to the vale I

[165]

had outraged. The moon was rising and silvering the smoke, and through the gaps I could see the tongues of fire. Somehow, I know not why, the lake, the stream, the garden-coverts, even the green slopes of hill, wore an air of loneliness and desecration.

And then my heartache returned, and I knew that I had driven something lovely and adorable from its last refuge on earth.

The Lemnian

Written in 1910, 'The Lemnian' is another story simultan-
eously published in *Blackwood's Magazine* and *The Atlantic
Monthly* – in January 1911 – and then included in *The Moon
Endureth* (1912). Together with Buchan's poem 'Atta's Song'
it appeared in *Rosemary* (1916), a collection of prose and
poetry from, among others, G.K. Chesterton, Walter de la
Mare, John Galsworthy, Sir Arthur Conan Doyle, Compton
Mackenzie and Arnold Bennett, published during the First
World War to raise money for the 'Not Forgotten Associ-
ation', a charity which provided support to the war wounded.

Part of the inspiration may have come from Gilbert
Murray's 1907 lectures about the *Iliad* in which he described
an outcast tribe which answered to babyish names like 'Atta'
and 'Babba'. The Carians were a simple people who lived in
south-west Asia Minor, the Pelasgians early inhabitants of
Greece, the Far-Darter was Apollo's name in the *Iliad* and
'klepht' was a common word for brigand.

HE PUSHED THE matted locks from his brow as he peered into the mist.
His hair was thick with salt, and his eyes smarted from the green-
wood fire on the poop. The four slaves who crouched beside the
thwarts – Carians with thin birdlike faces – were in a pitiable case,
their hands blue with oar-weals and the lash marks on their shoulders
beginning to gape from sun and sea. The Lemnian himself bore marks
of ill-usage. His cloak was still sopping, his eyes heavy with watching,
and his lips black and cracked with thirst. Two days before the storm
had caught him and swept his little craft into mid-Aegean. He was a
sailor, come of sailor stock, and he had fought the gale manfully and
well. But the sea had burst his water-jars, and the torments of drought
had been added to his toil. He had been driven south almost to Scyros,
but had found no harbour. Then a weary day with the oars had

brought him close to the Eubœan shore, when a freshet of storm drove him seaward again. Now at last in this northerly creek of Sciathos he had found shelter and a spring. But it was a perilous place, for there were robbers in the bushy hills – mainland men who loved above all things to rob an islander; and out at sea, as he looked towards Pelion, there seemed something adoing which boded little good. There was deep water beneath a ledge of cliff, half covered by a tangle of wildwood. So Atta lay in the bows, looking through the trails of vine at the racing tides now reddening in the dawn.

The storm had hit others besides him, it seemed. The channel was full of ships, aimless ships that tossed between tide and wind. Looking closer, he saw that they were all wreckage. There had been tremendous doings in the north, and a navy of some sort had come to grief. Atta was a prudent man, and knew that a broken fleet might be dangerous. There might be men lurking in the maimed galleys who would make short work of the owner of a battered but navigable craft. At first he thought that the ships were those of the Hellenes. The troublesome fellows were everywhere in the islands, stirring up strife and robbing the old lords. But the tides running strongly from the east were bringing some of the wreckage in an eddy into the bay. He lay closer and watched the spars and splintered poops as they neared him. These were no galleys of the Hellenes. Then came a drowned man, swollen and horrible: then another – swarthy, hook-nosed fellows, all yellow with the sea. Atta was puzzled. They must be the men from the East about whom he had been hearing. Long ere he left Lemnos there had been news about the Persians. They were coming like locusts out of the dawn, swarming over Ionia and Thrace, men and ships numerous beyond telling. They meant no ill to honest islanders: a little earth and water were enough to win their friendship. But they meant death to the ὕβρις of the Hellenes. Atta was on the side of the invaders; he wished them well in their war with his ancient foes. They would eat them up, Athenians, Lacedæmonians, Corinthians, Æginetans, men of Argos and Elis, and none would be left to trouble him. But in the meantime something had gone wrong. Clearly there had been no battle. As the bodies butted against the side of the galley he hooked up one or two and found no trace of a wound. Poseidon had grown cranky, and had claimed victims. The god would be appeased by this time, and all would go well.

Danger being past, he bade the men get ashore and fill the water-skins. 'God's curse on all Hellenes,' he said, as he soaked up the cold water from the spring in the thicket.

About noon he set sail again. The wind sat in the north-east, but the wall of Pelion turned it into a light stern breeze which carried him swiftly westward. The four slaves, still leg-weary and arm-weary, lay like logs beside the thwarts. Two slept; one munched some salty figs; the fourth, the headman, stared wearily forward, with ever and again a glance back at his master. But the Lemnian never looked his way. His head was on his breast, as he steered, and he brooded on the sins of the Hellenes. He was of the old Pelasgian stock, the first lords of the land, who had come out of the soil at the call of God. The pillaging northmen had crushed his folk out of the mainlands and most of the islands, but in Lemnos they had met their match. It was a family story how every grown male had been slain, and how the women long after had slaughtered their conquerors in the night. 'Lemnian deeds,' said the Hellenes, when they wished to speak of some shameful thing: but to Atta the shame was a glory to be cherished for ever. He and his kind were the ancient people, and the gods loved old things, as those new folk would find. Very especially he hated the men of Athens. Had not one of their captains, Miltiades, beaten the Lemnians, and brought the island under Athenian sway? True, it was a rule only in name, for any Athenian who came alone to Lemnos would soon be cleaving the air from the highest cliff-top. But the thought irked his pride, and he gloated over the Persians' coming. The Great King from beyond the deserts would smite those outrageous upstarts. Atta would willingly give earth and water. It was the whim of a fantastic barbarian, and would be well repaid if the bastard Hellenes were destroyed. They spoke his own tongue, and worshipped his own gods, and yet did evil. Let the nemesis of Zeus devour them!

The wreckage pursued him everywhere. Dead men shouldered the sides of the galley, and the straits were stuck full of things like monstrous buoys, where tall ships had foundered. At Artemision he thought he saw signs of an anchored fleet with the low poops of the Hellenes, and sheered off to the northern shores. There, looking towards Œta and the Malian Gulf, he found an anchorage at sunset. The waters were ugly and the times ill, and he had come on an enterprise bigger than he had dreamed. The Lemnian was a stout fellow, but he had no love for needless danger. He laughed mirthlessly as he thought of his errand, for he was going to Hellas, to the shrine of the Hellenes.

It was a woman's doing, like most crazy enterprises. Three years ago his wife had laboured hard in childbirth, and had had the whims of labouring women. Up in the keep of Larisa, on the windy hillside, there had been heart-searching and talk about the gods. The little olive-wood Hermes, the very private and particular god of Atta's folk, was good enough in simple things like a lambing or a harvest, but he was scarcely fit for heavy tasks. Atta's wife declared that her lord lacked piety. There were mainland gods who repaid worship, but his scorn of all Hellenes made him blind to the merits of those potent divinities. At first Atta resisted. There was Attic blood in his wife, and he strove to argue with her unorthodox craving. But the woman persisted, and a Lemnian wife, as she is beyond other wives in virtue and comeliness, excels them in stubbornness of temper. A second time she was with child, and nothing would content her but that Atta should make his prayers to the stronger gods. Dodona was far away, and long ere he reached it his throat would be cut in the hills. But Delphi was but two days' journey from the Malian coast, and the god of Delphi, the Far-Darter, had surprising gifts, if one were to credit travellers' tales. Atta yielded with an ill grace, and out of his wealth devised an offering to Apollo. So on this July day he found himself looking across the gulf to Kallidromos, bound for a Hellenic shrine, but hating all Hellenes in his soul. A verse of Homer consoled him – the words which Phocion spoke to Achilles. 'Verily even the gods may be turned, they whose excellence and honour and strength are greater than thine; yet even these do men, when they pray, turn from their purpose with offerings of incense and pleasant vows.' The Far-Darter must hate the ὕβρις of those Hellenes, and be the more ready to avenge it since they dared to claim his countenance. 'No race has ownership in the gods,' a Lemnian song-maker had said when Atta had been questioning the ways of Poseidon.

The following dawn found him coasting past the north end of Euboea in the thin fog of a windless summer morn. He steered by the peak of Othrys and a spur of Œta, as he had learned from a slave who had travelled the road. Presently he was in the muddy Malian waters, and the sun was scattering the mist on the landward side. And then he became aware of a greater commotion than Poseidon's play with the ships off Pelion. A murmur like a winter's storm came seawards. He lowered the sail, which he had set to catch a chance breeze, and bade the men rest on their oars. An earthquake seemed to be tearing at the roots of the hills.

The mist rolled up, and his hawk eyes saw a strange sight. The water was green and still around him, but shoreward it changed its colour. It was a dirty red, and things bobbed about in it like the Persians in the creek of Sciathos. On the strip of shore, below the sheer wall of Kallidromos, men were fighting – myriads of men, for away towards Locris they stretched in ranks and banners and tents till the eye lost them in the haze. There was no sail on the queer, muddy, red-edged sea; there was no man on the hills: but on that one flat ribbon of sand all the nations of the earth were warring. He remembered about the place: Thermopylæ they called it, the Gate of the Hot Springs. The Hellenes were fighting the Persians in the pass for their father-land.

Atta was prudent and loved not other men's quarrels. He gave the word to the rowers to row seaward. In twenty strokes they were in the mist again ...

Atta was prudent, but he was also stubborn. He spent the day in a creek on the northern shore of the gulf, listening to the weird hum which came over the waters out of the haze. He cursed the delay. Up on Kallidromos would be clear dry air and the path to Delphi among the oak woods. The Hellenes could not be fighting everywhere at once. He might find some spot on the shore, far in their rear, where he could land and gain the hills. There was danger indeed, but once on the ridge he would be safe; and by the time he came back the Great King would have swept the defenders into the sea, and be well on the road for Athens. He asked himself if it were fitting that a Lemnian should be stayed in his holy task by the struggles of Hellene and Barbarian. His thoughts flew to his steading at Larisa, and the dark-eyed wife who was awaiting his home-coming. He could not return without Apollo's favour: his manhood and the memory of his lady's eyes forbade it. So late in the afternoon he pushed off again and steered his galley for the south.

About sunset the mist cleared from the sea; but the dark falls swiftly in the shadow of the high hills, and Atta had no fear. With the night the hum sank to a whisper; it seemed that the invaders were drawing off to camp, for the sound receded to the west. At the last light the Lemnian touched a rock point well to the rear of the defence.

He noticed that the spume at the tide's edge was reddish and stuck to his hands like gum. Of a surety much blood was flowing on that coast.

He bade his slaves return to the north shore and lie hidden to await him. When he came back he would light a signal fire on the topmost bluff of Kallidromos. Let them watch for it and come to take him off. Then he seized his bow and quiver, and his short hunting-spear, buckled his cloak about him, saw that the gift to Apollo was safe in the folds of it, and marched sturdily up the hillside.

The moon was in her first quarter, a slim horn which at her rise showed only the faint outline of the hill. Atta plodded steadfastly on, but he found the way hard. This was not like the crisp sea-turf of Lemnos, where, among the barrows of the ancient dead, sheep and kine could find sweet fodder. Kallidromos ran up as steep as the roof of a barn. Cytisus and thyme and juniper grew rank, but above all the place was strewn with rocks, leg-twisting boulders, and great cliffs where eagles dwelt. Being a seaman, Atta had his bearings. The path to Delphi left the shore road near the Hot Springs, and went south by a rift of the mountain. If he went up the slope in a bee-line he must strike it in time and find better going. Still it was an eerie place to be tramping after dark. The Hellenes had strange gods of the thicket and hillside, and he had no wish to intrude upon their sanctuaries. He told himself that next to the Hellenes he hated this country of theirs, where a man sweltered in hot jungles or tripped among hidden crags. He sighed for the cool beaches below Larisa, where the surf was white as the snows of Samothrace, and the fisherboys sang round their smoking broth-pots.

Presently he found a path. It was not the mule road, worn by many feet, that he had looked for, but a little track which twined among the boulders. Still it eased his feet, so he cleared the thorns from his sandals, strapped his belt tighter, and stepped out more confidently. Up and up he went, making odd detours among the crags. Once he came to a promontory, and, looking down, saw lights twinkling from the Hot Springs. He had thought the course lay more southerly, but consoled himself by remembering that a mountain path must have many windings. The great matter was that he was ascending, for he knew that he must cross the ridge of Œta before he struck the Locrian glens that led to the Far-Darter's shrine.

At what seemed the summit of the first ridge he halted for breath, and, prone on the thyme, looked back to sea. The Hot Springs were hidden, but across the gulf a single light shone from the far shore. He guessed that by this time his galley had been beached and his slaves were cooking supper. The thought made him homesick. He had beaten and cursed these slaves of his times without number, but now in this strange land he felt them kinsfolk, men of his own household. Then he told himself he was no better than a woman. Had he not gone sailing to Chalcedon and distant Pontus, many months' journey from home, while this was but a trip of days? In a week he would be welcomed by a smiling wife, with a friendly god behind him.

The track still bore west, though Delphi lay in the south. Moreover, he had come to a broader road running through a little tableland. The highest peaks of Œta were dark against the sky, and around him was a flat glade where oaks whispered in the night breezes. By this time he judged from the stars that midnight had passed, and he began to consider whether, now that he was beyond the fighting, he should not sleep and wait for dawn. He made up his mind to find a shelter, and, in the aimless way of the night traveller, pushed on and on in the quest of it. The truth is his mind was on Lemnos, and a dark-eyed, white-armed dame spinning in the evening by the threshold. His eyes roamed among the oak trees, but vacantly and idly, and many a mossy corner was passed unheeded. He forgot his ill-temper, and hummed cheerfully the song his reapers sang in the barley-fields below his orchard. It was a song of seamen turned husbandmen, for the gods it called on were the gods of the sea . . .

Suddenly he found himself crouching among the young oaks, peering and listening. There was something coming from the west. It was like the first mutterings of a storm in a narrow harbour, a steady rustling and whispering. It was not wind; he knew winds too well to be deceived. It was the tramp of light-shod feet among the twigs – many feet, for the sound remained steady, while the noise of a few men will rise and fall. They were coming fast and coming silently. The war had reached far up Kallidromos.

Atta had played this game often in the little island wars. Very swiftly he ran back and away from the path up the slope which he knew to be the first ridge of Kallidromos. The army, whatever it might be, was on the Delphian road. Were the Hellenes about to turn the flank of the Great King?

A moment later he laughed at his folly. For the men began to appear, and they were crossing to meet him, coming from the west. Lying close in the brushwood he could see them clearly. It was well he had left the road, for they stuck to it, following every winding – crouching, too, like hunters after deer. The first man he saw was a Hellene, but the ranks behind were no Hellenes. There was no glint of bronze or gleam of fair skin. They were dark, long-haired fellows, with spears like his own, and round Eastern caps, and egg-shaped bucklers. Then Atta rejoiced. It was the Great King who was turning the flank of the Hellenes. They guarded the gate, the fools, while the enemy slipped through the roof.

He did not rejoice long. The van of the army was narrow and kept to the path, but the men behind were straggling all over the hillside. Another minute and he would be discovered. The thought was cheerless. It was true that he was an islander and friendly to the Persian, but up on the heights who would listen to his tale? He would be taken for a spy, and one of those thirsty spears would drink his blood. It must be farewell to Delphi for the moment, he thought, or farewell to Lemnos for ever. Crouching low, he ran back and away from the path to the crest of the sea-ridge of Kallidromos.

The men came no nearer him. They were keeping roughly to the line of the path, and drifted through the oak wood before him, an army without end. He had scarcely thought there were so many fighting men in the world. He resolved to lie there on the crest, in the hope that ere the first light they would be gone. Then he would push on to Delphi, leaving them to settle their quarrels behind him. These were the hard times for a pious pilgrim.

But another noise caught his ear from the right. The army had flanking squadrons, and men were coming along the ridge. Very bitter anger rose in Atta's heart. He had cursed the Hellenes, and now he cursed the Barbarians no less. Nay, he cursed all war, that spoiled the errands of peaceful folk. And then, seeking safety, he dropped over the crest on to the steep shoreward face of the mountain.

In an instant his breath had gone from him. He slid down a long slope of screes, and then with a gasp found himself falling sheer into space. Another second and he was caught in a tangle of bush, and then dropped once more upon screes, where he clutched desperately for handhold. Breathless and bleeding he came to anchor on a shelf of greensward and found himself blinking up at the crest which seemed to tower a thousand feet above. There were men on the crest now. He heard them speak and felt that they were looking down.

The shock kept him still till the men had passed. Then the terror of the place gripped him, and he tried feverishly to retrace his steps. A dweller all his days among gentle downs, he grew dizzy with the sense of being hung in space. But the only fruit of his efforts was to set him slipping again. This time he pulled up at a root of gnarled oak which overhung the sheerest cliff on Kallidromos. The danger brought his wits back. He sullenly reviewed his case, and found it desperate.

He could not go back, and, even if he did, he would meet the Persians. If he went on he would break his neck, or at the best fall into the Hellenes' hands. Oddly enough he feared his old enemies less than his friends. He did not think that the Hellenes would butcher him. Again, he might sit perched in his eyrie till they settled their quarrel, or he fell off. He rejected this last way. Fall off he should for certain, unless he kept moving. Already he was retching with the vertigo of the heights. It was growing lighter. Suddenly he was looking not into a black world, but to a pearl-grey floor far beneath him. It was the sea, the thing he knew and loved. The sight screwed up his courage. He remembered that he was a Lemnian and a seafarer. He would be conquered neither by rock, nor by Hellene, nor by the Great King. Least of all by the last, who was a barbarian. Slowly, with clenched teeth and narrowed eyes, he began to clamber down a ridge which flanked the great cliff of Kallidromos. His plan was to reach the shore and take the road to the east before the Persians completed their circuit. Some instinct told him that a great army would not take the track he had mounted by. There must be some longer and easier way debouching farther down the coast. He might yet have the good luck to slip between them and the sea.

The two hours which followed tried his courage hard. Thrice he fell, and only a juniper root stood between him and death. His hands grew ragged, and his nails were worn to the quick. He had long ago lost his weapons; his cloak was in shreds, all save the breast-fold which held the gift to Apollo. The heavens brightened, but he dared not look around. He knew he was traversing awesome places, where a goat could scarcely tread. Many times he gave up hope of life. His head was swimming, and he was so deadly sick that often he had to lie gasping on some shoulder of rock less steep than the rest. But his anger kept him to his purpose. He was filled with fury at the

Hellenes. It was they and their folly that had brought him these mischances. Some day . . .

He found himself sitting blinking on the shore of the sea. A furlong off the water was lapping on the reefs. A man, larger than human in the morning mist, was standing above him.

'Greeting, stranger,' said the voice. 'By Hermes, you choose the difficult roads to travel.'

Atta felt for broken bones, and, reassured, struggled to his feet.

'God's curse upon all mountains,' he said. He staggered to the edge of the tide and laved his brow. The savour of salt revived him. He turned to find the tall man at his elbow, and noted how worn and ragged he was, and yet how upright.

'When a pigeon is flushed from the rocks there is a hawk near,' said the voice.

Atta was angry. 'A hawk!' he cried. 'Nay, an army of eagles. There will be some rare flushing of Hellenes before evening.'

'What frightened you, Islander?' the stranger asked. 'Did a wolf bark up on the hillside?'

'Ay, a wolf. The wolf from the East with a multitude of wolflings. There will be fine eating soon in the pass.'

The man's face grew dark. He put his hand to his mouth and called. Half a dozen sentries ran to join him. He spoke to them in the harsh Lacedæmonian speech which made Atta sick to hear. They talked with the back of the throat, and there was not an 's' in their words.

'There is mischief in the hills,' the first man said. 'This islander has been frightened down over the rocks. The Persian is stealing a march on us.'

The sentries laughed. One quoted a proverb about island courage. Atta's wrath flared and he forgot himself. He had no wish to warn the Hellenes, but it irked his pride to be thought a liar. He began to tell his story hastily, angrily, confusedly; and the men still laughed.

Then he turned eastward and saw the proof before him. The light had grown and the sun was coming up over Pelion. The first beam fell on the eastern ridge of Kallidromos, and there, clear on the sky-line, was the proof. The Persian was making a wide circuit, but moving shoreward. In a little while he would be at the coast, and by noon at the Hellenes' rear.

His hearers doubted no more. Atta was hurried forward through the lines of the Greeks to the narrow throat of the pass, where behind a rough rampart of stones lay the Lacedæmonian headquarters. He was still giddy from the heights, and it was in a giddy dream that he traversed the misty shingles of the beach amid ranks of sleeping warriors. It was a grim place, for there were dead and dying in it, and blood on every stone. But in the lee of the wall little fires were burning and slaves were cooking breakfast. The smell of roasting flesh came pleasantly to his nostrils, and he remembered that he had had no meal since he crossed the gulf.

Then he found himself the centre of a group who had the air of kings. They looked as if they had been years in war. Never had he seen faces so worn and so terribly scarred. The hollows in their cheeks gave them the air of smiling, and yet they were grave. Their scarlet vests were torn and muddied, and the armour which lay near was dinted like the scrap-iron before a smithy door. But what caught his attention were the eyes of the men. They glittered as no eyes he had ever seen before glittered. The sight cleared his bewilderment and took the pride out of his heart. He could not pretend to despise a folk who looked like Ares fresh from the wars of the Immortals.

They spoke among themselves in quiet voices. Scouts came and went, and once or twice one of the men, taller than the rest, asked Atta a question. The Lemnian sat in the heart of the group, sniffing the smell of cooking, and looking at the rents in his cloak and the long scratches on his legs. Something was pressing on his breast, and he found that it was Apollo's gift. He had forgotten all about it. Delphi seemed beyond the moon, and his errand a child's dream.

Then the King, for so he thought of the tall man, spoke. 'You have done us a service, Islander. The Persian is at our back and front, and there will be no escape for those who stay. Our allies are going home, for they do not share our vows. We of Lacedæmon wait in the pass. If you go with the men of Corinth you will find a place of safety before noon. No doubt in the Euripus there is some boat to take you to your own land.'

He spoke courteously, not in the rude Athenian way; and somehow the quietness of his voice and his glittering eyes roused wild longings in Atta's heart. His island pride was face to face with a greater – greater than he had ever dreamed of.

'Bid yon cooks give me some broth,' he said gruffly. 'I am faint. After I have eaten I will speak with you.'

He was given food, and as he ate he thought. He was on trial before these men of Lacedæmon. More, the old faith of the islands, the pride of the first masters, was at stake in his hands. He had boasted that he and his kind were the last of the men; now these Hellenes of Lacedæmon were preparing a great deed, and they deemed him unworthy to share in it. They offered him safety. Could he brook the insult? He had forgotten that the cause of the Persian was his; that the Hellenes were the foes of his race. He saw only that the last test of manhood was preparing, and the manhood in him rose to greet the trial. An odd wild ecstasy surged in his veins. It was not the lust of battle, for he had no love of slaying, or hate of the Persian, for he was his friend. It was the joy of proving that the Lemnian stock had a starker pride than these men of Lacedæmon. They would die for their fatherland, and their vows; but he, for a whim, a scruple, a delicacy of honour. His mind was so clear that no other course occurred to him. There was only one way for a man. He, too, would be dying for his fatherland, for through him the island race would be ennobled in the eyes of gods and men.

Troops were filing fast to the east – Thebans, Corinthians.

'Time flies, Islander,' said the King's voice. 'The hours of safety are slipping past.'

Atta looked up carelessly. 'I will stay,' he said. 'God's curse on all Hellenes! Little I care for your quarrels. It is nothing to me if your Hellas is under the heel of the East. But I care much for brave men. It shall never be said that a man of Lemnos, a son of the old race, fell back when Death threatened. I stay with you, men of Lacedæmon.'

The King's eyes glittered; they seemed to peer into his heart.

'It appears they breed men in the islands,' he said. 'But you err. Death does not threaten. Death awaits us.'

'It is all one,' said Atta. 'But I crave a boon. Let me fight my last fight by your side. I am of older stock than you, and a king in my own country. I would strike my last blow among kings.'

There was an hour of respite before battle was joined, and Atta spent it by the edge of the sea. He had been given arms, and in girding himself for the fight he had found Apollo's offering in his breastfold. He was done with the gods of the Hellenes. His offering should go to the gods of his own people. So, calling upon Poseidon, he flung the little gold cup far out to sea. It flashed in the sunlight, and then sank in the soft green tides so noiselessly that it seemed as if the hand of the Sea-god had been stretched to take it. 'Hail, Poseidon!' the Lemnian cried. 'I am bound this day for the Ferryman. To you only I make prayer, and to the little Hermes of Larisa. Be kind to my kin when they travel the sea, and keep them islanders and seafarers for ever. Hail and farewell, God of my own folk!'

Then, while the little waves lapped on the white sand, Atta made a song. He was thinking of the homestead far up in the green downs, looking over to the snows of Samothrace. At this hour in the morning there would be a tinkle of sheep-bells as the flocks went down to the low pastures. Cool wind would be blowing, and the noise of the surf below the cliffs would come faint to the ear. In the hall the maids would be spinning, while their dark-haired mistress would be casting swift glances to the doorway, lest it might be filled any moment by the form of her returning lord. Outside in the chequered sunlight of the orchard the child would be playing with his nurse, crooning in childish syllables the chanty his father had taught him. And at the thought of his home a great passion welled up in Atta's heart. It was not regret, but joy and pride and aching love. In his antique island creed the death he was awaiting was not other than a bridal. He was dying for the things he loved, and by his death they would be blessed eternally. He would not have long to wait before bright eyes came to greet him in the House of Shadows.

So Atta made the Song of Atta, and sang it then, and later in the press of battle. It was a simple song, like the lays of seafarers. It put into rough verse the thought which cheers the heart of all adventurers – nay, which makes adventure possible for those who have much to leave. It spoke of the shining pathway of the sea which is the Great Uniter. A man may lie dead in Pontus or beyond the Pillars of Herakles, but if he dies on the shore there is nothing between him and his fatherland. It spoke of a battle all the long dark night in a strange place – a place of marshes and black cliffs and shadowy terrors.

'In the dawn the sweet light comes,' said the song, 'and the salt winds and the tides will bear me home ...'

When in the evening the Persians took toll of the dead, they found one man who puzzled them. He lay among the tall Lacedæmonians, on the very lip of the sea, and around him were swathes of their countrymen.

It looked as if he had been fighting his way to the water, and had been overtaken by death as his feet reached the edge. Nowhere in the pass did the dead lie so thick, and yet he was no Hellene. He was torn like a deer that the dogs have worried, but the little left of his garments and his features spoke of Eastern race. The survivors could tell nothing except that he had fought like a god and had been singing all the while.

The matter came to the ear of the Great King, who was sore enough at the issue of the day. That one of his men had performed feats of valour beyond the Hellenes was a pleasant tale to tell. And so his captains reported it. Accordingly when the fleet from Artemision arrived next morning, and all but a few score Persians were shovelled into holes, that the Hellenes might seem to have been conquered by a lesser force, Atta's body was laid out with pomp in the midst of the Lacedæmonians. And the seamen rubbed their eyes and thanked their strange gods that one man of the East had been found to match those terrible warriors whose name was a nightmare. Further, the Great King gave orders that the body of Atta should be embalmed and carried with the army, and that his name and kin should be sought out and duly honoured. This latter was a task too hard for the staff, and no more was heard of it till months later, when the King, in full flight after Salamis, bethought him of the one man who had not played him false. Finding that his lieutenants had nothing to tell him, he eased five of them of their heads.

As it happened, the deed was not quite forgotten. An islander, a Lesbian and a cautious man, had fought at Thermopylæ in the Persian ranks, and had heard Atta's singing and seen how he fell. Long afterwards some errand took this man to Lemnos, and in the evening, speaking with the Elders, he told his tale and repeated something of the song. There was that in the words which gave the Lemnians a clue, the mention, I think, of the olive-wood Hermes and the snows of Samothrace. So Atta came to great honour among his own people, and his memory and his words were handed down to the generations. The song became a favourite island lay, and for centuries throughout the Aegean seafaring men sang it when they turned their prows to wild seas. Nay, it travelled farther, for you will find part of it stolen by Euripides and put in a chorus of the *Andromache*. There are echoes of it in some of the epigrams of the *Anthology*; and, though the old days have gone, the simple fisherfolk still sing snatches in their barbarous dialect. The Klephts used to make a catch of it at night round their fires in the hills, and only the other day I met a man in Scyros who had collected a dozen variants, and was publishing them in a dull book on island folklore.

In the centuries which followed the great fight, the sea fell away from the roots of the cliffs and left a mile of marshland. About fifty years ago a peasant, digging in a rice-field, found the cup which Atta had given to Poseidon. There was much talk about the discovery, and scholars debated hotly about its origin. Today it is in the Berlin Museum, and according to the new fashion in archæology it is labelled 'Minoan', and kept in the Cretan Section. But any one who looks carefully will see behind the rim a neat little carving of a dolphin; and I happen to know that that was the private badge of Atta's house.

Space

Written in 1910, 'Space' was published in May 1911 in *Blackwood's Magazine* and the following month in *The Living Age*. It was one of the stories in *The Moon Endureth* (1912).

J'ai dit que nous pourrions concevoir, vivant dans notre monde, des êtres pensants dont le tableau de distribution serait à quatre dimensions et qui par conséquent penseraient dans l'hyperespace. Il n'est pas certain toutefois que de pareils êtres, en admettant qu'ils y naissent, pourraient y vivre et s'y défendre contre les mille dangers dont ils y seraient assaillis.

H. POINCARÉ: *Science et Méthode*

Le silence éternel de ces espaces infinis m'effraie.

PASCAL

LEITHEN TOLD ME this story one evening in early September as we sat beside the pony track which gropes its way from Glenaicill up the Correi na Sidhe. I had arrived that afternoon from the south, while he had been taking an off-day from a week's stalking, so we had walked up the glen together after tea to get the news of the forest. A rifle was out on the Correi na Sidhe beat, and a thin spire of smoke had risen from the top of Sgurr Dearg to show that a stag had been killed at the burn-head. The lumpish hill pony with its deer-saddle had gone up the Correi in a gillie's charge, while we followed at leisure, picking our way among the loose granite rocks and the patches of wet bogland. The track climbed high on one of the ridges of Sgurr Dearg, till it hung over a caldron of green glen with the Alt-na-Sidhe churning in its linn a thousand feet below. It was a breathless evening, I remember, with a pale-blue sky just clearing from the haze of the day. West-wind weather may make the North, even in September, no bad imitation of the Tropics, and I sincerely pitied the man who all these stifling hours had been toiling on the screes of Sgurr Dearg. By and by we sat down on a bank of heather, and idly watched the trough swimming at our feet. The clatter of the pony's hoofs grew fainter, the drone of bees had gone, even the midges seemed to have forgotten their calling. No place on earth can be so deathly still as a deer-forest early in the season before the stags have begun roaring, for there are no sheep with their homely noises, and only the rare croak of a raven breaks the silence. The hillside was far from sheer – one could have walked down with a little care – but something in the shape of the hollow and the remote gleam of white water gave it an air of extraordinary depth and space. There was a shimmer left from the day's heat, which invested bracken and rock and scree with a curious airy unreality. One could almost have believed that the eye had tricked the mind, that all was mirage, that five yards from the path the solid earth fell away into nothingness. I have a bad head, and instinctively I drew farther back into the heather. Leithen's eyes were looking vacantly before him.

'Did you ever know Hollond?' he asked.

Then he laughed shortly. 'I don't know why I asked that, but somehow this place reminded me of Hollond. That glimmering hollow looks as if it were the beginning of eternity. It must be eerie to live with the feeling always on one.'

Leithen seemed disinclined for further exercise. He lit a pipe and smoked quietly for a little. 'Odd that you didn't know Hollond. You must have heard his name. I thought you amused yourself with metaphysics.'

Then I remembered. There had been an erratic genius who had written some articles in *Mind* on that dreary subject, the mathematical conception of infinity. Men had praised them to me, but I confess I never quite understood their argument. 'Wasn't he some sort of mathematical professor?' I asked.

'He was, and, in his own way, a tremendous swell. He wrote a book on Number, which has translations in every European language. He is dead now, and the Royal Society founded a medal in his honour. But I wasn't thinking of that side of him.'

It was the time and place for a story, for the pony would not be back for an hour. So I asked Leithen about the other side of Hollond which was recalled to him by Correi na Sidhe. He seemed a little unwilling to speak ...

'I wonder if you will understand it. You ought to, of course, better than me, for you know something of philosophy. But it took me a long time to get the hang of it, and I can't give you any kind of explanation. He was my fag at Eton, and when I began to get on at the Bar I was able to advise him on one or two private matters, so that he rather fancied my legal ability. He came to me with his story because he had to tell some one, and he wouldn't trust a colleague. He said he didn't want a scientist to know, for scientists were either pledged to their own theories and wouldn't understand, or, if they understood, would get ahead of him in his researches. He wanted a lawyer, he said, who was accustomed to weighing evidence. That was good sense, for evidence must always be judged by the same laws, and I suppose in the long-run the most abstruse business comes down to a fairly simple deduction from certain data. Anyhow, that was the way he used to talk, and I listened to him, for I liked the man, and had an enormous respect for his brains. At Eton he sluiced down all the mathematics they could give him, and he was an astonishing swell at Cambridge. He was a simple fellow, too, and talked no more jargon than he could help. I used to climb with him in the Alps now and then, and you would never have guessed that he had any thoughts beyond getting up steep rocks.

'It was at Chamonix, I remember, that I first got a hint of the matter that was filling his mind. We had been taking an off-day, and were sitting in the hotel garden, watching the Aiguilles getting purple in the twilight. Chamonix always makes me choke a little – it is so crushed in by those great snow masses. I said something about it – said I liked open spaces like the Gornergrat or the Bel Alp better. He asked me why: if it was the difference of the air, or merely the wider horizon? I said it was the sense of not being crowded, of living in an empty world. He repeated the word 'empty' and laughed.

' "By 'empty' you mean," he said, "where things don't knock up against you?"

'I told him No. I mean just empty, void, nothing but blank æther.

' "You don't knock up against things here, and the air is as good as you want. It can't be the lack of ordinary emptiness you feel."

'I agreed that the word needed explaining. "I suppose it is mental restlessness," I said. "I like to feel that for a tremendous distance there is nothing round me. Why, I don't know. Some men are built the other way and have a terror of space."

'He said that that was better. "It is a personal fancy, and depends on your *knowing* that there is nothing between you and the top of the Dent Blanche. And you know because your eyes tell you there is nothing. Even if you were blind, you might have a sort of sense about adjacent matter. Blind men often have it. But in any case, whether got from instinct or sight, the *knowledge* is what matters."

'Hollond was embarking on a Socratic dialogue in which I could see little point. I told him so, and he laughed.

' "I am not sure that I am very clear myself. But yes – there *is* a point. Supposing you knew – not by sight or by instinct, but by sheer intellectual knowledge, as I know the truth of a mathematical proposition – that what we call empty space was full, crammed. Not with lumps of what we call matter like hills and houses, but with things as real – as real to the mind. Would you still feel crowded?"

' "No," I said, "I don't think so. It is only what we call matter that signifies. It would be just as well not to feel crowded by the other thing, for there would be no escape from it. But what are you getting at? Do you mean atoms or electric currents or what?"

'He said he wasn't thinking about that sort of thing, and began to talk of another subject.

'Next night, when we were pigging it at the Géant *cabane*, he started again on the same tack. He asked me how I accounted for the fact that animals could find their way back over great tracts of unknown country. I said I supposed it was the homing instinct.

' "Rubbish, man," he said. "That's only another name for the puzzle, not an explanation. There must be some reason for it. They must *know* something that we cannot understand. Tie a cat in a bag and take it fifty miles by train and it will make its way home. That cat has some clue that we haven't."

'I was tired and sleepy, and told him that I did not care a rush about the psychology of cats. But he was not to be snubbed, and went on talking.

' "How if Space is really full of things we cannot see and as yet do not know? How if all animals and some savages have a cell in their brain or a nerve which responds to the invisible world? How if all Space be full of these landmarks, not material in our sense, but quite real? A dog barks at nothing, a wild beast makes an aimless circuit. Why? Perhaps because Space is made up of corridors and alleys, ways to travel and things to shun? For all we know, to a greater intelligence than ours the top of Mont Blanc may be as crowded as Piccadilly Circus."

[185]

'But at that point I fell asleep and left Hollond to repeat his questions to a guide who knew no English and a snoring porter.

'Six months later, one foggy January afternoon, Hollond rang me up at the Temple and proposed to come to see me that night after dinner. I thought he wanted to talk Alpine shop, but he turned up in Duke Street about nine with a kit-bag full of papers. He was an odd fellow to look at – a yellowish face with the skin stretched tight on the cheek-bones, clean shaven, a sharp chin which he kept poking forward, and deep-set, greyish eyes. He was a hard fellow too, always in pretty good condition, which was remarkable considering how he slaved for nine months out of the twelve. He had a quiet, slow-spoken manner, but that night I saw that he was considerably excited.

'He said that he had come to me because we were old friends. He proposed to tell me a tremendous secret. "I must get another mind to work on it or I'll go crazy. I don't want a scientist. I want a plain man."

'Then he fixed me with a look like a tragic actor's. "Do you remember that talk we had in August at Chamonix – about Space? I daresay you thought I was playing the fool. So I was in a sense, but I was feeling my way towards something which has been in my mind for ten years. Now I have got it, and you must hear about it. You may take my word that it's a pretty startling discovery."

'I lit a pipe and told him to go ahead, warning him that I knew about as much science as the dust-man.

'I am bound to say that it took me a long time to understand what he meant. He began by saying that everybody thought of Space as an "empty homogeneous medium". "Never mind at present what the ultimate constituents of that medium are. We take it as a finished product, and we think of it as mere extension, something without any quality at all. That is the view of civilised man. You will find all the philosophers taking it for granted. Yes, but every living thing does not take that view. An animal, for instance. It feels a kind of quality in Space. It can find its way over new country, because it perceives certain landmarks, not necessarily material, but perceptible, or if you like intelligible. Take an Australian savage. He has the same power, and, I believe, for the same reason. He is conscious of intelligible landmarks."

'"You mean what people call a sense of direction," I put in.

'"Yes, but what in Heaven's name is a sense of direction? The phrase explains nothing. However incoherent the mind of the animal or the savage may be, it is there somewhere, working on some data. I've been all through the psychological and anthropological side of the business, and after you eliminate clues from sight and hearing and smell and half-conscious memory there remains a solid lump of the inexplicable."

'Hollond's eye had kindled, and he sat doubled up in his chair, dominating me with a finger.

' "Here, then, is a power which man is civilising himself out of. Call it anything you like, but you must admit that it is a power. Don't you see that it is a perception of another kind of reality that we are leaving behind us? ... Well, you know the way nature works. The wheel comes full circle, and what we think we have lost we regain in a higher form. So for a long time I have been wondering whether the civilised mind could not recreate for itself this lost gift, the gift of seeing the quality of Space. I mean that I wondered whether the scientific modern brain could not get to the stage of realising that Space is not an empty homogeneous medium, but full of intricate differences, intelligible and real, though not with our common reality."

'I found all this very puzzling, and he had to repeat it several times before I got a glimpse of what he was talking about.

' "I've wondered for a long time," he went on, "but now, quite suddenly, I have begun to know." He stopped and asked me abruptly if I knew much about mathematics.

' "It's a pity," he said, "but the main point is not technical, though I wish you could appreciate the beauty of some of my proofs." Then he began to tell me about his last six months' work. I should have mentioned that he was a brilliant physicist besides other things. All Hollond's tastes were on the borderlands of sciences, where mathematics fades into metaphysics and physics merges in the abstrusest kind of mathematics. Well, it seems he had been working for years at the ultimate problem of matter, and especially of that rarefied matter we call æther or space. I forget what his view was – atoms or molecules or electric waves. If he ever told me I have forgotten, but I'm not certain that I ever knew. However, the point was that these ultimate constituents were dynamic and mobile, not a mere passive medium but a medium in constant movement and change. He claimed to have discovered – by ordinary inductive experiment – that the constituents of æther possessed certain functions, and moved in certain figures obedient to certain mathematical laws. Space, I gathered, was perpetually "forming fours" in some fancy way.

'Here he left his physics and became the mathematician. Among his mathematical discoveries had been certain curves or figures or something whose behaviour involved a new dimension. I gathered that this wasn't the ordinary Fourth Dimension that people talk of, but that fourth-dimensional inwardness or involution was part of it. The explanation lay in the pile of manuscripts he left with me, but though I tried honestly I couldn't get the hang of it. My mathematics stopped with desperate finality just as he got into his subject.

'His point was that the constituents of Space moved according to these new mathematical figures of his. They were always changing, but the principles of their change were as fixed as the law of gravitation. Therefore, if you once grasped these principles you knew the contents of the void. What do you make of that?'

I said that it seemed to me a reasonable enough argument, but that it got one very little way forward. 'A man,' I said, 'might know the contents of Space and the laws of their arrangement and yet be unable to see anything more than his fellows. It is a purely academic knowledge. His mind knows it as the result of many deductions, but his senses perceive nothing.'

Leithen laughed. 'Just what I said to Hollond. He asked the opinion of my legal mind. I said I could not pronounce on his argument, but that I could point out that he had established no *trait d'union* between the intellect which understood and the senses which perceived. It was like a blind man with immense knowledge but no eyes, and therefore no peg to hang his knowledge on and make it useful. He had not explained his savage or his cat. "Hang it, man," I said, "before you can appreciate the existence of your Spacial forms you have to go through elaborate experiments and deductions. You can't be doing that every minute. Therefore you don't get any nearer to the *use* of the sense you say that man once possessed, though you can explain it a bit." '

'What did he say?' I asked.

'The funny thing was that he never seemed to see my difficulty. When I kept bringing him back to it he shied off with a new wild theory of perception. He argued that the mind can live in a world of realities without any sensuous stimulus to connect them with the world of our ordinary life. Of course that wasn't my point. I supposed that this world of Space was real enough to him, but I wanted to know how he got there. He never answered me. He was the typical Cambridge man, you know – dogmatic about uncertainties, but curiously diffident about the obvious. He laboured to get me to understand the notion of his mathematical forms, which I was quite willing to take on trust from him. Some queer things he said, too. He took our feeling about Left and Right as an example of our instinct for the quality of Space. But when I objected that Left and Right varied with each object, and only existed in connection with some definite material thing, he said that that was exactly what he meant. It was an example of the mobility of the Spacial forms. Do you see any sense in that?'

I shook my head. It seemed to me pure craziness.

'And then he tried to show me what he called the "involution of Space", by taking two points on a piece of paper. The points were a foot away when the paper was flat, but they coincided when it was doubled up. He said that there were no gaps between the figures, for the medium was continuous, and he took as an illustration the loops on a cord. You are to think of a cord always looping and unlooping itself according to certain mathematical laws. Oh, I tell you, I gave up trying to follow him. And he was so desperately in earnest all the time. By his account Space was a sort of mathematical pandemonium.'

Leithen stopped to refill his pipe, and I mused upon the ironic fate which had compelled a mathematical genius to make his sole confidant of a philistine lawyer, and induced that lawyer to repeat it confusedly to an ignoramus at twilight on a Scotch hill. As told by Leithen it was a very halting tale.

'But there was one thing I could see very clearly,' Leithen went on, 'and that was Hollond's own case. This crowded world of Space was perfectly real to him. How he had got to it I do not know. Perhaps his mind, dwelling constantly on the problem, had unsealed some atrophied cell and restored the old instinct. Anyhow, he was living his daily life with a foot in each world.

'He often came to see me, and after the first hectic discussions he didn't talk much. There was no noticeable change in him – a little more abstracted perhaps. He would walk in the street or come into a room with a quick look round him, and sometimes for no earthly reason he would swerve. Did you ever watch a cat crossing a room? It sidles along by the furniture and walks over an open space of carpet as if it were picking its way among obstacles. Well, Hollond behaved like that, but he had always been counted a little odd, and nobody noticed it but me.

'I knew better than to chaff him, and we had stopped argument, so that there wasn't much to be said. But sometimes he would give me news about his experiences. The whole thing was perfectly clear and scientific and above-board, and nothing creepy about it. You know how I hate the washy supernatural stuff they give us nowadays. Hollond was well and fit, with an appetite like a hunter. But as he talked, sometimes – well, you know I haven't much in the way of nerves or imagination – but I used to get a little eerie. Used to feel the solid earth dissolving round me. It was the opposite of vertigo, if you understand me – a sense of airy realities crowding in on you, – crowding the mind, that is, not the body.

'I gathered from Hollond that he was always conscious of corridors and halls and alleys in Space, shifting, but shifting according to inexorable laws. I never could get quite clear as to what this consciousness was like. When I asked he used to look puzzled and worried and helpless. I made out from him that one landmark involved a sequence, and once given a bearing from an object you could keep the direction without a mistake. He told me he could easily, if he wanted, go in a dirigible from the top of Mont Blanc to the top of Snowdon in the thickest fog and without a compass, if he were given the proper angle to start from. I confess I didn't follow that myself. Material objects had nothing to do with the Spacial forms, for a table or a bed in our world might be placed across a corridor of Space. The forms played their game independent of our kind of reality. But the worst of it was, that if you kept your mind too much in one world you were apt to forget about the other, and Hollond was always barking his shins on stones and chairs and things.

'He told me all this quite simply and frankly. Remember, his mind and no other part of him lived in his new world. He said it gave him an odd sense of detachment to sit in a room among people, and to know that nothing there but himself had any relation at all to the infinite strange world of Space that flowed around them. He would listen, he said, to a great man talking, with one eye on the cat on the rug, thinking to himself how much more the cat knew than the man.'

'How long was it before he went mad?' I asked.

It was a foolish question, and made Leithen cross. 'He never went mad in your sense. My dear fellow, you're very much wrong if you think there was anything pathological about him – then. The man was brilliantly sane. His mind was as keen as a keen sword. I couldn't understand him, but I could judge of his sanity right enough.'

I asked if it made him happy or miserable.

'At first I think it made him uncomfortable. He was restless because he knew too much and too little. The unknown pressed in on his mind, as bad air weighs on the lungs. Then it lightened, and he accepted the new world in the same sober practical way that he took other things. I think that the free exercise of his mind in a pure medium gave him a feeling of extraordinary power and ease. His eyes used to sparkle when he talked. And another odd thing he told me. He was a keen rock-climber, but, curiously enough, he had never a very good head. Dizzy heights always worried him, though he managed to keep hold on himself. But now all that had gone. The sense of the fullness of Space made him as happy – happier, I believe – with his legs dangling into eternity, as sitting before his own study fire.

'I remember saying that it was all rather like the mediæval wizards who made their spells by means of numbers and figures.

'He caught me up at once. "Not numbers," he said. "Number has no place in Nature. It is an invention of the human mind to atone for a bad memory. But figures are a different matter. All the mysteries of the world are in them, and the old magicians knew that at least, if they knew no more."

'He had only one grievance. He complained that it was terribly lonely. "It is the Desolation," he would quote, "spoken of by Daniel the prophet." He would spend hours travelling those eerie shifting corridors of Space with no hint of another human soul. How could there be? It was a world of pure reason, where human personality had no place. What puzzled me was why he should feel the absence of this. One wouldn't, you know, in an intricate problem of geometry or a game of chess. I asked him, but he didn't understand the question. I puzzled over it a good deal, for it seemed to me that if Hollond felt lonely, there must be more in this world of his than we imagined. I began to wonder if there was any truth in fads like psychical research. Also, I was not so sure that he was as normal as I had thought: it looked as if his nerves might be going bad.

'Oddly enough, Hollond was getting on the same track himself. He had discovered, so he said, that in sleep everybody now and then lived in this new world of his. You know how one dreams of triangular

railway platforms with trains running simultaneously down all three
sides and not colliding. Well, this sort of cantrip was "common form",
as we say at the Bar, in Hollond's Space, and he was very curious about
the why and wherefore of Sleep. He began to haunt psychological
laboratories, where they experiment with the charwoman and the odd
man, and he used to go up to Cambridge for *séances*. It was a foreign
atmosphere to him, and I don't think he was very happy in it. He
found so many charlatans that he used to get angry, and declare he
would be better employed at Mothers' Meetings!'

From far up the Glen came the sound of the pony's hoofs. The stag
had been loaded up, and the gillies were returning. Leithen looked at
his watch. 'We'd better wait and see the beast,' he said.

'... Well, nothing happened for more than a year. Then one
evening in May he burst into my rooms in high excitement. You
understand quite clearly that there was no suspicion of horror or fright
or anything unpleasant about this world he had discovered. It was
simply a series of interesting and difficult problems. All this time
Hollond had been rather extra well and cheery. But when he came in I
thought I noticed a different look in his eyes, something puzzled and
diffident and apprehensive.

' "There's a queer performance going on in the other world," he
said. "It's unbelievable. I never dreamed of such a thing. I – I don't
quite know how to put it, and I don't know how to explain it, but –
but I am becoming aware that there are other beings – other minds –
moving in Space besides mine."

'I suppose I ought to have realised then that things were beginning
to go wrong. But it was very difficult, he was so rational and anxious
to make it all clear. I asked him how he knew. There could, of course,
on his own showing be no *change* in that world, for the forms of Space
moved and existed under inexorable laws. He said he found his own
mind failing him at points. There would come over him a sense of fear
– intellectual fear – and weakness, a sense of something else, quite
alien to Space, thwarting him. Of course he could only describe his
impressions very lamely, for they were purely of the mind, and he had
no material peg to hang them on, so that I could realise them. But the
gist of it was that he had been gradually becoming conscious of what
he called "Presences" in his world. They had no effect on Space – did
not leave foot-prints in its corridors, for instance – but they affected

his mind. There was some mysterious contact established between him and them. I asked him if the affection was unpleasant, and he said "No, not exactly." But I could see a hint of fear in his eyes.

'Think of it. Try to realise what intellectual fear is. I can't, but it is conceivable. To you and me fear implies pain to ourselves or some other, and such pain is always in the last resort pain of the flesh. Consider it carefully and you will see that it is so. But imagine fear so sublimated and transmuted as to be the tension of pure spirit. I can't realise it, but I think it possible. I don't pretend to understand how Hollond got to know about these Presences. But there was no doubt about the fact. He was positive, and he wasn't in the least mad – not in our sense. In that very month he published his book on Number, and gave a German professor who attacked it a most tremendous public trouncing.

'I know what you are going to say – that the fancy was a weakening of the mind from within. I admit I should have thought of that, but he looked so confoundedly sane and able that it seemed ridiculous. He kept asking me my opinion, as a lawyer, on the facts he offered. It was the oddest case ever put before me, but I did my best for him. I dropped all my own views of sense and nonsense. I told him that, taking all that he had told me as fact, the Presences might be either ordinary minds traversing Space in sleep; or minds such as his which had independently captured the sense of Space's quality; or, finally, the spirits of just men made perfect, behaving as psychical researchers think they do. It was a ridiculous task to set a prosaic man, and I wasn't quite serious. But Hollond was serious enough.

'He admitted that all three explanations were conceivable, but he was very doubtful about the first. The projection of the spirit into Space during sleep, he thought, was a faint and feeble thing, and these were powerful Presences. With the second and the third he was rather impressed. I suppose I should have seen what was happening and tried to stop it; at least, looking back that seems to have been my duty. But it was difficult to think that anything was wrong with Hollond; indeed, the odd thing is that all this time the idea of madness never entered my head. I rather backed him up. Somehow the thing took my fancy, though I thought it moonshine at the bottom of my heart. I enlarged on the pioneering before him. "Think," I told him, "what may be waiting for you. You may discover the meaning of Spirit. You may open up a new world, as rich as the old one, but imperishable.

You may prove to mankind their immortality and deliver them for ever from the fear of death. Why, man, you are picking at the lock of all the world's mysteries."

'But Hollond did not cheer up. He seemed strangely languid and dispirited. "That is all true enough," he said, "if you are right, if your alternatives are exhaustive. But suppose they are something else, something . . ." What that "something" might be he had apparently no idea, and very soon he went away.

'He said another thing before he left. He asked me if I ever read poetry, and I said, Not often. Nor did he: but he had picked up a little book somewhere and found a man who knew about the Presences. I think his name was Traherne, one of the seventeenth-century fellows. He quoted a verse which stuck to my fly-paper memory. It ran something like this:

> Within the region of the air,
> Compassed about with Heavens fair,
> Great tracts of lands there may be found,
> Where many numerous hosts,
> In those far distant coasts,
> For other great and glorious ends
> Inhabit, my yet unknown friends.

Hollond was positive he did not mean angels or anything of the sort. I told him that Traherne evidently took a cheerful view of them. He admitted that, but added: "He had religion, you see. He believed that everything was for the best. I am not a man of faith, and can only take comfort from what I understand. I'm in the dark, I tell you . . ."

'Next week I was busy with the Chilian Arbitration case, and saw nobody for a couple of months. Then one evening I ran against Hollond on the Embankment, and thought him looking horribly ill. He walked back with me to my rooms, and hardly uttered one word all the way. I gave him a stiff whisky-and-soda, which he gulped down absent-mindedly. There was that strained, hunted look in his eyes that you see in a frightened animal's. He was always lean, but now he had fallen away to skin and bone.

' "I can't stay long," he told me, "for I'm off to the Alps to-morrow and I have a lot to do." Before then he used to plunge readily into his story, but now he seemed shy about beginning. Indeed, I had to ask him a question.

' "Things are difficult," he said hesitatingly, "and rather distressing. Do you know, Leithen, I think you were wrong about – about what I spoke to you of. You said there must be one of three explanations. I am beginning to think that there is a fourth . . ."

'He stopped for a second or two, then suddenly leaned forward and gripped my knee so fiercely that I cried out. "That world is the Desolation," he said in a choking voice, "and perhaps I am getting near the Abomination of the Desolation that the old prophet spoke of. I tell you, man, I am on the edge of a terror, a terror," he almost screamed, "that no mortal can think of and live."

'You can imagine that I was considerably startled. It was lightning out of a clear sky. How the devil could one associate horror with mathematics? I don't see it yet . . . At any rate, I— You may be sure I cursed my folly for ever pretending to take him seriously. The only way would have been to have laughed him out of it at the start. And yet I couldn't, you know – it was too real and reasonable. Anyhow, I tried a firm tone now, and told him the whole thing was arrant raving bosh. I bade him be a man and pull himself together. I made him dine with me, and took him home, and got him into a better state of mind before he went to bed. Next morning I saw him off at Charing Cross, very haggard still, but better. He promised to write to me pretty often . . .'

The pony, with a great eleven-pointer lurching athwart its back, was abreast of us, and from the autumn mist came the sound of soft Highland voices. Leithen and I got up to go, when we heard that the rifle had made direct for the Lodge by a short cut past the Sanctuary. In the wake of the gillies we descended the Correi road into a glen all swimming with dim purple shadows. The pony minced and boggled; the stag's antlers stood out sharp on the rise against a patch of sky, looking like a skeleton tree. Then we dropped into a covert of birches and emerged on the white glen highway.

Leithen's story had bored and puzzled me at the start, but now it had somehow gripped my fancy. Space a domain of endless corridors and Presences moving in them! The world was not quite the same as an hour ago. It was the hour, as the French say, 'between dog and wolf', when the mind is disposed to marvels. I thought of my stalking on the morrow, and was miserably conscious that I would miss my stag. Those airy forms would get in the way. Confound Leithen and his yarns!

'I want to hear the end of your story,' I told him, as the lights of the Lodge showed half a mile distant.

'The end was a tragedy,' he said slowly. 'I don't much care to talk about it. But how was I to know? I couldn't see the nerve going. You see I couldn't believe it was all nonsense. If I could I might have seen. But I still think there was something in it – up to a point. Oh, I agree he went mad in the end. It is the only explanation. Something must have snapped in that fine brain, and he saw the little bit more which we call madness. Thank God, you and I are prosaic fellows ...

'I was going out to Chamonix myself a week later. But before I started I got a post card from Hollond, the only word from him. He had printed my name and address, and on the other side had scribbled six words – '*I know at last – God's mercy. – H. G. H.*' The handwriting was like a sick man of ninety. I knew that things must be pretty bad with my friend.

'I got to Chamonix in time for his funeral. An ordinary climbing accident – you probably read about it in the papers. The Press talked about the toll which the Alps took from intellectuals – the usual rot. There was an inquiry, but the facts were quite simple. The body was only recognised by the clothes. He had fallen several thousand feet.

'It seems that he had climbed for a few days with one of the Kronigs and Dupont, and they had done some hair-raising things on the Aiguilles. Dupont told me that they had found a new route up the Montanvert side of the Charmoz. He said that Hollond climbed like a "*diable fou*", and if you know Dupont's standard of madness you will see that the pace must have been pretty hot. "But monsieur was sick," he added; "his eyes were not good. And I and Franz, we were grieved for him and a little afraid. We were glad when he left us."

'He dismissed the guides two days before his death. The next day he spent in the hotel, getting his affairs straight. He left everything in perfect order, but not a line to a soul, not even to his sister. The following day he set out alone about three in the morning for the Grèpon. He took the road up the Nantillons glacier to the Col, and then he must have climbed the Mummery crack by himself. After that he left the ordinary route and tried a new traverse across the Mer de Glace face. Somewhere near the top he fell, and next day a party going to the Dent du Requin found him on the rocks thousands of feet below.

'He had slipped in attempting the most fool-hardy course on earth, and there was a lot of talk about the dangers of guideless climbing. But I guessed the truth, and I am sure Dupont knew, though he held his tongue ...'

We were now on the gravel of the drive, and I was feeling better. The thought of dinner warmed my heart and drove out the eeriness of the twilight glen. The hour between dog and wolf was passing. After all, there was a gross and jolly earth at hand for wise men who had a mind to comfort.

Leithen, I saw, did not share my mood. He looked glum and puzzled, as if his tale had aroused grim memories. He finished it at the Lodge door.

'... For, of course, he had gone out that day to die. He had seen the something more, the little bit too much, which plucks a man from his moorings. He had gone so far into the land of pure spirit that he must needs go further and shed the fleshly envelope that cumbered him. God send that he found rest! I believe that he chose the steepest cliff in the Alps for a purpose. He wanted to be unrecognisable. He was a brave man and a good citizen. I think he hoped that those who found him might not see the look in his eyes.'

The Green Glen

Written in 1911 and published the following January in *Blackwood's Magazine*, 'The Green Glen' was collected in *The Moon Endureth* (1912). It was one of only two of his stories – the other was 'The Far Islands' – that Buchan included in an anthology, *Modern Short Stories* (1926), which he edited for Nelson. It also appeared in the 1928 *Nelson Annual* but has not been available since then.

I

I FIRST SAW the Glen when I was eleven years old, a small boy consumed with a passion for trout. Adventuring on a rusty bicycle I had penetrated to remote dales, and made baskets in streams which no *Anglers' Guide* ever heard of. One day I had fished the sources of the Cauldshaw, and, the sun being yet high, be-thought me of the Fawn, which flowed on the other side of the narrow watershed. I shouldered my rod and tramped up the mossy spaces of the burn-head, till I waded deep in the bracken of the ridge. There on the summit the heather ended as if ruled by a gardener's line. I was looking into a narrow glen which ran from a round hope till a broad green hill baulked the view. From beginning to end there was no house, not even a sheepfold or a dyke. I remember my amazement at its indescribable greenness. There was the yellow-green of moss, the old velvet of mountain turf, the grey-green of bent on the hill-brow; but all was green, without tree or crag or heather bush to distract the eye. Through the middle of it ran the Fawn, a very fishable stream to my notion, and I ran down the brae with hope high in my heart.

But I never cast a fly in those waters. Long before I was down the hill the eeriness and the solitariness of the place weighed on my mind. There was no man here, and no sign of man. There were no whaups crying, or grouse to upbraid my presence. It was still as the grave, but for the lilt of the stream; and it was terribly green. I remembered a line of a song that ploughmen used to whistle – 'The wild glen sae green' – and I thought how much deeper this green wildness was than any rock and heather. The still slopes and folds of hill seemed to my unquiet eye to stretch to eternity.

At the edge of the burn was a rude mound, embanked like some Roman fort. With a fluttering heart I began to put my rod together. The Fawn dashed and swirled in noble pools, but I could not keep my eyes on it. The green hills shut me in, and the awe of them brooded over me. I was mortally afraid, and not ashamed of my fear. I could not give a name to it, but something uncanny was in the air: not terrible exactly, or threatening, but inhumanly strange. I clutched my rod – the butt and middle piece were put together – and fled the way I had come. I do not think I stopped running till I fell panting by the side of the Cauldshaw among the friendly heather.

II

Twenty years later, when the doings of eleven are a faint memory, chance set me fishing the lower streams of the Fawn. It was a clear June day, but the waters were too low and my basket was light. I fished like an epicure, a cast in each pool sufficing for me; and presently I had rounded the shoulder of the green hill which cuts the valley in two. They call it the Green Dod, and there is no greener hill in that green country. I found myself in an upland glen, where the Fawn had sunk to a mountain burn. The place was very soothing and quiet, and idly I wandered on, drinking in the peace of the hills. Then something in the contours awakened a memory, and I recalled my boyish escapade. The years have their consolations, for what had once terrified now charmed. I laughed at the scared little sinner, whose trembling legs had once twinkled up those braes. I put by my rod and abandoned myself to the delights of the greenness. Far up on the hill shoulders white sheep were dotted, but the water-side was empty. Not even a water-crow was visible, and in the patches of bog there was no sign of snipe. The place was full of a delicious desolation. There were the strait green sides, the Green Dod at the foot, a green hope at the head, and only the clear singing water stirred in the sunny afternoon.

I found a seat on a mound, and basked in deep content. It was the height of pastoral, yet without sheep or shepherd. The Fawn was a true Border stream, jewelled in sunlight, but wan as death under grey skies. I wondered how I had hitherto missed this happy valley. Nature had wrought it in a kindly mood, and hidden it very far from men. It must, I thought, have had a gracious history. There was no terror in its solitude. I could not imagine the cry of death from the burn, or harsh deeds done on those green lawns. Who had owned it in old days? Perhaps some Roman, pushing north with his bronze soldiers against the Picts, had been caught by its grace, and christened it by the name of his woodland god. True Thomas may have walked by its streams. But its story must have been chiefly of elves and fairy folk, for it wore the fairy livery.

I looked at the mound on which I sat, and saw that it had once been the site of a dwelling. It was all crisp moorland turf, gemmed with eye-bright and milkwort, but the rampart had been made by man. Scraping with the butt-end of my rod, I laid bare a chiselled block. This had been no sheepfold or shepherd's cot, but a tower.

The discovery stirred a fresh strain of fancy. Some old raider had had his keep here, and filled the glen with ill-gotten cattle. I pictured the forays returning over the green hills in some autumn twilight. I saw beacons fired on the tops, and the winter snows reddened with blood. Just then a cloud came over the sun, and the grace of the valley vanished. Now the stream ran wan, and I saw that the glen was wild and very lonely. Terror had dwelt here as well as peace. I remembered the boy of eleven, who on this very mound had picked up his rod and run.

That evening at Hardriding I hunted the library for local histories. They could not tell me much, being mostly the casual compilations of local ministers. But I found one thing of interest. I had been right about True Thomas. It seemed that the Rhymer had honoured the Fawn with a couplet of doubtful Latin:

> *Ubi Faunus fluit*
> *Spes mortalis ruit.*

I had no notion what he meant, and suspected the hand of the Reverend Mr Gilfillan *circa* 1780.

III

A broken leg gave me some leisure that winter, and I spent it in searching for the history of what I had come to call the Green Glen.

For two hundred years back it was plain going. Along with a dozen other valleys it had been swept into the net of the noble house which had built its fortunes on the fall of the turbulent little Border septs. Earlier it had been by turns in the hands of two families, both long perished – Home of Hardriding and Douglas of Cauldshaw. That took me back to the fourteenth century or thereabouts, where the history stopped short. But I found a charter of Melrose a century before, from which it appeared that the lands of Fawn, 'the nether and hither glens thereof', had been in the hands of the monks, who had profited by the good grazing. A chapel of Our Lady had stood by the burnside, endowed with a hundred merks a year by a certain Simon de Fries in penance for the slaying of an erring wife. There my tale ended, but I hazarded a guess. Fifty years ago a slab was found near Hadrian's Wall with a list of stations on the great road which ran north to the land of the Picts. You will find it copied in the Berlin *Corpus*, and there is much dispute about the identification of the names. One of them is a certain *Fauni Castellum*, which scholars have fastened on a dozen places between Ardoch and Melrose. I was myself convinced that the castellum was the mound in the Green Glen, the more so as Mr Gilfillan reported a find there of gold coins of the Antonines in 1758. It is true that the place was some miles from the main line of transit, but it would command the hill-roads from the West. Besides, might it not have been a sacred place, half fort, half shrine, an outpost of the dying faith? Why, otherwise, the strange name of the woodland god?

These were all my facts – too few on which to spin the delicate web of history. But my imagination was kindled, and I set to work. If I were right, this glen had a virtue which had drawn to it many races. Little as the recorded history was, it was far more than the due of an inconsiderable howe of the hills. Rome had made it a halting-place and consecrated it to her gods; the Church had built a shrine in it; two famous clans had fought furiously for its sake. My first impression was justified, for it had been no common place. Some ancient *aura* had brooded over its greenness and compelled men's souls.

Bit by bit from monkish Latin, from fragments of ballads, from cumbrous family histories, and from musty chronicles, I built up the shadow of a tale. Rome gave me nothing – the fog of years lay too thick over that greatest of mortal pages; but I hazarded a guess that the broken satyr's head, found in some unknown Border earthwork and now in the Grange collection, had come from my glen. Perhaps the Melrose monks had found it and copied it in their gargoyles. But of the Christian shrine I had something to tell. The chapel seems to have had an ill reputation for a holy place. The chapter of Melrose in or about 1250 held an inquisition into the doings of a certain John of Fawn, who tended the shrine with unhallowed service. There were complaints of his successor, a monk who bore the name of Lapidarius; and the grand climax was reached in the fate of one Andrew de Faun, a priest, says the record, who had the unpleasing gift '*diabolos convocandi*'. He was hand in glove with Lord Soulis, whose castle of Hermitage lay some twenty miles over the hills. Of his iniquities it is recorded that the country folk grew weary, and one October night surprised him at the business. He confessed his sins under the pressure of boiling lead, was duly burned, and his ashes cast into Tweed to be borne to the cleansing sea.

To the monks succeeded the Barons, the first being the tragically fated house of Home. But side by side with the record of their moorland wars I found a ballad history. Fawn had caught the fancy of the wandering minstrel. The heroine of the ghastly 'Riding of Etterick' had eyes 'grey as Fawn'. (The other reading 'grey as a fawn' is obvious nonsense.) The tryst for true love on Beltane's E'en was the Fawn side, and it was in the Green Glen that young Brokyn found himself asleep on his return from Fairyland.

> And when ye come to Fawn water,

says the wise wife in 'May Margaret',

> I bid ye lout fu' low,
> And say three prayers to Christes grace
> Afore ye ride the flow.

In the lovely fragment, 'The Thorn of Life', there is a variant, not given by Child, which tells how on Midsummer morning the lady washed herself with dew 'clear as dawn' – an absurd literary phrase which spoils the poem. My emendation 'Fawn' is, I take it, certain. In the later riding ballads the name is still more frequent. The doomed raider in 'Carlisle Town' swears that Fawn will run red as blood ere his wrongs are forgotten. In 'Castle Gay' the dying Home craves, like King David, for a draught of Fawn water; and in 'Lord Archibald's

Goodnight' there is a strange line about 'the holy wells of Fawn'. No doubt the line is corrupt, but the form of the corruption testifies to the spell of the Green Glen.

The Homes of Hardriding marched through disorder and violence to catastrophe. Never more than a hill clan, and kin to no powerful house, they persisted for three centuries by sheer audacity and pride. They held the Fawn glen and built a tower in it, but their real seat was Hardriding in the lower valley. The wave of Douglas aggression flowed round them, but they stoutly resisted, and it was only the power of the great Warden of the Marches that seized Fawnside for the Cauldshaw branch of his house. The battle in which Piers Home died by the hand of young Cauldshaw was fought in the Green Glen. Presently the Douglases were in trouble with the King, and a younger Piers, under a King's commission, won back his lands and chased Cauldshaw into Northumberland. The Douglas clan was as often as not in treaty with the English Warden, while the Hardriding folk were vehemently Scottish, and, alone of their name, gave a good account of themselves at Flodden. The fortunes of the two houses see-sawed so long as lands were won and kept by the strong arm alone. By and by came the day of smooth things, when a parchment was more potent than the sword, and both Home and Douglas withered, like hill plants brought into a lowland garden.

It was all an unedifying tale of blood and treason, but in reading it I was struck by one curious fact. Every critical event in the fortunes of the two clans befell in the Green Glen. There the leaders died in battle or in duel, and there a shameless victor celebrated his mastery. It was, so to speak, the citadel, of which the possession was the proof of triumph. It can have had but little value in itself, for the tower by the burn was scarcely a fortalice, and was never seriously dwelled in. Indeed, it is referred to not as a castle but as a 'bower'. When a Douglas defied a Home he summoned him to meet him by the 'Bower o' Fawn'. This same Bower was the centre of a pretty tale, when for once the blood-stained record emerges into the clear air of pastoral. The Fawn glen did not always pass by war; once it fell to the Douglases by marriage. Marjory of Hardriding, walking one evening by the stream, fell in with the young Douglas, sore wounded in a forest hunt. In the Bower she tended his wounds, and hid him from her fierce clan. Love ripened, and one July morn came the heir of Cauldshaw to Hardriding gates on an errand of peace. But the Home was surly, and the Douglas retired with a bitter denial and an arrow in his corselet. Thereupon Maid Marjory took the matter into her own hands, and rode over the hills to her lover. A gallant lady this, for, after a hurried wedding at the Kirk o' Shaws, she returned with her man to the Fawn Bower to confront an angry father and six angrier brothers. She offered peace or war, but declared that, if war it should be, she herself would fight in the first rank of the Douglases. Whereupon, it is said, old Piers, struck with wonder and delight at the courage he had begotten, declared for peace, and the Green Glen was her dowry.

IV

The thing became an obsession with me, and I could not let this nook of history alone. Weary hours were spent in the search for Homes and Douglases. Why I wasted my time thus I cannot tell. I told myself it was part of the spell of the Green Glen. 'The place was silent and *aware*,' as Browning says. I could not think that the virtue had departed and that the romance of Fawn was a past tale. Now it had no visitants save a shepherd taking a short cut or a fisherman with a taste for moorland trout. But some day a horseman on a fateful errand would stir its waters, or the Bower witness a new pastoral. I told myself that the wise years might ordain a long interval, but sooner or later they would ring up the curtain on the play.

A needle in a haystack was a simple quest compared to mine. History, which loves to leave fringes and loose threads, had cut the record of Home and Douglas with her sharpest shears. The two families disappeared within the same decade. Cauldshaw had chosen the king's side in the Covenant wars, and the head of the house, Sir Adam, had been a noted persecutor of the godly. He came to his end by a bullet of the Black Macmichael's somewhere in the hills of Galloway. His son had fought in the Scots Brigade for the French king, and returned about 1710 to find an estate broken by fines and penalties. We see him last riding south with Mackintosh in the 'Fifteen, but history does not tell us of his fate. He may have died with Derwentwater, or, more likely, he may have escaped and lain low till the hunt passed. Cauldshaw was forfeited and sold, and there was an end of it. Thirty years later I find a Douglas, a locksmith in the High Street of Edinburgh, who may have been his son, since he was gently born and yet clearly of no other known Douglas sept. After that the shears are at work. My note at the end of my researches was, 'merged in the burgesses of Edinburgh'.

Hardriding showed a similar tale, save that the Homes stood for the Covenant. One of them, Piers or Patrick, swung in the Grassmarket, and was the subject of the eulogies of Wodrow and Patrick Walker. An odd type of saint, his godliness was proved chiefly by his ferocity against the King's officers, for whom he would lie in wait behind a dyke with a musket. He died gallantly, declaiming the 23rd Psalm. The Jacobite rising brought Hardriding round to the side of Cauld-shaw. Home and Douglas rode south together, and the fate of the first at any rate is clear. He fell in the rout of Preston, charging with a mouthful of oaths and texts. He left landless sons who disappear into the mist, and the ancient name of Home of Hardriding died in the land. David Hume, the philosopher, in his cups used to claim kin with the house, but it is recorded that David's friends did not take him seriously.

V

About that time I used to try to analyse the impression the Green Glen made upon me. I went to it often and in all weathers, but especially in the soft June days and the flaming twilights of October. At first I thought that the attraction was the peace of it, Words-worth's 'sleep that is among the lonely hills'. Certainly it was very quiet and hallowed, with that brooding stillness which is a positive thing and not a mere absence of unrest. I have gone there, worried and distraught, and returned at ease with the world. Once, I remember, I came to it after fighting a forlorn bye-election in an English slum, with my brain fagged and dull and my nerves a torment. The Glen healed me, plunging me into the deeps of cool old-world shadows. But I soon discovered that the charm was not an opiate, but a stimulant. Its spell was the spell of life. It stirred the blood, comforting failure and nursing hope, but it did not lull to sleep. Once after a bad illness I went to Hardriding to rest, but I could not face the Glen. It only fevered a sick man. Its call was to action, and its ancient genius had no love for weaklings.

Often I tried to test it, to see if others could feel as I did. I was ridiculously unsuccessful. The sportsmen who frequented Hardriding, finding no grouse in the Glen, fought shy of it, and, if chance took them there, lamented the absence of heather. 'Pretty place,' one young man observed to me, 'but no more Scotch than my hat. It might be Sussex. Where's the brown heath and shaggy wood? What! There isn't cover for a tomtit. It's a nasty big slice out of Harry's shooting to have that long bare place taking up room.' It was too remote for ladies to picnic in, but one who penetrated as far called it 'sweet', and said it reminded her of Dartmoor. The people of the neighbourhood were no better. Keepers took the same view as the Hardriding sportsmen, and the farmer whose lease covered it spoke of it darkly as 'Poverty Neuk'. 'Food for neither man nor beast,' he said. 'Something might be done with phosphates, but I've no money to spend. It would make a grand dam if any town wanted a water-supply.' Good business-like views, but no hint anywhere of the strangeness which to me had made it a kind of sanctuary.

There was one exception, the shepherd of the Nine Stane Rig. He was a young man, with a fiery red head and a taste for poetry. He would declaim Burns and Hogg with gusto, and was noted at 'kirns' and weddings for his robust rendering of songs like 'When the Kye come Hame', and 'Robin Tamson's Smiddy'. I used to accompany him sometimes on his rounds, and he spoke to me of the Green Glen.

'It's a bonny bit,' he once said, waving his arm towards the Green Dod. 'And there's ae queer thing about it. Sheep 'll no bide in it. Ye may pit a hirsel in it at nicht, and every beast 'll be on the tap o' the rig by the mornin'. How d'ye account for that? Mr Yellowlees says the feedin's no guid, and that it wants phosphates. I dinna agree wi' him. I've herdit a' my days, and I never saw better feedin' than by yon burnside. I've no just fawthomed it yet, but I've an idea o' my ain. I think the glen is an auld kirk-yaird. I mind when I herdit in Eskdalemuir there was a bit on the hill whaur Covenanters had been buried, and the sheep were aye sweir to gang near it. Some day I'm thinkin' o' gettin' a spade and howkin'. I micht find something queer ...'

VI

I came to regard the Green Glen as my own exclusive property, which shared with me a secret. It was a pleasant intimacy, and I had resigned myself to its limits, conscious that the curtain of the past was drawn too close to allow more than one little chink to be seen. Then one day Fate brought Linford across my path.

I had known him slightly for several years. I can see him now as I first knew him, a big solemn young man, too heavy for elegance, and an awkward weight for a horse. We first met one spring at Valescure, and a lonely fortnight established a kind of friendship between us. He was a modest being, full of halting sympathies and interests, for which he rarely found words. His family had been settled for two generations in Australia, sheep-farming in the good days when the big profits were made. His father had made a second fortune in a gold mine, and, disliking the land legislation of the country, had sold his farms and brought his boy to England. An undistinguished progress through a public school and Oxford had left him without a profession, and, his father having died, with no near relations, and a ridiculous amount of money. He should have been a soldier, but somehow had missed his chance. The man was in no way slack, but he gave me the impression of having no niche to fit into. He was very English in speech and manners, but he seemed to stand outside all the ordinary English occupations and look on. Not that he didn't do most things well. He was a magnificent shot, a first-rate horseman, and the best man to sail a boat I have ever met. He read much, had travelled considerably, and had a keen interest in scientific geography. I thought he had found a job when he took a notion of exploring the Brahmaputra gorges, but the expedition fell through and his interest flagged. He belonged to many clubs, and had a few hundred acquaintances; but beyond myself I don't think he had a friend.

He used to come to see me, and I tried to understand what puzzled him. For puzzled he was – not unhappy or disillusioned, but simply puzzled with life. Somehow he did not fit in with the world around him. I used to think it would have been better if he had never left Australia. There he had a ready-made environment; here in England he had to make his own, and he did not seem to have the knack of it. People liked him, and thought him, for all his stiffness, a good fellow. But he never accepted anybody or anything as his own; he was always the observant and sympathetic stranger. I began to realise that my friend, with all his advantages, was desperately homeless.

To myself, as I thought about him, I prescribed marriage. *Vix ea nostra voco* might have been his motto about most things, but in a wife he would find something his very own. The thing was obvious, but I saw also that he would be a hard fellow to marry. He was hopelessly shy and curiously unimpressionable. I do not remember that he ever

[207]

spoke to me of any woman, and he avoided every chance of meeting them. I only once saw his tall figure at a dance, when he looked like nothing so much as Marius among the ruins of Carthage.

Hunting was his main hobby, and one January I found myself staying under the same roof with him in the Cottesmore country. He was, as I have said, a bold and fine rider, but he had to know his horse, and on this occasion our host mounted both of us. There was an ugly banked fence where he misjudged his animal's powers, and came down in a heap on a hardish bit of ground. I thought his neck was broken, and prepared for the worst, as I helped three other white-faced men to get him clear. But it was only a slight concussion, a broken finger, and a dislocated shoulder. He had a bad night, but next day was little the worse for his fall, and, frost having set in, I spent most of the afternoon in his bedroom.

He wore a ring which I had often noticed, a little engraved carnelian in a heavy setting of Australian gold. In doctoring his hand it had been removed, and now lay on the dressing-table. We were talking idly of runs and spills, and, as we talked, I picked it up and examined it.

The stone was old and curious. There was no motto, and the carving seemed to be a heart transfixed by an arrow. I thought it the ordinary trumpery love token – Cupid and his darts – when I noticed something more. The heart was crowned, and the barb transfixing it was not an arrow but a spear.

The sight roused me to the liveliest interest. For the cognisance belonged to one house and one house alone. It was Douglas of Cauldshaw who had carried the family badge with this strange difference. Mary of Scots, it was said, had given him the spear, for to the last they had stood by that melancholy lady.

'Where did you get this?' I asked.

'What? The ring? It was my father's. An ugly thing.'

I looked at it again. 'It has an odd crest. Did you ever inquire about it?'

He said No. He knew little heraldry, and didn't want to pretend to what didn't belong to him. Then he corrected himself. He thought that the thing was a family relic, right enough. His father had got the stone in turn from his mother, and had had it reset. He thought, but he wasn't sure, that it had been a long time in his grandmother's family.

'What was her name?' I asked eagerly.

The answer was disappointing. 'Brown,' he said. 'They had the Wooramanga place.'

I asked if they came from Scotland. 'No,' he said. 'They were Yorkshire, I think. But wait a bit. I think – yes – I have heard my father say something about the Browns being Scotch – Brouns, you know.'

This was a false scent and I tried again. But Linford had nothing to tell me. He had no family papers or jewels or pictures, nothing but the one ring. I could see that he was puzzled at my interest, and to my horror offered to pay the Heralds' College to investigate matters. I made him promise to let the Heralds alone, and tried to get more about his grandmother. She had been a tall, thin old lady, as he remembered her, with a north-country accent. She had disliked Melbourne intensely. That was all he could tell; not a saying or a rhyme or a memory to link her with those who had borne the ring's cognisance.

I heard, however, another startling thing that afternoon. Linford, blushing delightfully, confessed that he was in love. He had no chance, of course, wasn't good enough, and all the rest of it. When I heard that the lady was Virginia Dasent I was inclined to agree with him. Miss Dasent was very high game for Linford to fly at – or for anybody.

VII

Language is too coarse a medium in which to give a true portrait of Miss Virginia. Airy diaphanous colours and the sharp fineness of marble are needed; and something more, something to recapture that grace, wild and birdlike and only half mortal, which for three seasons turned all our heads. She was an astounding success. Coming from nowhere, and as innocent as a child of ambition, she made every man her most hopeless and humble servant. I think her charm was her pure girlishness – neither childish nor womanly, you understand. She had the air of one who faces the world frankly but does not accept it. She was a changeling, a wanderer, a dainty solitary figure on the weary old roads of life. I remember thinking, when I first saw her, that she might have stood for a statue of incarnate Wonder.

I knew her a little, well enough to see the hopelessness of my friend's case. She was an American – from one of the Carolinas, I believe; and Lady Amysfort took her about in London. I do not think that they were related. I hope my friends beyond the Atlantic will forgive me for saying that Miss Virginia was like no American I have ever met. Not that she had any of the sad homeless vulgarity of the denationalised. She was a fervent patriot, and had a delicious variety of the national humour. But I could not fit her in with her great continent. Indeed, I could not place her anywhere in any society. She belonged to some fanciful world of her own; but all the time she seemed to me to be looking for something – perhaps for her lost material heritage.

I was more interested, however, in Linford than in Miss Dasent. I could find out no more from him about his forbears, but I wondered if the Glen could tell me anything. Supposing I took him there, unprepared, of course, by any warning of mine, might not he feel the spell of it? If he did, I would be convinced of the Douglas blood; for I was certain that not otherwise would so prosaic a being feel so subtle a charm.

I persuaded him to take the Hardriding shootings; with an option to purchase, too, for Harry's finances were now past praying for. The chance came two days before the Twelfth, when he and I were alone in the house. It was a mild, blue August day, with clear distances and a cool breeze, and as we rounded the Green Dod I thought that my Glen was nobly dressed for us. I had hoped for some cry of delight, but none came. Linford stalked through the bent, muttering something about black-game.

We came to the mound by the waterside, Maid Marjory's Bower, and stretched ourselves on the scented turf. Then a curious thing happened to me. A light wind came up the stream, rippling the pools and sending a grey shiver over the grasses. Suddenly I became oppressed with a mortal fear. I must have lain limp and white, looking dumbly at the opposite hill. I had no notion what I feared, but it was worse than my old boyish adventure, for, though I longed madly to flee, I knew I could not. The Green Glen was trying me, and if I failed I had lost its secret for ever. I shut my teeth, and for a second or two hung at the limit of my endurance. Then it all passed. I found myself lying back on the mound, desperately sleepy and dripping with sweat, as if I had run twenty miles.

I mopped my brow and looked at Linford. He was quite unperturbed, and had got out his pouch and was filling his pipe. He glanced at me curiously.

'You're in pretty bad condition, old chap,' he observed. 'You'll founder on the Twelfth if you drip like this in an afternoon saunter.'

He got up and stretched himself. 'Let's go back,' he said. 'There isn't a beast or bird in the place. I am glad I came here, for it will keep us from wasting time over it.'

I followed him, still shaky and acutely disappointed. The Glen had nothing to say to him. The ring was an accident, and the Cauldshaw stock was still to find. And yet, as we walked home, I began to doubt. The Glen had been not for Douglas or Home alone, but for both. What if a Home were needed to complete the circuit?

It was a possible explanation. Besides, the extraordinary seizure which had befallen me that afternoon seemed to argue that the visit had not been meaningless. I was perfectly well and normal, and I had sat on the mound a hundred times before. Might it not be that the Glen had been stirred, and was striving to tell us its secret? Then I began to laugh, and told myself that I was a fool to treat my fancies as solid facts.

VIII

That winter was made memorable to me, and a good many others, by Virginia Dasent. The Amysforts went to Egypt, leaving her very much to her own devices. She hunted a little and spent some time in country houses; but mostly she was to be found in London, a city for which she had an inordinate love. This was bad for Linford, who stayed devotedly in town, and being deprived of healthful exercise put on flesh and lost spirits. I found him in the club one afternoon in a very bad temper. I alone knew of his hopeless plight, and with me he did not trouble to keep up appearances.

'I get no forrarder,' he groaned. 'She tolerates me as she tolerates everybody else. Lord, how I hate that kind smile of hers! She isn't a woman, Jack. She's an adorable sort of bird that flits about and never settles. You know the way she holds her head forward and peers away beyond you. She's always preening for another flight.'

Love was making him a psychologist, for Miss Virginia's maddening charm lay in just that birdlike detachment. We had become very good friends, she and I; and often of a late afternoon we talked in the Amysforts' big ugly drawing-room. She liked me because I was interested in old things and odd bypaths, for I found that the child bubbled over with romance. A lonely girlhood in some Carolinian manor had given her fancy rich feeding. Half in a world of books, half in a world of pure dreaming, she took her airy way. She had about as much worldliness as St Theresa, and much less worldly knowledge. Frankly, I was a little afraid for her; some day disillusion would come, and come cruelly. There was a loneliness about her, as about Linford, but it was the loneliness of a happy preoccupation. Some day those wondering eyes would find the world less marvellous, and then her heart would break. Or would she carry her fresh childlike interest undimmed to the end? I could not tell, but I argued badly for Linford's chances. He was far too eligible – young, good-looking, preposterously rich. The man who was to win Miss Virginia's heart, I thought, must come riding in the fearless old fashion. Linford was as romantic in the ordinary sense of the word as a Republican senator of Virginia's native land.

That was my first impression, but I found cause to alter it slightly. As I came to know her better, new avenues opened up in her soul. She had an excellent brain, very clear, shrewd and subtle, and behind all her fancies I was aware of a solid rock of common-sense. She was not a ready talker, and never rhapsodised. Little odd phrases, a shrug and a laugh, gave the key to her whimsical world. But on a matter of prosaic fact I found her amazingly practical. More than once she offered me advice, with a little wise air which spoke of youth, but with a penetration, too, which took my breath away. I put my surprise into words. 'Of course I'm practical,' she said. 'I'm more than half Scotch, you know.'

I thought nothing of it at the time, for American girls have a habit of being either Scotch or early Norman. I remember asking her if she had ever been to Scotland, and she said – No; not yet. She had not had time. But some day ...

I was inclined to be a little angry with both her and Linford. He went about like a sheep, a ridiculous figure of purposeless melancholy, and the deeper he sank in this mood the worse it was for his chances. As for the lady, I began to think her almost inhuman. I wondered if she were not perfectly heartless, hollow within like an Ell-woman. She seemed unconscious of the havoc she was causing everywhere. I think I would have preferred a common flirt to that unearthly aloofness. But her eyes used always to make me revise my judgments: they were so innocent and young. Some day she would awaken, I told myself. Some day the sleeping princess would be kissed into life. But I was pretty certain that, unless a miracle happened, it would be none of Linford's doing.

It was one morning in the Park in early May that she exploded the mine under my feet. She had been riding with Linford, and turned, as I came up, to accompany me. I don't know what they had been talking about, but her eyes were shining, her colour high, and her lips very tight.

'We have been discussing Scotch places,' she volunteered. 'It is very tiresome. I wanted a place, and Mr Linford seems to have got a long lease of it. He offered to make it over to me, but of course that was impossible. It's a great nuisance, for I had set my heart on it.'

I asked the name, and even as I asked I think I guessed the answer.

'Hardriding,' she said. 'A little old place in the Borders. My family lived there long ago, and I have always meant to make a pilgrimage to it. Caroline Amysfort is going to Bayreuth, so I shall set up as hostess on my own account. If I can't get Hardriding I must have Cauldshaw. Will you come and stay with me?'

I listened to her, I hope, with an impassive face, but inwardly I was a volcano of excitement. Hardriding and Cauldshaw! Home and Douglas! Was the circuit by some amazing chance to be completed? I wondered how soon I could decently make an appointment with Miss Virginia and get the whole story. She was going away for the week end, but would be free on Tuesday, rather late. I hugged my impatience for three beastly days.

I had expected a fragment, and found instead a complete and well-authenticated tale. I blessed that lovable American seriousness about genealogies. There was the pedigree neatly inscribed, with excerpts from registers and letters, as business-like, as irrefutable, as a share certificate. After old Sir Piers fell at Preston his eldest son, Gideon, fled to France, and thence to the Canadas. He fought under the French flag, and rose to a colonelcy before he fell at Quebec. He had married a Frenchwoman, and their son – Lewis, I think – took to the sea and did good trade in the smuggling and privateering line along the New England coast. He settled in North Carolina, and, being rich from his ventures, bought a handsome property, and built a manor-house in the colonial style. With his grand-daughter the male line of Home –

Miss Virginia pronounced it to rhyme with 'loam' – ended. She married a Dasent, son of a neighbouring squire, and was Miss Virginia's grandmother. There it was, all set down in black and white, and very prettily she expounded it to me. I had found the Hardriding stock at last. It had come back to me out of the mist with ample credentials.

Miss Virginia at Cauldshaw, Linford at Hardriding, and between them the Green Glen! Surely the stage was being set at last for the play. My first impulse was to tell her the whole romance. I pictured her delight; I saw the prosaic Linford take on the colour of poetry. But a scruple deterred me. It would be breaking faith with the Green Glen. If the spell were there it needed no preparation of mine for its working. Those starry influences called for respectful treatment. I would go to Hardriding, and some day – some mellow autumn day – Miss Virginia would cross the hills, and Linford would be there by the Bower to meet her!

Meanwhile all that summer the course of true love ran badly. The two were friends after a fashion, but Linford was such a clumsy and uneasy being, and Miss Virginia so swift and evasive, that it seemed impossible that that friendship could ripen. I got very sick of the whole business, angry with Linford, and puzzled about the lady. At one moment I called her inhuman, at another angelic; but, whatever view one took (and after all they came to the same conclusion), she was the most heartbreaking beauty. Her wild childlike eyes looked through one as if to a pleasant country beyond. There is a Greek fable, isn't there? about some hero who needed the touch of his mother the Earth to give him strength. I wondered if she would ever find that earth-kinship, which means common humanity.

IX

In early August the Lammas floods were high, so that sultriness was purged from the air and the world left clean and rain-washed and sweet-scented. I was staying at Cauldshaw, in a small party which tried in vain to induce its dancing hostess to be still. She was in wild spirits, out at all hours, a crony of shepherds, already learned in the ways of the moors. She had come back, she said, to her own country, and lived every hour in a whirl of delight and wonder. The long round-shouldered hills, the clear burns, the homely simplicity of the old land ravished her heart. I counted the days till I could take her to the Green Glen.

Then the party melted away, and it was arranged that she should pay a visit of state to Hardriding. I also was bidden, and Linford spent his days in a fever of expectation. Miss Virginia was scrupulous about the details. She would walk across the hills by the old raiding road from Cauldshaw. I showed her the way, which traversed the Green Glen, and on the map I pointed out the Bower. She clapped her hands with delight at my tale – the barest sketch – of the Home doings. 'What an adventure!' she cried. 'I shall tell you all about it at dinner. I feel like a princess coming home to her kingdom.'

I sincerely hoped that she was. If the Fates were kind this airy spirit should feel the antique spell of earth, and I dared to think that two wanderers might find a home.

To this hour I remember every incident of that autumn day. It was the 3rd of September. The morning broke cold and misty, but by ten o'clock the sun had burned up the rime, and the hills slept in a bright windless calm. I was shooting with Linford, and set out from Cauldshaw at eleven o'clock. Miss Virginia was to leave after luncheon, and, if she followed my directions, would be at Hardriding by six. She would reach the Green Glen about four o'clock, and I laid my plans accordingly.

I shot vilely, for I was full of a curious sense of anticipation. So was Linford, but nothing could impair his skill. We talked very little, I remember; but it took some manœuvring on my part to have the afternoon beat where I wanted it. Linford would have had us try the moors near the house, for his mind was always turning to Hardriding; but after some persuasion I got him to keep to the hills by the Nine Stane Rig, where we looked down on the Green Glen. Had I told him that Miss Virginia was walking, he would have set off then and there to meet her, and spoiled everything. He kept asking me when she would start. 'She'll have to go round by the Red Ford,' he repeated, 'and that means Hardriding at tea-time. We needn't stay too long up here. Hardriding is her family place, so to speak, and I want to be there to welcome her.'

Shortly after three we stood on the summit of the Dun Rig, and as I watched the green shoulders of the Fawn Hope I saw a figure cross the sky-line. Then I told Linford the truth. I bade him go up the Glen to meet her and wait for her at the Bower. He looked at me shyly. 'You arranged all this?' he asked. 'Thanks very much, old man. You've been a pretty good friend to me.'

I set off for Hardriding without a glance behind. The Glen was now no place for me. Looking back at my frame of mind, I can see nothing but exhilaration. Some great thing was about to befall two people whom I loved. I had no doubt of the virtue of the place. By devious paths I had brought back to it its old masters. It had whispered its secret to me, and I had repaid it. For the moment I felt that time was not, that death was little, and change a mockery. The wise years let nothing die, and always the circle came full again, bringing back lost hopes and dreams. The still and golden afternoon spoke the same message to my heart. I felt the serene continuance of all things, the sense of something eternal behind the trivial ways of man.

I reached Hardriding a little after four, and according to my plan sat down to read and smoke. But I soon found that idleness was impossible. I was strung too high with expectation. I wandered into the library, and then into the garden, but my eyes were always turning to the shoulder of hill which marked the opening of the Fawn Glen. Then I resolved to go to meet Linford. Whatever had happened, it would be right for me to welcome Miss Virginia to Hardriding.

Before I had crossed the lawns my mood changed utterly. I suddenly became a prey to black forebodings. The doggerel Latin of True Thomas rang in my head like the croak of a raven:

> *Ubi Faunus fluit*
> *Spes mortalis ruit.*

I tried to laugh at it. I told myself that the verses were no doubt the work of a foolish eighteenth-century parson. What harm could follow the meeting of two friends in a hill glen where their forbears had fought and loved? But I reasoned in vain. A deadly depression overmastered me. The light had gone out of the sky, and the bent, all yellow in the westering sun, seemed wan as death.

> Where Fawn flows
> Man's hope goes.

The dolorous refrain would not leave me.

I emerged from the park into the water-meadows where Fawn runs deep among flags and meadow-sweet. Beyond them I came to the lower glen, where the fir-clad slopes leave a thin strip of pasture by the stream. Here I should have met the two, but there was no sign of them. I looked at my watch and found it after five.

Then I began to quicken my pace. My depression had turned to acute anxiety. Before me was half a mile of open strath, and then the Green Dod, where the Glen turned sharply to the right. I ran that half-mile with dread in my heart of what I might see beyond it. But when I came to the Green Dod there was still no sign of a human being. The Fawn flows round the shoulder of hill in a narrow defile, at the upper end of which begins the Green Glen. I resolved to wait there, for I realised that I could not enter the Glen. I can give no reason for this, but I knew the truth of it. My feet could not have carried me round the shoulder of hill.

I did not wait long. Suddenly down the defile came a single figure. It was Linford, but even to my distraught sight a different Linford from him I had known. As I have said he was a big fellow, a little ungainly, a little afraid of his size. But now he was a noble figure of a man, and as he strode along there was a strange mastery and dignity in him. But why was he alone? I blinked my eyes, for I saw that he was not alone. He carried in his arms something slim and white and very quiet. I crouched behind a boulder as he came near, but he had no eyes for anything but his burden. His head was bent over it, and his face was wild and drawn with grief. Then I saw that a fair head lay limply in the crook of his arm, and that the face was very pale . . .

The doctors called it heart failure. Miss Virginia, said one of them in a moment of poetry, had for years had a frail chariot for her body and the horses of her spirit had driven too fiercely. She must have had heart trouble, though no one had diagnosed it. The hill walk from Cauld-shaw had been too much for her. The same man spoke wisely about the evils of our modern life. 'Most people to-day,' he said, 'have temperaments that prey on their bodies. They must live at white heat and the shell cracks . . .'

Years afterwards, when time had taken the edge off his grief, Linford told me something of what happened. 'She met me, looking very well and jolly, and we walked to the place you call the Bower. You may laugh at me, but I tell you I had a presentiment that something was going to happen, but I couldn't be sure whether it was good or bad . . . She looked all round the Glen and sighed happily, as if she had found what she liked very much. Then suddenly she gave a little cry and went very white. I caught her, and saw that she was all in a shiver. She was staring at the burn, and her eyes were round and frightened like a deer's. Then she smiled again, and turned to me with a look – Oh, my God, I can never forget it! It was so kind and happy and . . . She must have cared for me all the time, and like a blind fool I didn't know it. She put her arms round my neck and said, "My ain true love" – I suppose she was quoting from a Scotch song. And just as I was bursting with joy I felt her cheek grow cold . . .'

Now it is a curious thing, but in the *Scotichronicon* of Hume of Calzeat – it is in manuscript, and I do not think any one living has read it besides myself – there is a version of the story of Maid Marjory. And according to that version, when the lady confronted her father in the Green Glen, she put her arm around the Douglas's neck, and said, 'My ain true love.'

The Riding of Ninemileburn

'The Riding of Ninemileburn' was published in *Blackwood's Magazine* in April 1912, *The Living Age* the following month, and was then included in *The Moon Endureth* (1912) but has not been in print for over eighty years.

———

SIM BENT OVER the meal ark and plumbed its contents with his fist. Two feet and more remained: provender – with care – for a month, till he harvested the waterside corn and ground it at Ashkirk mill. He straightened his back, better pleased; and, as he moved, the fine dust flew into his throat and set him coughing. He choked back the sound till his face crimsoned.

But the mischief was done. A woman's voice, thin and weary, came from the ben-end.

The long man tiptoed awkwardly to her side. 'Canny, lass,' he crooned. 'It's me back frae the hill. There's a mune and a clear sky, and I'll hae the lave under thack and rape the morn. Syne I'm for Ninemileburn, and the coo 'ill be i' the byre by Setterday. Things micht be waur, and we'll warstle through yet. There was mair tint at Flodden.'

The last rays of October daylight that filtered through the straw lattice showed a woman's head on the pillow. The face was white and drawn, and the great black eyes – she had been an Oliver out of Megget – were fixed in the long stare of pain. Her voice had the high lilt and the deep undertones of the Forest.

'The bairn 'ill be gone ere ye ken, Sim,' she said wearily. 'He canna live without milk, and I've nane to gie him. Get the coo back or lose the son I bore ye. If I were my ordinar' I wad hae't in the byre, though I had to kindle Ninemileburn ower Wat's heid.'

She turned miserably on her pillow and the babe beside her set up a feeble crying. Sim busied himself with stirring up the peat fire. He knew too well that he would never see the milk-cow till he took with him the price of his debt or gave a bond on harvested crops. He had

had a bad lambing, and the wet summer had soured his shallow lands. The cess to Branksome was due, and he had had no means to pay it. His father's cousin of the Ninemileburn was a brawling fellow, who never lacked beast in byre or corn in bin, and to him he had gone for the loan. But Wat was a hard man, and demanded surety; so the one cow had travelled the six moorland miles and would not return till the bond was cancelled. As well might he try to get water from stone as move Wat by any tale of a sick wife and dying child.

The peat smoke got into his throat and brought on a fresh fit of coughing. The wet year had played havoc with his chest, and his lean shoulders shook with the paroxysms. An anxious look at the bed told him that Marion was drowsing, so he slipped to the door.

Outside, as he had said, the sky was clear. From the plashy hillside came the rumour of swollen burns. Then he was aware of a man's voice shouting.

'Sim,' it cried, 'Sim o' the Cleuch ... Sim.' A sturdy figure came down through the scrog of hazel and revealed itself as his neighbour of the Dodhead. Jamie Telfer lived five miles off in Ettrick, but his was the next house to the Cleuch shieling.

Telfer was running, and his round red face shone with sweat. 'Dod, man, Sim, ye're hard o' hearing. I was routin' like to wake the deid, and ye never turned your neck. It's the fray I bring ye. Mount and ride to the Carewoodrig. The word's frae Branksome. I've but Ranklehope to raise, and then me and William's Tam will be on the road to join ye.'

'Whatna fray?' Sim asked blankly.

'Ninemileburn. Bewcastle's marching. They riped the place at cockcrow, and took twenty-six kye, five horse, and a walth o' plenishing. They were seen fordin' Teviot at ten afore noon, but they're gaun round by Ewes Water, for they durstna try the Hermitage Slack. Forbye they move slow, for the bestial's heavy wark to drive. They shut up Wat in the auld peel, and he didna win free till bye midday. Syne he was off to Branksome, and the word frae Branksome is to raise a Ettrick, Teviotdale, Ale Water, and the Muirs o Esk. We look to win up wi' the lads long ere they cross Liddel, and that at the speed they gang will be gey an' near sunrise. It's a braw mune for the job.'

Jamie Telfer lay on his face by the burn and lapped up water like a dog. Then without another word he trotted off across the hillside beyond which lay the Ranklehope.

Sim had a fit of coughing and looked stupidly at the sky. Here was the last straw. He was dog-tired, for he had had little sleep the past week. There was no one to leave with Marion, and Marion was too weak to tend herself. The word was from Branksome, and at another time Branksome was to be obeyed. But now the thing was past reason. What use was there for a miserable careworn man to ride among the swank well-fed lads in the Bewcastle chase?

And then he remembered his cow. She would be hirpling with the rest of the Ninemileburn beasts on the road to the Border. The case was more desperate than he had thought. She was gone for ever unless he helped Wat to win her back. And if she went, where was the milk for the child?

He stared hopelessly up at a darkening sky. Then he went to the lean-to where his horse was stalled. The beast was fresh, for it had not been out for two days – a rough Forest shelty with shaggy heels and a mane like a thicket. Sim set his old saddle on it, and went back to the house.

His wife was still asleep, breathing painfully. He put water on the fire to boil, and fetched a handful of meal from the ark. With this he made a dish of gruel, and set it by the bedside. He drew a pitcher of water from the well, for she might be thirsty. Then he banked up the fire and steeked the window. When she woke she would find food and drink, and he would be back before the next darkening. He dared not look at the child.

The shelty shied at a line of firelight from the window, as Sim flung himself wearily on its back. He had got his long ash spear from its place among the rafters, and donned his leather jacket with the iron studs on breast and shoulder. One of the seams gaped. His wife had been mending it when her pains took her.

He had ridden by Commonside and was high on the Caerlanrig before he saw signs of men. The moon swam in a dim dark sky, and the hills were as yellow as corn. The round top of the Wisp made a clear mark to ride by. Sim was a nervous man, and at another time would never have dared to ride alone by the ruined shieling of Chasehope, where folk said a witch had dwelt long ago and the Devil still came in the small hours. But now he was too full of his cares to have room for dread. With his head on his breast he let the shelty take its own road through the mosses.

But on the Caerlanrig he came on a troop of horse. They were a lusty crowd, well-mounted and armed, with iron basnets and corselets that jingled as they rode. Harden's men, he guessed, with young Harden at the head of them. They cried him greeting as he fell in at the tail. 'It's Long Sim o' the Cleuch,' one said; 'he's sib to Wat or he wadna be here. Sim likes his ain fireside better than the 'Bateable Land.'

The companionship of others cheered him. There had been a time, before he brought Marion from Megget, when he was a well-kenned figure on the Borders, a good man at weaponshows and a fierce fighter when his blood was up. Those days were long gone; but the gusto of them returned. No man had ever lightlied him without paying scot. He held up his head and forgot his cares and his gaping jacket. In a little they had topped the hill, and were looking down on the young waters of Ewes.

The company grew, as men dropped in from left and right. Sim recognised the wild hair of Charlie of Geddinscleuch, and the square shoulders of Adam of Frodslaw. They passed Mosspaul, a twinkle far down in the glen, and presently came to the long green slope which is called the Carewoodrig, and which makes a pass from Ewes to Hermitage. To Sim it seemed that an army had encamped on it. Fires had been lit in a howe, and wearied men slept by them. These were the runners, who all day had been warning the dales. By one fire stood the great figure of Wat o' the Ninemileburn, blaspheming to the skies and counting his losses. He had girded on a long sword, and for better precaution had slung an axe on his back. At the sight of young Harden he held his peace. The foray was Branksome's and a Scott must lead.

Dimly and stupidly, for he was very weary, Sim heard word of the enemy. The beasts had travelled slow, and would not cross Liddel till sunrise. Now they were high up on Tarras water, making for Liddel at a ford below the Castletown. There had been no time to warn the Elliots, but the odds were that Lariston and Mangerton would be out by morning.

'Never heed the Elliots,' cried young Harden. 'We can redd our ain frays, lads. Haste and ride, and we'll hae Geordie Musgrave long ere he wins to the Ritterford. Borrowstonemoss is the bit for us.' And with the light Scott laugh he was in the saddle.

They were now in a land of low marshy hills, which made ill-going. A companion gave Sim the news. Bewcastle had five-score men and the Scots fourscore and three. 'It's waur to haud than to win,' said the man. 'Ae man can tak' ten beasts when three 'ill no keep them. There'll be bluidy war on Tarras side ere the nicht's dune.'

Sim was feeling his weariness too sore for speech. He remembered that he had tasted no food for fifteen hours. He found his meal-poke and filled his mouth, but the stuff choked him. It only made him cough fiercely, so that Wat o' the Ninemileburn, riding before him, cursed him for a broken-winded fool. Also he was remembering about Marion, lying sick in the darkness twenty miles over the hills.

The moon was clouded, for an east wind was springing up. It was ill riding on the braeface, and Sim and his shelty floundered among the screes. He was wondering how long it would all last. Soon he must fall down and be the scorn of the Border men. The thought put Marion out of his head again. He set his mind on tending his horse and keeping up with his fellows.

Suddenly a whistle from Harden halted the company. A man came running back from the crown of the rig. A whisper went about that Bewcastle was on the far side, in the little glen called the Brunt Burn. The men held their breath, and in the stillness they heard far off the sound of hooves on stones and the heavy breathing of cattle.

It was a noble spot for an ambuscade. The Borderers scattered over the hillside, some riding south to hold the convoy as it came down the glen. Sim's weariness lightened. His blood ran quicker; he remembered that the cow, his child's one hope, was there before him. He found himself next his cousin Wat, who chewed curses in his great beard. When they topped the rig they saw a quarter of a mile below them the men they sought. The cattle were driven in the centre, with horsemen in front and rear and flankers on the braeside.

'Hae at them, lads,' cried Wat o' the Ninemileburn, as he dug spurs into his grey horse. From farther down the glen he was answered with a great shout of 'Branksome'.

Somehow or other Sim and his shelty got down the steep braeface. The next he knew was that the raiders had turned to meet him – to meet him alone, it seemed; the moon had come out again, and their faces showed white in it. The cattle, as the driving ceased, sank down wearily in the moss. A man with an iron ged turned, cursing, to receive Wat's sword on his shoulder-bone. A light began to blaze from down the burn – Sim saw the glitter of it out of the corner of an eye – but the men in front were dark figures with white faces.

The Bewcastle lads were stout fellows, well used to hold as well as take. They closed up in line around the beasts, and the moon lit the tops of their spears. Sim brandished his ash-shaft, which had weighed heavily these last hours, and to his surprise found it light. He found his voice, too, and fell a-roaring like Wat.

Before he knew he was among the cattle. Wat had broken the ring, and men were hacking and slipping among the slab sides of the wearied beasts. The shelty came down over the rump of a red bullock, and Sim was sprawling on his face in the trampled grass. He struggled to rise, but some one had him by the throat.

Anger fired his slow brain. He reached out his long arms and grappled a leather jerkin. His nails found a seam and rent it, for he had mighty fingers. Then he was gripping warm flesh, tearing it like a wild beast, and his assailant with a cry slackened his hold.

'Whatna wull-cat ...' he began, but he got no further. The hoof of Wat's horse came down on his head and brained him. A spatter of blood fell on Sim's face.

The man was half wild. His shelty had broken back for the hill, but his spear lay a yard off. He seized it and got to his feet, to find that Wat had driven the English over the burn. The cattle were losing their weariness in panic, and tossing wild manes among the Scots. It was like a fight in a winter's byre. The glare on the right grew fiercer, and young Harden's voice rose, clear as a bell, above the tumult. He was swearing by the cross of his sword.

On foot, in the old Border way, Sim followed in Wat's wake, into the bog and beyond the burn. He laired to his knees, but he scarcely heeded it. There was a big man before him, a foolish, red-haired fellow, who was making great play with a cudgel. He had shivered two spears and was singing low to himself. Farther off Wat had his axe in hand and was driving the enemy to the brae. There were dead men in the moss. Sim stumbled over a soft body, and a hand caught feebly at his heel. 'To me, lads,' cried Wat. 'Anither birse and we hae them broken.'

But something happened. Harden was pushing the van of the raiders up the stream, and a press of them surged in from the right. Wat found himself assailed on his flank, and gave ground. The big man with the cudgel laughed loud and ran down the hill, and the Scots fell back on Sim. Men tripped over him, and as he rose he found the giant above him with his stick in the air.

The blow fell, glancing from the ash-shaft to Sim's side. Something cracked and his left arm hung limp. But the furies of hell had hold of him now. He rolled over, gripped his spear short, and with a swift turn struck upwards. The big man gave a sob and toppled down into a pool of the burn.

Sim struggled to his feet, and saw that the raiders were beginning to hough the cattle. One man was driving a red spear into a helpless beast. It might have been the Cleuch cow. The sight maddened him, and like a destroying angel he was among them. One man he caught full in the throat, and had to set a foot on his breast before he could tug the spear out. Then the head shivered on a steel corselet, and Sim played quarterstaff with the shaft. The violence of his onslaught turned the tide. Those whom Harden drove up were caught in a vice, and squeezed out, wounded and dying and mad with fear, on to the hill above the burn. Both sides were weary men, or there would have been a grim slaughter. As it was, none followed the runners, and every now and again a Scot would drop like a log, not from wounds but from dead weariness.

Harden's flare was dying down. Dawn was breaking, and Sim's wild eyes cleared. He saw the press of cattle, dazed with fright, and the red and miry heather. Queer black things were curled and stretched athwart it. He noticed a dead man beside him, perhaps of his own slaying. It was a shabby fellow, in a jacket that gaped like Sim's. The face was thin and patient, and the eyes, even in death, looked puzzled and reproachful. It would be one of the plain folk who had to ride, willy-nilly, on bigger men's quarrels. Sim found himself wondering if he, also, had a famished wife and child at home. The fury of the night had gone, and Sim began to sob from utter tiredness.

He slept in what was half a swoon. When he woke the sun was well up in the sky and the Scots were cooking food. His arm irked him, and his head burned like fire. He felt his body and found nothing worse than bruises, and one long shallow scar where his jacket was torn.

A Teviotdale man brought him a cog of brose. Sim stared at it and sickened: he was too far gone for food. Young Harden passed, and looked curiously at him. 'Here's a man that hasna spared himsel',' he said. 'A drop o' French cordial is the thing for you, Sim.' And out of a leathern flask he poured a little draught which he bade Sim swallow.

The liquor ran through his veins and lightened the ache of his head.

He found strength to rise and look round. Surely they were short of men. If these were all that were left Bewcastle had been well avenged.

Jamie Telfer enlightened him. 'When we had gotten the victory, there were some o' the lads thocht that Bewcastle sud pay scot in beasts as weel as men. Sae Wat and a score mair rade off to lowse Geordie Musgrave's kye. The road's clear, and they'll be back ower Liddel by this time. Dod, there'll be walth o' plenishin' at the Ninemileburn.'

Sim was cheered by the news. If Wat got back more than his own he might be generous. They were cooking meat round the fire, the flesh of the cattle killed in the fight. He went down to the nearest blaze, and was given a strip of roast which he found he could swallow.

'How mony beasts were killed?' he asked incuriously, and was told three. Saugh poles had been set up to hang the skins on. A notion made Sim stagger to his feet and go to inspect them. There could be no mistake. There hung the brindled hide of Marion's cow.

Wat returned in a cloud of glory, driving three-and-twenty English beasts before him – great white fellows that none could match on the Scottish side. He and his lads clamoured for food, so more flesh was roasted, till the burnside smelt like a kitchen. The Scots had found better than cattle, for five big skins of ale bobbed on their saddles. Wat summoned all to come and drink, and Harden, having no fear of reprisals, did not forbid it.

Sim was becoming a man again. He had bathed his bruises and scratches in the burn, and Will o' Phawhope, who had skill as a leech, had set his arm and bound it to his side in splints of ash and raw hide. He had eaten grossly of flesh – the first time since the spring, and then it had only been braxy lamb. The ale had warmed his blood and quickened his wits. He began to feel pleased with himself. He had done well in the fray – had not young Harden praised him? – and surly Wat had owned that the salvage of so many beasts was Sim's doing. 'Man, Sim, ye wrocht michtily at the burnside,' he had said. 'The heids crackit like nits when ye garred your staff sing. Better you wi' a stick than anither man wi' a sword.' It was fine praise, and warmed Sim's chilly soul. For a year he had fought bitterly for bread, and now glory had come to him without asking.

Men were drawn by lot to drive the cattle, and others to form a rearguard. The rest set off for their homes by the nearest road. The shelty had been recovered, and Sim to his pride found himself riding in the front with Wat and young Harden and others of the Scott and Elliot gentry.

The company rode fast over the green hills in the clear autumn noon. Harden's blue eyes danced, and he sang snatches in his gay voice. Wat rumbled his own praises and told of the raid over Liddel. Sim felt a new being from the broken man who the night before had wearily jogged on the same road. He told himself he took life too gravely and let care ride him too hard. He was too much thirled to the Cleuch and tied to his wife's apron. In the future he would see his friends, and bend the bicker with the rest of them.

By the darkening they had come to Ninemileburn, where Harden's road left theirs. Wat had them all into the bare dwelling, and another skin of ale was broached. A fire was lit and the men sprawled around it, singing songs. Then tales began, and they would have sat till morning, had not Harden called them to the road. Sim, too, got to his feet. He was thinking of the six miles yet before him, and as home grew nearer his spirits sank. Dimly he remembered the sad things that waited his home-coming.

Wat made him a parting speech. 'Gude e'en to ye, cousin Sim. Ye've been a kind man to me the day. May I do as weel by you if ever the fray gangs by the Cleuch. I had a coo o' yours in pledge, and it was ane o' the beasts the Musgraves speared. By the auld law your debt still stands, and if I likit I could seek anither pledge. But there'll be something awin' for rescue-shot, and wi' that and the gude wark ye've dune the day, I'm content to ca' the debt paid.'

Wat's words sounded kind, and no doubt Wat thought himself generous. Sim had it on his tongue to ask for a cow – even on a month's loan. But pride choked his speech. It meant telling of the pitiful straits at the Cleuch. After what had passed he must hold his head high amongst those full-fed Branksome lads. He thanked Wat, cried farewell to the rest, and mounted his shelty.

The moon was rising and the hills were yellow as corn. The shelty had had a feed of oats, and capered at the shadows. What with excitement, meat, and ale, and the dregs of a great fatigue, Sim's mind was hazy, and his cheerfulness returned. He thought only on his exploits. He had done great things – he, Sim o' the Cleuch – and every man in the Forest would hear of them and praise his courage. There would be ballads made about him; he could hear the blind violer at the

Ashkirk change-house singing songs which told how Sim o' the Cleuch smote Bewcastle in the howe of the Brunt Burn – ash against steel, one against ten. The fancy intoxicated him; he felt as if he, too, could make a ballad. It would speak of the soft shiny night with the moon high in the heavens. It would tell of the press of men and beasts by the burnside, and the red glare of Harden's fires, and Wat with his axe, and above all of Sim with his ash-shaft and his long arms, and how Harden drove the raiders up the burn and Sim smote them silently among the cattle. Wat's exploits would come in, but the true glory was Sim's. But for him Scots saddles might have been empty and every beast safe over Liddel.

The picture fairly ravished him. It carried him over the six miles of bent and down by the wood of hazel to where the Cleuch lay huddled in its nook of hill. It brought him to the door of his own silent dwelling. As he pushed into the darkness his heart suddenly sank . . .

With fumbling hands he kindled a rushlight. The peat fire had long sunk and left only a heap of white ashes. The gruel by the bed had been spilled and was lying on the floor. Only the jug of water was drained to the foot.

His wife lay so still that he wondered. A red spot burned in each cheek, and, as he bent down, he could hear her fast breathing. He flashed the light on her eyes and she slowly opened them.

'The coo, Sim,' she said faintly. 'Hae ye brocht the coo?'

The rushlight dropped on the floor. Now he knew the price of his riding. He fell into a fit of coughing.